PATRICK & BEATRICE HAGGERTY LIBRARY

W9-CMP-218

ALMANAC OF AMERICAN WOMEN
IN THE 20TH CENTURY

PATRICK & BEATRICE HAGGERTY LIBRARY
MOUNT MARY COLLEGE
MILWAUKEE, WISCONSIN 53222

ALMANAC OF AMERICAN WOMEN IN THE 20TH CENTURY

Judith Freeman Clark

PRENTICE HALL PRESS

New York   London   Toronto   Sydney   Tokyo

Copyright © 1987 by Judith Freeman Clark
All rights reserved, including the right of reproduction
in whole or in part in any form.

Published by Prentice Hall Press
A Division of Simon & Schuster, Inc.
Gulf+Western Building
One Gulf+Western Plaza
New York, NY   10023

PRENTICE HALL PRESS is a trademark of Simon & Schuster, Inc.

Library of Congress Cataloging-in-Publication Data

Clark, Judith Freeman.
   Almanac of American women in the twentieth century.

   Includes index.
   1. Women—United States—History—20th century—
Chronology.   2. Feminism—United States—History—
20th century—Chronology.   I. Title.
HQ1420.C55   1987   305.4'0973   86-43172
ISBN 0-13-022658-0
ISBN 0-13-022641-6 (pbk.)

Designed by C. Linda Dingler

Manufactured in the United States of America

10 9 8 7 6 5 4 3 2

505.4
593
1987

For my children,
Timothy S. Hawkins
and
Stephanie E. Hawkins

ACKNOWLEDGMENTS

The interest and assistance of various people at different times made this book possible. I owe a great deal to the University of Massachusetts/Amherst History Department faculty, specifically to Professors Joyce Berkman, Robert Griffith, and Gerald McFarland, whose training has benefited me in a variety of ways, and to Professor Miriam Chrisman, whose scholarly standards have been a constant guide and challenge.

Both Elise Bernier-Feeley, head of reference services, and Elise Chase Dennis, reference librarian at the Forbes Library in Northampton, Massachusetts, cheerfully provided access to sources and encouraged me along the way. The staffs at both the Neilsen Library, Smith College, and the University of Massachusetts at Amherst, were indispensable. In particular, Susan Boone, at the Sophia Smith Collection, Smith College, provided invaluable photo-research assistance.

Many colleagues and friends helped me over the rough spots and acted as catalysts for my writing and research efforts. To Lynn Cadwallader, very special thanks for everything, always. Others to whom I owe particular gratitude include John Bowman, Elizabeth Frost Knappman, Erika Neumann, Susan Carter Sawyer, and Robert Wilson. My editor, Paul Aron, was extremely flexible and supportive, and a real help during the final stages of the project.

My daughter, Stephanie E. Hawkins, spent many hours reviewing photographs, checking facts, and helping to write photo captions—tasks she did willingly and very well. Finally and most important, my husband, Robin E. Clark, deserves special thanks. He read the manuscript at various stages and offered valuable suggestions for its improvement. Robin also provided me with the opportunity to work full time on completing this book—a gesture of confidence and caring on his part for which I will always be grateful.

CONTENTS

PREFACE

Since an understanding of the past relies on availability of information, it is relatively difficult for the average reader to evaluate women's true role in American history. Few women receive mention in standard history books, although some women considered outstanding have achieved recognition, including Abigail Adams, Phillis Wheatley, Emily Dickinson, Clara Barton, and Harriet Tubman in the eighteenth and nineteenth centuries. Recent trends toward a more inclusive and accurate treatment of American history are encouraging, but the efforts of a few conscientious historians still leave enormous gaps in our knowledge of women's contributions to American history.

The facts *are* available. There is a wealth of information about women in newspapers, magazines, letters, journals, and other print and nonprint sources. It was an awareness of this convenient, usable material, particularly with regard to the twentieth century, that prompted this book. To compile basic facts and detail women's lives from 1900 to 1987 was a beguiling challenge. It also provided a fascinating, confirming view of women's slow, often frustrating journey toward an as-yet unrealized equality.

Of course, it was impossible to report every issue, event, or incident concerning women between 1900 and 1987. To maintain a workable format, editing material for inclusion often meant being highly selective. Some points were quite pertinent to or representative of a given decade, and the process was simple. Often, though, it was a matter of choosing from among facts of equal importance. The more obvious was sometimes eliminated in favor of information that shed new light on previously elusive or unknown facts or individuals.

The almanac entries, biographies, and topic essays were written to be as inclusive as possible without straying too far from the generally significant. Thus, some detail has been eliminated, not because of any particular bias but due to the need to maintain a broad overview of women's history in general. Admittedly, some lightweight material was occasionally included. History can and should be a delight to read as well as informative.

This almanac is based on the premise that most readers know little about the day-to-day accomplishments and events that comprise women's history in twentieth-century America. The majority of women and their efforts have gone unnoticed and are undervalued in history books and elsewhere. Some women, such as U.S. Representative Jeannette Rankin and Nobel Peace Prize recipient Emily Greene Balch, were well known at one time but subsequently fell into a kind of historical limbo. Others, like Helen Gurley Brown and Shirley Temple Black, may be thought of in more narrow terms than their many accomplishments warrant. Still other women, like mountain climber Annie Smith Peck, Native American educator Ella Deloria, and the nation's first black woman millionaire, Sarah Breedlove Walker, receive little attention from historians.

Women in the United States have lacked a comprehensive, inclusive treatment of their very special history. With its focus on the recent past, this book addresses that void. It describes many women whose hard work, intelligence, courage, and talent transformed our nation during this century. Although it has been impossible to include *every* woman who contributed to that transformation, this almanac should help the reader gain a better understanding of how women changed—and were changed by—American history. A good history book sparks the imagination and propels a reader's curiosity. I hope this book does that for you.

JUDITH FREEMAN CLARK
NORTHAMPTON, MASSACHUSETTS

ALMANAC OF AMERICAN WOMEN IN THE 20TH CENTURY

I

THE FIRST DECADE
1900–1910

During the first decade of the twentieth century, American women followed examples set for them by pioneering women of years past. From 1900 to 1910 women promoted better working conditions, participated in sports events, worked for better schools, and demonstrated on behalf of woman suffrage. Labor activists led adult and child workers on strike in a quest for decent pay and a healthier workplace. Their demonstrations became common throughout the decade and eventually led to passage of child labor laws and other protective legislation. Teachers such as Mary McLeod Bethune endeavored to improve educational opportunities for all students, black and white. Bethune devoted her entire life to bringing learning to others, and Bethune-Cookman College is a vital memorial to her devotion.

The National American Woman Suffrage Association was founded to gain voting rights for women, and through this organization individuals like Carrie Chapman Catt paved the way for the Nineteenth Amendment. Other reforms received attention from women, including the temperance movement. Prohibition was the darling issue of thousands who felt it their duty to protect the nation's morals by denying alcoholic beverage sales. Spearheaded by the Women's Christian Temperance Union, and by Carry Nation, the ax-wielding antialcohol activitist, the crusade to make America "dry" culminated in passage of the Volstead Act in 1917.

Other significant changes in women's roles during the years 1900 to 1910 included increased participation in business, industry, and sports, and formation of women's medical units in the armed forces. As early as 1901 the federal government established the Army Nurse Corps, naming Dita H. Kinney as its head, and the U.S. Naval Observatory employed its first woman astronomer.

In business, the first woman bank president in the United States proved that women could operate independently, while the Manhattan Trade School for Girls opened in order to prepare women for gainful employment outside the home. In another sphere, the golfer Margaret Abbot became the first American woman to win an Olympic gold medal. Other sportswomen, such as tennis great May Sutton, competed at world-class events. Sutton became the first American woman to win at Wimbledon.

1

Although not an era of radical change, the first ten years of the twentieth century contain a myriad of indications of future transformations. More and more women felt free to choose library work, social work, medicine, and business as a life's profession in lieu of marriage. Gradually, American society became as accustomed to cheering women airplane pilots and to seeing motion picture actresses as it would decades later to celebrating accomplishments of women astronauts and to rallying around a major-party woman vice-presidential nominee. In many ways, this century *was* a new millenium that held special hope and promise for all American women, and they met its challenges with courage, creativity, and conviction.

2 January 1900
WOMEN'S ISSUES. A total of $300,000 has been collected in New York City to build a residential hotel for women. It will be located between Madison Avenue and 39th Street, and will provide space for working women who might otherwise be unable to find suitable quarters.

3 January 1900
POPULAR CULTURE. Florence E. Woods is the first woman to obtain a permit to drive her car in New York City's Central Park. "An automobile is the easiest thing in the world to handle," she said. "I am astonished that women seem so timid [about it]."

EDUCATION. Miss Maria Parloa, noted cookbook author and lecturer, addresses a meeting of the Household Economic Association in New York City.

5 March 1900
POPULAR CULTURE. Mrs. Finley J. Shepard donates $250,000 for the establishment of a Hall of Fame to commemorate famous Americans, both male and female.

23 June 1900
LABOR. The International Ladies' Garment Workers Union establishes that women seamstresses working at home average less than $.30 daily in earnings.

5 July 1900
POLITICS. In Kansas City, Missouri, Elizabeth Cohn is the first woman delegate to make a seconding speech at the Democratic National Convention. She seconds William Jennings Bryan's nomination for president of the United States.

20 July 1900
SCIENCE. The U.S. Naval Observatory in Washington, D.C., employs the first woman astronomer, Eleanor Annie Lamson.

10 November 1900
ARTS AND CULTURE. In the hit musical *Floradora,* a group of 6 young women sing, "Tell Me Pretty Maiden." The sextette later becomes a byword for similar performing teams relying heavily on sheer numbers rather than talent.

27 December 1900
REFORM. Carry Nation, temperance activist, marches on the Carey Hotel in Wichita, Kansas, and smashes all the liquor bottles in sight.

OTHER EVENTS OF 1900

EDUCATION. Trinity College, the first national Roman Catholic college for women, is founded by Sister Julia McGroarty in Washington, D.C.

Olympic Gold Medals
Margaret Abbot: golf

2 February 1901
MILITARY. The U.S. Army establishes the Army Nurse Corps.

15 March 1901
MILITARY. Dita H. Kinney is named head of the U.S. Army Nurse Corps.

24 June 1901
SCIENCE. Clara Maass, R.N., volunteers as a subject in yellow fever research, permitting herself to be bitten by suspected disease-bearing mosquitoes. Recovering, Maass is bitten again on 14 August, and dies of yellow fever 10 days

later, thus establishing a direct link between the insect and the illness.

29 August 1901
REFORM. Kansas-born temperance advocate Carry Nation appears in New York City. She proceeds, armed with a hatchet, to a saloon run by boxing champ John L. Sullivan.

15 September 1901
EDUCATION. In Groton, Massachusetts, Mrs. Edward Gilchrist Low offers the first course in landscape architecture for women at the Lowthorpe School of Architecture.

24 October 1901
POPULAR CULTURE. Anna Edson Taylor rides over Niagara Falls in a cushioned barrel as a fund-raising stunt. A reporter for the *Denver Republican* later comments that Taylor "seems to be taking a lot of credit that belongs to the barrel."

OTHER EVENTS OF 1901

EDUCATION. Florence R. Sabin is named the first woman professor at Johns Hopkins University School of Medicine in Baltimore, Maryland. In 1925, she becomes the first woman member of the National Academy of Science.

IDEAS/BELIEFS. Amelia Devine becomes the first woman Salvation Army bell-ringer in the United States.

Edith Wharton, 1862–1937

Raised in the atmosphere of restrained wealth that characterized "old money" society in the east, Edith Newbold Jones Wharton produced a body of fiction that reflected much of her life's experience. The only daughter of George and Lucretia (Rhinelander) Jones, she was born in New York City on 24 January 1862. As a child, she lived with her family in Europe, and returned to New York where she made her social debut when she was seventeen. By this time she had already begun to write, producing a privately published book of poems at age sixteen.

In April 1885 she married retired banker Edward Robbins Wharton of Boston, and the couple maintained a life-style that reflected their position of wealth and social standing. They traveled to Europe each winter and entertained in New York, Boston, and Newport. Wharton had begun to write in earnest, and claimed occasional publishing credits in *Harper's* and *Scribner's* magazines. In 1897, she collaborated with architect Ogden Codman, Jr., on a book, *The Decoration of Houses.*

In 1899, the Whartons moved to Lenox, Massachusetts, where they built a large estate, The Mount. Here she produced two volumes of stories, *The Greater Inclination* (1899) and *Crucial Instances* (1901). In 1902, she published *The Valley of Decision* and in 1905, her critically acclaimed novel *The House of Mirth.*

Wharton's skill in depicting situations and in describing moods can be seen in many of her works. Among them, *Tales of Men and Ghosts, Ethan Frome,* and *The Age of Innocence* are considered highly representative of her clarity and facility with language. She won the Pulitzer Prize in 1920 for *The Age of Innocence;* she was generally accepted as one of the preeminent woman novelists of her time.

Wharton moved with her husband to Europe in 1910, where he was hospitalized due to emotional collapse. The novelist divorced him in 1913 and was left with the freedom to indulge her taste for beautiful homes, varied friendships, and, above all, her connection with the world of letters. During World War I, Wharton worked tirelessly on behalf of refugees. Her efforts caused her to be made a chevalier of the French Legion of Honor and the Belgian Order of Leopold. She was by now a permanent resident of France, owning two homes there, one outside Paris, at St. Brice-sous-forêt, and the other at Hyères on the Riviera.

Due to her isolation from American society, she was less able to write accurately about life in the Unite l States, and she grew less convincing with her portraits of Americans, their customs, and their culture. Still, she contributed regularly to American magazines and published a number of novels. In 1930, she was elected to the National Institute of Arts and Letters, and in 1934, she became a member of the American Academy of Arts and Letters.

Wharton continued to support herself by writing, maintaining the luxurious standard of living to which she had become accustomed. She died at St. Brice on 11 August 1937.

---

12 January 1902
POPULAR CULTURE. Dr. Felix Adler, speaking to the Society of Ethical Culture in New York City, asserts that women are not oppressed and that ''marriage means accepting restrictions from which we cannot withdraw.''

6 February 1902
IDEAS/BELIEFS. The Young Women's Hebrew Association (YWHA) is established in New York City. Mrs. Israel Unterberg is the group's first president.

23 August 1902
EDUCATION. The *School of Cookery,* run by Fannie Farmer, is opened in Boston, Massachusetts. Farmer soon becomes a leader in culinary education and publishes a best-selling cookbook.

31 August 1902
POPULAR CULTURE. In Saratoga, New York, Mrs. Adolph Ladenburg rides astride her horse in public, creating a minor furor.

6 December 1902
WOMEN'S ISSUES. The first postage stamps issued with a woman's likeness appears. The woman is Martha Washington, wife of the country's first president.

OTHER EVENTS OF 1902

SUFFRAGE. The first international organization for woman suffrage is founded in Washington, D.C.

EDUCATION. The *Manhattan Trade School for Girls* opens in New York City. It is among the first opportunities offered to working-class girls seeking vocational training. Mary Schenk Woolman is director. The first class consists of 20 students.

3 March 1903
MEDICAL. North Carolina is the first state to pass laws authorizing the registration of licensed practical nurses.

11 March 1903
ARTS AND CULTURE. Dame Ethel Mary Smyth's opera *Der Wald* is the first written by a woman to be performed at the Metropolitan Opera House in New York City.

27 April 1903
POPULAR CULTURE. Lillian Russell creates a stir of publicity as she attends the opening of the Jamaica Race Track in Long Island, New York.

23 May 1903
LABOR. Thousands of children who work in textile mills in the Philadelphia area begin a strike, which becomes famous as the ''March of the Mill Children,'' led by labor activist Mother Jones.

Jane Addams, 1860–1935

Jane Addams, humanitarian who spoke out in favor of woman suffrage, at one of the many "Votes for Women" parades of the early twentieth century. (Photo courtesy Sophia Smith Collection, Smith College)

One of the great names in American settlement house work and the international peace movement, as well as a tireless worker on behalf of woman suffrage, Jane Addams brought to her career a superlative intellect, a passion for service, and an abundant capacity for hard work. Born to John and Sarah (Weber) Addams in Cedarville, Illinois, on 6 September 1860, she never really knew her mother. When she was a baby, Sarah Addams died, and within a few years John Addams married Anna Haldeman, a widow with two sons.

Addams suffered ill health during her childhood but overcame her weakness sufficiently to attend nearby Rockford Seminary, although her chief wish was to attend Smith College in Massachusetts. Her father, however, discouraged her pursuit of any career that was not considered genteel for a young woman of upper middle-class background. Addams therefore traveled to Europe, as did many of her age and station, and there she encountered London's settlement houses. This experience so fired her imagination that she and a traveling companion, Ellen Gates Starr, set up a similar establishment in the United States in 1889.

That Chicago, Illinois, settlement—Hull House—was a model and inspiration for hundreds of similar ventures that soon sprang up across the country. Addams herself was an inspiration. She dedicated her entire life to improving living conditions for the immigrant and the poor, and she worked tirelessly to ensure passage of legislation designed to improve the urban environment.

Addams was a prominent figure in the fight for woman suffrage and either founded or belonged to an enormous number of humanitarian and activist groups. Her memberships included the Woman's Peace Party of which she was elected national president in 1915, and the Women's International League for Peace and Freedom. Addams helped to found the latter in 1919.

Along with her influence on the fields of public health and human services, her major contribution to America was that she helped lend respectability to education and employment for women. Born during an age that frowned on women who ventured outside the home for anything other than church or charitable work, Addams defied tradition and became a model for future generations.

In addition to her work in the settlement and as a international figure, she wrote several books, including *Democracy and Social Ethics* and *Twenty Years at Hull House.* Addams' speeches and writings dealt head on with the need for new perspectives on women's roles. In *Newer Ideals of Peace,* published in 1907, she stated, "Old fashioned ways which no longer apply to changed conditions are a snare in which the feet of women have always become readily entangled." Addams' uncompromising attitude toward social justice helped thousands who would have been otherwise condemned to lives of poverty and ignorance, or simply profligacy and ennui.

In 1931, she was named co-recipient of the Nobel Peace Prize along with Nicholas Murray Butler. She was awarded $16,480 as a result of this coveted honor. She donated this money to the Women's International League, an act characteristic of Addams' deep desire to alleviate human oppression.

Jane Addams died of cancer on 21 May 1935, shortly after the twentieth-anniversary celebration of the Women's International League at which she was hailed as "the truest American" and "a pioneer who was still pioneering."

---

10 June 1903
EDUCATION. In Groton, Massachusetts, the first woman student at the landscape architecture school receives her certificate.

28 July 1903
BUSINESS. Maggie Lena Walker becomes the first woman bank president. She heads the St. Luke Penny Savings Bank in Richmond, Virginia.

6 November 1903
ARTS AND CULTURE. Maude Adams opens in Sir J. M. Barrie's *Peter Pan,* a play that runs continuously through 8 June 1907.

13 November 1903
EDUCATION. The New York Federation of Women's Clubs votes at their annual convention to establish a trade school for girls. The group also assumes management of an industrial school already established in Amsterdam, New York.

19 November 1903
LABOR. The Women's National Trade Union League is established. Mary Morton Kehew is president. The league changes its name in 1907 to the National Women's Trade Union League.

OTHER EVENTS OF 1903

LITERATURE. Helen Keller, blind and deaf since infancy, publishes her autobiography, *The Story of My Life.*

28 September 1904
POPULAR CULTURE. A New York City police officer arrests a woman who is smoking a cigarette while she rides along Fifth Avenue in an open car.

3 October 1904
EDUCATION. Mary McLeod Bethune opens her first school for black students in Daytona Beach, Florida.

2 November 1904
IDEAS/BELIEFS. Evangeline Booth is named commander of the United States Salvation Army. She is the daughter of Salvation Army founder, William Booth, who began the organization in Great Britain in 1865.

16 December 1904
POPULAR CULTURE. The Majestic Theater in New York City is the first in the nation to employ female ushers.

OTHER EVENTS OF 1904

SUFFRAGE. Anna Howard Shaw succeeds Carrie Chapman Catt as president of the National American Woman Suffrage Association, a post she holds until 1915.

ARTS AND CULTURE. Mary Evelyn Beatrice Longman's statue, *Victory*, wins a silver medal at the St. Louis Exposition.

LITERATURE. Popular author Gene Stratton Porter publishes her best-selling book, *Freckles*.

Olympic Gold Medals

Lydia Scott Howell: Archery—Double National; Double Columbia; women's team
Mrs. C. S. Woodruff: Archery—women's team
Miss L. Taylor: Archery—women's team

Olympic Silver Medals

Miss E. C. Cooke: Archery—Double Columbia
Mrs. H. C. Pollock: Archery—Double National

10 February 1905
WOMEN'S ISSUES. The New York Portia Club registers a protest against proposed legislation that would hold married women liable for household bills in the event that their husbands are unable to pay them.

17 February 1905
ARTS AND CULTURE. Helen F. Mears is the sculptor of a memorial to educator and temperance advocate Frances Willard. The statue is the first of a woman to be unveiled at the National Statuary Hall in Washington, D.C.

10 April 1905
WOMEN'S ISSUES. Anna Perry Bunell announces the establishment of the Purple Cross Society. This group is aimed at providing moral and financial support for working girls "to prevent them from becoming discouraged or losing their self-respect through loss of position or illness."

14 April 1905
WOMEN'S ISSUES. In Washington, D.C., Susan B. Anthony speaks out against a National Council of Women resolution. "I do not consider divorce an evil by any means," Anthony states. The ruling would cut women off from refuge from designing and brutal men, according to Anthony.

Ida M. Tarbell, 1857–1944

Journalist Ida Minerva Tarbell was born in Erie, Pennsylvania, on 5 November 1857. The daughter of Franklin and Esther (McCullough) Tarbell, she was educated at Allegheny College, where she received an A.B. in 1880. After teaching at Poland Union Seminary in Ohio she began to write for the *Chautauquan* magazine as a staff member in 1883. She left in 1891 to travel in Europe, where she studied at the Sorbonne and the College of France, and mingled with leading intellectuals. Soon, she was writing for *McClure's Magazine,* interviewing such notables as Dumas, Pasteur, and Zola.

Tarbell returned to the United States in 1894, and published material on Napoleon Bonaparte in *McClure's Magazine.* In 1900, she produced a popular collection of articles on Abraham Lincoln, and subsequently began research for a study of the Standard Oil Trust.

Since Tarbell had been raised in the area of Standard Oil headquarters, she claimed more than a journalist's interest in the project. In 1904, Tarbell published the detailed, often critical *History of the Standard Oil Company*. For this work, she was described as a "muckraker," along with other writers who began exposing big business corruption and questionable industrial practices. This label was used by President Theodore Roosevelt, who adapted it from a description of a character in *Pilgrim's Progress*.

In 1906, Tarbell and several colleagues from *McClure's Magazine* purchased *American Magazine,* and the group collectively wrote and edited for this publication until 1915. She was recognized then and later as a meticulously careful journalist who relied on solid research. One of Tarbell's chief values, however, was her ability to present a variety of topics in easily accessible language and style. Her works were widely read, and she was accepted as one of the most important journalists of the early twentieth century due to her writing for *McClure's Magazine, American Magazine,* and her larger work on Standard Oil. Following her tenure on *American Magazine,* Tarbell devoted herself to lecturing on a wide range of popular and controversial topics.

Associated with the Coit-Alber Lecture Bureau, she traveled extensively, speaking to audiences in different cities on the Chautauqua circuit. She continued these engagements until 1932, although she acknowledged that her schedule left little time for quality writing.

A committed pacifist, Tarbell nevertheless stood apart from actual involvement in peace activities. After World War I she was a reporter at the Paris Peace Conference. And although Tarbell was an independent career woman with a great sense of her abilities and contributions, she was never an avowed feminist. In fact, she spoke out on more than one occasion to defend the traditional, conventional roles of wife and mother.

In 1939, Tarbell published her autobiography, *All in the Day's Work,* and until the final decades of her life taught the writing of biography. She died in Bridgeport, Connecticut, on 6 January 1944.

---

24 April 1905
POPULAR CULTURE.   Lucille Mulhall, age 18, of Oklahoma Territory, appears at New York City's Madison Square Garden to demonstrate lassoing and steer roping along with other skills of the West.

30 April 1905
SUFFRAGE.   At a meeting of the College Equal Suffrage League of New York, speaker John Crosby states, "I am tired of discussing whether or not women ought to vote. If I were a woman and suffrage was denied me, I'd get up and make a howl."

7 June 1905
LABOR.   At the Women's International Union Label League convention in Chicago, Illinois, Sue M. Simpson wraps herself in the American flag and refuses to be expelled from the group's gathering. Simpson has been charged with writing to Samuel Gompers of the American Federation of Labor stating that the League conditions are "chaotic."

2 October 1905
SUFFRAGE.   Former President Grover Cleveland states in a *Ladies' Home Journal* article that " . . . sensible and responsible women do not want to vote. The relative positions to be assumed by men and women . . . were assigned long ago by a higher intelligence than ours."

OTHER EVENTS OF 1905

EDUCATION.   Children's librarian Annie Carroll Moore joins the staff of the New York Public Library. She remains involved with the children's division of the library until 1940, and becomes nationally known for her reform of library facilities for young people.

SPORTS. May G. Sutton is the first American woman to win at Wimbledon. She defeats Great Britain's Doris K. Douglas. Sutton maintains proficiency at tennis for 20 years, playing on the Wightman Cup team in 1925.

2 January 1906
WOMEN'S ISSUES. The New Hampshire State Supreme Court rules that women cannot hold commissions as notaries public in that state.

17 January 1906
WOMEN'S ISSUES. Underscoring the current feeling concerning working women, an editorial in the *New York Times* states: "no woman could go into the Pennsylvania Railroad expecting to become president thereof." It continues, "a nice girl . . . and all girls commercially employed are nice . . . is not thinking about spending her life in commercial employment."

6 March 1906
WOMEN'S ISSUES. Nora Stanton Blatch is the first woman to be elected a junior member of the American Society of Civil Engineers.

13 March 1906
DEATHS. Susan B. Anthony dies, leaving $10,000 to help promote woman suffrage in the United States. She is later named the "greatest woman that ever lived," by Carrie Chapman Catt during a speech at Columbia Teacher's College.

25 May 1906
SPORTS. Dr. Dudley Sargent, Physical Director at Harvard University, speaks to the Public School Physical Training Society in New York City. His topic focuses on the need for women to avoid certain types of sports and games—football, basketball, heavy gymnastics—because of their "inability to bear a prolonged mental and physical strain."

The new century offered women many opportunities, but even in 1906 attitudes concerning physical activity remained conservative. A simple walk in the country dictated long, cumbersome skirts, high-collared shirtwaists, and heeled shoes. (Photo courtesy Judith Freeman Clark)

IDEAS/BELIEFS. Anarchists Emma Goldman and Alexander Berkman are interviewed by a Chicago, Illinois, reporter and tell him, ''We are anarchists and don't believe in marriage.''

13 June 1906
EDUCATION. Simmons College in Boston, Massachusetts, holds graduation for the first class at this women's technical school.

11 August 1906
AVIATION. Mary P. Miller becomes the first woman airship (dirigible) passenger at Franklin, Pennsylvania.

26 August 1906
SUFFRAGE. Alice Stone Blackwell states her support of woman suffrage and her opposition to the Massachusetts Association Opposed to the Further Extension of Suffrage to Women. Blackwell claims the Massachusetts group has used questionable procedures in reporting its membership figures.

11 November 1906
EDUCATION. At a meeting of the College Entrance Examination Board, Smith College in Massachusetts is admitted to membership.

5 December 1906
MEDICAL. The new Woman's Hospital at 109th Street and Amsterdam Avenue in New York City opens. With a total cost of more than $1 million and a staff of 30 nurses and 10 doctors, the facility is the most up to date of its kind.

OTHER EVENTS OF 1906

EDUCATION. Mary Adelaide Nutting is the first nurse to obtain a professorship at Columbia University.

POPULAR CULTURE. Ida Tarbell becomes associate editor of *American Magazine*.

16 February 1907
SUFFRAGE. The Inter-Urban Political Equality Council, a group promoting equal rights for women, opens its headquarters in New York City. Council chairperson, Carrie Chapman Catt, speaks at the opening, stating, ''We are going to stay until all the women are converted.''

Elizabeth Gurley Flynn, 1890–1964

Prominent American Communist and labor organizer Elizabeth Gurley Flynn was born on 7 August 1890 in Concord, New Hampshire, the daughter of Thomas and Annie (Gurley) Flynn, both of whom were Socialists and Irish nationalists. The family moved in 1900 from New England to the South Bronx, New York, where Flynn attended grammar school, winning several debating medals. Influenced by the writings of William Morris and Edward Bellamy, she was active in Socialist party activities as a young girl. In 1906, she spoke at the Harlem Socialist Club; her topic was women and the effects of capitalism. That same year she was arrested for creating a disturbance while speaking in New York City's theater district. Flynn joined the International Workers of the World (IWW) in 1906 and participated in her first labor strike in 1907 in Bridgeport, Connecticut.

She dropped out of high school with her parents' blessings and devoted herself to furthering the Socialist cause. In January 1908, she married John Archibald Jones, a labor organizer at the Mesabi Iron Range in Minnesota. After the couple's son, Fred, was born in 1910, however, they lived apart and were divorced in 1920. For a number of years Flynn lived with Italian anarchist Carlo Tresca, whom she met in 1913. Although she was then legally married to Jones, she maintained an alliance with Tresca until 1925 when he fathered a child by her sister.

Elizabeth Gurley Flynn, labor activist, speaking at the Paterson, New Jersey, textile strike. (Photo courtesy Sophia Smith Collection, Smith College)

Flynn was active in all the major strikes promoted by the IWW in the Northeast. Chief among them were the 1912 Lawrence, Massachusetts, textile strike, and the Paterson, New Jersey, silk strike in 1913. In 1916, she participated in the Mesabi Range strike in Minnesota and helped fellow strikers by raising money for their legal expenses.

As disagreements developed between Flynn and IWW leader William (Big Bill) Heyward, she became less prominent in its activities, though still supporting its politics. In 1917, Flynn was indicted along with 168 other IWW members for violating the Espionage Act, and in 1918 she helped establish the Workers' Liberty Defense Union. This group's aim was to free those imprisoned during World War I under the Deportation Act of 1918.

In 1920, she helped found the American Civil Liberties Union (ACLU), and from 1926 and 1930 she was chairperson of the International Labor Defense. Between 1920 and 1927 Flynn worked to free anarchists Sacco and Vanzetti, and in 1926 she applied for membership in the Communist Party, U.S.A. She finally joined the party in 1937, and this move caused the ACLU to remove her from its membership in 1940, although that action was reversed in 1976.

During World War II Flynn worked tirelessly to promote the equality of women, urging establishment of federal day care centers and supporting the draft of women for factory work. In 1945, she attended the Women's Congress in Paris.

In March 1952, Flynn and twelve other Communists were tried, and in 1953 convicted, under the Smith Act, of advocating violent overthrow of the U.S. government. She was imprisoned at the Alderson, West Virginia, Women's Federal Reformatory from January 1955 to May 1957.

In 1961, Flynn was elected to chair the Communist Party, U.S.A., the first woman to hold this position. The State Department invoked the 1950 McCarren Act, relieving her of her passport in 1961. She brought a legal suit against the government, and the Supreme Court ultimately ruled in her favor. On 5 September 1964, Elizabeth Gurley Flynn died while on a visit to Moscow and was given a state funeral in Red Square.

17 February 1907
POPULAR CULTURE.   Prominent New York City women, including Mrs. John Jacob Astor, Mrs. Harry Payne Whitney, and Mrs. Walter Damrosch, organize a private group, The Colony Club. Its membership includes Maude Adams, Ethel Barrymore, Kate Douglas Wiggin, and Jeannette Gilder. The group is building a $1-million clubhouse on Madison Avenue.

11 March 1907
POPULAR CULTURE.   The Colony Club opens at 122 Madison Avenue. Elsie de Wolfe, club member, is responsible for the decor. Annual dues of $100, with a $150 initiation fee, make this club one of the most exclusive of women's society groups.

15 June 1907
IDEAS/BELIEFS.   Jane Addams is among the U.S. delegates to the Second Hague Peace Conference.

4 October 1907
POPULAR CULTURE.   Harriot Stanton Blatch, daughter of Elizabeth Cady Stanton, is barred from dining in the restaurant at the Hoffman House Hotel in New York City. Blatch is prohibited from dining there alone without a male escort. The New York Equal Suffrage League vows legal support for Blatch in her suit against the hotel.

20 October 1907
LITERATURE.   Book sales records in principal U.S. cities show that, between 1895 and 1907, female authors have become as popular as male authors.

25 October 1907
EDUCATION.   A report on Smith College students paying their way through school cites tutoring (at $.75 per hour) and waiting on tables at off-campus houses among the most popular types of employment.

26 October 1907
IDEAS/BELIEFS.   The first Woman's Missionary Conference is held at Yale University in New Haven, Connecticut. Male students at the school are warned against bothering the women.

9 December 1907
POPULAR CULTURE.   Emily Perkins Bissell designs and prints the first Christmas seals, selling them in order to help raise money for tuberculosis research.

16 December 1907
WOMEN'S ISSUES.   The first singer to broadcast over radio is Eugenia H. Farrar. At the Brooklyn Naval Yard, she takes part in ceremonies recognizing the departure of a fleet headed by Admiral "Fighting Bob" Evans.

Madame C. J. Walker, 1867–1919

Entrepreneur Madame C. J. Walker established a successful beauty business that had, by 1914, made her the nation's first black woman millionaire and the head of an operation rivaling those of Helena Rubenstein and Elizabeth Arden. Born near Delta,

Madame C. J. Walker, the first black woman millionaire in the United States. Her philanthropy was well known during her lifetime, and her business, the Walker Manufacturing Company, still produces her original formulas. (Photo courtesy Mme. C. J. Walker Mfg. Co. and the Collection of A'Lelia Bundles)

Louisiana, on 23 December 1867, Sarah Breedlove was orphaned as a child, married at age fourteen, and widowed by the time she was twenty years old. She then moved with her daughter, A'Lelia, to St. Louis, Missouri, where, for more than a decade, she worked as a washerwoman for $1.50 a day. But her ingenuity and sense of innovation enabled her, with capital assets under $5, to establish a small business in 1905.

She devised a system of hair care products and procedures that would prove to have wide appeal, and in 1906, she moved to Denver, Colorado. She met and married Charles J. Walker, a news reporter. Her hair care business expanded, and she opened a second office in 1908. Her daughter managed the latter and in 1910, Madame C. J. Walker, as she was known by this time, opened her corporate headquarters in Indianapolis, Indiana.

Walker's success was based largely on her policy of hiring "agents," young women who traveled to clients' homes and carried their hairdressing apparatus and products with them. Walker's agents were trained to be neat and thorough, and to maintain attractive appearances. They gained a reputation throughout the United States and in the Caribbean, as well as in Europe. Josephine Baker, the black entertainer, gave her wholehearted endorsement to Walker's products.

In addition to her thriving business, Walker was active in many different philanthropic activities. She helped support scholarships at several schools, and was known to spend $10,000 yearly on the education of young men and women. She was a supporter of the Tuskegee Institute and donated to numerous programs of the National Association for the Advancement of Colored People.

In 1914, Walker built a large home in New York City, and in 1917, she constructed Villa Lewaro, a $250,000, thirty-room country estate on the Hudson River. Walker's daughter, A'Lelia Walker Robinson Wilson Kennedy, was her mother's principal inheritor when the businesswoman died on 25 April 1919. Kennedy later opened her mother's spacious New York City home to a large number of black writers, artists, and musicians. In this way, Walker's work contributed in an important way to the Harlem Renaissance in the 1920s.

OTHER EVENTS OF 1907

MEDICAL. The American Hospital Association proposes a 3-tier system to license all nurses in the United States. The categories suggested are teaching nurse, bedside nurse, and attendant nurse.

POLITICS. Kate Barnard is elected Commissioner of Charities and Corrections for Oklahoma. She is the first woman ever elected to office in that state.

ARTS AND CULTURE. Julia Ward Howe is the first woman elected to the National Institute of Arts and Letters.

15 January 1908
WOMEN'S ISSUES. The first sorority for black women, Alpha Kappa Alpha, is founded in Washington, D.C.

21 January 1908
POPULAR CULTURE. The Sullivan Ordinance is passed in New York City, making it illegal for women there to smoke in public places.

10 March 1908
REFORM. The Children's Welfare Congress meets in Washington, D.C., to discuss pertinent issues regarding education of and legislation affecting children.

10 May 1908
POPULAR CULTURE. The first Mother's Day is proclaimed in Philadelphia, Pennsylvania.

13 May 1908
U.S. MILITARY. The Navy establishes a Nurse Corps. Esther Voorhees Hanson is its first superintendant.

27 August 1908
WOMEN'S ISSUES. Telephone operator Sarah J. Rooke of Folsom, New Mexico, dies in a flood after alerting and saving most of the townspeople.

OTHER EVENTS OF 1908

LABOR. In *Muller* v. *Oregon,* the U.S. Supreme Court affirms that a law limiting women's workdays to 10 hours each is constitutional.

ARTS AND CULTURE. The McDowell Colony, a retreat for artists, opens in Peterborough, New Hampshire, under the sponsorship of Marian Nevins McDowell, widow of composer Edward McDowell. She is well recognized for her patronage of the arts.

BUSINESS. Rose Markward Knox assumes control of Knox Gelatine Co., and later becomes a millionaire.

1 March 1909
EDUCATION. The University of Minnesota establishes the nation's first university school of nursing. Bertha Erdmann is the first director.

7 June 1909
POPULAR CULTURE. Actress Mary Pickford appears in her first motion picture, *The Violin Maker of Cremona.*

9 June 1909
POPULAR CULTURE. The first woman to attempt a transcontinental automobile trip leaves New York City. She arrives in San Francisco, California, on 6 August.

19 October 1909
EDUCATION. Due to the efforts of black educator Nannie Burroughs, the National Trade

and Professional School for Women and Girls opens in Washington, D.C. The school is funded partly by the National Baptist Women's Convention of which Burroughs is secretary until 1948.

27 October 1909
AVIATION. The first woman airplane passenger flies in College Park, Maryland.

22 November 1909
POPULAR CULTURE. Helen Hayes makes her stage debut in New York City at the Herald Square Theater, appearing in *In Old Dutch.*

24 November 1909
LABOR. In New York City, 20,000 waist- and dress-makers go on strike to demand a union contract, which will include higher wages and better work conditions.

20 December 1909
LABOR. In Philadelphia, Pennsylvania, waist- and dress-makers go on strike for union contracts.

OTHER EVENTS OF 1909

REFORM. The National Association for the Advancement of Colored People (NAACP) is founded. Among its leaders is Mary White Ovington, reformer and one of few whites committed to civil rights for black Americans. The NAACP grows to become an important forum for black women's rights.

BUSINESS. Rose O'Neill designs and writes about dolls called "Kewpies" from her home in Branson, Missouri.

2 January 1910
LABOR. At Carnegie Hall in New York City, a mass rally in support of striking dress-makers continues to prove the power behind the garment workers' protest.

Annie Smith Peck, 1850–1935

At a time when most women's outings were limited to family or neighborhood gatherings, Annie Smith Peck was climbing mountains. Peck was an active suffragist and respected lecturer, a woman of vigor and intelligence who was driven by curiosity and a desire to excel.

The only daughter of George Bacheler and Ann (Smith) Peck, she was born in Providence, Rhode Island, on 19 October 1850. As a child, many of Smith's activities centered on her brothers' pastimes and they were later to attribute her mountaineering skills to her early prowess in outdoor games.

Peck graduated with honors from the University of Michigan in 1878, and received her A.M. degree there three years later. She had a brief career as a teacher, at both girls' secondary schools and Smith College, but her main interest was mountain climbing.

In 1885, she entered the American School of Classical Studies in Athens, Greece, where she first became interested in mountaineering. While she lectured on the classics beginning in 1892, her climbing made her a minor celebrity in 1895 when she ascended the Matterhorn. In 1897, she went to Mexico where she became the first woman to climb Mount Orizaba.

Peck achieved a great deal of fame for her climbing feats. In 1900, by now a popular lecturer all over the United States, she became the nation's delegate to the Congrès Internationale de l'Alpinisme held in Paris, France. She climbed in South America, searching for a way to conquer the twin-peaked Peruvian mountain Huascarán,

Mountain climber and suffragist Annie Smith Peck, a founder of the American Alpine Club. (Photo courtesy Sophia Smith Collection, Smith College)

which was estimated to be about 24,000 feet high. In 1908, she ascended the north peak and received several awards, including a gold medal from the Peruvian government. In 1927, the northern peak of Huascarán was named for her.

Peck wrote extensively about her climbing. In 1911, she published *A Search for the Apex of America,* and in 1913 produced a guidebook, *The South American Tour.* Peck was a pioneer in women's mountaineering, and was a founder of the American Alpine Club in 1902. In 1917, she became a member of the Royal Geographic Society, and joined the Society of Woman Geographers in 1928.

When she was sixty-one years old, Peck unfurled a banner inscribed "Votes for Women" at the summit of Mount Coropuna in Peru to promote woman suffrage. And when she died on 18 July 1935, she was eighty-five years old, but had completed a climb of Mount Madison in New Hampshire only twenty-four months earlier.

6 February 1910
LABOR.   Striking Philadelphia garment workers settle their strike by means of arbitration.

15 February 1910
LABOR.   Garment workers in New York City end their general walkout without a comprehensive settlement.

11 June 1910
POPULAR CULTURE.   The Printers' Association of America launches efforts to deny illustration of women's skirts on billboards.

19 June 1910
POPULAR CULTURE.   Mrs. John Bruce Dodd helps establish the tradition of Father's Day, first observed in Spokane, Washington.

25 June 1910
LEGISLATIVE. The Mann Act is passed by the U.S. Congress, prohibiting interstate or foreign transport of females for immoral purposes.

1 September 1910
POPULAR CULTURE. Nan Jane Aspinwall is the first woman to make a solo transcontinental horseback ride from San Francisco, California, to New York City. The trip covers 4,500 miles and takes her 301 days. She arrives in New York City on 8 July 1911.

2 September 1910
WOMEN'S ISSUES. In Los Angeles, California, the first woman police officer, A. S. Wells, is appointed under civil service regulations.

16 September 1910
AVIATION. C. B. Harmon is the first woman to win a trophy for her balloon flight over Dayton, Ohio.

23 October 1910
AVIATION. Blanche Stuart Scott is the first woman pilot to make a public flight. In an Ely machine, she travels to a height of 12 feet.

8 November 1910
LEGISLATIVE. The state of Washington passes a constitutional amendment to permit woman suffrage.

During the first decade of the twentieth century, a woman's hat was an integral part of her street costume. Many hats sported bows, veils, fringe, tassels, and artificial birds. (Photo courtesy Judith Freeman Clark)

II

THE DEMAND FOR WOMAN SUFFRAGE
1911–1920

The culmination of women's efforts on behalf of voting occurred in August 1920 when the Nineteenth Amendment became law. Throughout the preceding ten years thousands of women, led by such notables as Alice Paul and Jane Addams, protested in orderly and disorderly fashion, demanding the right to vote. Once they had won that right, they established the League of Women Voters and worked to encourage American women to take advantage of their newly gained political power.

But this step forward was paralleled in other areas as well. Gradually, women were appointed and elected to public positions. During this decade the first woman civil service commissioner was named by President Woodrow Wilson, and in California, the first state attorney general assumed her post. Among the most remarkable of those women elected to office was Jeannette Rankin (R-Montana). She had the courage sufficient to cast one of only a few votes against U.S. entry into World War I. That she accomplished this prior to nationwide woman suffrage (Montana gave women the vote in 1914) is even more noteworthy.

Women continued to take their places in the ranks of commerce, industry, medicine, sports, and the military. During World War I, women worked as streetcar conductors and faced severe criticism from men who considered such tasks demeaning for women. The first birth control clinic opened under the direction of Margaret Sanger. And two women physicians were elected to the American College of Surgeons in 1914.

Swimmer Ethelda Bleibtrey, one of the first in a long line of American women championship swimmers, broke the world record for the 100-meter freestyle in 1920, and also brought home an Olympic gold medal in that event. Finally, the U.S. Marine Corps Reserve admitted the first woman, as did the U.S. Navy, and the U.S. Army School of Nursing opened at Walter Reed Army Hospital. These initial openings in the military permitted women opportunities to prove their worth in what was a particularly demanding male setting.

By World War II, women were integrated into civilian defense work as well as the military, areas that might have been closed to them had this earlier generation not paved the way for change. But it would take the test of time, and the support of all Americans, to enable women to effect any lasting changes in the economic, political, and cultural landscape of the nation.

Early Labor Activists and Organizers

One of the most well-publicized labor strikes in the United States involving women occurred on 25 November 1909. After a meeting of the International Ladies' Garment Workers Union (ILGWU) at which women garment workers in New York exchanged tales of poor working conditions and insufficient wages, more than 25,000 workers walked out on strike.

This "Uprising of the Twenty Thousand" as it was called, along with one of its chief organizers, Rose Schneiderman, received enormous attention. But six years earlier, in 1903, the Women's Trade Union League (WTUL) had been founded to aid in the organization of women workers. Schneiderman and Mary Anderson (later head of the federal Women's Bureau) were both active in the WTUL, and Schneiderman became a national president in 1926. Other women associated with the early labor movement were Leonora O'Reilly, Ella Bloor, Mary Kenny, Alice Hamilton, Mary McDowell, and Mary Dreier and her sister, Margaret Dreier Robins; many of them were also involved in the settlement house movement. Rose Pesotta was another woman active in labor efforts. She attended the Bryn Mawr Summer School for Women Workers in 1922, and by 1934 she was a vice-president in the ILGWU.

After the Triangle Shirtwaist Company fire on 25 March 1911 claimed the lives of 146 workers—mostly women and children—labor activists like Frances Perkins worked hard to obtain legislative labor reforms. But this type of activity could not quell demands for better conditions and fair wages. Labor unrest and strikes continued to disrupt production and call attention to workers' demands.

In 1912, when more than 10,000 textile workers in Lawrence, Massachusetts, went out on strike, Mother Jones was among the leaders of that group. Elizabeth Gurley Flynn also participated in this three-month walkout, as did birth control advocate Margaret Sanger. Flynn was also present at a similar labor strike in Paterson, New Jersey, in 1913.

Women labor activists found it difficult to make gains during the Depression years after an encouraging period in the 1920s. But formation of the Congress of Industrial Organizations (CIO) in 1934 gave important support to women workers. Unlike the American Federation of Labor (AFL), which ignored women workers, the CIO promoted their acceptance into unions. A case in point was the textile trades. The United Textile Workers (UTW) had not admitted women; however, formation of the Textile Workers Union of America resulted in an increase in membership. Union members from textile mills increased from 20,000 in 1936 to 120,000 in 1943.

A total of 800,000 women workers had been organized into unions by 1940, a figure that represents a 300 percent increase in a ten-year period. Much of this increase was due to the efforts of dedicated labor activists—women like Mary Barker and

Louise McClaren, who organized the Southern Summer School for Women Workers in Industry in Atlanta, Georgia; Selma Borchardt, a lawyer who worked with the American Federation of Teachers; and Gladys Dickason of the Amalgamated Clothing Workers of America. Without their energy, and the selfless work of thousands of unnamed others, organized labor in the United States might have been even slower to recognize and place a value on the contributions of women workers.

---

17 March 1911
POPULAR CULTURE. Mrs. Luther Halsey Gulick establishes the organization known as Campfire Girls in Lake Sebago, Maine.

25 March 1911
LABOR. The Triangle Shirtwaist Company fire claims the lives of 146 garment workers in New York City.

2 April 1911
LABOR. The Women's Trade Union League holds a memorial for the fire victims and a protest meeting at the Metropolitan Opera House in New York City. The group hopes to promote reform action in the aftermath of the Triangle Shirtwaist Company fire.

5 April 1911
LABOR. Eighty thousand people march for 4 hours on New York City's Fifth Avenue to attend the funeral of those who perished in the Triangle Shirtwaist Company fire late in March.

11 April 1911
WOMEN'S ISSUES. At a meeting of the Feminist Alliance, members draft a letter to President Wilson demanding passage of a constitutional amendment designed to prohibit job discrimination on the basis of gender.

24 May 1911
WOMEN'S ISSUES. Therese Hubbell West Elmendorf of Buffalo, New York, becomes the first woman president of the American Library Association.

9 June 1911
DEATHS. Temperance advocate Carry A. Nation dies.

1 August 1911
AVIATION. Harriet Quimby becomes the first woman airplane pilot to receive a license, issued by the Aero Club of America.

1 March 1912
WOMEN'S ISSUES. Isabella Goodwin, the first woman police detective, is appointed as a sergeant in the New York City Police Department.

12 March 1912
POPULAR CULTURE. Juliette Gordon Low founds the Girl Guides in America, later to be known as the Girl Scouts.

14 April 1912
INTERNATIONAL. Margaret "Molly" Brown rows a group of surviving passengers to safety after the ocean liner *Titanic* sinks, killing 1,502 people.

19 May 1912
SPORTS. Alpinist Dora Keen successfully reaches the summit of Mount Blackburn (16,390 feet) in Alaska. She is the first woman to do so.

20 May 1912
SPORTS. At a meeting of the Board of Governors of the New York Lawn Tennis Club, it is decided that tournaments for women players should be held.

29 May 1912
POPULAR CULTURE. Curtis Publishing Company in Philadelphia, Pennsylvania (home of *Ladies' Home Journal*) dismisses 15 women from their jobs after editor Edward Bok sees the women dancing the "turkey trot" during their lunch hour.

4 June 1912
REFORM. Julia Clifford Lathrop is named the first chief of the Children's Bureau, a branch of the Commerce and Labor Department. Lathrop's salary is $5,000 per year.

12 June 1912
POPULAR CULTURE. Lillian Russell retires from her stage career and marries Alexander P.

Moore. Russell says she will now be "just another housewife."

OTHER EVENTS OF 1912

SUFFRAGE. Progressive Party delegates vote in favor of a woman suffrage plank for their party campaign platform.

BUSINESS. Household efficiency expert Christine Frederick founds the League of Advertising Women in New York City.

IDEAS/BELIEFS. Henrietta Szold, a Zionist, founds Hadassah, a Jewish welfare organization.

6 January 1913
POLITICS. In Warrenton, Oregon, Clara Munson becomes the first woman to be elected mayor of a city west of the Rocky Mountains.

3 March 1913
SUFFRAGE. A demonstration is held in Washington, D.C., on behalf of woman suffrage. Alice Paul is the chief organizer of the event, which draws nearly 10,000 marchers.

The Settlement House Movement

Settlement houses in the United States were patterned after the great English settlement, Toynbee Hall, which was visited by many of America's settlement house founders. Among them was Jane Addams, who established Hull House in 1889. Several years before that, Lillian Wald had founded the Henry Street Settlement in New York City. Other early settlements were Denison House and Andover House in Boston, Massachusetts, and the Neighborhood Guild in New York City. Vida Scudder, later president of Wellesley College, helped organize the College Settlement Association in 1887, which opened yet another New York City settlement house.

Part of a larger reform movement that carried through to the early 1920s and beyond, settlement houses worked to improve living conditions for both immigrants and natives, though the former group seemed predominant in many cities. Located primarily in poor sections of urban areas, settlement houses also provided an outlet for talents and energies of women college graduates who looked for ways to use their education. This group of women increased steadily: In 1900, 5,237 women received B.A. degrees; by 1920 that number had grown to 16,642 women.

In 1891, there were six settlements in the United States; by 1900 there were one hundred. By 1910 there were more than four hundred such centers of reform nationwide, and it was clear by their growth that they were part of an established movement. At the settlements women taught a variety of classes. Sometimes they instructed immigrants in English; they organized kindergartens and young people's social clubs; they ran sewing and cooking classes. Settlement house workers often went into neighboring homes to dispense medical care or to give advice on everything from nutrition and well-baby care to waste disposal and personal hygiene. In 1902, Wald set up the first nursing system for public schools, based at her New York City settlement house.

In addition to working with disadvantaged groups, most settlement workers were involved in various lobbying efforts aimed at reform. A few, like Addams, developed a distinct political position. Others worked tirelessly, but maintained a quieter profile. Protective laws concerning child labor, sanitary conditions on city streets, and the quality of public education were a few of their concerns. Union meetings were held at Hull House, and Addams worked closely with labor leaders. Their interest in improving the quality of life for all people led many settlement workers to involvement in peace efforts. Wald and Fanny Garrison Villard marched in protest of war in August 1914. Addams helped found the Woman's Peace Party in 1915.

Some have questioned the efficacy of settlement house work in helping women break stereotypes of traditional, nurturing roles that they had held so long. Although it is true that the tasks and activities at many settlements were similar to those occupying the time of wives and mothers, settlement work encouraged development of broader opportunities for women. Many women active in settlement houses subsequently became leaders in the fight for woman suffrage. Some achieved high positions in municipal, state, and federal government, advocating a variety of reform and regulatory programs. Frances Perkins, the first U.S. woman cabinet member, worked at the Chicago Commons Settlement in 1905.

The settlement house movement helped professional women gain respectability. The growth of various organizations early in the century reflects this acceptance. The National Organization of Public Health Nurses (1912), the International Association of Policewomen (1915), the Federation of Teachers (1916), and the National Association of Deans of Women (1916), were by-products, in one way or another, of the tremendous surge in careers for women of which settlement work was among the very first.

Although estimates show that most women spent less than five years in settlement work before marrying, a romanticized view of their work and profession persists. Settlement house workers are often seen as dedicating their lives to their career, sacrificing everything for their cause.

But the value of settlement workers' efforts transcends their marital status, the length of time they spent at a settlement house, or their individual political views. What remains important is that settlement work established an urban reform niche for women that gradually extended to other disciplines. It helped them gain confidence and experience in a range of responsibilities, both civic and moral. And it provoked all women to examine their commitments while offering a viable opportunity to test their ideals and serve society while doing so.

---

19 April 1913
SUFFRAGE. Antisuffragists appear in protest of the Senate Woman Suffrage Committee at the nation's Capitol. The antisuffragists speak on behalf of women who feel that a woman's place is in the home. Among the protesters' comments is the statement that "the work of women has been fairly successful for the last 19 centuries."

5 May 1913
SUFFRAGE. Helen Keller announces her support for woman suffrage and states that she believes the women of America "cannot hope to get anything unless they are willing to fight and suffer for it."

12 June 1913
SUFFRAGE. Women in Springfield, Illinois, celebrate victory in the passage of a state woman suffrage bill.

21 June 1913
AVIATION. Georgia Broadwick is the first woman to make a parachute jump, over Los Angeles, California.

29 January 1914
LABOR. A group of unemployed women meet at Cooper Union to speak with Mayor Mitchell of New York City. The women plan to ask for state aid in finding suitable employment. Many of the women have complained about difficulties in finding decent wages. Some factory and shop positions pay as little as $5 per week, according to the women.

4 April 1914
POPULAR CULTURE. Actress Pearl White appears in New York City in the first motion picture serial, *The Perils of Pauline*.

New York City suffrage parade, May 1913. (Photo courtesy Sophia Smith Collection, Smith College)

7 May 1914
POPULAR CULTURE. President Wilson decrees that the second Sunday in May will now be a national holiday known as Mother's Day.

22 May 1914
WOMEN'S ISSUES. Labor organizer Mother Jones speaks out in favor of women's right to free speech.

Bohemian Women

Many writers, artists, actors, and others searching for a supportive, expansive environment in which to express themselves flocked to New York City's Greenwich Village in the decades prior to World War I. Among these seekers were a number of women whose contributions to the avant garde were both recognized and revered.

This curious American bohemia was fueled by certain realities: By 1910 more women than ever before were gainfully employed, and advanced degrees were more commonplace. Ten percent of all Ph.D.'s granted in 1910 went to women; by 1920 that number had risen to 15.1 percent.

Many of these well-educated women with a penchant for bohemian life-styles were strong supporters of feminist politics. They campaigned for woman suffrage and they demonstrated for peace. They decried poor working conditions and were obsessed with creative expression. And they documented their activities extensively on paper.

In publications like *The Masses,* into which Crystal Eastman poured so much energy, women expressed their views on politics, birth control, economics, suffrage, feminism, and world peace. Social workers like Lillian Wald worked in neighborhood settlements like the famous one on Henry Street. Activists like Henrietta Rodman promoted total independence of the American woman as outlined by Charlotte Perkins Gilman, partly through the Feminist Alliance, which Rodman helped found in 1914. Margaret Sanger and Emma Goldman were found in the Village too, dispensing advice on birth control and anarchy, respectively.

A well-known dramatic group in the Village during this period was the Provincetown Players. An experimental troupe dedicated to both entertainment and edification, the Provincetown Players had its inception when the Washington Square Players met in the summer of 1915 at the summer residence of Mary Heaton Vorse in Cape Cod, Massachusetts. By 1916, the renamed thespians held winter sessions in the Village. Ida Rauh, Crystal Eastman, Neith Boyce, Edna St. Vincent Millay, and Susan Glaspell were among the women in this highly original and creative gathering. They acted, directed, wrote, and, above all, they conceded nothing to the commonplace.

Dramatics, poetry, art, and politics kept the inhabitants of Greenwich Village in a flurry of intellectual activity. But after the United States entered World War I and women were granted the vote, the vital force seemed to go out of major issues occupying those living in the Village. The hopes of ardent pacifists and feminists were disappointed in the decade following the Treaty of Versailles and passage of the Nineteenth Amendment, and the utopian ideals of those who made Greenwich Village their home remained an unrealized, bohemian dream.

---

24 May 1914
SUFFRAGE. The National Association Opposed to Women Suffrage issues a bulletin that attacks woman suffrage. The organization warns that feminists favor "free love."

22 June 1914
MEDICAL. Alice Gertrude Bryant, M.D., and Florence West Duckering, M.D., become the first women members admitted to the American College of Surgeons, 2 years after the group's incorporation.

30 June 1914
SUFFRAGE. President Wilson asserts that the fight for woman suffrage should be won by individual states, not via a constitutional amendment.

16 July 1914
SUFFRAGE. William Jennings Bryan announces his support of woman suffrage saying, "Politics will not suffer by women's entrance into it."

13 October 1914
WOMEN'S ISSUES. Annette Abbott Adams is sworn in as attorney general of the Northern District of California. She is the first woman to be a federal prosecutor.

OTHER EVENTS OF 1914

EDUCATION. The University of Delaware establishes a Women's College. Delaware is the last state to provide an institution of higher learning for women.

16 September 1915
SUFFRAGE. Suffragist Sara B. Field leaves San Francisco, California, on a coast-to-coast trip, carrying a petition containing 500,000 names of women who support a woman-suffrage amendment to the U.S. Constitution. The petition is delivered to President Wilson on 6 December 1915.

23 October 1915
SUFFRAGE. Twenty-five thousand suffragists march in New York City, demanding voting rights for all American women.

11 February 1916
IDEAS/BELIEFS. Anarchist Emma Goldman is arrested for violating a New York state code prohibiting public lectures on various medical topics. Goldman is alleged to have spoken on issues related to birth control.

16 October 1916
MEDICAL. Margaret Sanger opens the nation's first birth control clinic in Brooklyn, New York.

17 October 1916
POPULAR CULTURE. Annette Kellerman appears in the motion picture, *A Daughter of the Gods.* Kellerman's lack of attire prompts extensive public debate and commentary on this new "sex" film.

Charlotte Perkins Gilman, 1860–1935

Few would dispute Charlotte Perkins Gilman's place at the head of the twentieth-century women's movement in the United States. She was a brilliant idealist whose efforts promoted economic equality for women, thereby encouraging their independence. Born 3 July 1860 in Hartford, Connecticut, Gilman claimed a distinguished lineage. Her father, Frederic Beecher Perkins, was the grandson of Lyman Beecher and nephew of both Henry Ward Beecher and Harriet Beecher Stowe. Her mother, Mary Fitch (Westcott) Perkins, was descended from the settlers of colonial Rhode Island. Despite their august forebears, her family experienced little financial stability. She worked as a governess and an art instructor during her adolescence, and in May 1884 she married artist Charles Walter Stetson. Their daughter Katherine was born a year later.

Soon, she began suffering from a nervous condition that ended in her complete collapse. Despite her husband's affectionate ministrations, she concluded her sanity depended on living apart from him. In 1888, she moved to California with her daughter, and in 1894 she and Stetson were divorced. Her ex-husband soon married Grace Ellery Channing, a close friend of Charlotte's, and Katherine, with her mother's blessing, went east to live with the couple.

Gilman had been supporting herself by lecturing and by writing since 1891, publishing poetry and short stories. She was a persuasive speaker, and in 1894 became active in promoting feminism in California.

Traveling to London in 1896, she was a delegate to the International Socialist and Labor Congress, although she was never a Socialist party member. In 1898, she published *Women and Economics,* a book that received wide acceptance and has come to represent much that was basic to the early feminist movement in this country. In the book, Gilman details the pervasive quality of male values in American life and the resulting limits on women's activities and opportunities.

On 11 June 1900, she married lawyer George Houghton Gilman, her first cousin. The couple had no children, although Katherine visited for several years prior to her own marriage. Once more, Gilman found it difficult to integrate domestic responsibilities with her career. She therefore employed a good friend, Helen Campbell, to run her home while she prepared her book, *Human Work,* for publication in 1904.

In 1909, Gilman began writing, editing, and publishing the *Forerunner,* which sought to promote a new social order with independence and equality for women in a variety of articles on social, political, and economic topics. The magazine ceased publication in 1916 with fewer than one thousand subscribers, although Gilman's efforts in this periodical were equal to writing about four books a year.

Gilman continued to write, publishing *The Man-Made World* in 1911, which discussed in detail the clash between male and female values. In 1913, she spoke at the International Suffrage Convention in Budapest, Hungary, and in 1915 she joined Jane Addams in helping to found the Woman's Peace Party.

In 1923, she wrote *His Religion and Hers,* although by the 1920s, feminism was less powerful. In 1932, Gilman learned she had breast cancer. Her husband died in 1934, and Gilman went to live with her married daughter in Pasadena, California. On 17 August 1935, she committed suicide.

Her suicide note asserted, "When all usefulness is over, when one is assured of an unavoidable and imminent death, it is the simplest of human rights to choose a quick and easy death in place of a slow and horrible one." Gilman thus acted on her philosophy that independence was chief among the courses of action critical to all individuals. Her last act was characteristic of her radical views and was in keeping with the position she had established for herself in the women's movement.

---

29 November 1916
SPORTS.   The Women's International Bowling Congress is organized. The group is incorporated on 20 October 1919.

5 December 1916
SUFFRAGE.   At the House of Representatives, members of the Congressional Union for Woman Suffrage unfurl a large banner that asks, "Mr. President, What Will You Do for Woman Suffrage?" Among those holding the banner in President Wilson's view are Florence B. Hilles of Wilmington, Delaware, and Dr. Caroline E. Spencer of Colorado.

22 March 1917
MILITARY.   Eighteen-year-old Loretta Walsh becomes the first U.S. Naval Petty Officer. She will be a recruiter for the Naval Coast Defense Reserve.

17 June 1917
AVIATION.   Pilot Julia Clark is the first woman airplane fatality. She is killed when her Curtis biplane crashes at the Illinois State Fairgrounds in Springfield.

10 July 1917
IDEAS/BELIEFS.   Anarchist Emma Goldman is sentenced to 2 years' imprisonment and fined $10,000 for obstructing the military draft.

14 July 1917
SUFFRAGE.   The National Women's party begins picketing the White House, demonstrating in favor of universal woman suffrage.

28 August 1917
SUFFRAGE.   Ten suffragists are arrested for demonstrating in front of the White House.

24 October 1917
MILITARY.   Abby Putnam Morrison is assigned to the Radio Bureau of the U.S. Navy as the first woman naval electrician.

6 November 1917
SUFFRAGE.   New York state passes a woman suffrage resolution, giving Empire State women the right to vote.

10 November 1917
SUFFRAGE.   In Washington, D.C., 41 women from 15 states are arrested as they picket with posters and placards in favor of woman suffrage.

Women and World War I

These young women were photographed at the Scott and Browne Plant, Bloomfield, New Jersey, in 1917, shortly after the United States entered World War I. (Photo courtesy Sophia Smith Collection, Smith College)

When the United States entered World War I in 1917, many American women faced personal dilemmas. They had been outspoken concerning peace in their general efforts to upgrade the world and improve it for future generations. Some, like Jane Addams and Emily Greene Balch, worked hard to promote peace as part of general reform issues. Others had waged a campaign to keep the nation out of war, and many of them, like Rose Pastor Stokes and Kate Richards O'Hare, were even jailed for their outspoken efforts.

But when the United States abandoned its neutral position and actually declared war in April 1917, women throughout the country bowed to the inevitable. Almost overnight they took up the cause of national defense and sought out ways to bolster the war effort. The Army Nurse Corps had been established in 1901, giving women the chance to serve both at home and in European medical facilities, as well as on board hospital ships.

Women filled in for men in a variety of ways on the home front. They were streetcar conductors, elevator operators, and munitions workers. Women also worked in steel mills, in the mines, and on farms, filling in for their absent husbands, fathers, brothers, and sons.

Despite wartime exigencies, however, women often found that they were unwelcome additions to the workforce. Male labor unions were loath to permit women to enter their ranks. By 1920, only one out of every fifteen women factory workers belonged to a union. And the average weekly earnings for female production workers was $18 for forty-three hours. Men averaged $32 for a forty-nine-hour week.

The federal government established the Women in Industry Service Bureau. Its function—to monitor the conditions of women in the workplace—was admittedly limited to the twenty-month duration of the war, which ended on 11 November 1918. But following the armistice, the bureau became a permanent government agency—the Women's Bureau of the U.S. Department of Labor. Employment figures gathered by this group show that in 1910, 8 million women were gainfully employed, but by 1920, that number had risen only slightly, to about 8,550,000.

In general, World War I did not usher in a new era for women at work. The conflict overseas, though it claimed 112,000 American lives, was too brief to provoke a major change in women's roles. They had no sustained opportunity to establish themselves in the workplace. And despite passage of the Nineteenth Amendment in August 1920, it would not be until after 1940 that patterns of women's employment would alter, again due largely to global war.

OTHER EVENTS OF 1917

LEGISLATIVE. The Volstead Act, requiring the prohibition of alcohol in the United States, is submitted for ratification by individual states.

WOMEN'S ISSUES. The first woman to be admitted to the American Bar Association is Mary Florence Lathrop.

BUSINESS. Bina West Miller establishes the Woman's Benefit Association for women's life insurance in Port Huron, Michigan.

DEATHS. Hawaii's Queen Liliuokalani dies at age 79.

29 March 1918
LABOR. The Bureau of Labor Statistics reports that 1,426,000 women have joined the work force since 1911. Women have replaced 1,413,000 men in jobs since 1914.

25 May 1918
MILITARY. The secretary of war authorizes the establishment of the Army School of Nursing at Walter Reed Army Hospital. The school's first director is Annie Warburton Goodrich.

12 August 1918
MILITARY. Opha May Johnson becomes a private in the U.S. Marine Corps Reserve. She is the first woman to join the Marine Corps.

30 September 1918
SUFFRAGE. President Wilson speaks to the U.S. Senate in support of woman suffrage, saying it is "a necessary war measure."

15 October 1918
WOMEN'S ISSUES. Kathryn Sellers is appointed the first woman judge of a juvenile court in Washington, D.C.

3 December 1918
LABOR. In Cleveland, Ohio, male members of the Union of Streetcar Conductors go on strike. They protest the continued employment of women streetcar conductors.

17 March 1919
LABOR. The War Labor Board rules in favor of the continued employment of women streetcar conductors in Cleveland, Ohio.

3 May 1919
AVIATION. Mrs. J. A. Hodges and Miss Ethel Hodges become the first commercial airplane passengers, flying from New York City to Atlantic City, New Jersey.

The Women's Christian Temperance Union

An outgrowth of the intense reformist impulse of the late nineteenth century, the Women's Christian Temperance Union (WCTU) was founded in 1873 in Hillsboro, Ohio. Its motto was "For God and Home and Every Land." Frances Willard, a Chicago educator and Dean of Women at Northwestern University, joined the WCTU in 1874 and became its first president. Willard left an indelible stamp on the organization which, by 1900, had grown to 150,000 members whose chief aim was to eradicate the sale of alcoholic beverages. Willard's stated purpose for the group was, in her words, "to protect the home." By 1911, the WCTU, which was ecumenical in spirit and far-reaching in scope and intention, claimed 245,000 women as members in various chapters in all states. It was by then the largest women's organization in the nation.

The fervor of WCTU meetings held significant appeal for many of its members, although some feared what they perceived as "radicalism." Willard's distinctly socialist leanings were rejected by some members of the WCTU, for whom a conservative reform approach was more palatable. The latter group broke with the main organization and established the National Women's Evangelical Temperance Union, which was short-lived.

Although some tactics used by WCTU members to advance their cause made them the object of derision, by 1919 they could point with pride to their accomplishments. Passage of the Volstead Act prohibited sale of liquor throughout the nation. At WCTU headquarters in Evanston, Illinois, the group subsequently established the Frances E. Willard Memorial Library for Alcohol Research. The organization also used two periodicals, *Union Signal* and *Young Crusader,* to reach the public and keep members informed.

In addition to its importance concerning alcoholic beverage consumption, the WCTU was the basic training ground for supporters of suffrage in the early twentieth century. Because of Willard's unsurpassed leadership skills, women belonging to the WCTU learned organizational strategies, means by which to widen their intellectual outlook, and—most important—how to effect reform. Aside from the abolitionist movement, temperance was the main issue around which women rallied most consistently and most effectively. Without the WCTU as a springboard to action, suffrage reform would have been far less likely to have occurred in the manner, and have the results, that it did.

4 June 1919
LEGISLATIVE. Congress proposes the Nineteenth Amendment to the Constitution, which would give women the right to vote.

21 October 1919
BUSINESS. Margaret P. Owen establishes a speed record for typewriting: She produces 170 error-free words in one minute.

19 November 1919
ARTS AND CULTURE. Sylvia Beach opens her bookshop, Shakespeare and Co., in Paris,

France. Beach subsequently publishes James Joyce's controversial novel, *Ulysses.*

1 December 1919
INTERNATIONAL. Lady Nancy Witcher Langhorne Astor becomes the first U.S. woman elected member of Parliament to the House of Commons, representing Plymouth, England.

OTHER EVENTS OF 1919

WOMEN'S ISSUES. Architect Julia Morgan is hired by William Randolph Hearst to build La

Casa Grande, with more than 100 rooms and a 25-stall garage.

ARTS AND CULTURE.   The National Academy of Design elects its first female member—Mary Evelyn Beatrice Longman, a sculptor.

BUSINESS.   Zonta International, an organization of business and professional women, is founded. One of its objectives is to improve the status of women.

27 March 1920
POPULAR CULTURE.   Actress Mary Pickford, "America's Sweetheart," marries actor Douglas Fairbanks.

9 April 1920
WOMEN'S ISSUES.   Marie Luhring is elected the first woman member of the Society of

Automotive Engineers. In June 1922, she receives a Master of Engineering from Cooper Union in New York City.

13 April 1920
WOMEN'S ISSUES.   Helen Hamilton Gardiner is named civil service commissioner by President Woodrow Wilson.

13 May 1920
LABOR.   In a letter to the Women's Bureau, the president of the Amalgamated Association of Street and Electric Railway Employees of America states that trolley cars are "no fit place for a woman to work."

Carrie Chapman Catt, 1859–1947

Pacifist and suffragist Carrie Clinton Lane Chapman Catt was born in Ripon, Wisconsin, on 9 January 1859, the only daughter of Lucius and Maria (Clinton) Lane. Her childhood was spent on a farm in Iowa; she was active, energetic, and an excellent student. Against her father's wishes she attended Iowa State College, graduating with a B.S. in November 1880, and became superintendant of schools in Mason City, Iowa, in 1883.

In 1885, Carrie Lane married Leo Chapman, a newspaper editor. After his death from typhoid in 1886, she worked as a news reporter and lecturer, and in 1887 joined the Iowa Woman Suffrage Association. In 1890, Carrie Chapman married George William Catt, a firm supporter of woman suffrage who gave her both financial backing and moral encouragement for her work. In 1895, she was named chairperson of the organization committee of the National American Woman Suffrage Association (NAWSA). She helped campaign for funds and garnered state-by-state support for votes for women.

In 1900, Susan B. Anthony named Catt to succeed her as president of NAWSA. Serving for four years, she resigned in 1904 due to her husband's failing health. But Catt had quite brilliantly imposed an efficient structure on the organization, permitting it to flourish as never before possible. Catt's husband died in 1905, and after that she worked diligently in New York state to organize the Woman Suffrage Party. In 1915, due in part to her able campaign efforts in New York state, she was once again elected to the presidency of NAWSA.

Catt favored a broad approach to the problem of legalizing votes for women. She supported passage of a federal suffrage amendment, but she also recognized that state ratification of such an amendment was crucial. Therefore, Catt advocated what came to be known as the "Winning Plan," a program designed to win the respect of political leaders across the nation.

Carrie Chapman Catt, women's rights advocate and peace activist. It was Catt's suggestion that a meeting of the nation's women's organizations might promote world peace, and, in 1915, this meeting resulted in the Woman's Peace Party. (Photo courtesy Sophia Smith Collection, Smith College)

She helped to found the Woman's Peace Party in 1915, but when the United States entered World War I she worked tirelessly on defense efforts. Still, she placed votes for women at the forefront of her activities, and when the Nineteenth Amendment was adopted, Catt was acknowledged, along with Susan B. Anthony, as having been responsible for that victory.

Catt was a leader of the International Woman Suffrage Alliance from 1904 to 1923, and she helped establish the League of Women Voters in 1919. A strong proponent of world peace, she worked on the Committee on the Cause and Cure of War between 1925 and 1939. Catt died of a heart attack on 10 March 1947.

23 July 1920
WOMEN'S ISSUES. A dispute grows over a Topeka, Kansas, city clerk's demands that women who register to vote must reveal their ages. A group of women organize a "21-plus" club in response to the requirement, stating that they cannot be required to give their real ages, only that they are over 21.

25 August 1920
SPORTS. Ethelda Bleibtrey breaks the world's record for the 100-meter freestyle swim. Her time is 1:13:6.

26 August 1920
SUFFRAGE. The Nineteenth Amendment to the U.S. Constitution is ratified, providing for woman suffrage nationwide.

2 November 1920
SUFFRAGE. In Savannah, Georgia, black women registered voters are denied ballots at several voting places in the city.

19 November 1920
WOMEN'S ISSUES. A justice of the peace in Chicago, Illinois, rules that women must remove

their hats in the courtroom. Two women who refuse to do so are fined $5 each.

OTHER EVENTS OF 1920

WOMEN'S ISSUES. The National League of Women Voters is founded to inform and educate the public concerning political issues.

Olympic Gold Medals

Aileen Riggin: Springboard diving
Ethelda Bleibtrey: Swimming—100-meter freestyle; women's freestyle relay

Olympic Silver Medals

Helen Wainwright: Springboard diving
Irene Guest: Swimming—100-meter freestyle; women's freestyle relay

Olympic Bronze Medals

Thelma Payne: Springboard diving
Frances Schroth: Swimming—100-meter freestyle; women's freestyle relay

III

THE EQUALIZING DECADE
1921–1930

The ten years between 1921 and 1930 have often been characterized as the "Roaring Twenties." But to describe women's activities as outrageous or frenetic during that time would be to present a more or less distorted picture of what really happened. Although the first Miss America Pageant and numerous dance marathons held across the nation suggested the frivolous, in the 1920s women broke new ground in politics, law, sports, and aviation, as well as in the area loosely termed popular culture.

During the previous decade, women had fought hard to win voting rights. And they had made some advances in public office, although only a few states had granted woman suffrage prior to 1920. Now, women attended national political party conventions both as delegates and alternates. There were other "firsts" for women during these years, including the appointment of a woman diplomat to the Foreign Service and the election of a woman governor in Wyoming. In 1922, the first woman associate justice of a state supreme court was named, and by 1925 Texas had designated an all-female state supreme court. In 1926, Attorney Violette Neatly Anderson became the first black woman to practice law before the U.S. Supreme Court.

Vital medical care came to the rural poor of Kentucky when Mary Breckenridge founded the Frontier Nursing Service in 1925. In Chicago that year, the Woman's World Fair displayed efforts and accomplishments of hundreds of women in business, industry, and the arts. Elsewhere, women began working as flight attendants on regularly scheduled airlines and as police officers in many cities. Gertrude Ederle became the first woman to swim the English Channel, thereby capturing the attention of the entire world. These women were part of a steadily increasing number who were integrated into America's work force. By the 1920s, this integration had occurred in ways that would have seemed shockingly inappropriate half a century earlier, but which were now accepted as commonplace.

Gertrude Stein, 1874–1946

Gertrude Stein when she was enrolled at Johns Hopkins University Medical School. (Photo courtesy Sophia Smith Collection, Smith College)

Known principally for her writing and for her famous Paris salon of the early twentieth century, Gertrude Stein was born in Allegheny, Pennsylvania on 3 February 1874, the daughter of German-Jewish parents. Her father, Daniel Stein, and mother, Amelia (Keyser) Stein, moved back to Europe briefly, then returned to the United States, settling in California.

In 1893, Stein became a student at Radcliffe College, graduating magna cum laude with an A.B. She attended Johns Hopkins University Medical School in 1897, but left in 1902 and moved to London with her brother Leo. Relocating in Paris, she and her brother began collecting the paintings of Braque, Cézanne, Renoir, Rousseau, and others. Their address, 27 rue de Fleures, was well known, both at that time and later, as a center of culture and a gathering place for those interested in abstract art.

In 1909, Stein self-published *Three Lives,* and in 1911 finished her book, *The Making of Americans* (which was not published until 1925). In the latter volume, Stein attempted an abstract approach to writing that she followed in 1914 with *Tender Buttons.* Perhaps the most important factor to influence her life and work beginning in 1909 was Stein's lesbian relationship with Alice B. Toklas. It was due to Toklas' support and encouragement that Stein was successful in her early writing. For many, the two women became almost one persona.

Stein was both appreciated and reviled, but no matter how the critics received her work, it was never ignored. During World War I, Stein and Toklas lived briefly in Mallorca and then returned to France where they drove an ambulance. After 1919, Stein focused her attentions on the writers Hemingway, Pound, Sherwood Anderson, and F. Scott Fitzgerald, influencing all of them.

In the mid-1920s, Stein lectured at both Cambridge and Oxford in England and published *Composition as Explanation* in 1926. By 1934, she had published *The Autobiography of Alice B. Toklas* and had produced the opera *Four Saints in Three Acts,* for which Virgil Thomson wrote the score. The *Autobiography* is particularly significant in its unusual narrative approach (it was written as a history of her own career as well as that of Toklas) and its detail about Paris in the pre- and postwar eras.

Stein and Toklas moved to a new address, V rue Christien, in 1937, but during the German occupation they lived alternately in the towns of Bilignin and Culoz. Stein brought out several works between 1940 and 1946, including *Brewsie and Willie* and *Wars I Have Seen.*

Nearing seventy and ill with cancer, Stein was hospitalized at Neuilly-sur-Seine. It was too late for surgery to save her, and she died late in the evening of 27 June 1946. Toklas was buried in 1967 next to Stein's grave at Père-Lachaise cemetery.

---

28 January 1921
HEALTH. A report issued by the House of Representatives notes that motherhood in 17 foreign countries is safer than in the United States. The report is part of research done in support of passage of the Sheppard–Towner Bill to provide funding for infant and maternity care.

15 February 1921
WOMEN'S ISSUES. The Suffrage Monument, named by the artist *The Woman Movement,* is dedicated in the nation's capital. Three portrait heads, of Susan B. Anthony, Elizabeth Cady Stanton, and Lucretia Mott, were carved by sculptor Adelaide Johnson.

28 March 1921
POPULAR CULTURE. Beachwear designers predict that American women will soon be wearing 1-piece, form-fitting swimsuits.

20 June 1921
POLITICS. Alice Robertson (R-Oklahoma) chairs the House of Representatives, the first time a woman has done so.

30 August 1921
LABOR. The wife of American Federation of Labor leader Samuel Gompers criticizes married women who work not out of necessity but out of choice. She tells an Atlantic City, New Jersey, audience that these women are denying jobs to men who need them.

8 September 1921
POPULAR CULTURE. The first national beauty pageant is held in Atlantic City, New Jersey. Margaret Gorman of Washington, D.C., is named the first winner of the Miss America Pageant.

2 November 1921
HEALTH. The American Birth Control League is founded by Margaret Sanger.

23 November 1921
HEALTH. The Sheppard–Towner Act becomes law. It provides for the "welfare and hygiene of maternity and infancy" and will allow up to $1 million a year in federal aid to mothers and children.

OTHER EVENTS OF 1921

BUSINESS. General Mills, Inc., creates Betty Crocker as an advertising strategy.

27 February 1922
SUFFRAGE. The U.S. Supreme Court makes a unanimous ruling in favor of the Nineteenth Amendment.

Margaret Sanger, 1879–1966

Unlike some reformers whose commitments to a cause have their inception in adult experience, Margaret Sanger saw from childhood the effects of a high fertility rate. One of eleven children born to Michael and Anne (Purcell) Higgins, she was born in Corning, New York, on 14 September 1879. Her mother, an overburdened housewife who died at age forty-nine, was outlived by Sanger's father, an outspoken man with a knack for political argument but no talent for wage earning.

However, it was from Michael Higgins that Sanger learned independence and acquired her questioning mind. In 1902, after attending Claverack College in New York and training at the White Plains Hospital School of Nursing, she married architect William Sanger. She became pregnant almost immediately, and her son Stuart was born in 1903. Another son, Grant, was born in 1908, and in 1910, the couple had a daughter, Peggy.

Disenchanted with the tedium of housework, she sensed a growing rift between herself and her husband. The couple moved to New York City from their home in Hastings-on-Hudson, and Sanger took up radical politics while working as a nurse on the Lower East Side.

Associated with the International Workers of the World's (IWW) efforts to achieve labor rights, she developed a growing concern for women's position in the economy. She soon established herself as a writer and speaker on sexual reform and women's right to control of their bodies.

In 1912, Sanger published articles on sexuality in the Socialist weekly *Call*. In 1913, the U.S. Postal Service refused, under the provisions of the Comstock Act, to mail one issue of the *Call* because of an article it carried that Sanger had written: the topic—syphilis.

Sanger felt keenly that the injustices she perceived were a result of women's ignorance and sexual misinformation. She therefore directed her efforts toward establishing birth control information centers in the United States. She traveled to Europe to research the subject of female birth control, and in 1914 returned home to publish *The Woman Rebel*. The U.S. Postal Service once more refused to mail her materials. Sanger continued her work and was indicted for having violated postal codes.

Sanger then went to Europe where she developed new strategies for disseminating information on sexuality. As a friend of Havelock Ellis, who had written *Studies in the Psychology of Sex,* she learned the importance of integrating a broad social science approach in her work. By incorporating newly defined principles of human sexuality in her efforts to educate the general public, she hoped to overcome puritanical attitudes about sex. In demystifying sexuality, making it seem more natural and less shrouded in taboo, she intended to generate a wider appeal for her crusade.

In New York City, while his wife was still in Europe, William Sanger was arrested for distributing *Family Limitation,* a pamphlet on birth control she had written. And in 1915, the couple's daughter Peggy died of pneumonia. Stricken, Sanger returned from Europe, and found that public opinion gradually came to side with her, due in part to her personal tragedy. The U.S. government subsequently dropped charges against Sanger concerning improper use of the mails.

Sanger was determined to see a properly equipped contraceptive clinic open in the United States. She had seen such clinics in the Netherlands, and in October 1916, she and her sister opened such a clinic in Brooklyn, New York. Nearly fifty women received birth control information before police closed the facility and jailed the "birth control sisters." The subsequent trial enabled Sanger to appeal to physicians for help in giving contraceptive advice to women. And in 1921, she had garnered enough philanthropic support to fund the establishment of the American Birth Control League.

Sanger divorced William in 1920. In 1922, she married J. Noah Slee, a millionaire who supported her activities. In 1923, she opened the Birth Control Clinic Research Bureau, the first in the nation to be staffed by physicians. In 1925, Sanger founded the Holland Rantos Company to manufacture diaphragms for women. In 1936, the outcome of a court case Sanger helped initiate finally permitted mailing contraceptives to physicians. Sanger's approach to birth control was criticized by some social scientists concerned with the low birth rate during the 1930s and 1940s, but by 1952, she helped found the International Planned Parenthood Federation. She was also instrumental in supporting development of the birth control pill. After several years of frail health, Sanger died of congestive heart failure on 6 September 1966.

Neysa McMein, 1888–1949

An important contributor to commercial illustration at a time when magazines relied heavily on original work, artist and illustrator Neysa McMein was born Marjorie McMein in Quincy, Illinois, on 24 January 1888, the daughter of Harry M. and Isabelle (Parker) McMein. After attending The Art Institute of Chicago, she sketched hats for Gage Brothers of Chicago. Soon after this, she left for New York City where she worked as a model, a hat designer, and—for about six weeks—as an actress.

In 1913, at the advice of a numerologist, she changed her name from Marjorie to Neysa. Enrolling in classes at the Art Students' League, she sold a fashion illustration in 1914 to *Designer* magazine, which was published by the Butterick Company, a pattern maker.

In 1915 McMein did her first cover for *Saturday Evening Post* magazine, and soon her work appeared in *Collier's, Photoplay, McClure's Magazine, Woman's Home Companion,* and other popular publications. In 1916, she became friendly with sculptor Sally James Farnham, and by 1923 she was, with Farnham's support and encouragement, under contract to *McCall's* magazine, designing all its covers until 1937, and earning $25,000 to $35,000 annually.

On 23 May 1923, she married John G. Baragwanath, but left soon after the wedding on a European tour with Alexander Woolcott, Jascha Heifetz, and several others. Baragwanath went on a business trip. Their daughter, Joan, was born in December 1924.

McMein's career peaked during the 1920s, when, in addition to magazine covers, she produced Palmolive Soap, Betty Crocker, and Lucky Strike ads. She also wrote songs and some articles, and spoke on radio broadcasts, discussing the American standard of feminine beauty. During both World Wars, McMein produced fourteen patriotic posters for the U.S. and French governments, and in 1918 was a YMCA entertainment lecturer in France. Hard-working yet sociable, McMein spent much time with other creative people, literary and artistic notables who gathered at New York City's Algonquin Hotel for lunch. Her studio was a popular spot for rather riotous get-togethers.

By the mid-1930s, McMein had begun to specialize in oil portraiture, since color photography had caused the magazine market to shrink somewhat. Among those who sat for McMein's portraits were Warren G. Harding, Charles Chaplin, Dorothy Parker, Edna St. Vincent Millay, Anne Morrow Lindbergh, Janet Flanner, Katherine Cornell, and Helen Hayes. Despite these famous patrons, McMein was never widely known for her painting, and is remembered today chiefly because of her many magazine covers and extensive illustrations produced during the pre–World War II era. She died of complications following cancer surgery on 12 May 1949.

---

9 April 1922
SPORTS. In reference to women's participation in swimming and track and field events, the Amateur Athletic Union announces that "the time has come for properly regulating the girls' athletics. Numerous requests have come in . . . asking that girls' events be put on field day programs." The result is the institution of the National Indoor and Outdoor Track Championships for Women.

5 June 1922
WOMEN'S ISSUES. Marie Luhring becomes the first woman to receive a Master of Engineering degree from Cooper Union in New York City.

Women may have won the right to vote in 1920, but they did not relinquish the roles of wife and mother. Many brides of the era chose knee-length wedding dresses, but clung to the traditional long veil and elaborate bridal bouquet. (Photo courtesy Judith Freeman Clark)

12 September 1922
RELIGION.   The Protestant Episcopal Church votes to remove the word "obey" from the marriage ceremony.

22 September 1922
LEGISLATIVE.   The Cable Act passes Congress; as a result, women who marry foreign citizens can maintain their U.S. citizenship.

3 October 1922
POLITICS.   Rebecca Felton becomes the first woman to occupy a U.S. Senate seat. She holds office for one day following the death of her husband.

13 October 1922
INTERNATIONAL.   Children's Bureau Chief Grace Abbott is appointed as unofficial U.S. Representative to the League of Nations.

7 November 1922
POLITICS.   Grace F. Kaercher of Ortonville, Minnesota, becomes that state's first woman elected to office. She is clerk of the state supreme court.

11 November 1922
MILITARY.   The Women's Overseas Service League publishes a list of 161 women known to have lost their lives in military service during World War I.

2 December 1922
LABOR.   The Government Printing Office announces that it will pay men and women equally for the same work.

5 December 1922
INTERNATIONAL.   Lucile Atcherson Curtis is the first woman in the Foreign Service. She is assigned to the Latin Affairs department.

Willa Cather, 1873–1947

Pulitzer Prize–winning author Willa Cather was born Wilella Cather on 7 December 1873, near the town of Winchester, Virginia. Her parents, Charles F. and Mary (Baak) Cather, called their daughter "Willie" as a child, a name she changed later to Willa.

In 1883, her family moved from the large, somewhat isolated farm of Willowshade in Virginia to Nebraska in the Great Plains. Previously educated at home, she began attending school in Red Cloud, Nebraska, where the Cather family finally settled. In 1891, she enrolled in the University of Nebraska at Lincoln, where she was discovered to have a talent for writing. At the university she adopted the mannerisms and style that were to characterize her life and writings.

After graduating in 1895, Cather worked for a newspaper in Lincoln, where she reviewed stage performances and developed an appreciation for the theatrical world. Cather moved to Pittsburgh, Pennsylvania, in 1896, where she worked for several publications, including the *Home Monthly*. In 1901, she began teaching high school. She also moved from a boarding house to the home of her friend Isabelle McClung. Cather devoted much of her spare time to writing. In 1902, she went with McClung to Europe, and published *April Twilights,* a book of verse, on her return to the United States in 1903. In 1905, she brought out a book of stories, *The Troll Garden.* S. S. McClure "discovered" Cather in 1906, and that year she joined the staff of *McClure's Magazine,* where she was managing editor from 1908 to 1912.

After her novel *Alexander's Bridge* was published in serial form in *McClure's Magazine,* she resigned her staff position and launched her career as a novelist. Drawing on her years of growing up on the Great Plains, Cather wrote of the struggles of early settlers in the American West. She described their virtues and the strengths of the pioneer tradition in contrast to what she saw as a new breed of grasping, shallow commercialists.

Cather's book *One of Ours* won the 1922 Pulitzer Prize for fiction. Other titles of this period include *O Pioneers!* (1913), *Song of the Lark* (1915), and *My Ántonia* (1918). Her postwar novels dealt with historical themes. Among the better known are *The Professor's House* (1925) and *Death Comes for the Archbishop* (1927).

In 1929, Cather was elected to the National Institute of Arts and Letters. By the 1930s, she was living in the east and spent some summer months in New Brunswick on Grand Manan Island. She was named to the American Academy of Arts and Letters in 1938. In her later years Cather felt increasingly alienated from a public who she felt was unable to understand or appreciate her work. She died in New York City on 24 April 1947, leaving a will that forbade publication of her private correspondence and prevented the sale of her novels for the purpose of making motion pictures.

---

16 December 1922
WOMEN'S ISSUES.   Florence E. Allen of Cleveland, Ohio, is appointed to the Ohio Supreme Court. She is the first woman ever to be named an associate state supreme court justice.

1 January 1923
RELIGION.   The Angelus Temple of Aimee Semple McPherson's Foursquare Gospel Church is dedicated near Echo Park in Los Angeles, California.

6 April 1923
SPORTS.   At the Conference on Athletics and Physical Recreation for Women and Girls, educators agree on formalizing guidelines for women's sports competition.

9 April 1923
LABOR.   The U.S. Supreme Court rules 5–3 that a minimum wage law for women and children is unconstitutional.

11 April 1923
SPORTS.   The National Committee on Women's Athletics of the American Physical Education Association endorses resolutions stating that schools should have year-round athletic activities for girls.

31 March 1923
POPULAR CULTURE.   Alma Cummings sets a world record at the nation's first dance

marathon. She dances with her partner nonstop for 27 hours.

6 October 1923
MEDICAL.   Microbiologist Dr. Gladys Henry Dick and her physician husband George announce their success in isolating the cause of scarlet fever. A test for treatment, prevention, and diagnosis of the disease, known as the Dick test, is later developed.

OTHER EVENTS OF 1923

LABOR.   According to the U.S. Department of Labor, a woman's total yearly expenditure for clothing averages $63.55. Her husband's clothing expenses total $71.38 annually, according to the same report.

SPORTS.   Mrs. George Wightman (née Hazel Hotchkiss) establishes the international women's tennis team competition known as the Wightman Cup. The first annual match between the United States and Great Britain is played at Forest Hills, New York, and the U.S. team wins 7–0.

POPULAR CULTURE.   Kate L. Butler of Dorchester, Massachusetts, wins $200 for coining the word ''scofflaw.'' The term was Butler's entry in a contest asking for the best word to ''stigmatize those who scoff at the Prohibition law.''

Edna St. Vincent Millay, 1892–1950

A poet of magnificent delicacy and fine precision, Edna St. Vincent Millay was among the foremost literary figures of her time. Born in Rockland, Maine, on 22 February 1892, Millay was the daughter of Henry T. and Cora (Buzzelle) Millay. Her interest in poetry began early, and in 1906, she won a Gold Badge from *St. Nicholas* magazine, which published her first verse in its October issue that year.

Vincent, as she was called by intimates, graduated from Camden Hills High School in 1909; in 1912, her poem *Renascence* was chosen for publication in *Lyric Year*. As a result, Vincent enjoyed much praise and publicity, and she was soon taken under the wing of an influential New Yorker, Miss Caroline B. Dow. By 1913, Vincent had entered Vassar College and was writing many of her finest lyric pieces. She received an A.B. from Vassar in 1917, despite her struggles with the college authorities over her somewhat too independent behavior. She also published her first book that year—*Renascence and Other Poems*.

Moving to Greenwich Village, which was the height of fashion for those with creative pretensions or genuine talent, Vincent shared an apartment with her sisters. The avant garde atmosphere of the Village appealed greatly to Millay, and she was soon acting (without pay) for the newly formed Provincetown Players on MacDougal Street. She also continued writing, mostly short stories under the pseudonym Nancy Boyd.

Often ill because of her high-strung nervous system, Vincent was earning a precarious living, a fact to which she often referred in letters to family and friends. She published *A Few Figs from Thistles* in 1920, which was instantly applauded by readers everywhere, and in 1919, a pacifist play, *Aria da Capo*. In 1921, she wrote *Second April* and also traveled to Europe, a trip made possible by a contract with *Vanity Fair* magazine, for which she was to write articles. In 1922 she won the Pulitzer Prize for her book, *The Harp Weaver and Other Poems*. She was married on 18 July 1923 to Eugen J. Boissevain.

Continuing an ambitious writing schedule, Vincent traveled around the world in 1925 with her husband, and afterward the couple bought a farm in Austerlitz, New York, near the Massachusetts border. In 1927, she became involved in an appeal in Boston to commute the death sentence of Nicola Sacco and Bartolomeo Vanzetti. She demonstrated, along with hundreds of others, and was arrested for her protests on behalf of these two immigrant workers. Her poem "Justice Denied in Massachusetts" expresses her strong feelings about the outcome of that famous case.

In 1927, Vincent also wrote the libretto for an opera, *The King's Henchman*, which was performed at the Metropolitan Opera House in New York City. Throughout the 1930s she produced an extensive array of poetry, including the volumes *Fatal Interview* and *Wine from These Grapes*.

Involved with the Writers' War Board and the Red Cross, Vincent and her husband experienced serious financial losses during World War II, largely because of reverses in Boissevain's foreign import business. In 1944, she suffered a nervous breakdown, and after her husband's death in 1949, although continuing to write, she remained alone at the Austerlitz farm. She died of a heart attack on 19 October 1950.

Mary Church Terrell, 1863–1954

As an early social reformer, black political activist, and suffragist, Mary Eliza Church Terrell was well known for her efforts to secure black women's rightful place in American society. Born on 23 September 1863, in Memphis, Tennessee, she was the daughter of Robert and Louisa (Ayres) Church. Her father, the son of a white man and a slave, became the South's first black millionaire in the 1880s, after investing in Memphis real estate. Her parents were separated in the late 1860s, and she and her brother lived with their mother, a hairdresser.

Sent to Ohio when she reached school age, Terrell was educated in a model program on the campus of Antioch College. After two years, she went to public school, then to Oberlin College. She chose the classical course of instruction there, and was active in swimming and skating. She was also the freshman class poet and an editor of the *Oberlin Review.*

Although her father encouraged her to remain at home in 1884 after her graduation, Terrell disregarded his wishes. Instead, she became a faculty member at Wilberforce University in Xenia, Ohio, earning $40 a month. In 1887, she went to Washington, D.C., where she taught at an all-black secondary school, and met Robert Heberton Terrell.

When they were married in October 1891, she was obligated to leave teaching since married women at that time could not hold positions in the district's schools. The couple had a daughter, Phyllis, born in 1898, and in 1905, they adopted Mary's niece.

Between 1895 and 1901, and then from 1906 to 1911, Terrell was a member of the District of Columbia Board of Education. In 1896, she became president of the National Association of Colored Women, and was voted to a life term as that group's honorary president in 1901. Terrell actively promoted woman suffrage, and in 1904 she spoke to the International Council of Women in Berlin, Germany. Her subject was the issues facing black women in America.

A charter member of the National Association for the Advancement of Colored People, she wrote extensively on black history. She was an active lobbyist for legislation that would benefit black Americans, and she campaigned extensively against lynching. In 1904, an article Terrell wrote, "Lynching From a Negro Point of View," was published by the *North American Review.*

Terrell picketed the White House with members of the National Women's party in 1919, and also went to Zurich, Switzerland, where she spoke at the Second Congress of the Women's International League for Peace and Freedom. She referred to the latter as an "illuminating and gratifying experience." Terrell was president of the Women's Republican League of Washington, and in 1929, she helped Ruth Hanna McCormick campaign for the U.S. Senate.

A diplomatic strategist, Terrell avoided unpleasant confrontations or hostility over issues of race. In 1940, she published *A Colored Woman in a White World,* a volume that took a conventional, noncontroversial view. By 1948, however, she had become the first black woman member of the American Association of University Women, and in 1950 she participated in a demonstration to desegregate the John R. Thompson restaurant in the nation's capital.

Terrell led civil rights demonstrations, picketing to desegregate many of Washington's lunchrooms. By that time Terrell was nearly ninety years old but steadfastly maintained her dignity and her quiet, but fierce, racial pride. She died of cancer on 28 July 1968 in Annapolis, Maryland.

---

24 April 1924
SPORTS. Chicago, Illinois, is the site of the first meeting of the Women's Division of the National Amateur Athletic Federation.

10 June 1924
POLITICS. One hundred eighteen women delegates and 279 women alternates attend the Republican National Convention.

24 June 1924
POLITICS. For the first time in history, 182 women delegates and 292 women alternates are among those attending the Democratic National Convention.

26 June 1924
RELIGION. The General Council of the Presbyterian Church in the United States denies women official recognition and full voting power in synods and presbyteries.

9 July 1924
POLITICS. Lena Jones Springs, of Lancaster, South Carolina, is the first woman to be nominated for vice-president on the Democratic party ticket. She receives only 18 votes.

23 August 1924
POLITICS. Miriam A. Ferguson, known as "Ma" Ferguson to her constituents, wins the Democratic nomination for governor of Texas with more than 80,000 votes.

29 August 1924
SPORTS. Katherine Howe of Dorset, Vermont, establishes a new women's record in the flight shoot at the 44th annual Archery Association's tournament at Deerfield, Massachusetts. Howe makes a shot of 255 yards, 11.5 inches.

20 September 1924
SPORTS. The Women's National Track and Field Championships are held at Forbes Field in Pittsburgh, Pennsylvania.

OTHER EVENTS OF 1924

Olympic Gold Medals

Caroline Smith: Platform diving
Elizabeth Becker: Springboard diving
Ethel Lackie: Swimming—100-meter freestyle
Martha Norelius: Swimming—400-meter freestyle
Sybil Bauer: Swimming—100-meter backstroke
  Swimming—400-meter freestyle relay team medal

Olympic Silver Medals

Elizabeth Becker: Platform diving
Aileen Riggin: Springboard diving
M. Wehselau: Swimming—100-meter freestyle
Helen Wainwright: Swimming—400-meter freestyle
Agnes Geraghty: Swimming—100-meter breaststroke

Olympic Bronze Medals

Caroline Fletcher: Springboard diving
Gertrude Ederle: Swimming—100-meter freestyle
Gertrude Ederle: Swimming—400-meter freestyle
Aileen Riggin: Swimming—100-meter backstroke

Isadora Duncan, 1878–1927

With her devotion to self-expression and freedom of movement, Isadora Duncan encouraged new aesthetic standards that would help revolutionize American dance in the twentieth century. She was born in San Francisco, California, on 27 May 1878. Her father Joseph and her mother Dora (Gray) Duncan were devotees of art and music. Her parents divorced when she was quite young, however, and her childhood was characterized by a bohemian, unstructured atmosphere riddled with debt.

Duncan held dance classes with her sister Elizabeth in San Francisco during the late 1880s and soon joined a traveling dance group. Subsequently she moved to Chicago and then to New York City, where she performed first with Augustin Daly's theater company and then alone, as an expressive dancer.

In 1900, Duncan danced in London for the first time. She became acquainted with scholars and artists whose interest in ancient Greece whetted her appetite for the classical. In 1903, she went to Athens and developed further her own distinctive style of interpretive dance. She danced in Germany and Budapest in 1902, and she met Hungarian actor Oscar Beregi. The two had a brief romance, but by 1905 she had borne a daughter by the English stage designer Edward Gordon Craig.

Duncan's intensely inspired dance and creative expression received minimal acceptance when she toured the United States during the summer of 1908. Accordingly, she returned to Europe, where she performed very successfully. She became notorious for her disregard of convention and her indifferent, independent attitude toward conservative views.

Duncan had a son, Patrick, by Paris Eugene Singer in 1910, but in 1913, both her children were tragically drowned in an automobile mishap by the Seine River. She became pregnant shortly after their deaths, but her child died at birth. Duncan soon began dancing again and established a school in Paris. During World War I she moved her students to New York, toured South America in 1916, and by 1917 had received a degree of acceptance in San Francisco, where her own career had begun some years before.

Trying to find a permanent home for her school of dance, she left unsympathetic American audiences and traveled first to France and then to Greece. Finally, in 1921, she went to Russia, where she performed brilliantly. Her hopes for funding were disappointed when the Soviet government would not underwrite her unconventional approach to dance. In May 1922, she married Russian poet Sergey Yesenin, who committed suicide in 1925 after several tempestuous years of matrimony with the individualistic Isadora.

Duncan found it increasingly difficult to find financial security. Although she was often in despair over her tumultuous personal life, she was still able to perform convincingly. In 1927, she danced in Paris at the Théâtre Mogador, proving her interpretive skills were as commanding as ever. Shortly after that appearance, on 14 September 1927, Duncan was killed when the flowing drapery of her shawl became caught in the wheel spokes of her car. Her neck was instantly broken. Following cremation, her ashes were buried near her childrens' graves in Père Lachaise cemetery in Paris.

Aimee Semple McPherson, 1890–1944

At the time of her death, Aimee Semple McPherson had succeeded in establishing an international organization that included two hundred mission stations, four hundred churches, three thousand ordained missionaries and ministers, and twenty-two thousand members. Born in Ontario, Canada, on 9 October 1890, she was the daughter of

James M. and Mildred (Pearce) Kennedy. Dedicated as a Salvationist by her mother, who had been raised in a Salvation Army family, she converted to the Pentecostal religion in 1908, and married evangelist Robert James Semple the same year.

She became a preacher of the Full Gospel Assembly in Chicago at age eighteen. In 1910, her husband died and her daughter, Roberta Star Semple, was born.

Semple married Harold McPherson in 1912, but the couple, with one son, Rolf, divorced in 1921. She returned to Ontario and began to preach, traveling to Providence, Rhode Island, in 1916, and conducting an extensive, two-year tour. In 1917, she started publishing the monthly magazine, the *Bridal Call*. She was known as a "miracle woman" due to her alleged faith-healing abilities, and she soon traveled to Los Angeles, where she received generous donations for the building of a five-thousand-seat Angelus Temple. This structure was dedicated in 1923.

McPherson preached three times each Sunday and daily throughout the week, devoting time to both healing and conversion. Her appeal was to the poor, whom she aided not only with spiritual guidance but by freely dispensing food and clothing to those in need. She also operated an employment bureau, arranged for free legal advice, and provided the disadvantaged with educational opportunities.

In the spring of 1926, McPherson was allegedly kidnapped while swimming in the Pacific Ocean, reappearing in Mexico a month later. Doubtful authorities investigated her story, and after extensive publicity some charged that she had gone into hiding with Angelus Temple member Kenneth Ormiston, with whom she was alleged to be romantically involved. McPherson was charged with conspiracy, although her case was eventually dropped for lack of evidence. Her personal life was as colorful and outrageous as her religious activities seemed to many non-Temple members. A nervous breakdown in 1930 was followed by her third marriage, in 1931, to Temple choir baritone David L. Hutton. They divorced in 1934.

Although "Sister Aimee" was passionately supported by Angelus Temple members, she was criticized by rivals as a twentieth-century "Jezebel" and called the "Barnum of Religion." McPherson died of a sleeping pill overdose on 27 September 1944 in Oakland, California.

ARTS AND CULTURE. Edith Wharton is given a gold medal by the American Academy of Arts and Letters.

RELIGION. Belle Carter Harmon is the first woman in the world to be ordained a deacon in the Methodist Episcopal Church.

5 January 1925
POLITICS. Nellie Tayloe Ross is inaugurated as the first woman governor—of Wyoming—in U.S. history.

8 January 1925
WOMEN'S ISSUES. The first state supreme court made up only of women is appointed in Texas.

3 March 1925
IDEAS/BELIEFS. The medical director of the Prudential Insurance Company of America states that wives can make their marriages happier by raising their standard of cooking.

20 March 1925
INTERNATIONAL. Pattie Hockaday Field of Denver, Colorado, is named the first woman vice consul and assigned to Amsterdam on 2 September 1925. She resigns on 27 June 1929.

18 April 1925
WOMEN'S ISSUES. The Woman's World Fair at Chicago, Illinois, is opened by Mrs. Calvin Coolidge. The fair is an exhibition of women's progress in 70 different industries.

7 December 1925
POLITICS. Edith Frances Nourse Rogers (R-Massachusetts), the first woman to serve 18 terms in Congress, begins her first term after being elected to replace her husband. She maintains her House seat until September 1960.

ARTS AND CULTURE. Hallie Flanagan founds the Vassar Experimental Theater. She later heads the Works Progress Administration Federal Theater Project during the Depression and is a leading supporter of dramatic innovation.

OTHER EVENTS OF 1925

MEDICAL. Mary Breckenridge establishes the Frontier Nursing Service in Kentucky.

Hazel Hotchkiss Wightman, 1886–1974

One of the earliest figures in women's tennis in the United States, Hazel Hotchkiss Wightman was best known for her success in establishing women's international tennis competition. She was the first to win the U.S. National Lawn Tennis Association singles, doubles, and mixed doubles championships three years in a row—1909, 1910, and 1911. Hotchkiss was born 20 December 1886, in Healdsburg, California, the only girl in a family of five children. Her parents, William and Emma (Grove) Hotchkiss, allowed her to play actively although she was a delicate child. Playing baseball and football prepared her for her first tennis tournament in 1902, and by 1909 she had won her first of forty-four national titles.

Hotchkiss was a rival of May G. Sutton (later Mrs. Thomas Bundy), also from California, and the two differed greatly in their style of playing. Hotchkiss introduced the volleying game; Sutton was a hardhitter. She also helped adapt clothing for women's tennis, appearing in sleeveless dresses at a time when female players generally wore corsets and long-sleeved, high-collared blouses complete with neckties.

Hotchkiss married George William Wightman in 1912 following her graduation from Berkeley. In 1913, the mother of an infant son, Wightman reigned victorious in a match at the Longwood Tennis Club in Chestnut Hill, Massachusetts. In 1919, she again won the National Singles title. The same year, she approached the International Lawn Tennis Federation with the idea of a women's competition patterned on the Davis Cup for men. After some delays, the first Wightman Cup Match for women of Great Britain and the United States was held at the West Side Tennis Club in Forest Hills, New York, in 1923. The Americans won that year, 7–0. She played in the match, and again in 1924, 1927, 1929, and 1931. In addition, she was captain of the American team thirteen times for the Wightman Cup matches.

A dedicated tennis instructor, beginning in the early 1920s, Wightman offered free tennis clinics at the Longwood Tennis Club starting in 1922. Still competing, she won the National Doubles championship in 1924, and again in 1928, each time with Helen Wills Moody as her partner. In 1924, Wightman won Olympic gold medals in doubles and mixed doubles, and won the mixed doubles match at Wimbledon. In 1927, she was National Squash champion, and was runner-up in the National Badminton Mixed championships.

She wrote a book, *Better Tennis,* in 1933. In 1940, she and her husband divorced, but she remained in Chestnut Hill, where she was also active in the Boston Red Cross. Wightman was elected to the International Tennis Hall of Fame in Newport, Rhode Island, in 1957. In 1973, a year before Wightman's death, Queen Elizabeth II of England named the tennis star an honorary Commander of the British Empire. She died of a heart attack on 5 December 1974.

---

29 January 1926
WOMEN'S ISSUES. Violette Neatly Anderson becomes the first black woman to practice law before the U.S. Supreme Court. She is from Chicago, Illinois.

12 March 1926
WOMEN'S ISSUES. Dr. Mary B. Harris is sworn in as the first superintendent of the Federal Industrial Institution for Women at Alderson, West Virginia. The first federal prison built exclusively for women, it cost more than $2 million to build and has no prison walls surrounding it and no guards.

15 June 1926
DEATHS. Noted Impressionist painter Mary Cassatt, a Pittsburgh, Pennsylvania, native, dies in Paris, France, where she had made her home since 1874.

6 August 1926
SPORTS. Gertrude Ederle is the first woman to swim from Gris-Nez, France, to Kingsdown, England. The Channel swim took Ederle 14 hours and 34 minutes to complete.

11 November 1926
EDUCATION. Margaret Newell H'Doubler is named chairperson of the first collegiate dance program in the nation at the University of Wisconsin at Madison.

OTHER EVENTS OF 1926

EDUCATION. Ellen Browning Scripps founds Scripps College in Claremont, California.

LITERATURE. Dorothy Canfield Fisher is named the first woman member of the selection board at Book-of-the-Month Club.

2 January 1927
POLITICS. The League of Women Voters releases a report disclosing that only 122 women have been elected to state legislatures in the past year, as opposed to 130 women in 1925.

14 March 1927
WOMEN'S ISSUES. Elsie Eaves is the first woman associate member of the American Society of Civil Engineers.

6 April 1927
SPORTS. Mrs. Herbert Hoover presides at a 2-day meeting in Washington, D.C., to discuss sports and athletics for women and girls in the United States.

30 June 1927
AVIATION. The first woman pilot's license is granted by the U.S. Commerce Department. The pilot is Phoebe F. Omlie, who receives commercial transport license no. 199.

Ethel Barrymore, 1879–1959

In her autobiography, Ethel Barrymore commented, "I had never known I was to go on the stage." But considering her origins, it is not surprising that within six years of her stage debut, Barrymore was playing lead roles in Charles Frohman's theater company. It seemed almost foreordained that she would become the grande dame of

American theater, born as she had been into the quintessentially American theater family, the Barrymores.

The only daughter of Maurice and Georgiana (Drew) Barrymore, she was born in Philadelphia, Pennsylvania, on 16 August 1879. Her parents were both actors, her maternal grandparents were in the theater, and her two brothers, Lionel and John, also achieved star status. Her career really began when she joined her uncles, actors Sidney Drew and John Drew, Jr., in New York, where she contracted with Charles Frohman, appearing in dozens of productions, usually in ingenue parts.

In 1909, she married Russell Griswold Colt, and the couple had three children, Samuel, born in 1901, Ethel, born in 1912, and John, born in 1913. She and Colt divorced in 1923.

Among Barrymore's most memorable stage roles was that of Emma McChesney in the play *Our Mrs. McChesney,* based on Edna Ferber's novels. She also starred in *The Lady of the Camellias* (1917) and in *Déclassée* (1919). In 1926, she made a Broadway hit in *The Constant Wife,* and later she played the Welsh schoolmistress in *The Corn Is Green,* staged in 1940.

Although her initial efforts were stage performances, Barrymore began making silent films in 1914. Appearing in many movies over a period of several decades, she won an Academy Award in 1944 for her screen portrayal of Ma Mott in *None but the Lonely Heart.* Later, in the early 1950s, she performed on television in a variety of dramatic and comedy roles.

Barrymore was admired for her ability to deliver humorous lines in a detached, almost bored manner that augmented their impact. She was equally at home, however, with Shakespearean drama. Part of a true theatrical dynasty, Barrymore died of a heart attack on 18 June 1959, in Beverly Hills, California.

---

7 December 1927
POPULAR CULTURE. Actress Helen Morgan opens in the Broadway play, *Show Boat,* adapted from Edna Ferber's novel of the same name.

19 January 1928
SPORTS. Eleanora Sears wins three of four matches to become the first woman to win the U.S. Women's Squash Racquets Singles championships.

4 May 1928
WOMEN'S ISSUES. Genevieve Cline is named the first woman associate federal court justice. She serves at the U.S. Customs Court in New York City.

1 June 1928
WOMEN'S ISSUES. Ruth B. Shipley is appointed as the first woman passport division chief by Secretary of State Frank B. Kellogg.

14 October 1928
POPULAR CULTURE. Cora Dennison becomes the first bride whose wedding, to James Fowlkes, is broadcast on television.

16 November 1928
RELIGION. In Oak Park, Illinois, the Woman's Home Missionary Society cancels a lecture after learning that the guest speaker, Maude Royden, smokes cigarettes.

OTHER EVENTS OF 1928

INTERNATIONAL. Doris Stevens is named the first woman president of the Inter-American Commission of Women, the Organization of American States.

MEDICAL. Alice Evans, a microbiologist credited with identifying the bacteria that causes brucellosis, is elected the first woman president of the Society of American Bacteriologists.

Not all flappers smoked cigarettes, but many shocked their elders by baring their arms, bobbing their hair, and roping strings of false pearls around their necks in a style considered quite daring. (Photo courtesy Judith Freeman Clark)

Olympic Gold Medals

E. Pinkston: Platform diving
Helen Meany: Springboard diving
Albina Osipowich: Swimming—100-meter freestyle

Martha Norelius: Swimming—400-meter freestyle
  Swimming—400-meter freestyle relay team medal
Elizabeth Robinson: Track—100 meters

Jessie Redmon Fauset, 1882–1961

Author, literary editor, and mentor to many black writers, Jessie Redmon Fauset was born on 26 April 1882 in Fredericksville, New Jersey. Her mother, Anna (Seamon) Fauset died when Fauset was a child, but her father, Redmon Fauset, an African Methodist Episcopal minister, was a loving, supportive parent. He encouraged her to become educated, and undoubtedly imparted to her a fierce sense of pride and desire to overcome racial prejudice.

In 1905, Fauset graduated from Cornell University and became a Latin and French teacher at the M Street High School in Washington, D.C. She also wrote pieces for *Crisis.* Soon, W. E. B. Du Bois, editor of the National Association for the Advancement of Colored People's (NAACP) journal, invited Fauset to join its staff. She became literary editor of *Crisis* in 1919, and received an A.M. degree in French from the University of Pennsylvania. Between 1920 and 1921, Fauset helped Du Bois with the NAACP children's publication, *The Brownie's Book,* and encouraged new black writers to submit their work to her. Many of these unknown authors were women. In 1921, Fauset attended the Pan-African Congress, and she traveled extensively through Europe and the Middle East from 1925 to 1926. These travel experiences were shared with her readers in *Crisis.*

During the period known as the Harlem Renaissance, Fauset was instrumental in both discovering and nurturing new literary talent, particularly among black poets and writers of fiction. She invited many of these authors, among them Langston Hughes and Nella Larson, to her home. In addition to her work as an editor, Fauset was an accomplished writer. Her fiction and poetry were widely read and usually depicted characters dealing in some way with racial prejudice.

Fauset had married Herbert Harris in 1929, when she was a teacher at DeWitt Clinton High School in New York City. In 1939, she moved with Harris to Montclair, New Jersey. After this time, her strong influence on black literary efforts lessened. In 1949, she spent a brief period teaching at Hampton Institute in Virginia. She died at her brother's home in Philadelphia on 30 April 1961.

Crystal Eastman, 1881–1928

Lawyer, feminist, and peace worker, Crystal Eastman was among the early group of activists whose efforts helped promote labor rights and civil liberties in the United States. Born in Marlborough, Massachusetts, on 25 June 1881, she was the daughter of Samuel and Annis (Ford) Eastman, both Congregational ministers. Her mother was a women's rights advocate, and her brother Max Eastman became a prominent Socialist writer and editor.

A dedicated student, she graduated from Vassar in 1903, and in 1904 earned a Master's degree in sociology at Columbia. She received an LL.B. from New York University Law School and then worked on the ''Pittsburgh Survey.'' She published the book *Work Accidents and the Law* in 1910, which was based on her investigation of urban industrialization.

Eastman was instrumental in bringing about the passage of a workmen's compensation law in New York state, as a member of the State Employers' Liability Commission. In 1911, she married Wallace Benedict, but the couple divorced by 1915. She joined the Political Equality League in 1912, and in 1913 helped establish the Congressional Union for Woman Suffrage. Eastman was an advocate of birth control, the economic independence of women, and, above all, human rights and peace.

In 1915, soon after her divorce from Benedict, she married Walter Fuller, an Englishman. They moved to Greenwich Village in New York City, where she was active in opposing the National Defense Bill. She also chaired the New York state

Woman's Peace Party, and gave numerous speeches against the war in Europe. After U.S. entry into World War I, she was an organizer of the Civil Liberties Bureau, which helped conscientious objectors.

Eastman was managing editor of the *Liberator,* and in March 1919, she helped organize the Feminist Congress in New York City. She moved to England in 1921 with her husband and two children, and became active in promoting labor reform there. In 1927, Eastman's husband died, and although she maintained a high level of involvement in reform work, failing health hampered her activism. She died of nephritis on 29 July 1928, at her brother's home in Erie, Pennsylvania.

Olympic Silver Medals

Georgia Coleman: Platform diving
Dorothy Poynton: Springboard diving
Elanora Garatti: Swimming—100-meter freestyle
Lillian Copeland: Field events—discus throw
   Track—100-meter relay team medal
   Track—400-meter relay team medal

Olympic Bronze Medals

Georgia Coleman: Springboard diving
Josephine McKim: Swimming—400-meter freestyle
Mildred Wiley: Field events—high jump

4 March 1929
WOMEN'S ISSUES. Lola M. Williams is the first woman to serve as secretary to a U.S. vice-president. She is on the staff of Charles Curtis.

16 May 1929
POPULAR CULTURE. The first Academy of Motion Picture Arts and Sciences Awards are presented. An Oscar for Best Actress goes to Janet Gaynor.

15 September 1929
LABOR. In Gastonia, North Carolina, 7 men are charged with the murder of female labor

striker Ella May Wiggins. She had been demonstrating on behalf of union organizing at a factory there.

20 November 1929
POPULAR CULTURE. Writer Gertrude Berg's radio program, "The Rise of the Goldbergs," premieres and is eventually broadcast by both CBS and NBC until 1945.

22 November 1929
POLITICS. Testifying during a tariff debate in the U.S. Senate, Ruth Peterson and Evelyn Southworth are the first women (other than members of Congress) to be permitted on the Senate floor.

OTHER EVENTS OF 1929

EDUCATION. Dorothy Harrison Wood Eustis establishes the first Seeing Eye dog class, in Nashville, Tennessee.

14 February 1930
WOMEN'S ISSUES. Annabel Matthews is confirmed by the Senate as the first woman tax appeals board member.

Eleanora Randolph Sears, 1881–1968

Known for her aggressive, nontraditional attitude toward women in sports, Eleanora Randolph Sears was the first national women's squash champion. In addition, she was a top-ranked tennis player and contributed generously to a number of other sports. Born in Boston, Massachusetts, on 28 September 1881, she was the only daughter of

Frederick and Eleanora (Coolidge) Sears. Her mother's family descended from Thomas Jefferson, and as a child she enjoyed many privileges of wealth, including travel to Paris where her grandfather was U.S. minister to France.

By 1903, Sears was an acknowledged tennis personality, and by 1911 she was winning national titles. She played with Hazel Hotchkiss Wightman and Molla Bjurstedt, winning the National Women's Doubles championships in 1911, 1915, 1916, and 1917. In 1916, she also won the Mixed Doubles championship with Willis Davis as her partner.

In 1918, Sears, who had been playing squash for ten years, won the first women's national squash championship. Although a leading member of "Boston Brahmin" society, she placed more emphasis on her many sports activities than she did on conventional feminine behavior. Prior to World War I, she appeared astride a horse, wearing riding trousers, an action that caused ministers to preach against her immoral behavior. Sears' principal interest was riding, and she maintained a large stable. She owned race horses and show horses, often riding at the National Horse Show at Madison Square Garden in New York City. Among her behind-the-scenes sports involvements was support of the U.S. Equestrian Team. She was also responsible for preventing the Boston Police Department from abandoning its use of mounted police officers. In the early 1960s she loaned the department horses from her own stables.

Sears was also very fond of walking long distances, which further contributed to her reputation as an eccentric. In 1926, she walked the forty-four miles between Providence, Rhode Island, and Boston, Massachusetts, in a little under ten hours. She was a member of the Boston Skating Club, having participated in the sport for decades. In 1961, after a plane crash killed nearly all the members of the U.S. Olympic Figure Skating team, Eleanora Sears spent a great deal of effort to help rebuild the team.

Sears accumulated more than 240 trophies from her sports participation over the years. At the time of her death on 27 March 1968, she had claimed proficiency in such diverse activities as riflery, polo, ice hockey, swimming, and sailing, as well as tennis, riding, squash, and long-distance walking.

---

4 March 1930
SPORTS. Emma Fahning is the first woman bowler to obtain a perfect score under the rules of the Women's International Bowling Congress, in Buffalo, New York.

12 March 1930
SPORTS. Stella Walsh breaks all records for the 220-yard dash with a time of 26:1:10.

3 April 1930
SPORTS. The University of Southern California polo team refuses to meet with the UCLA team until Barbara Rand, a UCLA polo player, is replaced by a man.

18 April 1930
WOMEN'S ISSUES. The first women state police officers, Lotta Caldwell and Mary

Ramsdell, are appointed to the Massachusetts State Police force.

15 May 1930
AVIATION. United Airlines employs its first flight attendant, Ellen Church, on flights from San Francisco, California, to Cheyenne, Wyoming.

AVIATION. Boeing Transport hires 8 trained nurses to act as attendants on air flights. They receive $125 per month for 100 hours of work.

2 June 1930
RELIGION. Sarah E. Dickson is elected the first woman Presbyterian elder at the Wauwatosa Presbyterian Church in Milwaukee, Wisconsin. She serves there until 1 January 1934.

9 June 1930
IDEAS/BELIEFS.   A New York State
Supreme Court judge notes that in homes
without children, divorce is likely to occur due
to the lack of a genuine home life. The judge
blames birth control for childless marriages that
lead to marital discord.

14 October 1930
POPULAR CULTURE.   Ethel Merman makes
her Broadway debut in George and Ira
Gershwin's musical comedy, *Girl Crazy.*

24 November 1930
AVIATION.   Ruth Nichols begins the first
transcontinental air flight by a woman. She
leaves Mineola, Long Island, in a Lockheed-
Vega, arriving in California 7 days later.

IV

WORKING AGAINST THE ODDS
1931–1940

During the 1930s American women faced many difficulties. The fiscal emergencies precipitated by the 1929 stock market crash had deepened into full-scale economic depression, causing some abrupt changes in the way women's roles were viewed. Perhaps the most noticeable of these shifts was the diminished opportunity for women in the workplace. Since most Americans felt that available jobs should go to male breadwinners, employment for women shrank in scope and quality. This attitude was further buttressed by federal policy denying government jobs to husbands and wives working in federal positions *if* those areas demanded layoffs. Still, there were American women who achieved prominence during the 1930s.

Through talent, perseverance, and sheer will, women like Eleanor Roosevelt and Frances Perkins became role models for other American women. Roosevelt, by virtue of her marriage to Franklin D. Roosevelt, was in the public eye and tried all her life to ease the plight of Americans who suffered from want and disadvantage. Frances Perkins became the first female cabinet member in U.S. history; she was chosen as secretary of labor due to her years of experience in public service and administration.

In 1931, another humanitarian and activist, Jane Addams, won the Nobel Peace Prize. This was the first time the award had ever gone to a woman. Just seven years later, Pearl S. Buck won the Nobel Prize for literature for her books on China. These firsts for women helped encourage others less well known to continue their fight against a relatively traditional, conservative societal order.

A major sports figure of the decade, Babe Didrikson, helped boost women's athletics. By winning several Olympic gold medals and many national championships, Didrikson lifted women's sports out of the realm of the unusual, although it would be several decades before professional athletics were open to women in any significant respect.

Less famous women also made their mark on America during the 1930s. One served as the first female foreign minister, another as the first member of a commodity stock exchange. Another was the first elected to the U.S. Senate, and yet another, Mother Cabrini, became the first American citizen to be beatified and to achieve sainthood.

Perhaps the woman who for many symbolized the pluck and courage that characterized the American spirit during the 1930s was Amelia Earhart Putnam. Her accomplishments in the field of aviation gave heart to all Americans during the Great Depression, but she held special interest for women whose lives were devoid of adventure and excitement. Earhart made the first transatlantic solo flight by a woman and the first transcontinental solo venture. She furthered women's involvement in aviation and helped promote this fledgling industry with her well-publicized flights. It was in part due to her pioneering efforts that women were chosen during World War II to head up aviation ferrying squadrons. Earhart's ambition and drive, like that of so many other American women during the Great Depression, were factors that gave the nation hope and a sense of shared purpose.

Elizabeth Arden, 1878–1966

Known for her ardent love of horses and for her gardening expertise, Elizabeth Arden became a recognized leader in the cosmetics industry. Born near Toronto, Canada, on or about 31 December 1878, she was christened Florence Nightingale Graham, and was the daughter of William and Susan (Todd) Graham. Until she moved to New York City at age thirty, she held a string of jobs and trained briefly as a nurse. In New York City she worked for the English cosmetics firm Eleanor Adair, but soon established her own Fifth Avenue salon with a partner, Elizabeth Hubbard. This partnership was brief, and Arden was soon sole proprietor. She changed the name of her shop to Elizabeth Arden, and with her new identity she traveled, in 1914, to Europe, where she researched various beauty techniques and products.

In 1915, Arden opened a larger shop, and by now had branches in Boston and in Washington, D.C. At these shops, she promoted not only the use of a special cleansing cream called Amoretta and another product called Ardena Skin Tonic but the use of facial massage as a beauty treatment. She was married on 29 November 1915 to Thomas J. Lewis, a banker who was a great help in running her business. The couple divorced in 1934, and she married again in 1942, this time to Prince Michael Evanoff.

In 1930, Arden purchased a horse farm in Maine, and subsequently ran her famous horses in the Kentucky Derby. Her horse Jet Pilot won the Derby in 1947. Arden divorced Prince Michael in 1944, after which she maintained sole proprietorship of her business until her death. She invested in art as well as in horses, and was well known for her activity in many civic and charitable organizations.

Arden was granted an honorary LL.D. from Syracuse University in 1949. When she died on 18 October 1966, she left most of her money to a niece, Patricia Young, although Arden provided numerous bequests to company employees. She also left $4 million to her sister Gladys. Without Arden's strong hand to guide it, the business was sold to Eli Lilly Company in order to meet government inheritance taxes.

OTHER EVENTS OF 1930

WOMEN'S ISSUES. The Association of Southern Women for the Prevention of Lynching is founded by Jessie Daniel Ames.

WOMEN'S ISSUES. Florence Bascom becomes the first female vice-president of the Geological Society of America. Bascom is the first woman to have received a Ph.D. from Johns Hopkins University.

POPULAR CULTURE. The Academy Award for Best Actress of 1929 goes to Mary Pickford for her role in the film *Coquette*.

9 January 1931
AVIATION. Evelyn "Bobby" Trout and Edna May Cooper complete an air flight of 122 hours and 20 minutes, setting a world record in the monoplane *Lady Rolph*.

16 March 1931
WOMEN'S ISSUES. Jean Wittich of Minneapolis, Minnesota, is the first woman to serve as a state budget commissioner. She remains in office until May 1933.

1 April 1931
SPORTS. Virne "Jackie" Mitchell, a 19-year-old woman, is signed up as pitcher for the Chattanooga, Tennessee, Baseball Club.

10 June 1931
POPULAR CULTURE. Wallis Warfield Simpson, an American divorcée, is presented at the Court of St. James in London, England, where she meets the Prince of Wales.

29 July 1931
SPORTS. Helen Wills Moody endorses short skirts and no stockings for female tennis players.

31 August 1931
AVIATION. Phoebe Omlie wins the National Air Race between Los Angeles, California, and Cleveland, Ohio. It is the first major aviation competition between men and women.

25 October 1931
AVIATION. Ruth Nichols flies nonstop from Oakland, California, to Louisville, Kentucky. The 1,977-mile flight is a world record of its kind.

13 November 1931
POLITICS. Hattie Wyatt Caraway is named to the U.S. Senate to fill a vacancy created by the death of her husband, Thaddeus Caraway. She is elected senator on 12 January 1932 and reelected in 1938, serving until January 1945.

Women and the New Deal

If the Depression years hit American women especially hard, its antidote—the New Deal—provided some relief. While nearly 25 percent of all Americans were out of work during the 1930s, women were *expected* to remain at home and not compete with men for the few jobs that were available. One piece of New Deal legislation, the Economy Act of 1932, did little, however, to aid women. The law was quite harsh in its dealings with women who happened to be federal employees. If their husbands also worked for the government, and if personnel cutbacks were deemed necessary, the *wives* were to be dismissed. This was true even if women had seniority or held positions of greater importance than their spouses held.

    If this particular New Deal bill was not designed to promote equality in the workplace, statistics for the period also paint a dismal picture of the percent of women then employed. In 1930, female professional workers represented 14.2 percent of the work force; in 1940, they represented only 12.3 percent. And in 1935, government projects employed 1.6 million people—of whom only 142,000, or about 9 percent, were women. And the number of female college teachers fell during the 1930s, from 32.5 percent at the beginning of the decade to 26 percent by its end.

But despite these gloomy realities, there were some bright spots during the troubled New Deal era. President Roosevelt appointed the first woman cabinet member, Frances Perkins, secretary of labor, and the first women ministers to foreign nations, Ruth Bryan Owen and Florence Jeffrey Harriman. And in the Works Progress Administration, another of President Roosevelt's projects, several women held executive positions: Rose Schneiderman became the only woman member of the Labor Advisory Board of the National Recovery Administration, for example. Mary Dewson helped organize women Democratic party members and received increased funding for her work from the president. By the 1936 Democratic Convention, a ruling passed that each delegate to the Platform Committee had to be joined by an alternate of the opposite gender, ensuring equal representation. Roosevelt was aided in his quest for a second term by more than sixty thousand women who actively promoted the New Deal and the Democratic party. An outcome of their support was reflected in the rise in women postmasterships—from 17.6 percent of those granted in 1930 to 26 percent in the period from 1932 to 1938.

Minimum wage laws passed during the New Deal also provided economic gains for women. The Fair Labor Standards Act meant increased wages in the textile trades, for example, where 40 percent of the workers were women. Labor unions were bolstered by passage of the Wagner Act, although unions were notoriously rigid in their exclusion of women workers. New Deal legislation, however, paved the way for increased union activity, which, in turn, set the stage for the formation of the Congress of Industrial Organizations (CIO). This group, after 1935, sought and actively represented women union members.

Of all New Deal activists, Eleanor Roosevelt was perhaps the quintessential advocate of women's rights. Persistent and scrupulously thorough, she investigated, collected facts and opinions, listened to Americans across the country, and then returned to the president and put the pressure on. She supported women's efforts wholeheartedly and expected that women should and could work hard to change America for the better. Although she was viewed as too conservative by some and as a political radical by others, Eleanor's friendships with many women in public office during the New Deal administration meant that she had an inside view of the specific needs of women's agencies. Eleanor Roosevelt's wise urgings were responsible for much of the funding and support women's programs received during her husband's term of office.

---

10 December 1931
INTERNATIONAL.   Jane Addams is the first American woman to be awarded the Nobel Peace Prize. She shares the honor with Nicholas Murray Butler.

15 December 1931
POLITICS.   U.S. Representative Mary T. Norton (D-New Jersey) is the first woman to

chair a congressional committee. She heads the District of Columbia Affairs committee until June 1937.

OTHER EVENTS OF 1931

POPULAR CULTURE.   Norma Shearer receives an Oscar for Best Actress of 1930 for the movie *The Divorcée*.

12 January 1932
POLITICS.   Hattie Wyatt Caraway (D-
Arkansas) is the first woman elected to the U.S.
Senate.

15 February 1932
POPULAR CULTURE.   "The Adventures of
Gracie," a radio program featuring comedienne
Gracie Allen and her husband George Burns,
premiers on CBS.

18 February 1932
SPORTS.   Florence Wolf Dreyfuss is elected
chair of the board of the Pittsburgh Pirates.

29 March 1932
IDEAS/BELIEFS.   The Chinese Women's
Association, Inc., is organized in New York
City. Its first president is Theodora Chan Wan.

9 May 1932
POLITICS.   Hattie Wyatt Caraway (D-
Arkansas) is the first woman to preside over the

U.S. Senate, but serves in this capacity for only
a brief time.

21 May 1932
AVIATION.   Amelia Earhart Putnam
completes the first transatlantic solo flight by a
woman. She flies from Harbor Grace,
Newfoundland, to Culmore, Ireland, completing
the 2,026-mile journey in 14 hours, 56 minutes.

28 May 1932
AVIATION.   In Port Bucyrus, Ohio, Laurette
Schimmoler is named the nation's first woman
airport manager. She earns $510 annually.

21 June 1932
AVIATION.   Amelia Earhart Putnam receives
the National Geographic Society Gold Medal for
her solo transatlantic flight.

Ella C. Deloria, 1888–1971

A Dakota Sioux, Ella C. Deloria devoted her life to the study and preservation of
Native American culture. She was born to Phillip and Mary (Sully) Deloria on 30
January 1888, at the Yankton Indian Reservation in what is now South Dakota. Deloria
studied at Oberlin College and received a B.S. from Columbia University in 1915.
At Columbia she became acquainted with anthropologist Franz Boas, who urged her
to investigate fully the Dakota language.

Although Deloria found only limited support for her studies, she was totally
absorbed in her work and derived much satisfaction from it. She interviewed many
Dakota Indians during her extensive field research projects and in 1931 published
Dakota Texts. This volume represented folk tales and legends Deloria had heard during
her visits to Dakota Indian reservations. Until Boas's death in 1942, Deloria worked
with him and with Ruth Benedict, his colleague. In 1941, Deloria and Boas published
a joint work, *Dakota Grammar*.

The detailed accounts of Dakota culture and language produced by Deloria have
subsequently proved invaluable to scholars of Native American life. Her careful efforts
were imbued with a concern for accurate interpretation. Deloria's scholarship resulted
in the most complete body of work to date on Dakota culture.

Devoted to her family as well as to her work, Deloria often lived with her sister,
the artist Mary Sully. The two women relied heavily on Deloria's meager income. In
1944, she published *Speaking of Indians,* with illustrations by her sister. Between
1955 and 1958, Deloria was director of the mission school at St. Elizabeth's in Wakpala,
South Dakota, founded by her father seventy years earlier. Subsequently, she was

assistant director of the W.H. Over Museum at the University of South Dakota, and from 1962 to 1966 she received some funding from the National Science Foundation in order to continue her research. After several more years of penurious living, Deloria died at age eighty-three in Tripp, South Dakota, on 12 February 1971.

Mary White Ovington, 1865–1951

At a time when few women of her background and breeding ventured outside the home for anything less tame than church work, Mary White Ovington became well known for her Socialist activities and, more important, for her dedication to civil rights. As a white woman, Ovington was among the minority in the National Assocation for the Advancement of Colored People (NAACP), yet without her the organization would have had difficulty surviving its early years. Born in Brooklyn, New York, on 11 April 1865, she was the daughter of upper middle-class parents, Theodore and Anne (Ketchum) Ovington. She was enrolled at Lacker Collegiate Institute between 1888 and 1891, and then attended Radcliffe College until 1893. In 1895, Ovington applied her reform interests to a position as head social worker at Greenpoint Settlement. She had left school by this time due to her father's financial reverses. In addition to her settlement work, Ovington was registrar at Pratt Institute.

In 1903, Ovington heard Booker T. Washington speak on northern racial discrimination. In 1904, she went to work at Greenwich House, another settlement, and began a study of black Americans' lives in New York City. She soon joined the Socialist party, which appeared to embrace principles that could effect positive change in society. Ovington wrote about her work in *Half a Man: The Status of the Negro in New York,* published in 1911. By this time, she was in contact with black scholar W. E. B. Du Bois, promoter of the Niagara Movement. She was one of few white associate members of this organization.

In 1909, Ovington helped found the NAACP. Its goals were considered radical in both black and the white communities of that time.

A major policymaker and officeholder in the NAACP, Ovington was active in the organization for nearly four decades. Early on, one of her chief contributions was to mediate a series of disputes between black leaders Du Bois and Oswald Garrison Villard. In 1919, Ovington became chairperson of the NAACP board of directors. By now there were forty-four thousand members nationwide. Ovington also worked to promote black woman suffrage, and later was instumental in the NAACP's pressuring of the U.S. government to terminate occupation of Haiti. Ovington was also an important figure in early efforts to press for school desegregation.

Resigning as chair of the NAACP board in 1932, Ovington became treasurer, but found herself increasingly at odds with Du Bois on the integration issue. Unlike Du Bois, who was a "partial segregationist," Ovington supported integration. She tried to temper radical elements within the organization with seemingly limited success.

Ovington wrote many book reviews during the 1920s in which she hailed artists of the Harlem Renaissance. She also published books on black leaders and on the NAACP itself, as well as several novels. Ovington retired from the NAACP in 1947. After suffering from poor health for several years, she died on 15 July 1951, in Newton Highlands, Massachusetts.

24 August 1932
AVIATION. Amelia Earhart Putnam completes the first transcontinental flight by a woman, leaving Newark, New Jersey, and arriving in Los Angeles, California, 19 hours and 5 minutes later.

12 October 1932
INTERNATIONAL. At the American Legation in Stockholm, Sweden, Frances Elizabeth Willis becomes the first woman chargé d'affaires, serving there for an interim period.

OTHER EVENTS OF 1932

POPULAR CULTURE. The Oscar for Best Actress of 1931 goes to Marie Dressler for her role in the film *Min and Bill*.

Olympic Gold Medals

Dorothy Poynton: Platform diving
Georgia Coleman: Springboard diving
Helene Madison: Swimming—100-meter freestyle
Helene Madison: Swimming—400-meter freestyle
Eleanor Holm: Swimming—100-meter backstroke
    Swimming—400-meter freestyle relay women's team medal
Jean Shiley: High jump

Lillian Copeland: Discus throw
Mildred Didrikson: Javelin throw
    Track—400-meter relay women's team medal

Olympic Silver Medals

Georgia Coleman: Platform diving
Katherine Rawls: Springboard diving
Lenore Knight: Swimming—400-meter freestyle
Mildred Didrikson: High jump
Ruth Osburn: Discus throw

Olympic Bronze Medals

Marion Roper: Platform diving
Jane Fauntz: Springboard diving
Eleanora Saville: Swimming—100-meter freestyle
W. von Bremen: Track—100-meter dash

13 January 1933
SPORTS. Babe Didrikson makes her first pro basketball appearance at a game between the Brooklyn Yankees (her team) and the Long Island Ducklings. She scores 9 of the points that the Yankees make, as they defeat the Ducklings, 19–16.

28 January 1933
SPORTS. Helen Wills Moody beats Phil Neer in a tennis match in San Francisco, California, while 3,000 fans look on.

Pearl S. Buck, 1892–1973

Few popular novelists have enjoyed the widespread acclaim that greeted Pearl Buck's work. The daughter of Presbyterian missionaries Absolom and Caroline (Stulting) Sydenstricker, she was born on 26 June 1892, in Hillsboro, West Virginia. Soon afterward her parents returned to their mission in China, taking their infant daughter with them. There, the child grew up in an atmosphere that blended the cultures of east and west.

In 1910, she returned to the United States and attended Randolph-Macon Woman's College in Virginia, graduating in 1914 with a B.A. degree. She went back to China to be with her mother who was fatally ill. In May 1917, she married John Lossing Buck, an American agricultural worker, in China. The couple had a daughter in 1920, and in 1922, Buck began writing articles and stories about China.

Buck returned to the United States in 1924. At that time she sought medical advice concerning her daughter, who was diagnosed as mentally retarded. Buck continued her writing, received an M.A. in English from Cornell University, and won the Messenger History prize for an essay, "China and the West." She also adopted another daughter, the first of several children she would take into her family.

Pearl Sydenstricker as she appeared in her 1914 graduation photograph in the *Helianthus*, the Randolph-Macon Woman's College yearbook. In 1938, Pearl Sydenstricker Buck was the first American woman to win the Nobel Prize for literature. (Photo courtesy Randolph-Macon Woman's College Archives)

Buck published several books prior to *The Good Earth* in 1931. This work, which was to be translated into nearly three dozen languages, became the basis for both a Broadway play and a Hollywood film. In 1932, she won the Pulitzer Prize for this compelling novel about Chinese peasant life. Although she wrote out of economic necessity, she found great fulfillment in her work. Drawing on her varied life experiences, as well as on her recollections of Chinese culture, Buck eventually published more than one hundred books.

Her marriage to John L. Buck ended in divorce in 1934, and the following year she married her publisher, Richard J. Walsh. She purchased a farm in Pennsylvania, which she maintained in addition to a New York apartment. She was by this time the mother of six adopted and two foster children.

Buck's writings encompassed American social themes as well as those dealing with China. In 1938, she was distinguished as the first American woman to be awarded the Nobel Prize for literature. She wrote many essays and novels between 1941 and 1946, hoping to promote a better understanding of war issues and the need for world peace. In 1941, she founded the East and West Association and helped publish *Asia* magazine until 1946. Buck was adept at writing both fiction and nonfiction works on women's lives, and she advanced her feminist opinions in *Of Men and Women* (1941). At one point she produced a series of historical novels dealing with the American West under the pseudonym John Sedges. During the 1950s, Buck wrote of concerns about nuclear technology, work that ultimately led her to become involved in the theater. Her play *Desert Incident*, which appeared in 1959, was not a critical success but did reflect her wide-ranging literary capabilities and social conscience.

Her interest in children, particularly those with special needs, caused her to support work for the mentally retarded. In 1949, she founded an adoption agency—Welcome House—to help place children of Asian-American parentage. In 1964, she established the Pearl S. Buck Foundation, also with the aim of supporting Amerasian children. Much of her humanitarian work was funded through her royalties. She was assisted in this area by close friend Theodore F. Harris, an organizational fund-raiser. Harris later wrote a two-volume biography of Buck.

By 1970, Buck had moved permanently to Vermont, where she owned property, continuing to write and to supervise her many projects. She died of lung cancer in Danby, Vermont, on 6 March 1973.

Dorothy Day, 1897–1980

Little in Dorothy Day's childhood predicted the deep and lasting influence she would later have as co-founder and leader of the Catholic Worker Movement. Born in Brooklyn, New York, on 8 November 1897, she was one of five children. Her parents, John and Grace (Satterlee) Day, provided a secure if somewhat austere family environment, but there was no religious training and no real expectation that Day would choose a career when she grew up. The family moved frequently and, while living in California, Day encountered Christianity in the form of a neighboring Methodist family. Day later was to recall that their piety and devotion impressed her greatly even though she was only a child.

In 1906, Day moved with her family to Chicago, where she joined the Episcopal Church. In 1914, she won a scholarship to the University of Illinois. Reading, studying, and contemplating society's ills, Day was influenced greatly by the writings of Jack London, Upton Sinclair, and Pyotr Kropotkin. In response to her growing awareness of poverty and the need for reform, she joined the Socialist party.

In 1916, Day began working as a reporter for the Socialist *Call*. She also joined the Anti-Conscription League. These activities helped forge Day's social conscience, and along with other suffragists she picketed the White House and was arrested. After her release from jail, where she participated in a hunger strike, Day worked briefly for Crystal Eastman's *The Liberator*, then worked for a year as a nurse at King's County Hospital in Brooklyn. She traveled to Europe in 1919, where she lived through what she describes in her autobiography as a time of "personal joy and heartbreak." Upon her return to the United States, Day moved to New Orleans, where she wrote for the *Item*. She subsequently moved back to New York and bought a house on Staten Island with proceeds from the sale of movie rights to her book *The Eleventh Virgin* (1924).

In 1925, Day became the common-law wife of anarchist Forster Batterham and in 1927 their daughter, Tamar Theresa, was born. Day soon found herself compelled to choose between her husband's beliefs and her growing Christian convictions. She was baptized a Roman Catholic on 18 December 1927. In her book *From Union Square to Rome* (1938), Day details this religious conversion and its significance in her life.

For several years Day supported herself by writing for *Commonweal*. In December 1932, she met Peter Maurin, a French-born Catholic reformer and grass-roots philosopher. His plans to care for the homeless and hungry coincided with Day's own ideas about social justice. On 1 May 1933, Day and Maurin first published *The Catholic Worker*. A year later they established St. Joseph's House of Hospitality in New York City. More than thirty of these homes for the unemployed and indigent opened across the United States during the Depression years.

Day was a staunch advocate of those who refused military service during the Vietnam conflict. She praised draft-card burners and others jailed for their antiwar principles and counseled thousands on pacifism. Day's death on 29 November 1980 deprived the Catholic Worker Movement of a courageous, defiant, and compassionate leader. But her imprint on the movement and her impact on social activism in the United States is indelible.

---

29 January 1933
DEATHS. Poet Sara Teasdale commits suicide.

4 March 1933
WOMEN'S ISSUES. Frances Perkins is sworn in as U.S. secretary of labor. She is the first woman cabinet member in U.S. history.

WOMEN'S ISSUES. The U.S. Postal Service announces that women are now eligible to be appointed postmistresses.

3 April 1933
POPULAR CULTURE. At a news conference, Eleanor Roosevelt announces that beer will be served at the White House.

12 April 1933
INTERNATIONAL. Ruth Bryan Owen is the first woman to represent the United States as foreign minister. She is named by President Roosevelt as envoy to Denmark and Iceland. Owen is the oldest daughter of William Jennings Bryan.

WOMEN'S ISSUES. Jeanie Rumsey Sheppard of New York is the first woman to serve on a state Alcoholic Beverage Control Board.

3 May 1933
WOMEN'S ISSUES. Nellie Tayloe Ross is named director of the U.S. Mint.

31 May 1933
POPULAR CULTURE. Sally Rand makes her debut at the Chicago Century of Progress Exposition, where she dances, appearing nude except for 2 fans.

16 June 1933
LABOR. Rose Schneiderman, long-time labor rights activist, is named to the National Recovery Administration's Labor Advisory Board.

26 June 1933
WOMEN'S ISSUES. The U.S. Consumers' Advisory Board is organized under the National Industrial Recovery Act. Its first chairperson is Mrs. Charles Carey Rumsey.

4 July 1933
AVIATION. At the National Air Race in Los Angeles, California, Mae Haizlip wins the Aero Trophy Race.

Frances Perkins, 1880–1965

Social reformer Frances Perkins was the first woman cabinet member in U.S. history. She was born Fannie Coralie Perkins on 10 April 1880, in Boston, Massachusetts. Her parents, Frederick and Susan (Bean) Perkins, were Congregationalists and Republicans. Educated in Worcester, Massachusetts, at Classical High School, Perkins was

Frances Perkins as she appeared at age eighteen, around the time that she enrolled at Mount Holyoke College. Perkins would later become the nation's first woman cabinet member, in the Roosevelt administration. (Photo courtesy Sophia Smith Collection, Smith College)

one of few female students. She subsequently enrolled at Mount Holyoke College, where she earned an A.B. in 1902 with a major in chemistry and physics.

After several years of teaching and volunteer work, she spent some time at Chicago's Hull House, which was located near the school where she was a biology and physics teacher. In 1907, Perkins joined the Philadelphia Research and Protective Association, and she also became a Socialist party member. However, she soon found practical, rather than ideal, solutions to social ills more palatable. Accordingly, in 1909, Perkins worked on a social survey of Hell's Kitchen in New York City, and earned an A.M. degree from Columbia University in 1910.

Perkins became secretary of the New York Consumer's League in 1910, and also taught at Adelphi College while she worked on behalf of woman suffrage. Perkins also worked for labor rights, and in 1912 her efforts to gain passage of a fifty-four-hour work week bill were rewarded when the legislation passed, albeit in slightly amended form. A few years later, she was also successful in gaining passage of progressive health and safety laws in New York.

On 26 September 1913, Frances married economist Paul Wilson. The couple had a daughter, whom they named Susanna, in 1916. Her husband eventually lost his life's savings through faulty investments, and by 1930 was frequently hospitalized for depression. He died in 1932.

Perkins received an appointment to the New York State Industrial Commission in 1918 after helping Al Smith win his campaign for governor. In 1920, she joined the Democratic party, traveling to San Francisco for her first of many Democratic

National conventions. That year she became executive secretary of the Immigration Education Council in New York, and in 1922 returned to the State Industrial Board (formerly the Commission). In 1926, Perkins was named board chair, and in 1928 she began service as state industrial commissioner, a post she held until 1933 thanks to the support of Franklin D. Roosevelt, who succeeded Al Smith as governor.

A friend of Eleanor's as well as Franklin Roosevelt's staunch political ally, Perkins was sworn in as secretary of labor on 4 March 1933. Until 1945 she played a significant role in shaping public policy. She was instrumental in writing the Federal Emergency Relief Act, Title II of the National Industrial Recovery Act, the Civilian Conservation Corps, the National Labor Relations Act, the Social Security Act, and the Fair Labor Standards Act. Frances Perkins held out time and again for the rights of laborers, often causing right-wing politicians to despair.

During her three decades of public service, Perkins helped to upgrade and consolidate many agencies designed to serve the interests of labor. She made important contributions to the Bureau of Labor Statistics and to the Women's and Children's Bureaus. Perkins was, however, generally unsympathetic to women workers' needs during the Depression. She then advised that married women should relinquish their jobs in favor of unemployed men. Later, she opposed child-care centers created under the Lanham Act during World War II. She also refused to endorse the Equal Rights Amendment.

After Franklin Roosevelt's death, Perkins served on the Civil Service Commission under President Truman. Later, in 1957, she became a professor at Cornell's School of Industry and Labor Relations. Perkins died in New York City on 14 May 1965.

Women in the 1930s on the Silver Screen

Hollywood films were an important diversion for Americans beginning in 1910 and throughout the 1920s. But by the 1930s movies dominated the public's leisure time and helped support the idea that the country, though hit by the Depression, was happy, healthy, and safe. In the 1930s between 60 and 90 million people attended movies; the price of admission was ten cents. For women, Hollywood provided employment in many areas. In 1928, for example, 20 percent of screenwriters' jobs were held by women. Among the many successful women screenwriters of the 1930s were Francis Marion, Zoe Akins, Bess Meredythe, and Dorothy Farmer. Anita Loos, famous in the 1920s for having written a screenplay for the 1928 version of *Gentlemen Prefer Blondes,* earned more than $2,500 a week.

Directing was also open to women. Dorothy Arzner began in 1918 as a typist, and then moved up to film editor. Eventually, she became chief editor at Paramount and was both writing and directing in 1927. Arzner became the well-respected director of such films as *Christopher Strong* (1933), starring Katharine Hepburn, and *The Bride Wore Red* (1937), with Joan Crawford.

Movie actresses in Hollywood numbered in the tens of dozens. In the 1920s, most people had seen Mary Pickford, Lillian and Dorothy Gish, and Clara Bow dozens of times. By the 1930s, other names had become pure box-office gold: Bette Davis, Claudette Colbert, Katharine Hepburn, Ruby Keeler, Ginger Rogers, Marlene Dietrich, Greta Garbo, Joan Crawford, Jean Harlow, Rosalind Russell, Norma Shearer. Among the most highly paid was Mae West who, by 1935, was earning $480,833 annually— reportedly the second highest income in America.

The themes of Hollywood films of this most prolific period covered a wide range. Some portrayed women as sexy, sultry bombshells, as in *The Blue Angel* (1930), with Marlene Dietrich. Others presented strong-willed heroines, such as Garbo's *Anna Karenina*. Despite these attempts at allowing women to portray three-dimensional characters on screen, there were limitations within the film industry. Many of the movies produced during the 1930s seem relatively tame, almost naive, when compared to films of subsequent decades. Yet, until Hollywood instituted the Production Code of 1934, movies showed women in a full range of emotional, physical, and intellectual postures. With the advent of the code, however, censors made unconventional or controversial films impossible. The decorous demands of the code ruled against violence and sex, while promoting the ideals of marriage, the family, Mom, and apple pie.

Although the Production Code of 1934 did not carry the force of law, it did institute a self-policing structure within the film industry. This self-censorship was especially obvious in terms of the way women were shown on screen. And among the best-remembered stars of that time were Judy Garland and Shirley Temple. *The Wizard of Oz* (1939), pure fantasy, sweetness, and light, is a good example of how hard Hollywood producers worked to transcend grim reality. They created Dorothy as an innocent, home-loving if slightly rebellious little girl whose adventures teach her the sanctity of the phrase, "there's no place like home."

Shirley Temple, the number-one draw at the box office from 1934 to 1938, was a film censor's delight. She was an innocent, curly-headed moppet—orphaned in many films—who only lacked a set of parents to make her life complete. And the charm that Shirley Temple radiated extended far beyond the movie theater. By 1940 she had made twenty-one films, and adoring fans willingly purchased Shirley Temple dolls, tea sets, dresses, jewelry, and other items that were sold nationwide.

The Depression decade is remembered for its impressive array of beautiful and talented actresses. Hollywood's ambitious production schedule resulted in hundreds of films every month that were eagerly watched by Americans who flocked to the movie theaters. Inside, they forgot, if briefly, the drabness of routine existence and sat for a few hours enchanted by the queens of the silver screen.

---

22 July 1933
ARTS AND CULTURE. Caterina Jarboro of the Chicago Opera Company is the first black prima donna of an opera company. She plays *Aida* at New York City's Hippodrome.

24 July 1933
AVIATION. Amy Johnson Mollison and her husband James make a nonstop flight from Wales to Connecticut in 39 hours, 3 minutes. They make a forced night landing and both suffer injuries.

OTHER EVENTS OF 1933

LABOR. Passage of the National Economy Act results in dismissal from government jobs for many women whose husbands also hold federal posts.

LEGISLATIVE. The Cable Act of 1922 is amended to permit American-born Asian women to regain American citizenship after terminating their marriages to foreign citizens.

POPULAR CULTURE. At the Academy Award presentations, Helen Hayes is named Best Actress of 1932 for her role in the motion picture *Sin of Madelon Claudet.*

30 January 1934
AVIATION. Anne Morrow Lindbergh is awarded the National Geographic Society Gold Medal. Lindbergh was co-pilot and radio operator of her husband's Aerial Survey. The award is presented on 31 March.

6 March 1934
AVIATION. Eleanor Roosevelt is the first president's wife to travel by airplane to a foreign country. She leaves Miami, Florida, on a trip to several countries in the Caribbean, returning on 16 March.

21 March 1934
SPORTS. Babe Didrikson pitches a full inning for the Philadelphia Athletics against the Brooklyn Dodgers.

9 April 1934
WOMEN'S ISSUES. Florence Ellenwood Allen is sworn in as an associate justice of the circuit court of appeals. She will serve in the sixth judicial court.

20 April 1934
POPULAR CULTURE. Child actress Shirley Temple appears for the first time on screen in the film *Stand Up and Cheer*.

22 May 1934
POLITICS. Mary Teresa Norton is elected the first woman state committee chair at the Democratic Convention in Trenton, New Jersey. Norton is a representative from the 13th New Jersey district.

Zora Neale Hurston, 1901–1960

Black folklorist and anthropologist Zora Neale Hurston was born in Eatonville, Florida, on 7 January 1901, although the facts concerning her birth are somewhat discrepant. The daughter of John and Lucy (Potts) Hurston, she was "passed around the family like a bad penny," in her words, after her mother's death in 1910. Hurston managed to get an education, however, receiving a high school diploma from Morgan College in Baltimore. She studied at Howard University from 1921 to 1924, moving to New York City in January 1925. She enrolled as a junior at Barnard College, studying anthropology under Franz Boas. In 1928, Hurston became the first black graduate of Barnard. She then received a two-year fellowship from the Rosewald Foundation; the grant enabled her to do graduate work in anthropology at Cornell.

During her academic career Hurston began what was to become her vocation—writing down folktales and telling stories about the black experience in America. Encouraged by leading figures of the Harlem Renaissance, among them Langston Hughes, Hurston became a consummate ethnographer whose work was an extension of her participation in the culture she studied. As a result of her research, she wrote a novel, *Jonah's Gourd Vine,* published in 1934, which the *New York Times* termed a "most vital and original book."

She married medical student Herbert Sheen in 1927; the couple divorced by 1931. In 1935, she published *Mules and Men,* a study of black folkways, having first produced a series of folk music programs in New York City and St. Louis, Missouri. She married again in 1939, but she and her second husband, Albert Price, subsequently divorced. In 1937, her second novel, *Their Eyes Were Watching God,* was published and received wide critical acclaim. More books followed, along with articles in the *American Mercury,* the *Saturday Evening Post,* the *Journal of American Folklore,* and *Survey Geographic.* In 1942, Hurston published her autobiography, *Dust Tracks on a Road.*

By the 1940s and 1950s, Hurston had become an outspoken critic of racial integration, which she felt would damage existing black culture and institutions. Despite her earlier prominence in Afro-American arts and letters, she died impoverished and virtually forgotten, on 3 February 1960, at a welfare home in Fort Pierce, Florida.

3 July 1934

FINANCE. Lydia Lobsiger, a widow in East Peoria, Illinois, is the first person to receive a check issued by the Federal Deposit Insurance Corporation (FDIC) following the suspension of the Fond du Lac State Bank. The FDIC was created in June 1933 to provide for safer banking.

13 July 1934

AVIATION. Cora Sterling is the first aerial police officer. Named to the Seattle (Washington) State Police Force, she holds a commercial transport license.

23 October 1934

AVIATION. Jeannette Piccard is the first woman to pilot a 175-foot hydrogen balloon into the stratosphere.

27 December 1934

POPULAR CULTURE. Isabel Smith and her husband open the first headquarters of the American Youth Hostels, Inc., in Northfield, Massachusetts.

31 December 1934

AVIATION. Helen Richey flies an airmail transport from Washington, D.C., to Detroit, Michigan. She is the first woman to assume this responsibility.

OTHER EVENTS OF 1934

LABOR. Writer Helena Hill Weed speaks out against clause #213 of the 1933 Economy Act, which states that if a husband and wife are both in the Civil Service, staff reduction guidelines would require dismissal of the woman over her husband.

POPULAR CULTURE. Academy Award-winning performers for 1933 include Katharine Hepburn for her role in *Morning Glory.*

11 January 1935

AVIATION. Amelia Earhart Putnam makes the first solo flight from Hawaii to North America.

10 July 1935

AVIATION. Pilot Laura Ingalls is the first woman to make a nonstop east-west transcontinental airplane flight.

3 September 1935

BUSINESS. Gretchen B. Schoenleber is the first woman stock exchange member (commodity exchange). She joins the N.Y. Cocoa Exchange, Inc.

11 November 1935

IDEAS/BELIEFS. Ella "Mother" Bloor is released from her most recent prison term. Often imprisoned for her communist activities, Bloor had been arrested for unlawful assembly.

Katharine Hepburn, 1909–

Among all female motion picture stars to come out of the Hollywood "system," few have enjoyed a career as rich and stable as that of Katharine Hepburn. Born in Hartford, Connecticut, on 8 November 1909, she was the daughter of Dr. Thomas N. and Katharine (Houghton) Hepburn. Although socially prominent and financially comfortable, the Hepburns were somewhat unconventional by early twentieth-century standards. Her mother was an early birth control advocate and suffragist, and her father was a famous urologist whose Spartan attitudes were inflicted on his children in the form of cold baths.

Hepburn attended Bryn Mawr College, hoping to become a doctor, but found that she had little genuine ability in chemistry and physics. Drama, her second choice, was looked at askance by her father, but she persevered, receiving a B.A. in 1928. She immediately entered summer stock upon graduation, and later that year married

Philadelphian Ludlow Ogden Smith. Although the couple divorced in 1934, they continued to remain on cordial terms.

By the autumn of 1928, Hepburn had appeared on Broadway in *Night Hostess* and *These Days*. In 1932, she landed a major role in *The Warrior's Husband* and soon received an offer from RKO Pictures in Hollywood; she worked for the studio for six years. Her first picture for RKO was *Bill of Divorcement* (1932), and in 1933 she was awarded an Oscar for best actress in *Morning Glory*. Subsequently, she appeared in *Little Women, Spitfire, The Little Minister, Alice Adams, Sylvia Scarlett, Christopher Strong, Mary of Scotland,* and *A Woman Rebels*. She was nominated for another Oscar for *Alice Adams*. In all of these films, Hepburn exercised the opportunity to portray vibrantly forceful women in ways that were often at odds with conventional standards of femininity.

Hepburn, however successful at the box office, was viewed warily by directors and producers because of her apparent ill will toward co-workers, the press, and studio executives. She persisted in a highly individual life-style and was recognized as an outspoken, totally truthful woman who worked hard and played hard. She went to Columbia Pictures, for whom she did *Holiday* in 1938, and returned to Broadway in 1939 to star as Tracy Lord in *The Philadelphia Story*. Since Hepburn owned the movie rights to this play, she sold them to MGM and won another Oscar nomination for her screen portrayal of Tracy Lord.

Hepburn's long and popular association with Spencer Tracy began on screen in 1942, when they acted together in *Woman of the Year*. Hepburn received her fourth Academy Award nomination for best actress. She and Tracy appeared in nearly a dozen films together until his death in 1967, and the two were quite openly, though discreetly, paired off the set despite Tracy's long-time marriage. This was yet another way in which Hepburn asserted herself and acted out her strongly individualistic personal style, which feminists lauded then and still do.

In 1952, Hepburn appeared in *The African Queen* opposite Humphrey Bogart and received another Oscar nomination. *Summertime* (1955), *The Rainmaker* (1956), and *Suddenly Last Summer* (1959) brought three more nominations.

Hepburn did not desert Broadway, however, and appeared in *As You Like It* in 1950, and in G. B. Shaw's *The Millionairess* in 1952. She also played at the American Shakespeare Festival in 1957 and 1960.

In 1967, Hepburn received her second Oscar as Best Actress in *Guess Who's Coming to Dinner*. She did *The Lion in Winter* (1968) and *The Mad Woman of Chaillot* (1969), winning her third Oscar for playing Eleanor of Aquitaine in the former. Among Hepburn's later films were *A Delicate Balance*, done for the American Film Theater, and *The Corn is Green*. Both were shown on television and were widely praised. In 1981, she starred opposite Henry Fonda in *On Golden Pond*, receiving yet another Oscar for best actress.

Cherishing her privacy, Hepburn has maintained a distance from the press, although she has agreed in later years to several taped interviews, one of which was with Barbara Walters in 1981. Afflicted with Parkinson's disease, Hepburn nevertheless has continued to approach life and her career with vigor. In early 1986, she appeared as narrator of a television special honoring Spencer Tracy. Hepburn is quick to point out that her years in acting—more than fifty at last count—have provided her with a satisfaction and sense of accomplishment she would not have found elsewhere.

19 November 1935
SCIENCE. Two botanists, Wanda K. Farr and Dr. Sophia H. Eckerson, announce their findings of research into the study of cellulose, discovering its double cell-wall structure.

23 November 1935
ARTS AND CULTURE. The opera *Gale,* sung at the Chicago City Opera, is the first to be written and conducted by a woman, Ethel Legins, in a major opera house.

OTHER EVENTS OF 1935

ARTS AND CULTURE. Hallie Flanagan is named head of the Federal Theater Project, which she runs until 1939.

POPULAR CULTURE The Oscar for Best Actress of 1934 goes to Claudette Colbert for *It Happened One Night.*

27 May 1936
SPORTS. Rollins College student Sally Stearns is the first woman coxswain of a male varsity team. They lose a race against Marietta College by 4 lengths.

30 June 1936
LITERATURE. Margaret Mitchell's novel *Gone With the Wind* is published; by 1955 it has sold 6 million copies.

19 October 1936
AVIATION. Reporter Dorothy Kilgallen loses an around-the-world airplane race to H. R. Elkins.

OTHER EVENTS OF 1936
Olympic Gold Medals

Dorothy Hill: Platform diving
Marjorie Gestring: Springboard diving
Helen Stephens: 100-meter dash
    Track—400-meter relay women's team medal

Olympic Silver Medals

Velma Dunn: Platform diving
Katherine Rawls: Springboard diving

Amelia Earhart Putnam, 1897–1937

Amelia Earhart's energetic curiosity led her from one project to another in a search for meaningful life's work. In 1917, she was an aide at a Canadian military hospital; in 1919, she enrolled in the pre-med program at Columbia University. Flying lessons followed and after her first solo flight in June 1921, Earhart barnstormed throughout southern California. Then, after a year spent visiting her sister at Smith College in Massachusetts, Earhart went to Boston, where she became a resident social worker at Denison House in 1926.

But the sky beckoned, and since the public's imagination had been stirred to a frenzy by Charles A. Lindbergh's transatlantic flight in 1927, Earhart was offered the chance to be the first woman to cross the Atlantic. As keeper of the flight log, however, and not as pilot, Earhart participated in this aviation stunt backed by publisher George Palmer Putnam. ''How could I refuse such a shining adventure?'' she commented later on this episode.

Earhart soon became known as ''Lady Lindy, First Lady of the Air.'' If the derivative title bothered her, she kept that to herself. For the next several years she promoted aviation, helping to found the ''Ninety-Nines,'' an international organization of licensed women pilots. She also became aviation editor of *Cosmopolitan* magazine. She seemed to embody the very essence of feminism with her cool demeanor, her flying escapades, and her keen intellect, and she once more made headlines by marrying

George Palmer Putnam on 7 February 1931. It was soon clear, however, that Earhart would not give up her flying career for a job as a housewife.

On 21–22 May 1932, Earhart became the first woman to pilot a plane across the Atlantic. She was subsequently awarded the Distinguished Flying Cross, the cross of the French Legion of Honor, and the National Geographic Society Gold Medal. Throughout all the publicity, she carried herself with what Anne Morrow Lindbergh once termed, "poise, equanimity." Earhart's accomplishment placed her even further into the public eye, which she likened to being "in a zoo." But responsibilities and honors continued, and she was appointed women's counselor at Purdue University in 1935.

In June 1937, after months of preparation, Earhart left on the first leg of an around-the-world flight. Several weeks into the journey, she radioed from a point in the mid-Pacific Ocean. After that radio message was received on 2 July 1937, the "First Lady of the Air" vanished. Neither she nor her plane was ever seen again.

Olympic Bronze Medals

Dorothy Hill: Springboard diving
Lenore Wingard: Swimming—400-meter freestyle
Alice Bridges: Swimming—100-meter backstroke
   Swimming—400-meter freestyle relay women's team medal

POPULAR CULTURE. Margaret Mitchell's *Gone With the Wind* film rights are sold to David Selznick for $50,000.

POPULAR CULTURE. The 1935 Oscar for Best Actress goes to Bette Davis for her performance in *Dangerous*.

15 March 1937
HEALTH. Roberta Pratt, a nurse from Raleigh, North Carolina, is on the staff of the first state contraceptive clinic set up for indigent women.

29 March 1937
LABOR. The U.S. Supreme Court upholds the Washington State minimum wage law for women. This reverses a decision of June 1936 in which similar New York state laws were declared invalid.

6 April 1937
WOMEN'S ISSUES. Julia Sims serves as foreman on the federal grand jury in the U.S.

district court in Newark, New Jersey. She is the first woman to act in this capacity.

24 May 1937
WOMEN'S ISSUES. New York state passes a law that will permit women to serve as jurors.

1 June 1937
AVIATION. Amelia Earhart Putnam boards her Lockheed Electra to begin an around-the-world flight.

22 June 1937
POLITICS. U.S. Representative Mary T. Norton (D-New Jersey) is named chair of the House Committee on Labor.

2 July 1937
AVIATION. Amelia Earhart's plane is lost near Howland Island in the Pacific Ocean.

4 September 1937
SPORTS. Doris Kopsky of Belleville, New Jersey, is named the first woman bicycle champ by the National Amateur Bicycle Association. She completes a 1-mile ride in 4 minutes, 22.4 seconds.

8 September 1937
WOMEN'S ISSUES. Anne I. Farley of the Bronx, New York, is selected as the first woman juror in New York state.

Mary McLeod Bethune, 1875–1955

Educator, federal official, and civil rights activist Mary McLeod Bethune was born on 10 July 1875, in Mayesville, South Carolina, the daughter of Sam and Patsy (McIntosh) McLeod. Her parents, former black slaves, owned a tiny farm and were hardworking. They raised corn, cotton, and seventeen children. As a child, she obtained limited schooling at a Presbyterian mission school to which she walked five miles each morning. At fifteen she received a scholarship to Scotia Seminary in Concord, North Carolina, graduating in 1893. Although she planned to become a missionary to Africa, McLeod was instead persuaded to be a teacher.

In 1895, after graduating from Moody Bible Institute in Chicago, she took a teaching position at Hanes Institute in Augusta, Georgia. In 1898, she married Albertus Bethune, who had also been a teacher, and the couple had a son, Albert McLeod Bethune, in 1899.

Bethune taught in Palatka, Florida, at a Presbyterian school for black students until 1904. At this time she invested just $1.50 and started her own school for girls. It was modeled after Scotia Seminary, and on 3 October it opened with six students.

As a result of her boundless ambition and dedication to education, Bethune was successful in garnering much support for her little school. In two years, she had 250 pupils. By 1911 the Daytona Normal and Industrial Institute, as the school was known, had established a hospital for blacks. By 1923 there were eight buildings and a faculty of thirty-five. In 1923, the school became coeducational after its merger with Cookman Institute in Jacksonville. Most of this rapid expansion and successful growth was due to Bethune's fund-raising abilities and her skills as an administrator. In 1929, the school became Bethune–Cookman College, and it began conferring four-year teaching degrees in 1943. Bethune was president until 1942, despite the demanding federal position she had assumed (at President Roosevelt's request) in 1938 as part of the National Youth Administration (NYA).

Bethune was a tireless speaker on behalf of black women's rights. Between 1917 and 1924, she was president of the Florida Federation of Colored Women; in 1920, she helped found the Southeastern Federation of Colored Women. In 1924, Bethune was named president of the National Association of Colored Women, which was then the most influential organization of its kind. In 1935, President Roosevelt named Bethune to a thirty-five member advisory committee as part of the NYA, and there she continued to champion the needs of black Americans, particularly with regard to education and employment. Later she helped unite all major black women's organizations, forming the National Council of Negro Women (NCNW). She was NCNW president until 1949.

Throughout Roosevelt's administration, Bethune was a devoted New Deal supporter and a close associate of Eleanor Roosevelt. After her retirement in 1949, she continued her speaking engagements on behalf of black civil rights. She went to Liberia in 1952 as U.S. representative at President William Tubman's inauguration. Bethune died of a heart attack on 18 May 1955, and was buried on the Bethune–Cookman College campus.

OTHER EVENTS OF 1937

WOMEN'S ISSUES.   Twelve New York City women become the first female members of the New York City Bar Association.

POPULAR CULTURE.   Academy Awards go to Luise Rainer for Best Actress of 1936 in *The Great Ziegfeld,* and Gale Sondergaard, Best Supporting Actress in *Anthony Adverse.*

13 January 1938
SPORTS.   Missouri's all-women's basketball team, the All-American Redheads, meets a male team at the Pan Pacific Auditorium in Los Angeles, California. Four of the women players are more than 6 feet tall.

5 May 1938
MEDICAL.   At a meeting of the American Pediatric Association and the Society for Pediatric Research, Dr. Dorothy H. Andersen presents the results of her medical research identifying the disease cystic fibrosis.

4 June 1938
AVIATION.   Marjorie Shuler is the first woman to fly around the world in a commercial plane.

13 September 1938
POLITICS.   Elizabeth Hawley Gasque (D-South Carolina) is the first female representative not sworn in. Until January 1939 she fills a vacancy caused by her husband's death, but never participates in the 75th Congress as it is not in session.

13 October 1938
SPORTS.   Mrs. Payne Whitney is the first woman to receive a life membership in the Thoroughbred Club of America in Lexington, Kentucky.

9 November 1938
POPULAR CULTURE.   Mary Martin makes her debut in the muscial comedy *Leave it to Me.* She introduces the hit song "My Hearts Belongs to Daddy."

13 November 1938
RELIGION.   Mother Frances Xavier Cabrini is beautified. She is the first American woman citizen to become a saint.

10 December 1938
INTERNATIONAL.   Pearl S. Buck is the first woman to receive the Nobel Prize for literature. She is awarded $37,975 and a gold medal for her novels about China.

Eleanor Roosevelt, 1884–1962

From a sheltered girlhood, this remarkably strong-willed woman emerged as a crusader for the needs of the downtrodden and dedicated her life to helping others. The daughter of aristocratic Elliot and Anna (Hall) Roosevelt, she was born in New York City on 11 October 1884. She and her brother Hall were orphaned when she was ten, and until the age of fifteen she lived with her maternal grandmother. Prior to entering Allenswood, a private girls' school outside of London, England, Roosevelt's life was characterized by a total lack of warmth and affection. At the school, however, she found friendship and also loving guidance under the tutelage of Marie Souvestre, the school's headmistress. The three years she spent at the school always remained among her most cherished memories.

Returning to the United States, she was obliged to make her formal debut at seventeen, but subsequently devoted herself to settlement work, joining the National Consumers' League. On 17 March 1905, she married her distant cousin Franklin Roosevelt, and the couple had six children, all born between 1906 and 1916. During these years and beyond, her mother-in-law dominated Roosevelt's home life and contributed

Eleanor Roosevelt, U.S. delegate to the
United Nations Commission on Human
Rights, at a U.N. press conference in
1952. (Photo courtesy United Nations)

none of the caring support that the young wife and mother both needed and deserved.

Her husband's increasing involvement in politics placed Roosevelt in a role of prominence that she managed efficiently along with her domestic duties. During World War I she was active in the Red Cross and later was prominent in the League of Women Voters. She joined the Women's Trade Union League in 1922 and worked hard for fair labor legislation in New York state.

In 1921, FDR contracted polio, and Roosevelt became virtually indispensable to her husband's position as Democratic party leader in New York. She found that she was a spokesperson for minority groups and for women. She helped her husband, then governor of New York, recognize the needs of women workers, and she acted as an example to others to speak out for and act on their political beliefs.

A formidable political activist, Roosevelt found many ways to further women's demands after the 1932 presidential election. She spoke nationally on a variety of subjects pertinent to general relief during the Depression. In 1930, she began writing a syndicated news column and also spoke on radio programs. Since Roosevelt's sympathy and compassion were genuine, many credit her with greatly influencing the president's New Deal programs in ways that other advisors found impossible to manage.

Although there were emotional storm clouds on the horizon, she never permitted her personal difficulties to interfere with her public responsibilities. Her heartbreak over her husband's extramarital involvement with Lucy Mercer seems to have further fueled her passion to serve all humanity. A proponent of civil rights, Roosevelt resigned from the Daughters of the American Revolution in 1939 when that group prohibited opera singer Marian Anderson from performing at Constitution Hall in Washington, D.C. At Roosevelt's urging the concert was held instead at the Lincoln Memorial, where the black contralto sang for a crowd of seventy-five thousand people.

Between 1936 and 1940, she was a staunch supporter of the American Student Union and the American Youth Congress, both of which were committed to social welfare. During World War II, Roosevelt worked to promote women's integration in the war effort. She also acted as an advocate for Jewish war refugees. After her husband's death, she pressed for fair labor practices and for civil rights. She was named a delegate to the United Nations' Charter Commission, and was a shaping force in that body's early years. Despite her refusal to run for public office, Roosevelt proved she was a continuing influence in both Republican and Democratic presidential administrations by virtue of the enormous public influence she held.

World peace and the alleviation of human suffering were her chief postwar concerns. She traveled worldwide, and in 1962 spoke vehemently in support of black civil rights workers. President John F. Kennedy named Roosevelt chair of the Commission on the Status of Women in 1961, although she retired in August 1962. She died of tuberculosis on 7 November 1962, at age seventy-eight.

OTHER EVENTS OF 1938

POLITICS. Democrat Crystal Bird Fauset is elected to the House of Representatives in Pennsylvania. She is the first black woman elected to an American state legislature.

POPULAR CULTURE. The Academy Award for Best Actress of 1937 goes to Luise Rainer for her role in *The Good Earth*. Alice Brady receives an Oscar for Best Supporting Actress in *In Old Chicago*.

3 January 1939
WOMEN'S ISSUES. The first female page in the U.S. House of Representatives, Gene Cox, age 13, serves on the first day of the 76th Congress and receives $4.

4 January 1939
EDUCATION. Dr. Freida Wünderlich is the first woman dean of a graduate school, at the New School for Social Research. She heads the Graduate Faculty of Political and Social Sciences.

9 April 1939
ARTS AND CULTURE. Marian Anderson sings at the Lincoln Memorial in Washington, D.C., performing before a crowd of 75,000 people. Because of her race, Anderson was denied the opportunity to sing at Constitution Hall by the Daughters of the American Revolution (DAR). Eleanor Roosevelt resigns from the DAR in protest.

28 May 1939
EDUCATION. Helen Hadassah Levinthal is the first Jewish woman to receive a degree—Master of Hebrew Literature—from a recognized theological college, The Jewish Institute of Religion.

22 June 1939
POPULAR CULTURE. The first beauty contest is televised from Flushing, New York, during the New York World's Fair.

30 June 1939
ARTS AND CULTURE. The Federal Theater Project, under the direction of Hallie Flanagan, ends when it no longer receives funding from the U.S. Congress.

22 July 1939
WOMEN'S ISSUES. In New York City, Jane Matilda Bolin is the first black woman judge to be appointed to the court of domestic relations.

25 August 1939
POPULAR CULTURE. Judy Garland appears as Dorothy in the motion picture *The Wizard of Oz*. She wins a special Academy Award for this performance.

Mary Anderson, 1872–1964

Throughout the early to mid-twentieth century, Mary Anderson helped organize and strengthen the Federal Women's Bureau—an agency designed to further the position of working women. She was born on 27 August 1872, in Lidköping, Sweden, the daughter of Magnus and Matilda (Johnson) Anderson, and at sixteen years old emigrated with her sister to the United States. Anderson settled in Chicago, where she worked in a shoe factory.

In 1899, Anderson joined the International Boot and Shoe Workers Union and was quickly elected to a leadership position. In 1905, she joined the Women's Trade Union League (WTUL) and became a close friend of its president, Margaret Dreier Robins. A strike by clothing workers in Chicago during 1910–1911 resulted in a paid League position as a union organizer, and in that capacity Anderson traveled extensively. She met with workers in forty shops owned by Hart, Schaffner, and Marx, urging them to join the union.

Anderson continued on the WTUL payroll until World War I, when she obtained a subcommittee position with the U.S. Council of Defense. In 1915, she became a naturalized American citizen, and was named assistant director of the Women in Industry Service, a branch of the Department of Labor, in 1918.

Anderson succeeded in her Defense Department job because she was a seasoned labor organizer and experienced administrator. In 1919, she was a WTUL representative to the Paris Peace Conference, and soon after her return, in August 1919, she was named head of the Women in Industry Service. This wartime board was converted in June 1920 to permanent agency status and became the Women's Bureau of the Department of Labor. Anderson was appointed its director. The Women's Bureau was quickly hailed as one of the foremost agencies advocating for women workers. Anderson's efficiency and ability to oversee a large staff helped her become well known and well respected throughout the federal government.

Although a strong supporter of woman suffrage, Anderson opposed National Women's party efforts to promote passage of an Equal Rights Amendment (ERA). Anderson, a hard-working advocate of women workers, feared the threat posed to protective legislation if the ERA passed. A friend of both Franklin and Eleanor Roosevelt, Anderson was named head of the U.S. delegation to the International Labor Organization in 1933.

As Women's Bureau chief during the early years of World War II, Anderson attempted to gain expanded funding for the Bureau's war-related activities. The Women's Bureau was heavily involved in the complexities of establishing guidelines for women defense workers. Unfortunately, due to a variety of reasons, the Bureau failed to obtain the needed monies. Anderson retired in 1944 and was succeeded by Freida Miller.

Anderson was granted an honorary degree from Smith College in 1941. In 1962, she was given the Department of Labor's Award of Merit. She died at age ninety-one on 29 January 1964.

13 October 1939
AVIATION. Evelyn Pinckert Kilgore is the first licensed woman airplane instructor to receive certification by the Civil Aeronautics Authority.

2 December 1939
POLITICS. Ruth Hanna McCormick Simms is co-manager of Thomas Dewey's presidential campaign. She is the first woman to assume authority for a presidential campaign.

OTHER EVENTS OF 1939

POPULAR CULTURE. Oscars for 1938 go to Bette Davis for her Best Actress performance in *Jezebel* and to Fay Bainter, in the same film, for Best Supporting Actress.

2 January 1940
POPULAR CULTURE. Mary Brooks Picken compiles *The Language of Fashion*, the first dictionary completely edited by a woman.

8 April 1940
POLITICS. Republican Margaret Chase Smith from Skowhegan, Maine, is elected to the 76th Congress to fill a slot left open by her husband's death.

30 April 1940
SPORTS. Belle Martell of Van Nuys, California, is the first licensed woman prize-fight referee. She first officiates on 2 May.

10 November 1940
IDEAS/BELIEFS. Eleanor Roosevelt addresses 1,800 people attending the 20th Annual Conference of the United Parents Associations of New York. Her speech at the Hotel Pennsylvania emphasizes "a great obligation to prepare young people for the kind of world they must face."

25 November 1940
POPULAR CULTURE. Well-known radio commentator and journalist Mary Margaret McBride signs a contract with CBS for a national 15-minute radio broadcast.

OTHER EVENTS OF 1940

RELIGION. Dr. Aurelia H. Reinhardt of Oakland, California, is named the first woman moderator of the Unitarian Churches of America.

POPULAR CULTURE. Oscars go to Vivien Leigh and Hattie McDaniel, Best Actress and Best Supporting Actress of 1939, respectively, for *Gone With the Wind*.

Margaret Bourke-White, 1904–1971

Known for her internationally acclaimed photographs, which brought the plight of sharecroppers and soldiers alike to the attention of millions, Margaret Bourke-White broke into a difficult technical field when many of her contemporaries opted for less challenging assignments. She was born on 14 June 1904, in New York City. Her father, Joseph White, was an engineer; her mother, Minnie (Bourke) White, worked on books for the blind.

Attending Columbia University from 1922 to 1923, Bourke-White studied engineering, biology, and photography. At the University of Michigan between 1923 and 1925 she took yearbook photographs. She also married Everett Chapman, although they divorced in 1926. She then began using the hyphenated name by which she was subsequently known. Still involved in photography, Bourke-White studied briefly at Western Reserve University, ultimately graduating from Cornell in 1927. She then moved to Cleveland, where she applied her skills and interests as a photographer to industrial projects.

In 1929, she was hired by *Fortune* magazine and moved to New York City, establishing a commercial studio there. In 1930, she traveled to the Soviet Union and published a book about her trip, *Eyes on Russia,* in 1931. Bourke-White was one of a group of photographers whose mid-1930s coverage of the Dust Bowl captured the plight of thousands of poverty-stricken Americans. In 1935, her photographs of dam construction in Montana resulted in a cover story for the premier issue of *Life* magazine on 23 November 1936. Bourke-White collaborated with writer Erskine Caldwell the same year to produce a book about Southern sharecroppers. The result, published in 1937 as *You Have Seen Their Faces,* became a classic of the genre. Bourke-White and Caldwell were married in 1939, and they worked together on several other books before their divorce in 1942.

Following the Japanese attack on Pearl Harbor, Bourke-White was named an official U.S. Air Force photographer and was sent to cover troop action, first in England and then in North Africa. She followed General Patton's Third Army during the final days of the war. This experience led to one of her most famous books of photographs, *The Living Dead of Buchenwald.*

After World War II, Bourke-White was sent by *Life* magazine to India, where she did numerous photographs of Gandhi. She also traveled to South Africa and covered the Korean conflict on film as well. By the mid-1950s, Bourke-White's work was curtailed by her ongoing battle with Parkinson's disease. She died on 27 August 1971 in Stamford, Connecticut.

V

WOMEN IN THE MILITARY AND BEYOND
1941–1950

For all Americans, the event carrying the most significance during the 1940s was U.S. entry into World War II. And the war marked even greater opportunities for women, particularly in the workplace. The best example of this is the defense industry, where women made up the greatest proportion of all workers during the war years. The armed forces expanded, too, accommodating women by adding the Women's Auxiliary Army Corps (WAAC, later the WACs), Women Appointed for Voluntary Emergency Service (WAVES), the Women's Auxiliary Ferrying Squadron (WAFS), and the Coast Guard Women's Reserve (SPARS). By the end of the decade all of these units had been racially integrated, providing at least a minimum standard of racial equality on which the rest of society might pattern itself.

In medicine, an American woman doctor was, with her husband, corecipient of the Nobel Prize. Another became the first female member of the Association of American Physicians. By 1949, Harvard Medical School broke with tradition and admitted its first women students and paved the way for greater equality in the medical profession.

A black woman tennis star, Althea Gibson, was the first to become a member of the U.S. Lawn Tennis Association. During these years, sports superstar Babe Didrikson Zaharias joined the ranks of pro golfers and signed a $300,000 movie contract. Another woman was the first Sullivan trophy winner, the award given by the Amateur Athletic Union to the outstanding amateur athlete of the year.

Late in the 1940s, women assumed positions on the Federal Communications Commission and as head of the U.S. Treasury, firsts in both areas. By 1950 the U.S. Senate passed a version of the Equal Rights Amendment and sent it to the House for further action. The same year, Anna Rosenberg was named the first woman assistant secretary of defense. The decade led the way in important respects for women's assumption of more meaningful roles. But it would be at least another dozen years before American women could expect that their responsibilities were able to bring them anything more than cursory power.

Jeannette Rankin, 1880–1973

On 6 April 1917, Jeannette Rankin (D-Montana) announced her opposition to U.S. entry into World War I. "I want to stand by my country, but I cannot vote for war," she said. Five days before this statement, Rankin had been introduced as the first woman ever elected to the U.S. House of Representatives. But her rigid peace stance came as little surprise to those who knew her. Her election campaign had been run on the progressive Republican platform, which included support from "preparedness that will make for peace."

Rankin was born on a ranch six miles from Missoula in the Montana Territory on 11 June 1880. Her father, John Rankin, and her mother, Olive (Pickering) Rankin, had seven children, and all were encouraged to be successful. She attended public school and graduated from the University of Montana in 1902 with a B.S. in biology.

Like many college-educated women of her generation, Rankin enjoyed a brief career in social work following training at the New York School of Philanthropy in 1908. She then joined the Washington state woman suffrage efforts while she was a student at the University of Washington. Her positive experience there (Washington granted woman suffrage in 1910) led her to campaign for similar rights in her home state of Montana. In 1913, Rankin was named field secretary of the National American Woman's Suffrage Association, and one year later her efforts were rewarded in part as Montana gave women the vote. She had to wait until 1920, however, for this right to be extended to all women in all states.

Due to Montana's enfranchisement of women, Rankin mounted a successful bid for a seat in the U.S. House of Representatives in 1916. Later, however, her intransigent position on war caused her defeat in the 1918 U.S. Senate race in Montana. A committed pacifist, Rankin traveled to Zurich in 1919 as a delegate to the Second International Congress of Women. In 1924, she bought a home near Athens, Georgia, where she formed the Georgia Peace Society in 1928. For the next twelve years Rankin made a monumental effort to secure world peace.

Retaining her Montana residency, Rankin was once again elected to the U.S. House of Representatives in 1940. She opposed American involvement in war, arguing forcibly against the military draft and the Lend-Lease bill. On 8 December 1941, Rankin cast the single vote against a U.S. declaration of war on Japan. This distinguished her as the only member of Congress to directly oppose U.S. participation in both World Wars. Although this position cost her any hope of reelection, Rankin was undaunted. She sustained her pacifist efforts, and in 1967 formed the Jeannette Rankin Brigade, which demonstrated in Washington, D.C., against the Vietnam War in January 1968.

Rankin, feisty and outspoken throughout her sixty-five years of activism, died on 18 May 1973. In May 1985, she was honored with a lasting memorial at the nation's Capitol. A bronze likeness of Rankin now occupies the Statuary Hall there, which is reserved for each state to memorialize two of its most revered citizens.

Women in Defense Work, 1941–1946

Wartime provokes change, and after Pearl Harbor women faced many opportunities as a result of a changing American economy. The Depression had severely curtailed women's employment, and by 1940 the number of working women in America had dropped to 1910 levels. Sadly, it was war that energized the economy and pushed women out of the home and into the workplace. Overall, the war years saw 6 million women go to work. The number of women in the labor force increased by 50 percent compared to prewar years, and the number of working wives doubled. Women's union membership quadrupled.

The largest employer in America was the defense industry. Rosie the Riveter, popularized on posters and in songs, became a living, breathing reality in defense plants across the nation. Women rolled up their sleeves, donned overalls, and began making ships, planes, and tanks. They were hired by munitions plants and for work in government offices. In September 1939, only thirty-six women worked in ship construction. By December 1942 the shipbuilding industry employed 160,000 women. The aircraft industry employed only 143 women in April 1941, but eighteen months later, 65,000 women had jobs building planes.

War spelled emergency. This shifted attitudes about women's capabilities as suddenly—almost overnight—women working outside the home were praised and applauded for their efforts. Female gender stereotypes faded as the urgency accompanying defense work accelerated. A whole new way of viewing women's lives and their work evolved. Each morning millions of women packed lunches and punched time clocks. A mystique grew about the woman defense worker. Movie screens showed her larger than life, and stories and books embroidered strength and pathos onto the fabric of her days, imbuing her tasks with home-front heroism.

But defense work did more than break down female stereotypes. It also smashed civilian wages standards. In munitions plants and aircraft factories women workers averaged 40 percent higher pay than in civilian jobs. A woman shipbuilder, for example, earned $37 a week—in the same city, a waitress earned $14.

And although women may have been unprepared for defense work, they adapted quickly. They were deft and learned rapidly. Furthermore, federal officials bolstered their egos with statements such as "Our country was not built the soft way." Women responded to the challenge with energy and drive, producing ships, planes, and the other necessities of war.

When the war was over, America had changed. Women had found that defense work was a step in the right direction, and it seemed unlikely that they would return contentedly to hearth and home. America had won the war but had established a new battlefield—women's struggle for permanent recognition in the work force had begun.

6 January 1941
SPORTS. Tennis player Alice Marble makes her professional debut at Madison Square Garden.

3 July 1941
SPORTS. Eleanor Dudley wins the first women's national intercollegiate golf championship at Ohio State University.

11 September 1941

SPORTS. Seventeen-year-old Myrtle Chick announces her intention of organizing a girl's football team after being denied the opportunity to play on the Medfield High School (Massachusetts) football team.

12 November 1941

AVIATION. Alma Heflin, a test pilot for Piper Aircraft Corp., completes the first test flight of standard production aircraft.

19 November 1941

POPULAR CULTURE. Actress Linda Darnell is the first woman to sell securities on the New York Stock Exchange, selling U.S. Defense Bonds and Stamps.

7 December 1941

MILITARY. Captain Annie Fox will receive the first Purple Heart awarded to a nurse for her service under attack at Pearl Habor in the Hawaiian Islands.

8 December 1941

POLITICS. The first U.S. representative to vote twice against U.S. entry into war is Montana Democrat Jeannette Rankin.

OTHER EVENTS OF 1941

POPULAR CULTURE. At the Academy Awards presentations, Ginger Rogers is named Best Actress of 1940 for her role in *Kitty Foyle*. Jane Darwell is named Best Supporting Actress for her part in *The Grapes of Wrath*.

16 January 1942

DEATHS. Actress Carole Lombard (wife of Clark Gable) is killed in a Nevada plane crash during a trip to sell war bonds.

25 January 1942

AVIATION. American aviator Jacqueline Cochran begins a tour to recruit 375 women pilots for the British Air Transport Auxiliary. Cochran has the backing of both the U.S. War Department and the president in this venture.

Millions of American teenagers found film stars like Linda Darnell, Ginger Rogers, and Carole Lombard the ultimate role models. Bobby-soxers pin-curled and waved their hair a la Darnell and hoped for dance partners as suave as Fred Astaire. (Photo courtesy L. Elizabeth Bartlett)

Alice Paul, 1885–1977

Best known as author of the Equal Rights Amendment, feminist Alice Paul was born in Moorestown, New Jersey, on 11 January 1885. The daughter of wealthy Quakers William M. and Tacie (Perry) Paul, she graduated from Swarthmore College in 1905. She then studied at the New York School of Social Work, living for a time at the New York College Settlement. An ardent suffragist, Paul went to England to practice settlement work and was imprisoned for her suffrage activities several times there between 1906 and 1909. During one of her imprisonments she was force-fed for more than three weeks because of her refusal to eat. In 1907, Paul received an M.A. from the University of Pennsylvania; she received a Ph.D. from the same school in 1912.

When a group of militant suffragists separated from the National American Women's Suffrage Association in 1913 at a Denver convention, Paul led the secession. Along with this group of secessionists she helped establish the Congressional Union for Woman Suffrage (CUWS) and was its national chairperson until 1917. At that time, the CUWS members formed the National Women's party with Paul as chair of its executive committee until 1921. During these years, she received three prison sentences for her demonstrations on behalf of women's voting rights. Prior to passage of the Nineteenth Amendment, she was among picketers outside the White House who carried banners proclaiming "How Much Longer Must Women Wait?"

Between 1922 and 1928 Paul received three law degrees—an LL.B. from Washington College of Law and an LL.M. and a D.C.L. from American University. At the same time, she worked to further women's rights and in 1923 promoted introduction of a Constitutional amendment known as the Equal Rights Amendment (ERA). Paul was involved in women's equality on an international scale as well. Between 1930 and 1933 she worked on the Inter-American Commission of Women. She also worked for an Equal Rights Treaty to be supported by all nations, and helped organize the World Women's Party, representing that group in Geneva, Switzerland.

In 1942, she was elected chairperson of the National Women's party and saw the ERA rewritten by the Senate Judiciary Committee in 1943. The following year, due to her efforts, the ERA was endorsed as a plank in the campaign platforms of both the Democratic and Republican parties. In 1945, Paul worked to incorporate an equal rights statement into the United Nations Charter. After the resolution was adopted by the United Nations Assembly in December 1946, she said that she believed "all member nations will bring their laws in regard to suffrage up to the standard of equality recommended by the Assembly." Although Paul consistently stated that she felt passage of the Nineteenth Amendment was "the most useful [thing] I ever did . . . because that was a big transformation for the country to have one-half the country enfranchised," she still hoped for passage of an ERA.

After 1941, Paul lived at the National Women's party headquarters in Washington, D.C., a building purchased in 1921 with money donated by Mrs. O. H. P. Belmont. As her health declined and she required more privacy, she moved in 1972 to Ridgefield, Connecticut, where she suffered a stroke two years later. Paul was honored in January 1977 by the National Organization for Women with a nationwide observance of her ninety-second birthday. Confined to a wheelchair, she was nevertheless pleased to be promoting passage of the ERA. She died on 10 July 1977, at the Greenleaf Extension Nursing Home in her hometown of Moorestown, New Jersey.

2 March 1942
MILITARY. The U.S. War Department issues a statement promoting the hiring of women for industrial jobs. Ford Motor Company is advised to hire 12,000–15,000 women for its Willow Run bomber plant. Willow Run currently has 28 female employees.

13 March 1942
MILITARY. Julia Otteson Flikke of the Army Nurse Corps is the first woman to receive a rank—that of colonel—corresponding to regular U.S. Army ranking.

14 May 1942
MILITARY. Oveta Culp Hobby is named director of the newly created Women's Auxiliary Army Corps. She assumes rank equivalent to that of colonel in the U.S. Army.

6 June 1942
AVIATION. Parachute rigger Adeline Gray of the Pioneer Parachute Company in Manchester, Connecticut, is the first person to jump with a nylon parachute.

20 July 1942
MILITARY. The first class of women officer candidates for the Women's Auxiliary Army Corps (WAAC) begins at Fort Des Moines, Iowa. The WAAC accepts both black and white women.

30 July 1942
MILITARY. The agency Women Appointed for Voluntary Emergency Service (WAVES) is created by President Roosevelt. Mildred McAfee is sworn in as lieutenant commander of the WAVES.

24 August 1942
MILITARY. Engineer Jean Hales is appointed junior inspector by the 12th naval district. She is the first woman in the navy named to this post.

7 September 1942
MILITARY. Dr. Caroline J. Gaskill of Peekskill, New York, is the first woman doctor commissioned into the WAVES. She enrolls at the National Naval Medical Center in Bethesda, Maryland, in November.

10 September 1942
AVIATION. Nancy Harkness Love becomes commander of the Women's Auxiliary Ferrying

Squadron (WAFS). Love received her commercial pilot's license while a student at Vassar College from 1931 to 1934.

9 October 1942
MILITARY. The WAVES opens training programs for enlisted women.

13 November 1942
MEDICAL. The first 2 women medical technicians report to the National Naval Medical Center after a 30-day course at the U.S. Naval Training School at Smith College in Northampton, Massachusetts.

23 November 1942
MILITARY. The Coast Guard Women's Reserve (SPARS) is formed and placed under the command of Lieutenant Commander Dorothy Constance Stratton.

7 December 1942
MILITARY. Yeoman Third Class Dorothy Edith Tuttle is the first recruit for the SPARS.

OTHER EVENTS OF 1942

POPULAR CULTURE. The Oscar for Best Actress of 1941 goes to Joan Fontaine for her role in *Suspicion*. Mary Astor receives an Academy Award for Best Supporting Actress in *The Great Lie*.

29 January 1943
MILITARY. Ruth Cheney Streeter is the first woman major in the U.S. Marine Corps Women's Reserve. She serves as director of the Reserves until her resignation in 1945.

13 February 1943
MILITARY. The U.S. Marines announce the need for 19,000 women in the Women's Reserve.

26 March 1943
MILITARY. Second Lieutenant Elsie Ott of the Army Nurse Corps is the first woman to receive an air medal for "meritorious achievement" while participating in an aerial flight.

3 April 1943
POPULAR CULTURE. The first of the *New York Times* Youth Forum programs, led by

Dorothy Gordon, is broadcast on radio station WQXR.

21 June 1943
MILITARY. Edith Greenwood, R.N., receives the Soldier's Medal. She is the first woman to be so honored. She displayed heroism in saving patients' lives in a fire at an Arizona hospital.

1 July 1943
MILITARY. President Roosevelt signs a law creating the Women's Army Corps (WACs). This law will enable the training and enlistment of American women for the duration of World War II and for 6 months afterward. The WACs replaces the Women's Auxiliary Army Corps formed in 1942.

12 July 1943
MILITARY. Two Navy nurses are the first to receive certificates after they complete the submarine-escape test at the 100-foot deep training tank in New London, Connecticut.

29 July 1943
MILITARY. The first Women's Army Corps

Service Medal is authorized for the Women's Auxiliary Army Corps and the Women's Army Corps.

4 August 1943
MILITARY. Ensign Rosalie Thorne is the first woman awarded the Navy Expert Pistol Shot Medal. Thorne qualifies by obtaining 211 points out of a possible score of 240.

11 September 1943
SPORTS. Agnes Rifner, a 16-year-old girl at New Castle High School in Indiana, is named fullback of the football team.

22 September 1943
POPULAR CULTURE. Entertainer Kate Smith completes a radio War Bond Marathon. After 13 hours of nonstop appeal, listeners purchase $39 million in war bonds.

19 October 1943
POLITICS. Hattie Wyatt Caraway (D-Arkansas) presides as president pro tem of the U.S. Senate in the absence of Vice-President Henry A. Wallace.

Despite the exigencies of war, young girls in World War II America spent plenty of time at the local soda fountain and considered saddle shoes the last word in fashion. (Photo courtesy Maureen Scanlon)

17 November 1943
MILITARY. Private Margaret Maloney is the first Women's Army Corps member to receive the Soldier's Medal.

OTHER EVENTS OF 1943

WOMEN'S ISSUES. In Asheville, New York, the fire department is composed entirely of 13 women who serve, without pay, while men are in the armed services.

POPULAR CULTURE. Oscars for 1942 go to Greer Garson and Teresa Wright for their roles in the motion picture *Mrs. Miniver*. Garson is Best Actress; Wright is Best Supporting Actress.

29 February 1944
POLITICS. Dorothy Vredenburgh is named the first secretary of a national political party. She serves at the Democratic National Convention in Chicago, Illinois, from 19 to 21 July.

17 April 1944
LABOR. In Seattle, Washington, a restaurant owner advertises for a dishwasher. His message reflects the currently acute labor shortage: "Woman wanted to wash dishes. Will marry if necessary."

19 April 1944
MILITARY. Dr. Hilda Thelander is the first woman physician in the U.S. Navy Medical Corps Reserve.

1 June 1944
MILITARY. Lieutenant Sara G. Krout is the first woman dentist to serve in the U.S. Navy.

15 August 1944
MILITARY. The first U.S. Navy ship with a male-female company is the *Sanctuary*. It is a hospital ship with 2 women officers and 60 enlisted women on board.

27 September 1944
MILITARY. For her outstanding services in North Africa, Lieutenant Colonel Westray B. Boyce is awarded the Legion of Merit Medal. She is the first woman WAC member to receive the award.

19 October 1944
MILITARY. Black women are admitted to the WAVES. The first black women are sworn in on 13 November and the first officers graduate at Smith College in December.

1 November 1944
POPULAR CULTURE. The play *Harvey,* by Mary Chase, opens at the 48th Street Theater in New York City. The play wins the Pulitzer Prize in 1945.

22 November 1944
MILITARY. Ensign Margaret Moon is the first Coast Guard Women's Reserve officer to be assigned overseas. She is sent to Hawaii.

28 December 1944
MILITARY. The Distinguished Flying Cross is presented posthumously to Lieutenant Aleda E. Lutz of the Army Nurse Corps.

31 December 1944
MILITARY. Oveta Culp Hobby, director of the Women's Army Corps, is presented with the U.S. Army's Distinguished Service Medal. She is the first woman recipient.

Mildred Didrikson Zaharias, 1914–1956

Defying convention even as a child, Mildred Ella Didrikson became one of the greatest and most versatile sportswomen ever known. She was born in Port Arthur, Texas, on 26 June 1914. Her father, Ole, was a carpenter. Her mother, Hannah (Olson) Didrikson, had won skating contests as a girl in her native Norway. Called "Baby" at home, Didrikson was an avid baseball player who reminded her friends of Babe Ruth; The nickname they dubbed her with was to follow her to fame.

At Beaumont Senior High School, Didrikson played forward on the girls' basketball team and was noticed by Melvin J. McCombs, coach of the Golden Cyclone Athletic Club. This semipro team was owned by Employers Casualty Company of Dallas, Texas, where she was hired as a typist in February 1930. Within two years, Didrikson helped the Cyclones win a national championship.

Didrikson went on to compete in track and field, and soon became a champion in that area. She set records in many events, including the broad and high jumps. She won—singlehandedly—the team championship in the national Amateur Athletic Union competitions in 1932. That year she came home from the Olympics with gold medals for hurdles and the javelin throw, and with a silver medal for the high jump.

Turning pro in December 1932, she played with the Babe Didrikson All-American Basketball Team, and even pitched a preseason exhibition game for the St. Louis Cardinals, having added baseball to her roster of sports activities. In 1935, she won the Texas Women's Amateur golf championship and turned to professional golf after the U.S. Golf Association prevented her from entering any more amateur competitions.

Didrikson played exhibition golf with Gene Sarazen and earned nearly $1,000 a week. She also received a retainer from the Wilson sporting goods company during this period. On 23 December 1938, she married wrestler George Zaharias, who urged her to drop out of the pro golf circuit. By 1946 she had become the only three-time winner of the Associated Press Woman Athlete of the Year Award, which she was ultimately to receive three more times. She had also garnered the All American Open and National Women's Amateur Golf titles by this point in her career.

Didrikson turned pro again in 1947 and helped found the Ladies Professional Golf Association in January 1948. She became ill a few years later, and although hospitalized after hernia surgery she continued to play golf. She won the U.S. Women's Open title for the third time in 1954, but was very ill with cancer of the colon. She died in Galveston, Texas, on 27 September 1956.

OTHER EVENTS OF 1944

MILITARY. Lieutenant Cordelia Cook, an army nurse, receives the first Bronze Star presented to a woman.

POPULAR CULTURE. Academy Awards for 1943 go to Jennifer Jones, Best Actress in *The Song of Bernadette,* and Katina Paxinou, Best Supporting Actress in *For Whom the Bell Tolls.*

4 January 1945
SPORTS. Swimmer Ann Curtis, 8-time National Amateur Athletic Union titlist, is the first woman to be awarded the Sullivan trophy.

16 February 1945
MILITARY. Elizabeth Lutz of Pittsburgh, Pennsylvania, is the first woman U.S. Army Corps veteran to obtain a loan under the so-called "G.I. Bill of Rights." She receives $7,500 to purchase a house.

8 March 1945
MILITARY. Phyllis Mae Daily is the first black woman nurse sworn into the Navy Nurse Corps.

26 June 1945
INTERNATIONAL. The charter of the United Nations is the first federal treaty signed by a woman, Virginia C. Gildersleeve. She is a delegate to the United Nations Conference on International Organization.

12 July 1945
MILITARY. Oveta Culp Hobby resigns from active duty as commander of the WACs.

19 August 1945
SPORTS. Mildred Dietz, of St. Louis, Missouri, is named bicycle champ of the National Amateur Bicycle Association. She wins again in August 1946, making her the first woman to win twice.

29 August 1945
MILITARY.   Enlistment in the WACs is officially closed.

29 October 1945
WOMEN'S ISSUES.   Anna Rosenberg is the first woman to receive the Medal of Freedom, which was established on 6 July 1945, to award civilians for meritorious service to the nation.

10 November 1945
WOMEN'S ISSUES.   A statement issued by the National Association of Day Nurseries asserts the rising demand for daytime care of young children whose mothers work in munitions plants.

Emily Greene Balch, 1867–1961

It is not difficult to explain Emily Greene Balch's 1946 Nobel Peace Prize: Balch had, from an early age, been groomed for a life of humanitarian service and dedication to high ideals. A social worker and pacifist, she was born in Jamaica Plain, Massachusetts, on 8 January 1867, the daughter of Francis and Ellen (Noyes) Balch. Both of her parents were highly educated Unitarians with demanding personal standards that they passed along to their daughter.

Balch attended Bryn Mawr, graduating in 1889 with an A.B. degree in economics. Thereafter, she worked in New York City as a social worker, then, using an award she had received at Bryn Mawr, traveled to Paris to study at the Sorbonne. She returned to Boston in 1891, where she worked for the Children's Aid Society. In 1892, she helped found Denison House, a Boston settlement. Deciding to advance her interest in social reform by teaching, Balch attended graduate school at the University of Chicago, Harvard University, and the University of Berlin.

In 1896, Balch joined the faculty of Wellesley College, and taught economics. Maintaining an active interest in social welfare, she helped found the Women's Trade Union League of Boston in 1902. By 1906 she had spoken out in favor of Socialist principles; this statement denied her quick promotion on the Wellesley faculty. Balch was an American delegate to the International Congress of Women at the Hague in 1915; afterwards, she devoted her time and energy to militant pacifist activities. She was on leave from Wellesley from 1916 to 1918, and in the following year her college contract was not renewed.

In 1921, Balch joined the Society of Friends with whom she was living in London, England. In 1922, she resigned her position as secretary-treasurer of the Women's International League for Peace and Freedom, a post she had held since 1919. Her health failing, she continued peace work, and in 1935 was Armistice Day speaker at Wellesley, her former employer. In 1946, she was honored with the Nobel Peace Prize, which she shared with YMCA official John R. Mott. Balch continued to be active in various organizations despite poor health, and was honorary chair of the Women's International League during her later years. In 1959, she helped organize a centenary celebration in honor of Jane Addams' birth. She died in a nursing home, after a severe bout with pneumonia, on 10 January 1961.

14 December 1945
MILITARY. Captain Su Dauser is the first woman member of the Navy Nurse Corps to receive the Distinguished Service Medal.

25 December 1945
MILITARY. In Honolulu, Hawaii, hundreds of military wives arrive to meet their husbands who are stationed at Pacific outposts.

OTHER EVENTS OF 1945

POPULAR CULTURE. Academy Awards go to Ingrid Bergman as Best Actress of 1944 for her role in *Gaslight,* and to Ethel Barrymore for Best Supporting Actress in *None but the Lonely Heart.*

10 January 1946
MILITARY. The last WAVES class graduates from the Hospital Corps school in Bethesda, Maryland.

11 February 1946
MILITARY. Reports issued by the U.S. Coast Guard, Army, Navy, and Marine Corps indicate that all women's auxiliary military forces are being cut back. Present law states that these auxiliary bodies will be terminated in 6 months.

18 February 1946
POLITICS. Lawyer and former World War I ambulance driver Helen Gahagan Douglas (D-Georgia) is elected to the House of Representatives.

11 March 1946
POPULAR CULTURE. A national outcry against a new policy of no longer labeling flour sacks with brightly printed labels comes from farm women. They object to the policy since they use the colored muslin sacks for clothing, curtains, and other decorative purposes.

24 July 1946
MILITARY. The WAC Integration Act is introduced in the Senate. It will establish the WACs as part of the regular U.S. Army.

OTHER EVENTS OF 1946

HISTORY. Mary R. Beard publishes *Woman as Force in History.*

POPULAR CULTURE. Academy Awards for Best Actress and Best Supporting Actress of 1945 go to Joan Crawford in *Mildred Pierce,* and Anne Revere in *National Velvet,* respectively.

3 June 1947
ARTS AND CULTURE. "Theater '47," the brainchild of theater-in-the-round producer Margo Jones, opens the State Fair Association grounds in Dallas, Texas.

14 August 1947
SPORTS. Babe Didrikson Zaharias quits her role as an amateur golfer and accepts $300,000 in movie contracts.

Agnes de Mille, 1905–

As a young girl, Agnes de Mille spent some of her happiest hours dancing and performing skits with her sister. Those around her expected de Mille to mature into a woman whose interests rested in more conventional areas, but she insisted on dance and drama instruction. Her adamance paid off, and by her early twenties she was regarded as a talented dancer and choreographer with an unparalleled gift for imitation and innovation. She was born on 18 September 1905, in New York City, the daughter of playwright William Churchill and Anna (George) de Mille. Her uncle was filmmaker Cecil B. de Mille, and her maternal grandfather was economist Henry George.

Although discouraged from becoming a performer, she showed an early interest in dance. Meeting notables such as Ruth St. Denis and Ted Shawn, as well as having watched Pavlova dance, further fueled de Mille's enthusiasm for a stage career. She graduated from the Hollywood School for Girls and majored in English at UCLA, from which she graduated cum laude in 1927. The following year she went to New York City, staging a series of dance concerts in which she presented character sketches with a strong dramatic emphasis.

Critically acclaimed, de Mille began choreographic work in 1929, and by 1932 took her dance sketches to Europe. She was eventually invited to study with the Ballet Rambert and to dance at the Mercury Theatre in London. In 1936, de Mille choreographed *Hamlet* on Broadway and created the dances for the 1937 version of *Romeo and Juliet* filmed by MGM. That year she and several associates formed the London-based Dance Theatre. Returning to the United States after her Dance Theatre project failed, de Mille taught ballet in 1938, and the next year joined the American Ballet Theater as resident choreographer. She held this position for five years.

On 16 October 1942, de Mille enjoyed instant and total praise with her portrayal of the Cowgirl in her ballet *Rodeo*. She had written and choreographed this piece for the Ballet Russe de Monte Carlo, on tour in the United States. Music for the ballet was written by the American composer Aaron Copland. On 14 June 1943, de Mille married Walter J. Prude shortly after her triumphant production of all the dances for the Broadway show *Oklahoma!*

This success was followed by a string of similar first-rate Broadway productions, including *One Touch of Venus* (1943), *Bloomer Girl* (1944), *Carousel* (1945), and *Brigadoon* (1947). She also staged dances for *Gentlemen Prefer Blondes* (1949), *Paint Your Wagon* (1951), and *Kwamina,* for which she won a Tony Award in 1961. Chief among her best-known balletic works is *Fall River Legend,* which premiered in 1948. *Legend* tells the tragic story of Lizzie Borden, the young woman charged with killing her father and stepmother in 1892. It was considered a showcase of de Mille's dramatic skills and choreographic talent.

In 1973, de Mille established the Heritage Dance Theatre at the North Carolina School of the Arts. And although she suffered a debilitating stroke on 15 May 1975, the night of the Heritage Theatre's premiere, she nevertheless resumed her professional activities less than two years later.

In 1980, de Mille received the Kennedy Center Career Achievement Award; in 1982, she was the recipient of the Elizabeth Blackwell Award. De Mille has published several autobiographical works, including *And Promenade Home* (1956), *Where the Wings Grow* (1978), and *Reprieve* (1981), which concerns her fight to regain normal activities after a stroke.

---

23 August 1947
POPULAR CULTURE. President Harry S Truman's daughter Margaret gives a piano concert at the Hollywood Bowl in California.

23 October 1947
INTERNATIONAL. Dr. Gerty Thersa Cori and her husband Carl are the first husband-and-wife team in the United States to receive a joint Nobel Prize. They are awarded the Nobel Prize in medicine for their work in human enzymes.

OTHER EVENTS OF 1947

MILITARY. The Army–Navy Nurse Act is passed, securing permanent, full military rank for women. Colonel Florence A. Blanchfield is superintendent of the Army Nurse Corps and is the first woman in the United States to hold a regular army commission.

POPULAR CULTURE. Filmmaker Maya Deren is the first woman and the first American to win the Cannes Grand Prix Internationale for Avant-Garde Film.

POPULAR CULTURE. Oscars for 1946 go to Best Actress Olivia de Havilland in *To Each His Own,* and to Best Supporting Actress Anne Baxter in *The Razor's Edge.*

6 January 1948
SCIENCE. At the 114th meeting of the American Association for the Advancement of Science, Dr. L. W. Sontag reports that women relax and recover more quickly from stress than do men. This explains in part why women are less likely than their male counterparts to develop stomach ulcers, according to Dr. Sontag.

19 January 1948
WOMEN'S ISSUES. U.S. Judge Dorothy Kenyon meets with the United Nations Commission on the Status of Women.

12 February 1948
MILITARY. The first black nurse is integrated into the Army Nurse Corps.

3 March 1948
POLITICS. Vera Conrad, president of the Women's Clubs of America, calls on women nationwide to support a female candidate for U.S. president. Among her personal nominees are Clare Boothe Luce and Eleanor Roosevelt.

5 March 1948
LABOR. Former Secretary of Labor Frances Perkins states that "Unless a woman can earn $4,000 a year . . . it is absurd, anti-social, and uneconomic for her to work outside the home."

5 April 1948
WOMEN'S ISSUES. The U.S. Postal Service announces it will issue a 3-cent commemorative stamp in honor of "100 years of progress" by American women.

Whether or not most American women agreed with Frances Perkins' opinions on working wives, the postwar period saw a great increase in weddings. The rush to the altar coincided with the return of GIs from the military and would result in the jump in the nation's birthrate during the 1950s. (Photo courtesy L. Elizabeth Bartlett)

Child Care

Since 1900, growing numbers of American women have tried to provide for careful nurturing of their children while trying to function as part-or full-time wage earners. But the concept of child care has never been an acceptable alternative for most mothers and fathers who work outside the home. In particular, Americans have rejected the idea of federally supported child care, preferring to leave the burden of locating, financing, and monitoring child care to parents. During the Depression, the government provided some support through Works Progress Administration (WPA) funding, primarily to low-income families whose children attended government day-care centers. Most Americans felt, however, that married women with children belonged at home.

But when the country entered World War II, there was substantial evidence that the government needed to reexamine its position on child care. The War Production Board acknowledged the importance of developing adequate day care for children so that mothers could work in defense plants. And although President Roosevelt hoped local community action would meet the needs of working mothers, he provided $400,000 in federal matching grants to cities and towns for day-care projects in August 1942. Also, the WPA, until its abolition in 1943, permitted defense workers' children to attend day-nurseries for a small charge.

In 1943, the Lanham Act, providing funds for building defense facilities, also provided for the construction and operation of day-care centers. Unfortunately, the Lanham Act required completion of an extensive application process, and because of the bureaucratic red tape accompanying it, many feared that the Lanham Act did more to hinder than to help in building day-care facilities. The Federal Works Administration (FWA) did provide funding for child care, however, spending almost $50 million during the war years.

The Federal Children's Bureau did little to promote federally supported day care, and other government agencies, such as the FWA or the Office of Education, engaged in debilitating internal arguments on the subject. Ultimately, by the summer of 1943, there were only sixty-six day-care centers in operation nationwide, although estimates showed that at least six hundred areas in the country needed child care. One deterrent to child care was cost. Until a government-imposed ceiling on $.50 per child per day was mandated, most mothers could not afford day care.

The FWA hoped to have space for 750,000 children by 1944, but by February of that year only 65,717 were actually enrolled. Even by the spring of 1945, a mere 100,000 children were in federal day-care centers—about 10 percent of the number estimated to need care. There was no good solution to the problem. When the war ended in 1945, the government quickly withdrew federal funding for day-care centers, since women were no longer employed in the once-vital defense plants. And although the Children's Bureau supported federally funded day care, it acknowledged the difficulties inherent in such funding. Public opinion tended to side with conservative, traditional views about women as homemakers. In fact, one New York newspaper stated in 1947 that child care was "conceived by leftists operating out of Communist 'social work cells.' "

By the late 1960s and early 1970s, the question of day care had once more become a pressing one. Although a federally sponsored day-care bill was passed by

Congress, President Nixon vetoed the measure. He took the position that such care would threaten the sanctity of the family. But unhappily, the lack of adequate day-care facilities for children of working parents, combined with the rising divorce rate had by the late 1970s and early 1980s created a crisis in thousands of families. Some experts said that the economic burden of day care was untenable, particularly for single mothers. Fully one-half of a working mother's income was often going to pay for the care of her children. And the reality facing women, no matter what their income level, was that dollar for dollar they earned consistently less than their male counterparts. The child-care dilemma in the United States was, and remains, a critical one for the majority of working mothers.

5 April 1948
ARTS AND CULTURE. Indiana-born Janet Flanner, who writes under the pen name Genêt for *New Yorker* magazine, receives the French Légion d'Honneur. Although she had been cited for the award in 1947, she failed to attend the presentation ceremony.

6 April 1948
SPORTS. Babe Didrikson Zaharias is barred from the National Open golf tournament when the U.S. Golf Association states that the contest is limited to men.

18 May 1948
AVIATION. Jacqueline Cochran, flying an F-86 Sabre jet, breaks the sound barrier. She is the first woman to do so.

28 June 1948
RELIGION. Helen Kenyon is elected the first woman moderator of the General Council of Congregation Christian Churches.

1 July 1948
POLITICS. In response to Harry S Truman's expressed interest in her as a possible vice-presidential running mate, Eleanor Roosevelt replies that she is not seeking public office "at any time."

2 July 1948
BUSINESS. At a Chicago, Illinois, meeting, 600 women meet for the National Secretaries Association convention. They discuss the desirability of attaining a "certified professional secretary" status similar to that of accountants.

6 July 1948
WOMEN'S ISSUES. Freida Barkin Hennock

is sworn in as the first woman member of the Federal Communications Commission.

7 July 1948
MILITARY. Six women are sworn into the regular U.S. Navy in Washington, D.C. They are transferred from the Naval Reserve.

30 July 1948
IDEAS/BELIEFS. Elizabeth Bently, a former Communist, testifies before Congress that she obtained classified information from U.S. government officials during the war.

26 August 1948
INTERNATIONAL. Mildred E. Gillars, known as "Axis Sally," is flown to the United States from Berlin, West Germany. She will face charges of espionage and treason for wartime propaganda broadcasts.

18 September 1948
MEDICAL. At a meeting of the Oregon Medical Society in Medford, Oregon, Dr. Leslie Swigart Kent becomes the first woman president of a state medical society.

15 October 1948
MILITARY. Dr. Frances L. Willoughby is the first woman doctor in the regular U.S. Navy.

OTHER EVENTS OF 1948
Olympic Gold Medals
Ann Curtis: Swimming—400-meter freestyle
　　Swimming—400-meter freestyle relay
　　women's team medal
Alice Coachman: High jump
Gretchen Fraser: Skiing—slalom

Olympic Silver Medals

Gretchen Fraser, Skiing—downhill combination

Olympic Bronze Medals

Ann Curtis: Swimming—100-meter freestyle
Suzanne Zimmermann: Swimming—100-meter
backstroke
Audrey Patterson: Track—200-meter dash

3 January 1949
POLITICS.   Margaret Chase Smith (R-Maine)
is elected to the Senate, where she remains until
June 1973. She is the first woman to serve in
both the House and the Senate, having been
U.S. representative from Maine.

23 January 1949
SPORTS.   With 295 strokes, Patty Berg ties
the record for 72 holes at the Tampa Women's
Open Golf Tournament.

7 April 1949
POPULAR CULTURE.   Mary Martin opens
on Broadway in *South Pacific.*

31 May 1949
POPULAR CULTURE.   Thirty-five thousand
fans celebrate Mary Margaret McBride's 15th
anniversary as a radio broadcaster.

3 June 1949
WOMEN'S ISSUES.   Georgia Neese Clark is
nominated as the first woman treasurer of the
United States. She is confirmed by the Senate on
9 June.

7 June 1949
HEALTH.   Lucile Petry of Lewisburg, Ohio,
is named the first woman assistant surgeon
general of the U.S. Public Health Service.

28 June 1949
MEDICAL.   Twelve women are the first to
receive medical degrees from Harvard Medical
School. They were admitted in 1945 during
World War II. Contrary to the fears of some,
none of the women flunked out and 2 graduated
cum laude.

31 October 1949
FINANCE.   Georgia Neese Clark, first woman
treasurer of the United States, speaks to 105
women at the 27th annual convention of the

Association of Bank Women (ABW). According
to the ABW, 10 percent of all bank executive
jobs—and 60 percent of all bank jobs—are held
by women.

16 November 1949
POLITICS.   At the Mayflower Hotel in
Washington, D.C., President Truman speaks to
assembled members of the Women's National
Democratic Club. He points out that "2 percent
more women vote than men."

OTHER EVENTS OF 1949

SCIENCE.   Winifred Gordring is named the
first woman president of the Paleontological
Society.

POPULAR CULTURE.   Academy Awards for
1948 go to Jane Wyman as Best Actress for her
role in *Johnny Belinda,* and to Claire Trevor,
Best Supporting Actress in *Key Largo.*

25 January 1950
WOMEN'S ISSUES.   A proposed Equal
Rights Amendment is passed by the U.S.
Senate, 63–19, and is sent to the House of
Representatives for action. All dissenting votes
in the Senate are cast by Democrats.

27 April 1950
POPULAR CULTURE.   Elizabeth Bender
Cloud of West Linn, Oregon, is named Mother
of the Year by the American Mother's
Committee in New York. Cloud is one-half
Native American.

1 May 1950
LITERATURE.   Black poet Gwendolyn
Brooks of Chicago, Illinois, wins the Pulitzer
Prize for her collection of poems, *Annie Allen.*

3 May 1950
MEDICAL.   Dr. Helen B. Taussig becomes
the first woman member of the Association of
American Physicians.

8 May 1950
MILITARY.   Lieutenant Commander Bernice
Rosenthal Walters, Medical Corps, U.S. Naval
Reserve, is the first woman to be assigned to a
naval vessel, the hospital ship *Consolation.*

Gwendolyn Brooks, 1917–

Gwendolyn Brooks had achieved distinction for her poetry as early as the mid-1940s. She was the first black woman to receive the Pulitzer Prize for poetry in 1950. (Photo courtesy The Contemporary Forum)

When Gwendolyn Brooks was a child growing up on the south side of Chicago, her parents encouraged a love of literature both by reading aloud and by providing her with plenty of books of her own. Born on 7 June 1917, in Topeka, Kansas, she was the daughter of David A. and Keziah (Wims) Brooks. Much of the young girl's time was spent writing, and at age thirteen she published a poem, "Eventide," in *American Childhood* magazine. Later, she went to Wilson Junior College, majoring in English literature, and graduated in 1936. Brooks joined the National Association for the Advancement of Colored People in the late 1930s and worked as publicity director for the organization's Youth Council. She met writer Henry Blakely, whom she married on 17 September 1939.

Brooks began studying poetry under Inez Cunningham Stark in 1941. She soon won several important awards, including the major prize given at the Writer's Conference in Chicago. By the mid-1940s, she had published in *Harper's, The Saturday Review of Literature*, and the *Yale Review*. In 1945, she published her first book of poems, *A Street in Bronzeville*, about black Americans and poverty. She was also named one of *Mademoiselle* magazine's "Ten Women of 1945."

By the time Brooks had published her second book, *Annie Allen*, in 1949, she had received two Guggenheim Fellowships and a grant from the National Institute of Arts and Letters. *Annie Allen* won the Pulitzer Prize in 1950; it was the first time this award had gone to a black woman. A number of other books, all dealing with the black struggle in America, followed. They included a novel, *Maud Martha* (1953), a collection of juvenile poems, *Bronzeville Boys and Girls* (1956), and *The Bean Eaters,* a volume containing reflections on racial injustice, which was published in 1963.

Brooks taught writing at several institutions, including the University of Wisconsin, Chicago's Columbia College, and Elmhurst College. In 1967, she met a group of militant black writers while attending a writer's conference in Tennessee, and after this encounter she became even more supportive of black youths who wished to express their racial pride via the arts. Brooks' contribution of both time and money for a variety of poetry competitions was one expression of her concern. Another was her activities with a community theater group known as the "Kuumba Workshop."

In 1968, she published *In the Mecca,* a poem that brought her renewed praise for her treatment of the black urban experience. Until this time, Brooks had worked with Harper & Row publishers in New York City. Subsequently, however, she allowed her work to be published only by a small, black-owned publishing house, Broadside Press. Brooks was named Poet Laureate of the state of Illinois in 1968 (an honor previously bestowed on Carl Sandburg). Continuing to write, she published an autobiographical work, *Report from Part One* in 1972, and *A Capsule Course in Black Poetry Writing* in 1975. In 1976, she was the first black woman named to the National Institute of Arts and Letters.

In 1985, Brooks was named the Poetry Consultant at the Library of Congress. She was the first black woman (and sixth woman) to be honored with this premier appointment among poets in the United States. In addition to this position, which requires one year's residence in Washington, D.C., at the Library of Congress, she has been working on a sequel to her autobiography.

Lillian Hellman, 1905–1984

A consummate craftsperson whose subtle yet direct observations on human nature are revealed in her many books and plays, Lillian Hellman spent much of her adult life attempting to prod her audience to action. She wrote with a vengeance, lived an existence characterized both by a desire for privacy and a thirst for public recognition, and remains one of the century's most significant female dramatists.

Born in New Orleans, Louisiana, on 20 June 1905, she was the only child of Max and Julia (Newhouse) Hellman. Although the family moved to New York City when she was just a child, they maintained close connections with New Orleans. Hellman attended public school in both Louisiana and New York.

In 1925, Hellman became a book reviewer for the *New York Herald Tribune* after studying for several years at New York University. In 1930, she went to California, where she worked as an MGM script reader, returning to New York City in 1932. During these years Hellman published several short pieces, and in 1934 she finished her first play, *The Children's Hour.* Produced by Herman Shumlin, the play opened on Broadway in November 1934 and ran for 691 performances before going on national tour.

Hellman's intellectual curiosity and left-leaning politics prompted her to travel to France and Russia in 1936, and to Spain in 1937, at the time of that country's civil war. In 1939, *The Little Foxes*, a play revolving around the intricacies of Southern family relations, opened on Broadway. Later, *The Little Foxes* was made into a movie; Bette Davis played the lead role. Hellman won the New York Drama Critics Circle Award in 1941 for her play, *Watch on the Rhine*, which was later made into a successful motion picture.

In 1945, Hellman again traveled to the Soviet Union, this time as an invited guest of Stalin's government. Her companion of many years, Dashiell Hammett, counseled her against the trip but she went anyway. She later wrote about her experiences in the Soviet Union in *An Unfinished Woman* (1969), a work that won the National Book Award in 1970. Throughout the late 1940s and early 1950s Hellman continued to produce a variety of dramatic pieces, including *Another Part of the Forest, The Autumn Garden*, and *The Lark*. In 1950, she received an honorary degree from Tufts University. In 1952, she helped stage a revival of *The Children's Hour*, starring Patricia Neal. Hellman wrote *Toys in the Attic* in 1960, another play that won the Drama Critics award. In 1974 she brought out *Pentimento*.

Because of her outspoken sympathy for Loyalist Spain during the 1930s and her several trips to Communist nations, Hellman became a captive player in the drama of the McCarthy era. Although Hammett was imprisoned for his political views, Hellman was spared that ordeal. But following a House Un-American Activities Committee investigation in 1952, her income went from $150,000 a year to virtually nothing. Hellman described these experiences in her book, *Scoundrel Time*, which was published in 1976.

Outspoken in expressing and defending her opinions, Hellman found it difficult in later years to accept views that conflicted with her own. Shortly before her death she became engaged in a well-publicized feud with writer and critic Diana Trilling. Hellman also sparred with novelist Mary McCarthy, and in 1980 sued that writer over comments made during a television interview. Prior to final judgment of the lawsuit against McCarthy, Hellman died on 30 June 1984. At the time of her death she lived alone on Martha's Vineyard in Massachusetts. She left no survivors but is remembered by millions for her insightful commentary on American life, so carefully expressed in her plays and books.

---

24 May 1950
LABOR. According to a *Wall Street Journal* report, the number of U.S. women working has increased 24 percent in the past 10 years. The number of working wives has increased by 90 percent. More than 18 million women now work outside the home—29 percent of the U.S. labor force.

25 May 1950
SCIENCE. The first U.S. Agriculture Gold Medal goes to Lucy Maclay Alexander for her research and applications concerning meat and poultry cookery.

2 June 1950
INTERNATIONAL. As the General Federation of Women's Clubs convention in Boston, Massachusetts, ends, it pledges support of President Truman's "4-Point" program of aid to underdeveloped nations.

5 June 1950
SPORTS. The Women's International Bowling Congress announces it no longer restricts nonwhites from membership.

7 June 1950
WOMEN'S ISSUES. Ruth Schick Montgomery is named president of the Women's National Press Clubs.

14 June 1950
LABOR. After 47 years of work on behalf of working women, the National Women's Trade

Union League is dissolved. Independent leagues will continue service in New York, Chicago, and Milwaukee.

16 July 1950
INTERNATIONAL.   Marguerite Higgins, a reporter for the *New York Herald Tribune,* has her Korean credentials restored after having been expelled from that country along with all other U.S. women except nurses. Higgins states that she should be permitted to remain since she was in Korea "as a correspondent and not as a woman."

29 July 1950
MILITARY.   According to Associated Press reports, a total of 22,000 women are now on active duty with the military. Another 25,000 are in reserve units.

8 August 1950
SPORTS.   Florence Chadwick is the first American woman to swim from Gris-Nez in France to Dover, England. She makes the swim in 13 hours, 28 minutes. In September 1951, Chadwick swims from St. Margaret's Bay, England, to Gris-Nez in 16 hours, 22 minutes.

26 August 1950
SPORTS.   Gertrude Moran signs a contract for $75,000 a year to tour with Bobby Riggs' pro tennis troupe.

VI

THE POSTWAR DECADE
1951–1960

During the decade following World War II, American women achieved some notable firsts and continued to play important roles in government, sports, religious life, medicine, and other areas. Despite a well-publicized increase in the birthrate during the 1950s, American women represented a substantial percentage of the U.S. work force. By 1958 there was a record number of women—twenty—in the U.S. House of Representatives. During this decade more women than at any time before entered college.

Oveta Culp Hobby was President Eisenhower's choice for secretary of the Department of Health, Education, and Welfare; she became the second female cabinet member in U.S. history. Eisenhower also made Clare Boothe Luce U.S. ambassador to Italy, another first for American women. Only slightly less significant on the international scene, at least to many observers, was Grace Kelly's storybook wedding to Prince Rainier of Monaco in 1956. Women were first given regular commissions in the U.S. armed forces as medical officers during the 1950s. Both Judaism and Christianity saw women assume important leadership roles: A woman became cantor in an American synagogue, and another was the first female Presbyterian minister.

Black women made history during these years, pushing for civil rights, achieving fame in the arts and in sports, and working for equality in the workplace. Autherine Lucy became the first black student admitted to the University of Alabama. Tennis star Althea Gibson was the first black woman to win at Wimbledon. In track, Wilma Rudolph became an Olympic medalist, competing in both 1956 and in 1960.

At the end of the decade, however, perhaps the most symbolic of achievements by women was made by Jerrie Cobb. She ushered women into what was a new era for all Americans: In 1960, Cobb became the first woman chosen for astronaut training. Her selection paved the way for others to join in exploration of what was described as the "last frontier." A little more than two decades later, Americans witnessed an even greater triumph as the first woman went into space. Far from being a placid decade characterized by traditional wife-and-mother roles, the 1950s proved to be yet another period when American women broke new ground and contributed their wealth of experience and talent to the general growth of the nation.

28 August 1950
POPULAR CULTURE. Actress Jean Muir is dropped from the cast of ''The Aldrich Family,'' a television program. Muir is accused of being a Communist sympathizer.

29 August 1950
SPORTS. Althea Gibson is the first black player to compete in a tournament of the U.S. Lawn Tennis Association.

9 November 1950
POLITICS. As a result of the recent elections, there are now 9 women in the U.S. House of Representatives and 1 woman in the Senate.

15 November 1950
WOMEN'S ISSUES. Anna M. Rosenberg is sworn in as the first woman assistant secretary of defense, succeeding Paul H. Griffith. Rosenberg's previous appointments include regional director of the National Recovery Administration, Social Security board member, and a seat on the War Manpower Commission.

OTHER EVENTS OF 1950

POPULAR CULTURE. Academy Awards go to Olivia de Havilland as Best Actress of 1949 for her role in *The Heiress,* and to Mercedes McCambridge as Best Supporting Actress in *All the King's Men.*

9 January 1951
IDEAS/BELIEFS. Elizabeth T. Bently, a former Soviet spy courier, testifies that she began transmitting secret U.S. information to the Russians in 1942. Bentley writes a book about her experiences, *Out of Bondage.*

11 January 1951
IDEAS/BELIEFS. Hadassah, the Women's Zionist Organization of America, presents the $1,000 Henrietta Szold Award to Harry S Truman.

26 January 1951
RELIGION. In Meridian, Mississippi, Paula Ackerman is the first woman to serve a Jewish congregation as spiritual leader with a rabbi's duties and authority.

6 March 1951
LABOR. The Child Welfare League of America advises that defense industry plants should not operate child-care centers as a way of luring mothers into factory work.

3 April 1951
BUSINESS. After disagreements with her uncle, owner of the Washington, D.C. *Times-Herald,* Ruth McCormick Miller resigns as editor of the paper.

Anne Morrow Lindbergh, 1906–

Raised in a sheltered world of privilege and wealth, Anne Spencer Morrow found herself an important public figure in February 1929 upon the announcement of her engagement to America's most popular hero, Charles A. Lindbergh, Jr. Born in Englewood, New Jersey, on 22 June 1906, she was one of four children. Her father, Dwight W. Morrow, was a lawyer with J. P. Morgan & Co. and later U.S. ambassador to

Mexico. Her mother, Elizabeth (Cutter) Morrow, was an educator who later was acting president of Smith College.

Morrow was a shy, self-conscious student; she graduated from Smith in 1928. Her chief pleasure and release up until that time was writing. And after her marriage to Lindbergh, although she found flying wonderfully freeing, her journals supplied her with a necessary outlet and refuge from the public adulation that surrounded the couple following their wedding on 27 May 1929. Tragedy struck the Lindberghs in March 1932 when their first child, a twenty-month-old son was kidnapped and murdered. Heartbroken and terrified, Lindbergh went with her husband on a half-year transcontinental air trip. By this time she had become an accomplished pilot and navigator, and was indispensable to her husband's work. In 1933, she was awarded the Cross of Honor by the U.S. Flag Association.

Still, she found time to write and in 1934, the National Geographic Society's magazine published her article, "Flying Around the North Atlantic." The year before she had been the first woman to receive the National Geographic Society's Hubbard medal. In 1935, she published *North to the Orient,* and late in that year, she and Charles, along with their young son, Jon (born only months after his brother's abduction and death), moved to England, where they lived for several years in relative seclusion.

Lindbergh published *Listen! The Wind* in 1938. The Lindberghs had moved to France, where Charles worked on aviation intelligence missions for the U.S. government. The couple's visits to Germany in the late 1930s prompted later accusations of pro-Nazi leanings, about which she wrote in *The Flower and the Nettle* (1979), a collection of her letters and journals from 1936 to 1939. This volume had been preceded by three similar ones—*Bring Me a Unicorn* (1972), *Hour of Gold, Hour of Lead* (1973), and *Locked Rooms and Open Doors* (1974). In 1980, she published an additional volume in this series of diaries, *War Within and Without.*

Just before the outbreak of World War II, the Lindberghs returned to the United States. By 1945, the family had grown to include five children, and although busy with maternal duties, she managed to write, contributing poetry to the *Atlantic Monthly* and publishing *Gift from the Sea,* an instant and perennial best seller, in 1955. Although a few critics viewed Lindbergh's work as inept or naive, the public embraced her writings, and she later wrote several novels. In 1969, she published *Earthshine,* a book about conservation.

Lindbergh spoke at an environmental conference held at her alma mater in 1970, the same year she received an honorary doctorate from Smith. Since her husband's death in 1974, Lindbergh lives alone in Connecticut, writing and maintaining close contact with her children and grandchildren.

---

5 April 1951
INTERNATIONAL. Ethel Rosenberg is sentenced to death along with her husband Julius. The Rosenbergs were convicted of transmitting classified information about atomic weapons to the Soviets.

4 May 1951
MILITARY. The U.S. Air Force announces that it will begin recruiting 40,000 women for the WAF to add to the 7,000 women currently enlisted in that program.

27 May 1951
POLITICS. The National Women's party elects Ethel E. Murrell as its chairperson at a meeting in Washington, D.C.

29 May 1951
DEATHS. Legendary comedienne Fanny Brice dies in Los Angeles, California. She is nearly 60 years old and has suffered a stroke.

As a new decade opened, it held the promise of better times—the Depression was only a dim memory, and the war was over. Leisure time meant trips to the beach, with all the paraphernalia such an outing entailed: radio, beach ball, umbrella. (Photo courtesy L. Elizabeth Bartlett)

18 June 1951
LABOR. The U.S. Bureau of Labor Statistics notes that nearly 19 million women are in the labor force. Another 40 million women of working age are not working outside the home.

11 August 1951
WOMEN'S ISSUES. Assistant Secretary of Defense Anna Rosenberg announces that 48 women were appointed to 1-year terms on the Defense Advisory Committee on Women in the Armed Forces.

14 August 1951
IDEAS/BELIEFS. The Women's Christian Temperance Union (WCTU) convenes at Boston, Massachusetts, and reelects Mrs. Leigh Colvin as its president. The WCTU boasts 400,000 members.

5 September 1951
SPORTS. Maureen Connolly, 16 years old, is the youngest winner of the U.S. women's singles amateur lawn tennis title.

26 September 1951
MILITARY. The Defense Department announces that the U.S. military wants to recruit at least 72,000 women by June 1952. The greatest number of all these sought—46,000— are to be enlisted in the WAF. The WACs seek 30,000 recruits, and the WAVES and Marines are also hoping for several thousand recruits.

1 October 1951
INTERNATIONAL. Eugenie Anderson, U.S. ambassador to Denmark, signs a treaty of friendship, commerce, and navigation between the United States and that country. She is the first woman ambassador to sign a treaty of this type.

Oveta Culp Hobby, 1905–

Even as a young girl, Oveta Culp Hobby showed an interest in legal issues, which was later to serve her well in her work for both state and federal governments. Born in Killeen, Texas, on 19 January 1905, she was the daughter of lawyer Isaac W. and Emma (Hoover) Culp. By the age of twenty, she had studied law at the University of

Texas Law School and had become parliamentarian of the Texas House of Representatives. She discharged her responsibilities there from 1925 to 1931, and again from 1939 to 1941. Culp also worked with the Texas State Banking Department and was active in local Democratic politics. In 1928, she worked at the National Democratic Convention in Houston. The following year she ran unsuccessfully for the Texas state legislature.

She married former Texas Governor William P. Hobby on 23 February 1931. He was publisher of the *Houston Post,* and she held positions as research editor, book editor, and assistant editor. In 1938, Oveta Hobby was made executive vice-president of the newspaper and soon became its full-time manager. In addition to her newspaper work, Hobby was president of the Texas League of Women Voters, director of the National Bank of Cleburne, Texas, and was on the Board of Regents at Texas State Teachers College.

By 1941 Hobby had been named to a $1-a-year position in President Roosevelt's administration as head of the Women's Division of the War Department's Public Relations Bureau. Working under General Marshall, Hobby helped set up the Women's Auxiliary Army Corps (WAAC) of which she became director and colonel. In September 1942, the WAAC announced plans to recruit 12,200 volunteers. In October, Hobby traveled with Eleanor Roosevelt to Great Britain, where the pair gathered information about women in the British military. In 1943, the WAAC became the Women's Army Corps (WAC) and was given full military status for the duration of the war. When she retired in July 1945, the WAC had about one hundred thousand members.

Hobby returned to Houston and became active in civic life after the war. She was a 1948 consultant-alternate to the Freedom of Information Conference in Geneva, Switzerland, and in 1952 became co-editor and publisher of the *Houston Post.* That year, Hobby announced her support of Dwight Eisenhower for president several months before the Republican National Convention. Due to her support of Eisenhower in the *Houston Post* and her influence throughout the South, she helped assure Eisenhower substantial backing at election time. By 25 November 1952, Hobby had been named the president-elect's choice for a federal position—head of the Federal Security Agency (FSA), succeeding Oscar Ewing.

In the spring of 1953, the FSA had been transformed into a cabinet-level department. On 11 April 1953, Hobby was sworn in as secretary of the Department of Health, Education, and Welfare, only the second woman in U.S. history to hold a cabinet post. During her tenure in the Eisenhower administration, she displayed conservative opinions and took a traditional, laissez-faire approach to government's role in the private sector. She also spoke out against the possibility of a federally backed health insurance plan.

After leaving government service in 1955, Hobby joined the *Houston Post* company once again, as board chairperson and editor. She was also director of KPRC-AMTW and Channel Two TV Company. From 1978 to 1983, Hobby was chair of the board of H&C Communications, Inc., in Houston, where she currently chairs the executive committee.

---

24 November 1951
EDUCATION. The U.S. Office of Education reports that 717,705 women are enrolled in college in 1951 compared to 727,270 in 1950.

OTHER EVENTS OF 1951

POPULAR CULTURE. Oscars go to Judy Holliday, Best Actress of 1950 for her performance in *Born Yesterday,* and Josephine Hull, Best Supporting Actress in *Harvey.*

8 January 1952
INTERNATIONAL. Mary McLeod Bethune attends the inauguration of Liberia's President Tubman. Bethune is the official U.S. representative to that event in Monrovia.

29 January 1952
LITERATURE. Rachel Carson receives the National Book Award for *The Sea Around Us,* voted best nonfiction work of 1951.

25 February 1952
LABOR. According to the International Labor Organization, there are 19 million women in the U.S. labor force—30 percent of the total of all Americans working.

6 May 1952
RELIGION. The Methodist General Conference ends its meeting in San Francisco, California, and refuses to admit women to annual conferences as ministerial members.

19 May 1952
LEGISLATIVE. The U.S. House of Representatives passes a bill that will allow the military to commission women as doctors, dentists, veterinarians, and osteopaths.

17 June 1952
MILITARY. The Senate passes a bill authorizing the U.S. Army, Navy, and Air Force to commission women as various medical specialists, including doctors and dentists. The legislation goes to President Truman for his signature.

21 June 1952
SPORTS. Stenographer Eleanor Engle has her player's contract with the Harrisburg Senators minor league baseball team vetoed. George Trautman, league president, terms the contract "a travesty on pro baseball."

24 June 1952
MILITARY. President Truman signs into law a bill authorizing women to receive medical commissions in the armed forces.

26 June 1952
EDUCATION. In support of equal pay and better job opportunities for women, the National Federation of Business and Professional Women speaks out in favor of equal education for women.

7 July 1952
POLITICS. At the Chicago GOP Convention, there are 128 women delegates and 252 women alternates out of 1,206 total delegates.

10 July 1952
WOMEN'S ISSUES. The Republican Party platform adopted by acclamation includes a plank supporting the Equal Rights Amendment.

21 July 1952
POLITICS. The Democratic National Convention in Chicago, Illinois, is attended by a total of 525 women delegates and alternates, 145 more than at the GOP Convention. The Women's Division of the Democratic National Committee notes that women of voting age outnumber men by nearly 1.75 million.

26 August 1952
SPORTS. Patty Berg sets a golf record by shooting 64 for 18 holes at a Richmond, California, tournament.

3 December 1952
LABOR. The Labor Department reports that one-third of all U.S. women over age 14 work outside the home. The median annual wage in 1950 was $1,230 for women and $2,659 for men.

OTHER EVENTS OF 1952

MEDICAL. Dr. Virginia Apgar of Columbia-Presbyterian Medical Center presents her scoring system to evaluate newborn infants' health. The system becomes widely used and is known as the Apgar Score.

Olympic Gold Medals
Patricia McCormick: Platform diving
Patricia McCormick: Springboard diving
    Track—100-meter relay women's team medal
Andrea Mead Lawrence: Skiing—giant slalom
Andrea Mead Lawrence: Skiing—slalom

Olympic Silver Medals

Paula Myers: Platform diving

Tenley Albright: Figure skating

Olympic Bronze Medals

Juno Irwin: Platform diving

Zoe Ann Jensen: Springboard diving

E. Kawamoto: Swimming—400-meter freestyle

Sonya Klopfer: Figure skating

3 February 1953

IDEAS/BELIEFS. Prominent American Communist Elizabeth Gurley Flynn declines a Federal judge's proposal that she and 12 others arrested for conspiracy be deported to Russia. "We have no desire to enjoy the fruits of socialism in a land where we did not work for it," Flynn asserts. She and the others receive 3-year jail sentences and fines of $6,000 apiece.

15 February 1953

SPORTS. Tenley Albright is the first American woman to win the world figure skating championship.

18 February 1953

ARTS AND CULTURE. Author Rachel Carson is elected to the National Institute of Arts and Letters.

3 March 1953

INTERNATIONAL. The first U.S. woman to be sworn in as ambassador to a major world power—Italy—is Clare Boothe Luce.

11 March 1953

MILITARY. First Lieutenant Fae Adams receives the first regular U.S. Army commission ever given to a woman.

11 April 1953

WOMEN'S ISSUES. Oveta Culp Hobby is sworn in as the second woman cabinet member in the United States. Hobby has been named President Eisenhower's secretary of health, education, and welfare.

14 April 1953

WOMEN'S ISSUES. Health, Education, and Welfare Secretary Oveta Culp Hobby names Jane M. Spaulding as her assistant. Spaulding is finance chair and executive board member of the National Association of Colored Women.

18 June 1953

MILITARY. The Senate passes a bill permitting mothers of dependent children to be eligible for military reserve duty. It also bars involuntary discharge of women reserves for motherhood. The Defense Department opposes this legislation.

19 June 1953

DEATHS. Ethel Rosenberg is executed at Sing-Sing Prison in Ossining, New York.

6 July 1953

DEATHS. Puerto Rican poet and activist Julia de Burgos dies in New York City.

The Baby Boom

According to most experts in demography, the post–World War II baby boom occurred between 1946 and 1957. Far from being dry and dull, statistics for these years outline the colorful reality of American women's lives in the decade after the war. In 1940, the fertility rate among American women averaged 1.9 children for each adult female. That number grew until it reached 2.3 by 1959. By the mid-1950s, women graduating from college in 1944 produced more children in ten years than the class of 1921 produced in twenty-five years. Furthermore, by 1955 30 percent of all first-born babies had mothers who were nineteen years old or younger. These statistics indicate that marriage and motherhood were top priorities for the period.

In 1945, there were 1,613,000 American marriages; by 1946 that number had jumped to 2,291,000. And there were 2,858,000 babies born in 1945 compared to

The nationwide trend known as the "Baby Boom" meant innumerable scenes like this one in suburban America. Families with an only child became rare; three, four, five, and more siblings grew common. (Photo courtesy L. Elizabeth Bartlett)

one year later when 3,411,000 American babies arrived. Immediately following the end of World War II, American women seemed to be jumping into matrimony. They also appeared to be moving, with their families, to the suburbs—areas that most people considered to be optimum for raising children. Advertisements that appeared in the late 1940s and throughout the 1950s show families with between three and seven children. This reflected the fact that between 1940 and 1960 the birthrate for third children doubled. It tripled for fourth children during those years. It is no wonder that the suburbs grew five times faster than cities did between 1950 and 1968.

Some less apparent facts of the baby boom years, particularly in the twelve months following the war's end, have to do with divorce. In 1945, there were 485,000 divorces, up from 264,000 in 1940. But one year later, in 1946, the divorce rate climbed to 610,000, suggesting that the return of many GIs signaled the end of some American marriages.

Perhaps the major misconception about the baby boom years has to do with American women and work. Even with the closing of the defense plants, many women opted to continue working. They did not all rush home, have babies, and raise children for fifteen or twenty years, although many did. In 1947, 16,323,000 American women over age fourteen were in the labor force. Before Pearl Harbor, only 12,840,000 American women worked outside the home. And of all working women in 1947, 40.9 percent were married, with husbands present—fully 20 percent of all American women of that time compared to 14.7 percent of the same group in 1940.

Even more telling are figures for married mothers with children under age six. In 1948, 1,226,000 American mothers worked—10.8 percent of all married mothers. The statistics show growth by 1957 to 2,208,000 working mothers, or 17 percent of the total number of married mothers (with children under age six) in the population. In general, the figures for working women with children older than six years indicate greater labor force participation for this period. So while the baby boom had an enormous impact, it did not prevent all mothers from working during the postwar years. In fact some feel that the growing consumer culture of the postwar period led more women to work in order to provide their families with material advantages that a single-income household could not afford. It is very possible that the baby boom actually prompted women to seek employment outside the home.

Clare Boothe Luce, 1903–

During the decades in which most American women maintained a low profile, Clare Boothe Luce appeared as a vibrant, opinionated, exceedingly savvy political and literary figure. She was both beautiful and intelligent, shrewd and compassionate. Her role as U.S. ambassador to Italy made her a world-renowned personality, and she perhaps embodied the full range of attitudes and abilities that the women's movement was later to extol. The daughter of a violinist, William F. Boothe, and Anna (Snyder) Boothe, she was born on 10 April 1903, in New York City. Her parents separated when she was a child; she was raised, along with her brother, by her beautiful but impecunious mother. By the age of twelve, she had landed several dramatic roles as understudy for such box office attractions as Mary Pickford.

In 1915, Boothe attended a private Episcopal high school on Long Island, and later attended the Castle School in Tarrytown, New York. She graduated at the head of her class in 1919. That year, she accompanied her newly remarried mother to Europe. Sailing home, Boothe charmed millionairess, society leader, and prominent suffragist, Mrs. O. H. P. Belmont, and she was quickly hired as Belmont's secretary. Boothe was courted by and married to millionaire George T. Brokaw on 10 August 1923. The couple's daughter, Ann, was born in August 1924. They eventually divorced due to Brokaw's alcohol dependency.

Witty and self-confident, Boothe was soon writing for *Vogue* and *Vanity Fair* magazines. In 1934, she met Henry Luce, the driving force behind *Fortune, Life,* and *Time* magazines. The two were married in 1935, the year her first play opened on Broadway. In 1936, that first play, *Abide with Me,* was followed by *The Women.* The latter was a critical success, although some were mildly shocked by its sharply frank treatment of women's behavior and attitudes. By 1939 Luce was working as a *Life* correspondent, and in Europe she witnessed the German invasion of Belgium. She returned to the United States to write a book on these experiences, *Europe in the Spring.*

Luce's involvement in Republican politics did not interrupt her ongoing work for *Life:* A cover story she wrote about General MacArthur appeared on the 8 December 1941 issue of the magazine, the same week as the attack on Pearl Harbor. In 1942, she mounted a successful campaign for U.S. representative from Fairfield, Connecticut, a seat formerly held by her stepfather, Dr. Albert E. Austin. Tragedy struck Luce when her only daughter was killed in a 1944 auto accident. Nevertheless, she campaigned for and won reelection to her congressional seat that year, but by 1946 had resigned from politics. Chief among her reasons for this retirement was grief over her daughter's death, a sorrow that later led her to convert to Roman Catholicism.

Luce devoted herself to writing, producing articles, scripts, and a *McCall's* magazine column. In 1952, she became involved once again in politics, attending the 1952 Republican Convention as a delegate. In 1953, her efforts for Eisenhower were rewarded when the president named her U.S. ambassador to Italy. She was the first woman to represent the United States to a major foreign power. Although some questioned her fitness for the post, those who knew her recognized that her gender was no barrier to effectiveness. In Italy, she found her work challenging yet satisfying. When she left in 1956, she had been presented with Italy's Order of Merit.

Returning to private life once more, Luce and her husband established residence in Arizona, where she wrote extensively. She also traveled during this time and received many awards and citations, including the Laertare Medal, which was given to Luce in 1957 in recognition of her qualities as an outstanding Roman Catholic layperson. Luce continued to be known as a woman of conservative values whose intelligence and determination could be counted on to see a project through to completion.

Named as a possible U.S. ambassador to Brazil in 1959, she was never formally appointed for fear that her reputation as a vehement anti-Communist would somehow compromise U.S. relations with South American nations. In 1964, she campaigned on behalf of presidential-hopeful Barry Goldwater. After her husband's death in 1967, Luce moved to Hawaii, where she and Henry had planned to retire together. But in 1982, Luce returned to the mainland, making her home in Washington, D.C. She was soon asked by President Reagan to serve on his Foreign Intelligence Advisory Board, and in 1983 was awarded the Presidential Medal of Freedom. In 1984, Luce was awarded an honorary LL.D. by the University of Southern California Medical School.

---

11 July 1953
INTERNATIONAL. Frances E. Willis is nominated U.S. ambassador to Switzerland. She is the first woman to work her way up as a career diplomat, and the third U.S. female ambassador.

7 August 1953
MILITARY. Staff Sergeant Barbara Barnwel' of the U.S. Marine Corps Reserve receives the first Navy-Marine Corps Medal for heroism.

20 August 1953
HEALTH. According to advance publicity information on Dr. A. C. Kinsey's report, *Sexual Behavior in the Human Female,* 50 percent of American women admitted to having premarital sexual intercourse.

2 September 1953
DEATHS. Jane Norman Smith, a leader in the National Women's party and its national president from 1927 to 1930, dies in Windsor, Vermont.

7 September 1953
SPORTS. Maureen Connolly is the first woman tennis player to win the grand slam—she took the Australian, French, British, and U.S. championship titles.

12 September 1953
POPULAR CULTURE. In Newport, Rhode Island, Jacqueline Lee Bouvier marries U.S. Senator John F. Kennedy (D-Massachusetts).

18 November 1953
DEATHS. Composer and folk music scholar Ruth Crawford Seeger dies of cancer at her home in Chevy Chase, Maryland.

OTHER EVENTS OF 1953

LITERATURE. Simone de Beauvoir's book *The Second Sex* is published in the United States.

POPULAR CULTURE.   Academy Awards go to Shirley Booth, Best Actress of 1952 for her performance in *Come Back, Little Sheba,* and Gloria Grahame, Best Supporting Actress in *The Bad and the Beautiful.*

1 January 1954
WOMEN'S ISSUES.   Anna Moscowitz Kross, the first woman to run a prison system, is named commissioner of corrections in New York City.

5 January 1954
POLITICS.   Senator Margaret Chase Smith (R-Maine) receives the Chi Omega award for her work in Congress and her anti-McCarthy declaration.

14 January 1954
POPULAR CULTURE.   New York Yankee Joe DiMaggio marries film star Marilyn Monroe.

6 February 1954
IDEAS/BELIEFS.   The Women's Patriotic Defense Conference on National Defense ends a 3-day meeting after pressing for U.S. withdrawal from the United Nations.

15 February 1954
AVIATION.   The Air Line Stewards and Stewardesses Association appeals for mediation in its dispute with American Airlines regarding company policy that stewardesses must retire at age 32.

20 July 1954
SPORTS.   Maureen Connolly, tennis champ, injures her right leg while horseback riding.

13 September 1954
EDUCATION.   Stern College for Women in New York City is the first such degree-granting liberal arts institution under Jewish auspices. Its first class has 33 students.

7 October 1954
ARTS AND CULTURE.   Contralto Marian Anderson is the first black singer to sign a contract with the Metropolitan Opera in New York City.

2 November 1954
POLITICS.   Vermont is the first state to elect a woman lieutenant governor. She is Consuelo Northrop Bailey, a Republican.

4 November 1954
POLITICS.   Reports from the 84th Congress indicate that as a result of the recent election, a record 15 women are now members of Congress.

8 November 1954
POLITICS.   Hazel H. Abel of Nebraska is the first woman senator to succeed another woman senator, Eve Bowring.

OTHER EVENTS OF 1954

SPORTS.   National Lawn Tennis Hall of Fame and Tennis Museum opens in Newport, Rhode Island.

POPULAR CULTURE.   The Academy Awards for 1953 go to Audrey Hepburn as Best Actress for her role in *Roman Holiday,* and to Donna Reed, as Best Supporting Actress in *From Here to Eternity.*

5 January 1955
POLITICS.   Reports from Congress indicate there are a record 18 women members—16 in the House and 2 in the Senate. Mrs. Joseph Farrington (R) is a nonvoting delegate to the Senate from Hawaii.

7 January 1955
ARTS AND CULTURE.   Marian Anderson makes her debut with the Metropolitan Opera in New York City. She appears in Verdi's *Masked Ball.*

19 January 1955
IDEAS/BELIEFS.   Annie Lee Moss, Defense Department secretary, twice suspended from her job after Senator Joseph McCarthy identified her as a Communist, has her employment reinstated by Defense Secretary Charles E. Wilson. The witness who identified Moss as a Communist admitted to never having actually seen Moss.

8 March 1955
HEALTH.   A House Commerce Committee learns from Health, Education, and Welfare Secretary Oveta Culp Hobby that 9 million Americans suffer from serious mental disorders.

29 March 1955
EDUCATION. Health, Education, and Welfare Secretary Oveta Culp Hobby tells a House Education Committee that by 1960, American schools will face a classroom shortage of 176,000 spaces.

4 June 1955
MEDICAL. The American Society for the Study of Sterility approves artifical insemination as a ''moral and desirable form of medical therapy.''

13 July 1955
WOMEN'S ISSUES. Effective 1 August, Oveta Culp Hobby will resign from her post as secretary of health, education, and welfare. She will succeed her husband (ex-Texas Governor William Hobby) as president of the Post Publishing Company in Houston, Texas. Marion Bayard Folsom will succeed Hobby in the HEW slot. She is sworn in on 1 August.

14 September 1955
BUSINESS. Freida Kirchwey, long-time editor and publisher of *The Nation,* announces her resignation. She is succeeded by Carey McWilliams.

15 September 1955
RELIGION. Mrs. Betty Robbins sings her first service as the first woman cantor in the United States. The services are held on the eve of Rosh Hashanah at a Long Island, New York, synagogue.

13 October 1955
MEDICAL. Dr. Emma Sadler Moss becomes president of the American Society of Clinical Pathologists. She is the first woman elected to head a major national medical society.

12 November 1955
INTERNATIONAL. The American Women's Association Eminent Achievement Award goes to Frances E. Willis, U.S. ambassador to Switzerland.

14 November 1955
LABOR. Helen Keller receives an award from President Eisenhower's Commission on Employment of the Handicapped. Keller, 75 years old, has recently published *Teacher,* a

biography of Annie Sullivan Macy, who taught Helen to read Braille.

15 December 1955
EDUCATION. Faculty members at the University of North Carolina Women's College vote to endorse the racial integration of classes.

20 December 1955
EDUCATION. Health, Education, and Welfare Secretary Marion B. Folsom announces that the administration will ask for an increase in the $200-million budget currently earmarked for new school construction.

OTHER EVENTS OF 1955

POPULAR CULTURE. Esther Pauline Friedmann Lederer publishes her first advice column, ''Ann Landers Says,'' in the *Chicago Sun-Times.*

POPULAR CULTURE. Academy Awards for 1954 go to Grace Kelly, Best Actress in the film *The Country Girl,* and to Eva Marie Saint, Best Supporting Actress in *On the Waterfront.*

5 January 1956
LABOR. In his State-of-the-Union message, President Eisenhower calls for legislation requiring ''equal pay for equal work without discrimination because of sex'' in the District of Columbia.

13 January 1956
IDEAS/BELIEFS. A Gallup poll indicates that the most admired woman in the United States is Eleanor Roosevelt.

26 January 1956
EDUCATION. In order to help prepare more teachers for work in understaffed schools, Brooklyn College opens classes during special ''mothers' hours.'' This permits women with children to attend college classes while their children are in school.

27 January 1956
SPORTS. Roxanne Anderson, the newly appointed manager of the U.S. Women's Olympic track and field team, expresses her confidence in the American athletes' abilities at the upcoming Melbourne Games.

1 February 1956
EDUCATION. Autherine Lucy is the first black student admitted to the University of Alabama.

22 February 1956
DEATHS. Fashion designer Hattie Carnegie dies in New York City.

19 April 1956
POPULAR CULTURE. Grace Kelly, Academy Award–winning actress, marries Prince Rainier III of Monaco in a ceremony at the Cathedral of St. Nicholas in Monte Carlo. Princess Grace's likeness appears on a postage stamp in Monaco. The stamp is sold only on the day of the wedding.

17 July 1956
LEGISLATIVE. The Senate passes a Social Security bill under which women could receive full retirement benefits at age 62. The new plan would take effect 1 July 1957.

20 September 1956
POLITICS. A Gallup poll indicates that 53 percent of women favor Republican candidates Eisenhower and Nixon; 38 percent favor Democrats Stevenson and Kefauver.

24 October 1956
RELIGION. Reverend Margaret E. Towner is the first woman to be ordained a minister in the Presbyterian Church.

11 November 1956
POPULAR CULTURE. The U.S. Census Bureau announces that American women outnumber men by 1,381,000.

27 November 1956
MILITARY. Lieutenant Colonel Mary Milligan will succeed Colonel Irene Galloway as Women's Army Corps director. Milligan will be sworn in on 4 January 1957.

1 December 1956
BUSINESS. Josephine P. Bay is the first woman president of a major stock brokerage firm—A. M. Kidder & Company, Inc., in New York City.

OTHER EVENTS OF 1956

SPORTS. At the National Lawn Tennis Hall of Fame in Newport, Rhode Island, May Sutton Bundy is the first woman to be enshrined as a member.

Olympic Gold Medals
Patricia McCormick: Platform diving
Patricia McCormick: Springboard diving
Shelley Mann: Swimming—100-meter butterfly
Mildred McDaniel: High jump
Tenley Albright: Figure skating

Olympic Silver Medals
Juno Irwin: Platform diving
Jeanne Stunyo: Springboard diving
Nancy Jane Ramey: Swimming—100-meter butterfly
Carin Cone: Swimming—100-meter backstroke
    Swimming—400-meter freestyle relay
    women's team medal
Willye White: Long jump

Olympic Bronze Medals
Paula J. Myers: Platform diving
Sylvia Ruuska: Swimming—400-meter freestyle
Mary Jane Sears: 100-meter butterfly
    Swimming—400-meter freestyle relay
    women's team medal

1 January 1957
SPORTS. Patricia McCormick is named the Associated Press Outstanding Female Athlete of 1956. She is also winner of the Sullivan Award given by the Amateur Athlete Union on 5 January.

16 January 1957
WOMEN'S ISSUES. President Eisenhower speaks out in support of the Equal Rights Amendment saying, "Congress should make certain that women are not denied equal rights with men."

19 January 1957
SPORTS. U.S. champion figure skater and Olympic gold medalist Tenley Albright announces her retirement. She will enter Harvard Medical School.

20 January 1957
SPORTS. Patricia McCormick makes her debut as the first American woman bullfighter in Cuidad Juarez, Mexico.

11 February 1957
MILITARY. Lieutenant Commander Mary Lou McDowell is the first woman presiding law officer in a U.S. naval court martial.

31 March 1957
POPULAR CULTURE. According to a Gallup poll, 50 percent of all American women drink alcohol.

3 April 1957
WOMEN'S ISSUES. President Eisenhower names Anne Williams Wheaton as the first woman White House associate press secretary.

26 April 1957
MILITARY. Naomi M. McCracken is the first woman officer at the Air Force Academy. She serves as assistant director of cadet records.

6 July 1957
SPORTS. Althea Gibson is the first black woman player to win a Wimbledon title in the women's tennis singles.

21 July 1957
SPORTS. Althea Gibson is the first black woman to win a major U.S. tennis title by capturing the national clay court singles championship.

5 August 1957
WOMEN'S ISSUES. A proposed Equal Rights Amendment is approved by the Senate Subcommittee on Constitutional Revision, but the amendment goes no further.

21 August 1957
SPORTS. Greta Anderson Sonnichsen of Long Beach, California, wins the 22-mile international mass swim across the English Channel in 13 hours, 53 minutes.

28 August 1957
WOMEN'S ISSUES. The witchcraft convictions of 6 women in 1692 in Salem, Massachusetts, are reversed by a measure signed by Governor Foster Furcolo.

14 September 1957
CIVIL RIGHTS. The National Association for the Advancement of Colored People's Arkansas branch president, Mrs. Daisy Getson Bates, criticizes Arkansas Governor Orval

Faubus and his position on desegregation of Little Rock, Arkansas, public schools. Faubus is against racial integration.

23 September 1957
CIVIL RIGHTS. Daisy Bates states that black students at Central High School in Little Rock, Arkansas, will return to class when President Eisenhower gives ''assurance that they will be protected from the mob.''

28 September 1957
INTERNATIONAL. Eleanor Roosevelt conducts an interview with Soviet premier Nikita Khrushchev at his home in Yalta.

2 November 1957
CIVIL RIGHTS. Daisy Bates, chair of the National Association for the Advancement of Colored People (NAACP) Arkansas branch, is arrested, along with other NAACP members, for refusing to comply with Little Rock's City Council demands to submit NAACP records for scrutiny.

5 November 1957
WOMEN'S ISSUES. Mary V. Beck is elected Detroit's first woman city council president.

4 December 1957
MILITARY. Commander Winifred Redden Quick is sworn in as director of the WAVES.

OTHER EVENTS OF 1957

SPORTS. Mary K. Browne and Hazel Hotchkiss Wightman are enshrined in the National Lawn Tennis Hall of Fame Tennis Museum.

POPULAR CULTURE. Ingrid Bergman is awarded an Oscar for Best Actress of 1956 for her performance in *Anastasia*. The Oscar for Best Supporting Actress goes to Dorothy Malone in *Written on the Wind*.

11 February 1958
AVIATION. Ruth C. Taylor, a registered nurse from Ithaca, New York, is the first black woman flight attendant. She is hired by Mohawk Airlines.

22 March 1958
SPORTS. Shirley Hereford of Cleveland, Ohio, sets a record broad jump distance of 9.5

feet at the U.S. Indoor Track and Field Championships in Akron, Ohio.

24 April 1958
POLITICS.   At its 23rd national convention, the League of Women Voters supports the current U.S. foreign policy.

3 May 1958
DEATHS.   Lena Kaplan, a founder in 1912 of Hadassah (the Women's Zionist Organization of America), dies in New York City.

7 May 1958
WOMEN'S ISSUES.   Marion B. Folsom resigns as secretary of the Department of Health, Education, and Welfare, effective 1 August, due to illness. She will be replaced by Dr. Arthur S. Fleming, president of Ohio Wesleyan University.

19 June 1958
EDUCATION.   Stern College for Women awards 26 B.A. degrees at its first commencement exercises.

17 September 1958
HEALTH.   In early tests, a birth control pill has proved 100 percent effective. Tests involving more than 3,000 women indicate a pregnancy rate of 9.3 percent—the same as is standard for other contraceptive methods.

23 September 1958
AVIATION.   The Civil Aeronautics Association reports that of a total 809,349 licensed pilots in the United States, one-fortieth are women.

28 October 1958
BUSINESS.   Mary G. Roebling is the first woman director of a stock exchange. She is with the Trenton Trust Company and is 1 of 32 governors of the American Stock Exchange in New York City.

4 November 1958
POLITICS.   According to a report from Congress, the number of women in the House of Representatives is at a record high. Three women members are newly elected: Jessica

Weiss (R-New York), Catherine May (R-Washington), and Edna O. Simpson (R-Illinois).

POLITICS.   A Census Bureau report indicates that there are 54,700,000 voting-age women in the United States.

22 December 1958
CIVIL RIGHTS.   The Arkansas Supreme Court upholds rulings that Mrs. Daisy Getson Bates and Mrs. Birdie Williams be fined $25 each for refusing to release records of the National Association for the Advancement of Colored People to the Little Rock and the North Little Rock city councils.

29 December 1958
DEATHS.   Choreographer and dancer Doris Humphrey, a colleague of Ruth St. Denis and Ted Shawn, dies in New York City.

OTHER EVENTS OF 1958

IDEAS/BELIEFS.   The American Association of Retired Persons (AARP) is founded by educator Ethel Andrus, who becomes the organization's first president.

SPORTS.   Molla Bjurstedt Lammory and Maud Burger Wallach are inducted into the National Lawn Tennis Hall of Fame.

POPULAR CULTURE.   Academy Awards go to Joanne Woodward, Best Actress of 1957, in *The Three Faces of Eve,* and to Miyoshi Umeki, Best Supporting Actress, in *Sayonara.*

7 January 1959
DEATHS.   Lillian Trumble Bradley Broadhurst, the first woman Broadway theatrical director and playwright, dies at age 75 in Santa Barbara, California. She had begun her work as a director in 1919.

20 January 1959
WOMEN'S ISSUES.   President Eisenhower gives the President's Award for Distinguished Civilian Service to Hazel K. Stiebeling, director of the Agriculture Department's Institute of Home Economics.

Hannah Arendt, 1906–1975

A controversial philosopher whose theories on political action and the human condition are at once profound and sensitive, Hannah Arendt was recognized as one of the century's most important contributors to intellectual discourse. Born in Germany on 14 October 1906 to Russian-Jewish parents Paul and Martha (Cohn) Arendt, she was a bright child whose intellect manifested itself early. Her father died in 1913, and her mother remarried in 1920, bringing two stepsisters into Arendt's life.

Arendt entered Marburg University in Germany in 1924, studying philosophy, New Testament theology, and Greek. In 1929, after transferring to Heidelberg, she received a Ph.D. in philosophy. At Marburg and at Heidelberg, she studied with Martin Heidegger and Karl Jaspers, two scholars who influenced her later work.

Arendt married writer Gunther Stern in 1929. Four years later she interrupted her writing to flee Germany after being imprisoned for one week by the Gestapo. Arendt moved to Paris and became active in several Jewish organizations. She met Henrich Blücher and, as her marriage to Stern had ended in 1936, she and Blücher were married in 1940. Shortly afterward, in 1941, they escaped from occupied Paris and went to the United States, accompanied by Arendt's mother. Despite little economic security, she, her husband, and her mother were established in New York City, where Arendt published short essays in various magazines and Blücher held a string of different jobs to help make ends meet.

Between 1944 and 1948, Arendt worked for the Conference on Jewish Relations at Brooklyn College and continued writing articles, which were published in *Partisan Review, The Nation,* and the *Review of Politics.* Arendt's first major published work, *The Origins of Totalitarianism,* appeared in 1951. This volume was the first postwar work to explore the subject of totalitarianism, and did so in meticulous detail and depth. Arendt was aided in this effort by Blücher, who continued to be her close collaborator and supporter until his death in 1970.

Arendt became an American citizen the same year her first book was published, and due to the success of her work she received a lion's share of publicity. Public acclaim made her uncomfortable; she was known to her friends and family as an intensely private person. In 1952, Arendt received a Guggenheim fellowship and by 1958 had published *The Human Condition,* another major work, which focuses on political activity and action from ancient to modern times. The book is an important outline of how Western political thought and culture developed.

A widely respected historian and considered to be the most important American philosopher of the century, Arendt became the first woman full professor at Princeton University in 1959. She soon published *On Revolution* (1963) and in 1964 brought out, in book form, a series of reports on the Jerusalem trial of Nazi Adolf Eichmann. Originally written for *The New Yorker,* these pieces, which were published as *Eichmann in Jerusalem: A Report on the Banality of Evil*, were rejected violently by some of Arendt's Jewish friends and critics. Many felt that Arendt had not sufficiently acknowledged Eichmann's evil or personal culpability in the death of 6 million Jews during World War II.

Arendt continued publishing throughout the 1960s, and in 1967 was named professor at the New School for Social Research in New York City. Late in her career, she received several awards, including the Danish government's Sonning prize. Arendt died of a heart attack in New York City on 4 December 1975. Her final work, published posthumously in 1979—*The Life of the Mind*—was conceived as a counterpart to *The Human Condition*.

---

26 February 1959
BUSINESS. Josephine Bay is named chair of American Export Lines, Inc. She is the first woman to control a major U.S. steamship company.

11 March 1959
ARTS AND CULTURE. Lorraine Hansberry's *A Raisin in the Sun* opens at the Ethel Barrymore Theater in New York City. The first Broadway play by a black woman, it runs for 530 performances and wins the New York Drama Critics Circle Award on 7 April.

28 April 1959
INTERNATIONAL. Clare Boothe Luce is considered for confirmation as U.S. ambassador to Brazil, although there is widespread Senate disapproval of her appointment.

1 May 1959
INTERNATIONAL. After having received confirmation from the U.S. Senate as U.S. ambassador to Brazil, Clare Boothe Luce resigns the post before actually serving. Many fear her harshly critical views concerning Communism would jeopardize U.S. relations with South American nations.

15 May 1959
HEALTH. Lucille Petry Leone, assistant surgeon general of the U.S. Public Health Service, is named president of the National League for Nursing.

8 June 1959
RELIGION. In Boston, Massachusetts, Kathryn F. Cook is chosen as president of the Mother Church, First Church of Christ, Scientist.

14 June 1959
CIVIL RIGHTS. In Tallahassee, Florida, 4 white males are found guilty of raping a 19-year-old black college student. The jury recommends mercy—no death penalty—because

the woman had received no physical injury. A spokesperson for the National Association for the Advancement of Colored People points out that "Florida has maintained an excellent record of never executing a white for the rape of a [black]."

17 July 1959
DEATHS. Black jazz singer Billie Holiday dies in a New York City hospital after years of struggling with drug and alcohol dependencies.

EDUCATION. Mary Jean Belitz gives up her title as Miss Omaha when she is told by a Duchesne College official that she would be barred from reentry as a student. Belitz was to have appeared in a bathing suit at the Miss Nebraska contest.

8 August 1959
HEALTH. Katherine Oettinger, U.S. Children's Bureau chief, reports that 20,000 unwed mothers annually sell their babies on the "black market" at prices from $1,500 to $3,000. Her report also points out that about 5,000 girls under age 15 annually give birth to illegitimate babies.

11 August 1959
CIVIL RIGHTS. The home of Daisy Getson Bates, Arkansas head of the National Association for the Advancement of Colored People, is sprayed with bullets from a speeding car.

12 August 1959
CIVIL RIGHTS. In Little Rock, Arkansas, Elizabeth Eckford, 17, attends Central High School. She is 1 of the group of 9 students whose attempt to integrate Central High closes the school.

7 September 1959
POPULAR CULTURE. American primitive painter Grandma Moses (Anna M. Robertson Moses) celebrates her 99th birthday.

30 November 1959
ARTS AND CULTURE.   Martha Graham, choreographer and modern dance pioneer, wins the 9th Annual Capezio Award.

22 December 1959
IDEAS/BELIEFS.   For the 11th year in a row, the Gallup poll reports that Eleanor Roosevelt is voted the ''most admired woman'' by Americans.

OTHER EVENTS OF 1959

SPORTS.   Helen Wills Moody Roark is enshrined as a member of the National Lawn Tennis Hall of Fame in Newport, Rhode Island.

POPULAR CULTURE.   Academy Awards go to Susan Hayward as Best Actress of 1958 for her role in *I Want to Live!,* and to Wendy Hiller, Best Supporting Actress in *Separate Tables.*

18 January 1960
WOMEN'S ISSUES.   Women representing 17 national groups meet in New York City to form the National Organization of Women Equality Council to help fight school segregation. This plan is organized by Thelma Richman, president of the American Jewish Congress Women's Division.

30 January 1960
SPORTS.   Carol Heiss wins the women's singles championships in figure skating.

VII

DEMANDS FOR PEACE AND EQUALITY
1961–1970

The turbulence that marked American society in the 1960s was reflected no less emphatically in the changes characterizing women's roles. Drawing strength from the past, many American women sought new opportunities, demanded increased workplace participation, and achieved positions of power and influence previously denied them. Shirley Chisholm became the first black woman in Congress upon her election in 1968, proving the power of the ballot and signaling the beginning of a new phase in American government. The first woman was named permanent ambassador to the United Nations, and the President's Commission on the Status of Women was formed by President Kennedy in 1961. When he was assassinated two years later, a woman officiated at the swearing-in of Lyndon B. Johnson, the first and only time a woman judge has done so.

A recurring theme during the 1960s was a public outcry for world peace. American women helped lead this demand when they joined together in Women Strike for Peace, an organization founded by Dagmar Wilson. This group was behind the major disarmament and antiwar demonstrations throughout the decade and helped give women valuable political experience and public exposure. Some other firsts for women during the decade include the first black woman ambassador to a major foreign post (Patricia Roberts Harris), the first woman member of the New York Stock Exchange, and the first female jockey to race in the Kentucky Derby.

Perhaps the most important change for all women was validated in 1965: A court ban on contraceptives was lifted by the U.S. Supreme Court. This ruling lifted a prohibition against women's reproductive freedom that had stood in force since 1879, and the change was to be a pivotal factor in continued advances women enjoyed in all areas of society in subsequent decades.

Wilma Rudolph, 1940–

Despite the crippling effects of pneumonia and scarlet fever that prevented her from walking until the age of eight, Wilma Rudolph became the first American woman to win three Olympic gold medals in track and field at a single year's games. Born on 23 June 1940 in St. Bethlehem, Tennessee, she was one of eight children. Her father, Ed Rudolph, was a porter; her mother, Blanche, was a domestic worker who spent one day a week driving her four-year-old daughter ninety miles to Nashville for physical therapy to counter the effects of her illnesses. Because of this devotion and due to help from older siblings, Rudolph was able to play basketball by age eleven, and by fourteen was an accomplished high school athlete. During her sophomore year she set a state record in girls' basketball, scoring 803 points in twenty-five games.

By now 5'11'' tall, she joined the school track team in 1955 after Ed Temple, the Tennessee State University track coach, saw her play. Rudolph trained with Temple during the summer. In 1956, she qualified for the U.S. Olympic team and won a Bronze medal in the 400-meter relay at Melbourne. After graduating from the all-black Burt High School in 1957, Rudolph joined the student body at Tennessee State, where she continued under Temple's training.

Although she suffered several injuries in early 1960, Rudolph appeared at the Olympic Games in Rome, where she amazed spectators by winning three gold medals. In the 100-meter dash, 200-meter dash, and 400-meter relay, she either met or exceeded world records. Nicknamed *La Gazelle, La Perel Noire,* and *La Gazella Nera* by the European press, she returned home in triumph. Associated Press named Rudolph America's Female Athlete of the Year for 1960, and in 1960 she finished second to Rafer Johnson for the Sullivan Award, which was given by the Amateur Athletic Union. In December 1960, United Press International named Rudolph Athlete of the Year.

In February 1961, Rudolph ran at the Millrose Games at Madison Square Garden in New York City; she was the first woman in thirty years to do so. She tied her own world record of 6.9 seconds for the 60-yard dash. Shortly after, she ran the 70-yard dash in 7.8 seconds, another world record, in Louisville, Kentucky. In July 1961, she went to West Germany and set still another record for the 100-meter dash, which she completed in 11.2 seconds. She won the Sullivan Award in 1961.

Rudolph's records remained unbroken through the 1964 Olympic Games. She retired in 1962 and acted as U.S. Goodwill Ambassador to French West Africa during the early 1960s. In 1972, Rudolph, married now to William Eldridge and the mother of five, was invited to Munich by the German Olympic Organizing Committee to be a liaison officer with television crews during the Games. A strong supporter of amateur athletics, Rudolph has urged changes in the way U.S. amateur standards are set. "We're not building a system that will make prolonged use of the talent we have," she said in an interview during the 1970s. In 1980, Rudolph co-hosted an NBC radio program that preceded the Olympic Games, and promoted juice products to sponsor those Games. She also wrote an autobiography, which was later produced by NBC-TV.

She is president of the nonprofit Wilma Rudolph Foundation, which is committed to helping motivate young people through athletics. Rudolph believes strongly in teaching youth to respect hard work and to be dedicated to a goal. After three years, the foundation has gone from a program involving two hundred children to one serving more than one thousand youths. With characteristic modesty, Rudolph says of her accomplishments, both past and current, ''I just want to be remembered as a hardworking lady with certain beliefs.''

---

21 February 1960
AVIATION. Jerrie Cobb, of Oklahoma City, Oklahoma, is the first woman to undergo exams at Lovelace Foundation in Albuquerque, New Mexico, for astronaut training.

2 May 1960
ARTS AND CULTURE. Margaret Leech is awarded the 1959 Pulitzer Prize in history for *In the Days of McKinley,* making her the first woman to win 2 such prizes. Her first was awarded in 1941 for *Reveille in Washington.*

6 July 1960
SPORTS. Dr. Barbara Moore completes a cross-country walk from New York City to Los Angeles, setting a woman's record for such an event. She travels 3,207 miles in 86 days.

OTHER EVENTS OF 1960

Olympic Gold Medals
Wilma Rudolph: Track—100-meter dash
Wilma Rudolph: Track—200-meter dash
   Track—400-meter relay women's team medal
C. von Saltza: Swimming—400-meter freestyle
Carolyn Schuler: Swimming—100-meter butterfly
Lynn Burke: Swimming—100-meter backstroke
   Swimming—400-meter freestyle relay
   women's team medal
   Swimming—400-meter medley relay women's
   team medal
Carol Heiss: Figure skating

Olympic Silver Medals
P. Jean Pope: Springboard diving
C. von Saltza: Swimming—100-meter freestyle
P. Jean Pope: Platform diving

Olympic Bronze Medals
Earlene Brown: Shot put

ARTS AND CULTURE. Writer Esther Forbes is elected the first woman member of the American Antiquarian Society.

INTERNATIONAL. Women Strike for Peace is formed to protest nuclear testing worldwide.

27 January 1961
ARTS AND CULTURE. Acclaimed black soprano Leontyne Price makes her debut as Leonora in *Il Trovatore* at New York City's Metropolitan Opera. She is the first black artist to sing a major role there since Marian Anderson's triumphant appearance in 1955.

13 March 1961
WOMEN'S ISSUES. Eleanor Roosevelt gives President Kennedy a 3-page list of women who are ''qualified for top federal jobs.'' The Associated Press reports that only 9 women are among 240 Kennedy appointees chosen to date.

IDEAS/BELIEFS. Elizabeth Gurley Flynn, labor organizer and activist, is elected chair of the national committee of the Communist Party U.S.A.

2 June 1961
INTERNATIONAL. Crowds cheer in Paris as First Lady Jackie Kennedy appears while accompanying her husband on a trip to France.

26 July 1961
WOMEN'S ISSUES. Anne X. Alpern, Pennsylvania's first woman attorney general, is named the state's first woman supreme court justice. She will serve the remaining 5 months of a term vacated by Chief Justice Charles A. Jones. The chief justice slot goes to Justice John C. Bell, Jr.

18 October 1961
LABOR. According to a U.S. Labor Department report, only 2 percent of all women in the work force hold more than 1 job.

1 November 1961
INTERNATIONAL. Fifty thousand women demonstrate worldwide in a show of force by Women Strike for Peace led by Dagmar Wilson, an activist who promotes commitment to

opposition to nuclear weapons. Fifteen hundred women walk to the White House and to the Soviet Embassy in Washington, D.C., to ask Mrs. Kennedy and Mrs. Khrushchev to stop war.

20 November 1961
WOMEN'S ISSUES. The Supreme Court upholds a Florida law exempting women from jury duty unless they volunteer. Florida is 1 of 18 states allowing women this exemption. Three states—Alabama, Mississippi, and South Carolina—bar women from juries.

14 December 1961
DEATHS. Noted American artist and primitive painter Grandma Moses dies at age 101.

WOMEN'S ISSUES. President Kennedy issues Executive Order 10980, forming the President's Commission on the Status of Women. Eleanor Roosevelt is named chair of this group, which will study ways to eliminate "all barriers to the full partnership of women in our democracy."

OTHER EVENTS OF 1961

POPULAR CULTURE. Academy Awards for Best Actress and Best Supporting Actress of 1960 go to Elizabeth Taylor, *Butterfield 8,* and Shirley Jones, *Elmer Gantry,* respectively.

14 January 1962
INTERNATIONAL. About 175 women demonstrate for peace and disarmament in Nassau, New York.

15 January 1962
INTERNATIONAL. A group of 500 women demonstrate at the United Nations headquarters in New York City in support of world peace.

INTERNATIONAL. About 1,700 women arrive in Washington, D.C., aboard a "Peace Train Special," from New York. They demonstrate at the White House for peace and in opposition to nuclear testing.

16 January 1962
POLITICS. Representative Martha Griffiths (D-Michigan) is the first woman on the House Ways and Means Committee.

12 February 1962
WOMEN'S ISSUES. At a swearing-in ceremony at the White House, Eleanor Roosevelt becomes chair of the President's Commission on the Status of Women. This commission has been formed at the request of President Kennedy, who supports a drive to prevent "discrimination by law or by implication" against working women.

26 February 1962
INTERNATIONAL. In a letter from President Kennedy to Congress, the president notes that the average age of women Peace Corps workers is 25 and that one-third of all 2,400 volunteers to the Peace Corps are women.

26 April 1962
INTERNATIONAL. Three thousand members of Women Strike for Peace march to United Nations headquarters to protest against U.S. atmospheric testing of nuclear weapons.

2 July 1962
WOMEN'S ISSUES. In a compromise vote, Eleanor P. Sheppard is elected the first woman mayor of the Richmond, Virginia, city council. She was elected on the 25th ballot.

17 July 1962
AVIATION. House of Representatives hearings begin on complaints of sex discrimination against women in the National Aeronautics and Space Administration's space program. Jerrie Cobb, a woman pilot, testifies that of 25 women who applied to the program, 13 had been found qualified to become astronauts.

24 July 1962
WOMEN'S ISSUES. President Kennedy issues an order to bar discrimination against women either appointed to or receiving promotions within the government service.

25 July 1962
LEGISLATIVE. The U.S. House of Representatives passes by voice vote a bill requiring companies doing interstate business and employing 25 or more persons to pay equal wages to men and women doing the same work in the same plant location. The bill also bars labor unions from forcing discrimination on the basis of gender.

Rachel Carson, 1907–1964

Although a quiet, unassuming researcher dedicated to studying the intricacies of ecological balance, Rachel Carson sparked a heated debate over proper use of the pesticide DDT. Her book *Silent Spring,* published in 1962, promoted public knowledge of the problems inherent in DDT and warned of the threat posed by indiscriminate use of poisonous chemicals. She was born on 27 May 1907, in Springdale, Pennsylvania. Her parents, Robert W. and Naria (McLean) Carson, sent her to public schools. Her mother encouraged Carson's literary talents and her love of nature to the extent that, in 1917, she began sending written material to *St. Nicholas* magazine.

Carson entered the Pennsylvania College for Women after her high school graduation; she graduated with a B.A. in science in 1929. She then entered Johns Hopkins University to do graduate study. She taught summer school there, and in 1931 joined the zoology staff at the University of Maryland. In 1932, Carson received an M.A. from Johns Hopkins.

Carson was hired as an aquatic biologist by the U.S. Bureau of Fisheries in 1936. She carried out research on a variety of topics and published many brochures aimed at promoting the nation's wildlife resources. In 1941, Carson published her first book, *Under the Sea Wind,* which dealt with the Atlantic coastal sea floor. In 1951, *The Sea Around Us* appeared, a book on which Carson had worked intermittently during the war years. Several chapters of this book came out first in research journals as short articles. Prior to the publication of *The Sea Around Us,* Carson received a $1,000 award from the Westinghouse Foundation for her science writings. Ever thrifty and undemanding where material things were concerned, she purchased only a new microscope and a small cottage in Maine with the earnings from her books.

In 1951, Carson received a Guggenheim Fellowship, which helped her research her next book, *Edge of the Sea,* published in 1955. She won the National Book Award in 1952, and in 1953 was named a member of the National Institute of Arts and Letters. Her constant study of and appreciation for the natural world caused her to become the spokesperson for a national movement aimed at control of chemical pesticides. In 1942, DDT was introduced, and although Carson acknowledged the necessity of controlling insects, she was concerned about effects of chemicals on the ecology.

Some observers compared Carson to Carry Nation, the aggressive ax-wielding temperance advocate, but Carson was shy, reserved, and nonmilitant. After her book *Silent Spring* appeared in 1962, she found herself at the center of the pesticide controversy. In 1963, she helped with a "CBS Reports" television series, acting as technical advisor on issues related to the environment and public policy. She testified before a Senate Committee on the Chemical Pesticides Coordination Act that year. This legislation was responsible for warning labels on chemical products.

Despite increasing ill health, Carson continued her dialogue with both the public and private sector, arguing against indiscriminate use of chemicals in the environment. Confined to a wheelchair and suffering from bone cancer, Carson stayed involved in the world around her until her death on 14 April 1964, in Silver Spring, Maryland.

5 September 1962
LEGISLATIVE. A Senate subcommittee approves a bill that will give women in interstate commerce equal pay for equal work. The bill had been previously passed by the House of Representatives.

3 October 1962
LEGISLATIVE. The U.S. Senate fails to take action on a bill that would provide equal pay for equal work done by women in interstate commerce.

10 October 1962
WOMEN'S ISSUES. Kathryn E. Graham is confirmed as treasurer of the United States.

12 October 1962
LABOR. The U.S. Labor Department reports that an unexpected rise in the nation's unemployment rate in August was due to an unaccountable influx of women into the labor market. The report notes that nine-tenths of those women had found jobs.

21 October 1962
DEATHS. Suffragist, social worker, and former Social Security Board member, Mary "Molly" Dewson, dies at her home in Castine, Maine.

28 October 1962
INTERNATIONAL. About 8,000 members of 20 peace and disarmament groups, including Women Strike for Peace, demonstrate at United Nations headquarters in New York City.

7 November 1962
POLITICS. As a result of the 6 November elections, all 10 incumbent women representatives win their races for reelection. One new representative is elected—Charlotte Reid (R-Illinois). The total number of women in Congress falls, however, from 20 to 13 due to the retirement of 8 women in the House. Neither of the 2 women senators is currently up for reelection.

13 December 1962
INTERNATIONAL. The House Un-American Activities Committee holds hearings on Women Strike for Peace. There are charges of possible Communist infiltration into the organization, founded by homemaker Dagmar Wilson.

OTHER EVENTS OF 1962

WOMEN'S ISSUES. Mildred Jeffrey and Myra Wolfgang help establish the Michigan Commission on the Status of Women. It is the first state commission of its kind in the nation.

SPORTS. Helen Hull Jacobs is inducted into the National Lawn Tennis Hall of Fame.

POPULAR CULTURE. Oscars for Best Actress and Best Supporting Actress of 1961 go to Sophia Loren in *Two Women* and Rita Moreno in *West Side Story,* respectively.

4 January 1963
POLITICS. According to the *Congressional Quarterly,* the typical member of Congress is a white male.

17 March 1963
RELIGION. Mother Elizabeth Ann Seton is beatified by Pope John XXIII.

18 April 1963
IDEAS/BELIEFS. The Women's National Press Club announces establishment of the Eleanor Roosevelt Award to be given annually to an American woman involved in humanitarian works.

17 May 1963
LEGISLATIVE. The Senate passes a bill requiring equal pay for equal work and sends it to the House.

12 June 1963
POPULAR CULTURE. Elizabeth Taylor appears at the premier showing of *Cleopatra,* which runs 4 hours and 3 minutes and cost $40,000,000 to make.

9 July 1963
CIVIL RIGHTS. At a White House gathering, 300 leaders of 93 women's organizations representing about 50 million women meet with President Kennedy to discuss his different programs in support of civil rights.

18 August 1963
CIVIL RIGHTS. The National Women's Committee for Civil Rights is formed at President Kennedy's suggestion. The group expresses desire to begin programs to help black students attending newly desegregated schools.

1 September 1963
MILITARY. Mildred Irene Clark is sworn in as chief of the Army Nurse Corps. Colonel Clark is the 12th chief of the Corps and succeeds Colonel Margaret Harper, who had been named to that post in 1959.

14 September 1963
HEALTH. Mrs. Andrew Fischer of Aberdeen, South Dakota, gives birth to quintuplets. The babies are the first set of quints born in the United States to survive.

15 September 1963
CIVIL RIGHTS. A bomb explodes at a black church in Birmingham, Alabama (the Sixteenth Street Church), killing 4 black children attending Sunday School—Addie Mae Collins, Denise McNair, Carol Robertson, and Cynthia Wesley.

11 October 1963
WOMEN'S ISSUES. *American Women,* the final report of the President's Commission on the Status of Women, is given to President Kennedy at a White House ceremony. The report notes that jury duty and personal property rights are 2 major areas of injustice to women under present law. The commission advocates initiation of test court cases to help provoke definitive Supreme Court decisions in these matters.

LABOR. A report by the U.S. Census Bureau shows that women in the nation outnumber men by nearly 4 million. Statistics indicate that there are currently 44 million American homemakers and 24 million paid workers, out of which 3,250,000 are labor union members. Other figures show that 234 women are state legislators, 11 are U.S. representatives, and 2 are U.S. senators.

1 November 1963
WOMEN'S ISSUES. President Kennedy creates a Citizen's Advisory Council on the Status of Women. Its executive secretary is Catherine East.

4 November 1963
SPORTS. The first National Institute on Girls' Sports opens at the University of Oklahoma, in Norman, Oklahoma.

14 November 1963
POLITICS. President Kennedy comments on the possibility of Senator Margaret Chase Smith (R-Maine) running for president in the 1964 elections. ''I would not look forward to campaigning against Margaret Chase Smith . . . I think she is very formidable,'' says Kennedy.

22 November 1963
WOMEN'S ISSUES. Federal Justice Sarah T. Hughes administers the oath of office to Lyndon B. Johnson as he becomes president of the United States following the assassination of President Kennedy.

OTHER EVENTS OF 1963

LABOR. The Equal Pay Act is passed, effective June 1964.

MILITARY. The Memorial Bell Tower at the Cathedral of the Pines, in Rindge, New Hampshire, is built in remembrance of women who served during America's participation in various wars.

SPORTS. Sarah Palfrey Danzig is inducted into the National Lawn Tennis Hall of Fame.

Mary Kay Ash, 1916(?)–

Combining shrewd business sense and a belief in women's abilities bordering on the evangelical, Mary Kay Ash is the chief executive officer of a worldwide cosmetics company. Born in Hotwells, Texas, on 12 May 1916(?), she was the daughter of Edward A. and Lula (Hastings) Wagner (she consistently declines to reveal the exact year of her birth). She was an ambitious student who constantly strove for excellence, but her family's financial situation precluded her attending college. Married at seventeen, she soon had three children but found it necessary to contribute to her family income and did so by selling books door-to-door. She subsequently became a dealer for Stanley Home Products.

As unit manager at Stanley from 1938 to 1952, she excelled in direct sales. She and her husband divorced shortly after World War II, and while she had attended the University of Houston for a year, she knew that her real talent was in selling. Subsequent to her work with Stanley, she worked at World Gift Company from 1952 to 1963. By the early 1960s, she felt ready to retire from sales—or so she thought. Soon, she was ready to direct her considerable energy for organizing and marketing toward launching her own cosmetics business.

As had several early cosmetics pioneers, she discovered a "magic" formula for skin care cream, purchased the rights to its manufacture, and was in business by September 1963. Disregarding the advice of accountants and lawyers, she set up incentive programs that ranged from gold-plated goblets to pastel pink Cadillacs. She eliminated assigned sales territories and conceived of home beauty demonstrations at which her products would be sold to small groups of women. But most significantly, she designed an organization that specifically aimed at encouraging women to excel and to become financially successful.

Her emphasis on women's abilities stemmed in part from her innate optimism. But her desire to develop business options for women also originated as a result of her personal experiences during the 1930s, 1940s, and 1950s. She pointed out that when she began her business in 1963, it was clear to her that "women's brains were worth only fifty cents on the dollar in a male-run corporation." Her response to this kind of gender discrimination was to generate ample opportunities for women in the following decades. After the death of her second husband, only weeks before the opening of her business in 1963, she relied on her youngest son to assist her with business details. Within five years, "Beauty by Mary Kay," as the company was then called, was a raging success, largely due to her knack for management.

In January 1966, she married Melville J. Ash, and continued her relentless encouragement of her sales force to do their very best. By 1979, her company had sold $54 million in cosmetics. In 1981, she published her autobiography, a carefully edited glimpse at the reasons for her financial success. In 1984, she wrote *Mary Kay on People Management,* a book that further explained her business principles—based on putting God first, family second, and career third.

Mary Kay Cosmetics, Inc. (the current name of her company), had grown by 1984 to a value of $238 million, with a sales force of 200,000 worldwide. Ash continues a grueling personal schedule, which includes rising daily at 5 A.M. and overseeing all aspects of the corporation, based in Dallas, Texas, that bears her name.

POPULAR CULTURE. At the Academy Award presentations, Anne Bancroft receives an Oscar for Best Actress of 1962 in *The Miracle Worker.* Best Supporting Actress is Patty Duke for her role in the same film, a story about Helen Keller.

11 January 1964

SPORTS. Peggy Fleming wins the women's senior title in the U.S. Figure Skating Championships in Cleveland, Ohio.

27 January 1964
POLITICS. At a Women's National Press Club luncheon, Senator Margaret Chase Smith (R-Maine) announces her decision to enter the New Hampshire and Illinois presidential primaries.

4 March 1964
WOMEN'S ISSUES. President Johnson announces that 10 women have been named to major government posts in his administration. They include Rose McKee, director of the Office of Public Information in the Small Business Administration; Dr. Eleanor Poland, a specialist in the Department of Health, Education, and Welfare's research grants projects; and Virginia Mae Brown, a member of the Interstate Commerce Commission.

19 March 1964
AVIATION. Jerrie Mock begins a solo flight around the world at her hometown airport in Columbus, Ohio.

17 April 1964
AVIATION. Jerrie Mock flies around the world in a single-engine Cessna 180—the first such solo flight by a woman. President Johnson subsequently names her vice-chair of the Federal Aviation Administration's Women's Aviation Advisory Committee.

24 May 1964
ARTS AND CULTURE. The 18th Annual Antoinette Perry ("Tony") Awards for distinguished American theater are presented. Among the winners are Carol Channing, musical star in *Hello, Dolly;* Sandy Dennis, actress in *Any Wednesday;* and Eva Le Gallienne, who receives a special award for distinguished contributions to the theater.

15 July 1964
POLITICS. Senator Margaret Chase Smith (R-Maine) receives 27 votes in nomination before the first ballot at the GOP Convention in San Francisco, California.

27 August 1964
DEATHS. Gracie Allen dies of a heart attack in Hollywood, California.

14 September 1964
IDEAS/BELIEFS. Helen Keller receives the Presidential Medal of Freedom along with 4 other women—Dr. Lena Edwards, Lynn Fontanne, Dr. Helen B. Taussig, and Leontyne Price.

Women as Consumers

Women emerged as an identifiable consumer group in the United States as early as 1900. In colleges and universities, domestic science and home economics courses flourished, helping to educate women for their roles as consumers. In Boston, Simmons College established a School of Household Economics in 1902, and Columbia University in New York City opened its School of Household Arts in 1909. The latter boasted about four hundred students in its first year of operation. At the federal level, the U.S. Department of Agriculture applauded the scientific approach to domestic affairs as being "in the same category with medicine, engineering, and agriculture." By 1910, newspapers in most areas devoted space to household hints, often publishing regular features on child care, family nutrition, household purchasing, and home care. Along with these articles ran advertisements for an increasing array of consumer goods aimed directly at the wife and mother.

In Chicago, Illinois, Christine Frederick, a well-known advisor on consumer issues, published *Household Engineering: Scientific Management and the Home* in 1919. She followed this with *Selling Mrs. Consumer* ten years later, a book designed to instruct advertisers in the most effective methods of reaching women in the household market. Another, even more famous proponent of scientific homemaking—and, indirectly, the consumerism that accompanied such an occupation—was Lillian Gilbreth, author of *The Home-Maker and Her Job* (1927) and *Management in the Home* (1954). Gilbreth consulted with many colleges and universities as they set up curricula in home economics, advising as early as 1926 about the most effective ways to manage and run the American home.

Women's magazines reflected the increased awareness of women as a consumer group. By the 1920s, *Ladies' Home Journal* placed great emphasis on domestic responsibilities and household efficiency. In 1929, an editorial in that magazine stated that homemaking "is today an adventure—an education in color, in mechanics, in chemistry." Like *Woman's Home Companion, Good Housekeeping,* and *McCall's, Ladies' Home Journal* also enjoyed a circulation of around 2 million by 1920. And advertising revenues for these four magazines totaled a combined $75 million per year.

Throughout the 1930s and into the mid-1940s, women's roles as consumers were shaped by the Depression, and then by World War II. But beginning in the postwar years, manufacturers, marketing specialists, and advertisers began to bombard wives and mothers with the same message: BUY. Purchases of every kind, from household appliances to cosmetics, food, and clothing, were assumed to be made by women. And the vast majority of advertising imagery of the period emphasized this assumption.

In the 1950s, *McCall's* gathered a 100-member "Better Living Congress"—a group of homemakers whose opinions on domestic economy were later incorporated into editorial and advertising strategies. Yet by the 1960s and 1970s, women as consumers were beginning to demand a real voice. They formed groups that challenged the prevailing view of women as housewives intent mainly on sparkling linoleum or making the perfect cup of coffee. By 1972, legal action was brought against WABC-TV in New York in part due to failure "to ascertain women's needs and interests in programming." The New York chapter of the National Organization of Women filed a petition with the Federal Communications Commission after research, a part of which was a study of 1,241 television commercials. The group found that in 42.6 percent of these advertisements, women were shown doing household tasks; in 37.5 percent women were shown as domestic adjuncts to men; and in 16.7 percent women were shown as sex objects. The majority of commercials sold either domestic or cosmetic goods.

Several years earlier, a group called Consumer Action Now (CAN) was founded by Ilene Goldman and Lola Redford. This organization was one of many groups of concerned women consumers that hoped to promote a more sound consumer attitude, in this case about the environment. Specifically, CAN worked at educating homemakers about the environmental impact of household purchases, and by 1974 was a major force behind the promotion of solar energy.

---

28 October 1964
INTERNATIONAL. Marietta Peabody Tree is the first woman permanent ambassador to the United Nations. She has served at the United Nations since 1961 as a delegate from the United States.

7 December 1964
VIETNAM WAR. At a closed session of the House Un-American Activities Committee, 2 women are charged with contempt of Congress for refusing to reply to questions concerning their actions in the Women Strike for Peace

group. The women are Dagmar Wilson, founder of Women Strike for Peace, and Donna Allen, a member.

OTHER EVENTS OF 1964

MEDICAL. Hattie Alexander, M.D., is named the first woman president of the American Pediatric Society. Alexander is known for her work in the diagnosis and treatment of meningitis.

HEALTH. The first shelter for battered women opens in Pasadena, California.

SPORTS. Alice Marble is inducted into the National Lawn Tennis Hall of Fame.

Olympic Gold Medals

Lesley Bush: Platform diving
Virginia Duenkel: Swimming—400-meter freestyle
Sharon Stouder: Swimming—100-meter butterfly
Cathy Ferguson: Swimming—100-meter backstroke
Donna de Varona: Swimming—400-meter individual medley
    Swimming—400-meter freestyle relay women's team medal
    Swimming—400-meter medley relay women's team medal
Wyomia Tyus: Track and Field—100-meter dash
Edith McGuire: Track and Field—200-meter dash

Olympic Silver Medals

Jeanne Collier: Springboard diving
Sharon Stouder: Swimming—100-meter freestyle
Claudia Kolb: Swimming—200-meter breaststroke
Sharon Finneran: Swimming—400-meter individual medley
Edith McGuire: Track and Field—100-meter dash
    Track and Field—100-meter relay women's team medal
Francine Fox and Glorianne Perrier: Canoeing— kayak pairs

Olympic Bronze Medals

Patsy Willard: Springboard diving
Kathleen Ellis: Swimming—100-meter freestyle
Kathleen Ellis: Swimming—100-meter butterfly
Virginia Duenkel: Swimming—100-meter backstroke

Martha Randall: Swimming—400-meter individual medley
Marcia Jones: Canoeing—kayak singles

POPULAR CULTURE. Oscars for 1963 go to Patricia Neal, Best Actress, in *Hud,* and to Margaret Rutherford, Best Supporting Actress, in *The V.I.P.s.*

4 January 1965
POLITICS. As the 89th Congress opens, 10 women are in the House and 2 are in the Senate. Of these women, Patsy Mink is the first woman Japanese-American representative from Hawaii.

12 January 1965
DEATHS. Playwright Lorraine Hansberry dies of cancer at age 34.

20 February 1965
POLITICS. Elly Peterson is elected Michigan GOP chair. She is former assistant chair of the GOP National Committee.

24 March 1965
CIVIL RIGHTS. Viola Luizzo, a white civil rights worker from Detroit, Michigan, is killed by racists on the road to Selma, Alabama, after a march to support equal voting rights for black Americans.

18 April 1965
ARTS AND CULTURE. Singer Marian Anderson formally ends her 30-year career in a concert at New York City's Carnegie Hall.

19 May 1965
INTERNATIONAL. President Johnson names Patricia Roberts Harris as U.S. ambassador to Luxembourg. She is the first black woman to be assigned to a major diplomatic berth.

7 June 1965
JUDICIAL. In a landmark case, *Griswold* v. *State of Connecticut,* the U.S. Supreme Court finds that a Connecticut law, passed in 1879, banning contraceptives, is unconstitutional. The law was found to have violated the First, Third, Fourth, Fifth, Ninth, and Fourteenth Amendments to the U.S. Constitution.

17 July 1965
SPORTS. Wyomia Tyus equals the women's world record for the 100-yard dash at Kingston, Jamaica. Her time is 10.3 seconds.

5 August 1965
WOMEN'S ISSUES. Irene Parsons is named assistant administrator for personnel of the Veterans Administration. She is the first woman to be named to this post in the federal government's third-largest agency.

Helen Taussig, 1898–1986

One of the first students at Radcliffe College, Helen B. Taussig was the daughter of Harvard economics professor Frank W. Taussig and his wife, the former Edith Guild. She was born on 24 May 1898 and was influenced early by her academic home surroundings. Although she enjoyed Radcliffe, which she attended from 1917 to 1919, she transferred to and received a B.A. from the University of California. She then studied at Harvard Medical School and entered Boston University Medical School in 1922. Her early research on the heart prompted her to continue her medical studies at Johns Hopkins University, from which she graduated in 1927.

Taussig interned at Johns Hopkins in pediatrics, and in 1930 was appointed staff doctor as well as head of the Children's Heart Clinic of Harriet Lane Home (the pediatrics section) there. Taussig's abiding medical interest had always been children's heart disease. In 1945, she and Dr. Alfred Blalock coauthored a paper that detailed surgical treatment of pulmonary stenosis—the cyanosis-causing disorder that resulted in "blue babies." The paper's publication in the *Journal of the American Medical Association* led the way for thousands of successful operations on children who would otherwise have died or led lives as invalids.

In 1946, Taussig published *Congenital Malformations of the Heart,* the results of studies in changes of heart size and shape. She was also a leader in warnings against the drug thalidomide—the tranquilizer associated with severe birth defects. Taussig was instrumental in passage of more stringent Food and Drug Administration laws concerning the testing and marketing of drugs in the wake of the thalidomide tragedies in Germany and in the United States.

In 1965, Taussig became the first female president of the American Heart Association. Taussig received the Albert Lasker Award in 1954, the Women's National Press Club Award in 1947, the Chevalier Legion d'Honneur in 1947, the Mead-Johnson Award in 1948, and the Eleanor Roosevelt Achievement Award in 1957. In 1963, she was honored by the American Association of University Women with an achievement award, and in 1964, she received the Presidential Medal of Freedom. She was also the first woman member of the Association of American Physicians.

In 1967, Taussig was named honorary chair of the Committee of Responsibility of War-Injured Children, Vietnam. In 1973, she was the Frances R. Seybold lecturer at Texas Medical Center in Houston, Texas. She received the Science Achievement Award from the American Medical Association in 1977 and a presidential citation from the American College of Cardiology in 1980.

In 1973, the American Heart Association established the Helen Brooke Taussig lectureship in honor of her contributions to the field. Taussig never married and stated many times that it would probably have been difficult for her to maintain a career and a family. She died in an auto accident near her home in Kennett Square, Pennsylvania, on 20 May 1986.

Katherine Anne Porter, 1890–1980

Katherine Anne Porter was a well-known author long before her best-selling novel *Ship of Fools* was published in 1962. The daughter of Harrison B. and Mary Alice (Jones) Porter, she was born on 15 May 1890, in Indian Creek, Texas. She received an education at private schools. Porter worked as a reporter for the *Rocky Mountain News* in Denver, Colorado, and in 1922 traveled to Mexico, where she studied Mexican art and continued to write, publishing her first short story in *Century* magazine in 1923.

Porter traveled to Europe on a Guggenheim Fellowship in 1931, and two years later published *Katherine Anne Porter's French Song-Book*. She married American diplomat Eugene Pressly the same year. During her Atlantic voyage to Europe, Porter had kept a journal, which she later drew on heavily while writing *Ship of Fools*. Her introduction to Nazi Germany during this trip caused her considerable distress, and she included these feelings in her book. In 1937, she published a novel, *Noon Wine.*

Porter divorced Pressly, and in 1938 married Albert Erskine, Jr. At this time she was writing short stories, some of which were collected in *Pale Horse, Pale Rider*. Her work was greeted by critics as flawless, yet she acknowledged that she seldom revised her writing after the first draft.

Porter began work on her best-known book, *Ship of Fools,* in 1940—and it took her twenty years to complete the novel. Meanwhile, she was occupied with a variety of tasks, including Hollywood scriptwriting and teaching and lecturing at colleges and universities. In 1942, she divorced her second husband. In 1944, she published another collection of stories, *The Leaning Tower; The Days Before,* a book of essays and articles, was published in 1952.

Porter was awarded the gold medal of the Society for the Libraries of New York University in 1940. From 1950 to 1952, she shared the vice-presidency of the National Institute of Arts and Letters with Glenway Westcott, and in 1962 received the American Academy of Arts and Sciences Emerson–Thoreau medal for prose fiction. *Ship of Fools* became an instant best-seller and was a Book-of-the-Month Club selection. Screen rights were sold for $500,000, and the movie version of the novel opened in July 1965. One year later, Porter was named to the fifty-member American Academy of Arts and Letters. She was awarded both the 1966 Pulitzer Prize and National Book Award for *Collected Stories of Katherine Anne Porter.* The National Institute of Arts and Letters honored Porter the following year with its gold medal, given at five-year intervals in recognition of a writer's lifelong works.

By 1964, Porter had curtailed her writing activities due to failing health, although she still wrote from her home in the Georgetown area of Washington, D.C. In 1977, she suffered a stroke. That year she published her final work, *The Never-Ending Wrong,* a book about anarchists Sacco and Vanzetti. Her health continued to decline until her death on 18 September 1980, at a nursing home in Silver Spring, Maryland.

Like their mothers' generation, the daughters of bobby-soxers found their teenage years shadowed by war. But even in the mid-1960s, most high school girls were principally concerned with the Beatles, high school football games, and the Junior Prom. (Photo courtesy Judith Freeman Clark)

16 October 1965
VIETNAM WAR.   At a parade down Fifth Avenue in New York City, 10,000–14,000 marchers protest U.S. involvement in the Vietnam War. Among speakers at the demonstration is Donna Allen of Women Strike for Peace.

4 November 1965
LABOR.   The Equal Employment Opportunity Commission (EEOC) makes public a report that 1,383 complaints of employment discrimination have been filed with the EEOC in its first 100 days of operation. Sixteen percent charge gender discrimination—14 complaints were filed by women, 7 by men.

SPORTS.   Lee Breedlove sets a women's land speed record at 308.56 miles per hour.

22 November 1965
LABOR.   The Equal Employment Opportunity Commission (EEOC) publishes guidelines clarifying the fair employment practices section (Title VII) of the 1964 Civil Rights Act. Earlier, the EEOC had said that refusal to hire or promote a woman because of "attitudes of fellow workers or clientele" was unlawful under Title VII.

27 November 1965
VIETNAM WAR.   Mrs. Coretta Scott King speaks out at an antiwar demonstration at the White House in Washington, D.C. Members of Women Strike for Peace also participate in this group demonstration of about 35,000 people.

13 December 1965

POPULAR CULTURE. According to a Gallup poll, Jacqueline Kennedy is the woman most admired by Americans in 1965. Ladybird Johnson is second on the list.

OTHER EVENTS OF 1965

SPORTS. Pauline Betz Addie and Ellen Forde Hansell Allerdice are inducted into the National Lawn Tennis Hall of Fame.

POPULAR CULTURE. Oscars go to Julie Andrews, Best Actress of 1964 in *Mary Poppins*, and to Lila Kedrova, Best Supporting Actress, in *Zorba the Greek*.

11 January 1966

VIETNAM WAR. Women Strike for Peace launches a "continuous lobby" in Congress to insist on full debate of the U.S. policy on Vietnam prior to further military appropriations.

2 February 1966

VIETNAM WAR. Two hundred members of Women Strike for Peace participate in a vigil in front of United Nations Plaza in New York City.

Betty Friedan, 1921–

It is impossible to discuss origins of the post–World War II feminist movement without acknowledging Betty Friedan's role as a driving force behind its growth. With the publication of *The Feminine Mystique* in 1963, Friedan became an almost instant celebrity. Dealing with the pressures educated women face when coping with society's expectations of feminine behavior, Friedan's book was decried by some but looked upon by others as a prophecy. In detailing the dehumanizing aspects of post–World War II womanhood, the book also outlined a plan to help women break free of sexual stereotypes.

Born Betty Naomi Goldstein in Peoria, Illinois, on 4 February 1921, she grew up in a quiet, Jewish home. Her parents, Harry and Miriam (Horwitz) Goldstein were indifferent to the intellectual pursuits their daughter found so fulfilling. She attended Smith College, graduating summa cum laude in 1942 after helping to found the literary magazine there. She then attended graduate school at the University of California at Berkeley. In June 1947, she married Carl Friedan.

Ten years later, after having three children, Friedan began research into the various difficulties—emotional and otherwise—that faced the American homemaker. Her work resulted in *The Feminine Mystique*. Soon, Friedan was sought after as a lecturer, and as she traveled throughout the country speaking, she determined the need for a national organization dedicated to women's rights. In October 1966, Friedan and a handful of other concerned women founded the National Organization for Women (NOW), one of the chief forces behind enforcing provisions of the 1964 Civil Rights Act. NOW was also instrumental in campaigning for passage of the Equal Rights Amendment. By 1970, the organization claimed a membership of six thousand men and women.

Friedan's time was absorbed by her work on behalf of women, and in 1969 she and her husband divorced. She was one of the prime movers behind the women's strike on 26 August 1970, a nationwide demonstration that demanded free abortion, free child care, and equal job opportunities for all women. In 1971, Friedan joined Bella Abzug, Shirley Chisholm, and Gloria Steinem to form the National Women's Political Caucus. Its purpose was to help elect women to political office in 1972.

During the summer of 1975, Friedan traveled to Mexico City, Mexico, where she attended the United Nations–sponsored International Woman's Year Conference. She spoke out in support of women's rights and expressed her concern at the many incidents marring the group meeting there. Friedan published *It Changed My Life* in 1976, which detailed her involvement in the growing feminist movement from the early 1960s onward. And in 1980, she went to a conference on world feminism in Copenhagen, Denmark, a follow-up of the Mexico City gathering of 1975. In 1981, she published *The Second Stage,* another in-depth study of feminism and its effects on American society.

For a variety of reasons, Friedan gradually grew less closely associated with the top-ranking politicians in NOW. Increasingly, she viewed feminist struggles as part of a larger global struggle for equality for all people. In 1984, Friedan attended a United Nations-sponsored meeting in Nairobi, Kenya, which would cap the decade-long work on world feminism. Friedan's experiences in Kenya fueled her desire to effect further change for American women, and she continues to write and speak, eloquently and forcefully, on feminist and human issues.

---

7 February 1966
JUDICIAL. A 3-judge Federal court in Montgomery, Alabama, rules that state laws excluding women from jury service "shall be of no effect on and after June 1, 1967." The court rules that statutes barring women from jury duty "deny to women the equal protection of the laws in violation of the 14th Amendment."

9 February 1966
VIETNAM WAR. About 1,500 members of Women Strike for Peace picket the White House, then move on to the Senate and House office buildings at the Capitol.

31 March 1966
HEALTH. The U.S. Department of Health, Education, and Welfare approves the supply of birth control instruction and contraceptives to all U.S. women who request them. This family planning information will be distributed through programs funded by several millions of federal dollars.

15 May 1966
VIETNAM WAR. Women Strike for Peace joins a Washington, D.C., demonstration of nearly 11,000 who protest the war in Vietnam.

14 June 1966
DEATHS. Mary Heaton Vorse, militant liberal active in the strikes of the 1920s and 1930s, dies in Provincetown, Massachusetts.

30 June 1966
VIETNAM WAR. Ten Women Strike for Peace members meet with U.S. Ambassador to the United Nations Arthur J. Goldberg after a demonstration at the U.S. Mission to the United Nations. Women Strike for Peace leaders term their talk "disappointing" following the meeting.

10 July 1966
DEATHS. Malvina Hoffman, who studied with Rodin and was considered the nation's most important woman sculptor, dies of a heart attack at her studio in New York City.

22 December 1966
DEATHS. Lucy Burns, a suffragist and founder of the Congressional Union for Woman Suffrage, dies in Brooklyn, New York.

OTHER EVENTS OF 1966

WOMEN'S ISSUES. At the Third National Conference of Governors' Commission on the Status of Women, 28 women form a new group called The National Organization for Women (NOW). Founders include Betty Friedan, Katherine Clarenbach, Caroline Davis, Pauli Murray, and Alice Rossi.

POPULAR CULTURE. Academy Awards for 1965 go to Julie Christie, Best Actress in *Darling,* and to Shelley Winters, Best Supporting Actress, in *A Patch of Blue.*

Dian Fossey, 1932–1985

Dedicated conservationist and researcher, and the world's foremost expert on mountain gorillas, Dian Fossey was born in San Francisco, California, in 1932. She received a B.A. in occupational therapy from San Jose State College in 1954 and by 1956 was based at Louisville, Kentucky, where she worked for the Kosair Crippled Children's Hospital. Despite a comfortable beginning to her career, Fossey's overriding interest in the study of gorillas led her to Africa in 1963. She spent seven weeks on safari, financing her trip with a loan of $8,000. Early in her trip she met and conferred with anthropologist Louis B. Leakey at Olduvai Gorge in Tanzania, and with Jane Goodall, a British specialist on primates. Both Leakey and Goodall encouraged Fossey to pursue her interest and she went to Zaire, where she first saw the objects of her study.

Satisfied that she was making the correct decision concerning her career, she returned to the United States until 1966, when she decided to begin long-term investigation of mountain gorillas in their natural habitat. Although she received funding from several private sources, including the National Geographic Society, Fossey's initial research station was simple. She worked alone in Zaire's Parc National des Virungas, to which she had gone on her second African trip, attempting to establish contact with the gorillas. By imitating their behavior and habits, Fossey was eventually able to make regular observations of three separate family groups.

Fossey encountered difficulty with Zaire's government within the first year of her work, however. In July 1967, she was expelled from the mountain area by armed guards and warned not to return. Despite this threat to her personal safety, she was back at her work in September 1967, this time in neighboring Rwanda, where she set up the Karisoke Research Center.

Eventually, Fossey identified fifty-one mountain gorillas living in four distinct family groups. She learned that, contrary to popular misconceptions, these enormous animals (males of the species often weigh 400 pounds and stand more than six feet tall) were vegetarians. She also learned that they were basically peaceful in their behavior and that they had more than a dozen different vocalizations used in communicating. She also determined that they were in danger of imminent extinction, threatened by both big-game hunters and encroaching agricultural development in their natural habitat.

Two decades earlier, estimates of the mountain gorilla population were 50 percent higher than the 242 primates that Fossey found. She therefore launched a worldwide campaign to prevent hunters and zoos from further decimating the gorillas' numbers. In addition, she tried to persuade native Rwandans from taking over gorilla lands for farmland. In 1983, Fossey published *Gorillas in the Mist,* a popular treatment of her findings, based in part on doctoral work that she completed in 1974 at Great Britain's Cambridge University. She was on the faculty at Cornell University from 1980 to the time that she returned to Karisoke Research Center several years later.

On 24 December 1985, Fossey was found murdered at her home in the Parc National des Volcans. There was no way of determining who had killed *Nyiramachabelli*—"the old lady who lives in the forest without a man"—but those who knew her stated that she had no valuables and little money. Some suspect that her death may have been the result of increased tension over land use.

15 February 1967
VIETNAM WAR. Women Strike for Peace organizes a rally of 2,500 women in front of the Pentagon. A delegation of 6 women meets with a Pentagon official to protest the "killing of innocent women and children in Vietnam."

23 March 1967
MILITARY. Hearings before a Senate subcommittee take place in which Sargent Shriver, head of the Office of Equal Opportunity, proposes that women register with the Selective Service at age 16 for nonmilitary forms of service to the nation.

30 August 1967
LABOR. Eleven people picket the classified advertising office of the *New York Times* in protest of male-female labeling of help wanted advertising.

20 September 1967
VIETNAM WAR. About 500 members of Women Strike for Peace clash with police in front of the White House. Three women are arrested but later released.

21 October 1967
LABOR. The Office of Equal Opportunity publishes the results of a survey indicating that white-collar jobs in New York City are held by 38,534 black women but by only 16,173 black men. For white women, the figure is 432,583 compared to 519,226 white males in white-collar jobs.

8 November 1967
LEGISLATIVE. Passage of a bill to remove legal limitations on strengths of women in armed service (formerly at 2 percent of the total armed service population) and promotion of women in the service, goes through Congress.

8 December 1967
VIETNAM WAR. Women Strike for Peace is among the organizations that have held STOP-THE-DRAFT week demonstrations nationwide.

28 December 1967
BUSINESS. Muriel Siebert is the first woman owner of a seat on the New York Stock Exchange. She pays $445,000 plus a $7,515 initiation fee for the seat.

OTHER EVENTS OF 1967

SPORTS. Kathy Switzer is the first woman to run in the Boston Marathon.

SPORTS. Louise Brough Clapp and Margaret Osborne DuPont are inducted into the National Lawn Tennis Hall of Fame.

ARTS AND CULTURE. An exhibition of the work of photographer Diane Arbus opens at The Museum of Modern Art.

Coretta Scott King, 1927–

Described by some as the "keeper of the flame," Coretta Scott King—widow of civil rights leader Martin Luther King, Jr.—has spent the years since her husband's death working to further the causes he championed. Born in Heiberger, Alabama, on 27 April 1927, she was the daughter of Obie and Bernice Scott. A bright child, she attended the Lincoln School in Marion, Alabama, graduating at the head of her class in 1945. She then attended Antioch College in Ohio and after graduating with a major in music and education she entered the New England Conservatory of Music in Boston, Massachusetts. At the Conservatory, Scott took voice lessons and sang in the chorus and in the choir at historic Old South Church in Boston's fashionable Back Bay.

While a student in Boston, Scott met Martin Luther King, Jr., a philosophy major at Boston University. The couple married on 18 June 1953, and by 1954 they had returned to the South and were living in Montgomery, Alabama. King was soon busy with four children, and though she had relinquished a full-time music career, she continued singing informally. She also worked closely with her husband, supporting his nonviolent peace efforts.

In 1962, King taught music at Morris Brown College in Atlanta, Georgia, where the family had moved in 1960. She was a delegate to the Women Strike for Peace contingent that attended the 1962 Disarmament Conference in Geneva, Switzerland. She also accompanied her husband to Oslo, Norway, when he received the Nobel Peace Prize in 1964. With the death of her husband on 4 April 1968, King devoted herself to raising their children and to keeping his memory and all he had worked for alive. King kept speaking engagements that her huband had made before his death, and at the Washington, D.C., Poor People's Campaign in June 1968, she called on Americans to fight racism and poverty.

King has served on the board of directors of many national groups, including the Southern Christian Leadership Committee and the National Organization for Women. Most of her time, however, was spent working toward the establishment of the Atlanta-based Martin Luther King, Jr. Center for Non-Violent Social Change. After more than a decade of fund-raising, King had the satisfaction of seeing the $8.5-million Freedom Hall Complex open in June 1982.

King, president of the organization that built the center, intended that the facility should be the center of educational programs designed to promote nonviolence. The center has attracted more than three hundred thousand visitors annually to its multiple-building complex, including an auditorium, conference center, and library. Much of the success of this venture has been due directly to King's unfailing devotion to the purposes that her husband had set out to achieve.

King is optimistic about the center's future, and she and a staff that includes her oldest daughter Yolanda hope that they can obtain funding necessary to its continued functioning. King pours her considerable energies and talents into the Center for Non-Violent Social Change. It has been her way of ensuring a proper memorial to her late husband and providing for the needs of future generations.

POPULAR CULTURE. At the Monterey International Pop Festival, singer Janis Joplin becomes famous for singing "Love Is Like a Ball and Chain."

POPULAR CULTURE. Academy Awards for 1966 go to Elizabeth Taylor, Best Actress, in *Who's Afraid of Virginia Woolf?* and to Sandy Dennis, Best Supporting Actress in the same film.

15 January 1968
VIETNAM WAR. About 5,000 women, led by Jeannette Rankin (87-year-old former U.S. representative from Montana), demonstrate against the Vietnam War. This "Jeannette Rankin Brigade," demonstrating at the foot of Capitol Hill, includes women from all over the nation. Coretta Scott King is among the demonstrators.

16 January 1968
AVIATION. An Eastern Airlines' spokesperson tells the Equal Employment Opportunity Commission that only 42 of 703 women flight attendants are black.

21 January 1968
HEALTH. The Food and Drug Administration announces that intrauterine devices (IUDs) are safe, highly effective birth control devices only "slightly less reliable" than oral contraceptives, which sometimes cause dangerous side effects in some women.

26 January 1968
LABOR. Elizabeth J. Kuck is confirmed as a member of the Equal Employment Opportunity Commission. She succeeds Aileen C. Hernandez.

8 April 1968
CIVIL RIGHTS.   Coretta Scott King takes her slain husband's place in front of 42,000 silent marchers in Memphis, Tennessee. She speaks to a city hall crowd after the march saying, "How many must die before we can really have a free and true and peaceful society?"

9 April 1968
CIVIL RIGHTS.   Coretta Scott King is named to a 53-member board of directors of the Southern Christian Leadership Committee.

27 April 1968
IDEAS/BELIEFS.   At a gathering of nearly 87,000 people in New York City, Coretta Scott King speaks to a Vietnam War protest rally, one of 17 such rallies held nationwide.

12 May 1968
WOMEN'S ISSUES.   A 12-block Mother's Day march of "welfare mothers" from 20 U.S. cities is held in Washington, D.C. Coretta Scott King leads the march accompanied by Ethel Kennedy and several other prominent women and about 5,000 participants.

Peggy Fleming, 1948–

Undefeated amateur figure skating champion Peggy Fleming put on her first pair of skates at age nine. Born in San Jose, California, on 27 July 1948, she moved to Cleveland, Ohio, with her parents, Albert E. and Doris (Deal) Fleming, and her three sisters. Her father was a strong supporter of Fleming's skating talent, and the family soon returned to California, where she began skating in earnest.

In 1960, Fleming won the Pacific Coast Juvenile Figure Skating Championship, and for the next several years she won championships steadily. In January 1964, Fleming won the first of five national ladies figure skating championships; at age fifteen, she became the youngest ever to win. Fleming placed sixth at the 1964 Olympic Games in Innsbruck, Austria, and after returning to the United States she entered Hollywood Professional School as an alternative to conventional high school classes. This enabled her to spend a maximum amount of time training.

In March 1964, Fleming took third place at the international figure skating championships. She and her family moved to Colorado Springs, where she coached with Carlo Fassi. In February 1966, when Fleming traveled to the world figure skating championships in Davos, Switzerland, she easily won the title. But while there, she learned of her father's heart attack and death. Despite sorrow over this loss, she took the national title once again in 1967, along with the North American title and another world championship.

But Fleming's real grace, style, and technical perfection were showcased most clearly at the 1968 Olympic Games in Grenoble, France. She won a gold medal by an 88.2-point margin. She was the only first-place winner for the United States at that year's winter Games. In March 1968, Fleming claimed her third world figure skating championship in Geneva, Switzerland. At that time, she also announced her retirement from amateur skating. In April 1968, she signed a contract with NBC and in November debuted on a television special, "Here's Peggy Fleming." She subsequently went on the Pro Skate circuit, and was married in 1971. In 1976, she announced her retirement from the Holiday on Ice troupe due to the fact that she was pregnant. Her son was born in 1977.

23 May 1968
WOMEN'S ISSUES.   About 250 welfare mothers march to the Longworth House Office Building to meet with Senator Wilbur Mills, chair of the House Ways and Means Committee.

28 May 1968
POLITICS.   Democrat Katherine Peden, ex-state commerce commissioner for Kentucky, defeats 11 opponents to become the first woman to win a statewide primary race. Peden receives 42 percent of the total vote.

4 June 1968
DEATHS.   Actress and star of early motion pictures, Dorothy Gish, dies in Rapello, Italy.

15 June 1968
IDEAS/BELIEFS.   Rose Kennedy, mother of slain presidential candidate Robert F. Kennedy, pledges the family to ''carry out the principles for which Bobby stood.''

19 June 1968
CIVIL RIGHTS.   On Solidarity Day, Coretta Scott King, widow of slain civil rights leader Martin Luther King, Jr., addresses a gathering at the Lincoln Memorial in Washington, D.C., as part of the Poor People's Campaign.

12 July 1968
HEALTH.   A Presidential Advisory Committee recommends repeal of laws making abortions illegal.

29 July 1968
MEDICAL.   In Houston, Texas, Beth Brunk receives a heart from Betty O'Neal in the first woman-to-woman heart transplant operation.

1 December 1968
IDEAS/BELIEFS.   The Women's Equity Action League (WEAL) is incorporated in Cleveland, Ohio. Within 3 years, WEAL has units in 40 states.

OTHER EVENTS OF 1968

SPORTS.   At Newport, Rhode Island, Maureen Connolly Brinker and Eleanora Sears are inducted into the National Lawn Tennis Hall of Fame.

Olympic Gold Medals

Sue Gossick: Springboard diving
Jan Henne: Swimming—100-meter freestyle
Debbie Meyer: Swimming—200-meter freestyle
Debbie Meyer: Swimming—400-meter freestyle
Debbie Meyer: Swimming—800-meter freestyle
Sharon Wichman: Swimming—200-meter breaststroke
Kaye Hall: Swimming—100-meter backstroke
Pokey Watson: Swimming—200-meter backstroke
Claudia Kolb: Swimming—200-meter individual medley
Claudia Kolb: Swimming—400-meter individual medley
   Swimming—400-meter freestyle relay women's team medal
   Swimming—400-meter medley relay women's team medal
Wyomia Tyus: Track and Field—100-meter dash
Madeline Manning: Track and Field—800-meter run
   Track and Field—400-meter relay women's team medal
Peggy Fleming: Figure skating

Olympic Silver Medals

Susan Pedersen: Swimming—100-meter freestyle
Jan Henne: Swimming—200-meter freestyle
Linda Gustavson: Swimming—400-meter freestyle
Pam Kruse: Swimming—800-meter freestyle
Ellie Daniel: Swimming—100-meter butterfly
Susan Pedersen: Swimming—200-meter individual medley
Lynn Vidali: Swimming—400-meter individual medley
Barbara Ferrell: Track and Field—100-meter dash
Mary Meyers/Dianne Holum/Jenny Fish: Speed skating—3-way tie for 500-meter

Olympic Bronze Medals

Ann Peterson: Platform diving
K. O'Sullivan: Springboard diving
Linda Gustavson: Swimming—100-meter free-style
Jane Barkman: Swimming—200-meter freestyle
Sharon Wichman: Swimming—100-meter breaststroke
Susie Shield: Swimming—100-meter butterfly
Ellie Daniel: Swimming—200-meter butterfly

Jane Swagerty: Swimming—100-meter backstroke
Kaye Hall: Swimming—200-meter individual medley
Dianne Holum: Speed skating—1,000-meter

POPULAR CULTURE. Women picket outside the Atlantic City, New Jersey, site of the Miss America pageant, terming the beauty pageant offensive to women.

POPULAR CULTURE. Oscars for 1968 go to Katharine Hepburn, Best Actress, in *Guess Who's Coming to Dinner* and to Estelle Parsons, Best Supporting Actress, in *Bonnie and Clyde*.

3 January 1969
POLITICS. As the 91st Congress convenes, Representative Shirley S. Chisholm (D-New York) takes her place as the first black woman in Congress.

10 January 1969
ARTS AND CULTURE. The Museum of Modern Art in New York City announces that it has acquired Gertrude Stein's 47-work painting collection for a reported $6.5 million.

28 January 1969
HEALTH. A report by nutrition experts testifying before the Senate Nutrition Committee reveals that malnutrition in pregnant women results in a high mortality rate for their children.

30 January 1969
RELIGION. The U.S. National Conference of Catholic Bishops announces that women will be allowed to participate actively in certain portions of the Roman Catholic mass.

22 February 1969
SPORTS. Barbara Jo Rubin is the first winning woman jockey at a U.S. thoroughbred race track with parimutuel betting, in Charles Town, West Virginia.

15 March 1969
RELIGION. Episcopal Deaconess Phyllis Edwards breaks precedent when she performs a marriage ceremony in San Francisco, California.

25 March 1969
ARTS AND CULTURE. The Solomon R. Guggenheim Museum in New York City anounces that it will acquire the 263-piece collection of art patron Peggy Guggenheim.

26 March 1969
VIETNAM WAR. Nearly 1,300 black-clad women march on the White House and the Capitol building in a strike sponsored by Women Strike for Peace. Bella Abzug, spokesperson for the group, says that the "moratorium on war criticism is over." In her maiden speech, Representative Shirley S. Chisholm (D-New York) says that she will vote against all defense money bills that come before the House of Representatives.

10 April 1969
EDUCATION. Katherine Graham, president and publisher of the *Washington Post,* is elected the first woman trustee of the University of Chicago.

22 June 1969
DEATHS. Singer and actress July Garland, famous as Dorothy in the film *The Wizard of Oz,* dies in London, England, following an overdose of barbiturates.

7 July 1969
SPORTS. Seventeen-year-old Ruth White becomes the first black national fencing champion at a major U.S. fencing match in Van Nuys, California.

18 July 1969
DEATHS. Mary Jo Kopechne, an aide to Senator Edward M. Kennedy, dies after an accident in which the senator's car plunges off a bridge on Chappaquiddick Island in Massachusetts.

Women and Peace

As women, we feel a peculiar moral passion of revolt against both the cruelty and waste of war.

The preamble to Woman's Peace Party resolutions in 1915 summed up the convictions of its organizers. Established by pacifists who believed they could prevent the United States from entering into World War I, the Woman's Peace Party elected Jane Addams national president. Women marched in support of peace in 1915; they published *Four Lights* (a pacifist journal), hoping to convince Americans that war should be avoided, and some, like Crystal Eastman (publisher of *Four Lights*), were jailed for their efforts to keep the country out of war.

In 1919, Florence Kelley helped found the Women's International League for Peace and Freedom. When another war loomed on the horizon several decades later, women continued to speak out for peace just as Kelley, Addams, and others had done earlier in the century. However, like their predecessors, organizations such as America First (established in the late 1930s) had only limited success in promoting an isolationist policy. Speakers for America First included the novelist Kathleen Norris and Anne Morrow Lindbergh—a well-known author, accomplished pilot, and wife of aviator Charles Lindbergh.

After World War II, many American women helped to promote disarmament in the hopes of promoting world peace. Threats of nuclear war provoked pacifists to demonstrate against the stockpiling of atomic weapons and in favor of bans on nuclear arsenals. By the 1960s, groups like Another Mother for Peace, and Women Strike for Peace—founded by Dagmar Wilson in September 1961—protested in major U.S. cities, hoping to end the Vietnam conflict. Jeannette Rankin, former U.S. representative from Montana, led antiwar demonstrations. In January 1968, Rankin led thousands who marched in the nation's capital, emphasizing American women's desires for peace. As the Vietnam conflict grew, women proponents of peace continued to demonstrate; many even engaged in illegal draft-protest activities. Catholic activist Dorothy Day counseled young men against military draft registration, joining the ranks of hundreds of women who risked arrest in connection with such actions. The efforts of these individuals were rewarded in 1974, at least in part, by the conclusion of the war in Southeast Asia; however, thousands of women continued to remain active in peace groups throughout the late 1970s and early 1980s as the specter of war loomed great in Central and South America, and in the Middle East.

25 July 1969
SPORTS. Sharon Adams completes a 5,618-mile trip from Japan to San Diego, California, in a 31-foot ketch. The crossing takes 74 days.

23 August 1969
SPORTS. Audrey McElmory of La Jolla, California, wins the world road race cycling championship at Brno, Czechoslovakia. This is the first U.S. title since 1912.

2 September 1969
RELIGION. At its general convention in South Bend, Indiana, the Episcopal Church refuses to consider the question of ordaining women as priests.

15 October 1969
VIETNAM WAR. A nationwide antiwar protest takes place with rallies, marches, and memorial services. Women Strike for Peace is one of the chief organizers of the Vietnam Moratorium Day.

27 October 1969
POLITICS. Helen Delich Bently is named chair of the Federal Maritime Commission. She is the first woman to serve in this capacity, and remains in office until November 1975.

4 December 1969
RELIGION. Atheist Madalyn Murray O'Hair has a lawsuit dismissed by U.S. district court. O'Hair attempted to bar the broadcast of prayers and Bible readings by U.S. astronauts.

22 December 1969
EDUCATION. Jacqueline Grennan Wexler is named the ninth president of Hunter College of the City University of New York.

OTHER EVENTS OF 1969

WOMEN'S ISSUES. The Interstate Association of State Commissions on the Status of Women is organized.

SPORTS. Doris J. Hart and Marie Wagner are named to the National Lawn Tennis Hall of Fame.

POPULAR CULTURE. Oscars for 1968 go to Katharine Hepburn in *The Lion in Winter* and Barbra Streisand in *Funny Girl*—a tie for Best Actress—and to Ruth Gordon, Best Supporting Actress, in *Rosemary's Baby*.

15 January 1970
POPULAR CULTURE. Diana Ross, lead singer of the Supremes, makes her final appearance as a member of that Motown group in a performance at the Frontier Hotel in Las Vegas, Nevada.

Helen Gurley Brown, 1922–

Helen Gurley Brown, whose best seller *Sex and the Single Girl* helped revolutionize the way American women viewed their relationships with men. (Photo courtesy Klaus Luca)

Author, editor, and publisher of *Cosmopolitan* magazine, Helen Gurley Brown was born on 18 February 1922, in Green Forest, Arkansas. She was the daughter of Ira M. and Cleo (Sisco) Gurley, and in order to escape her family's relative poverty she became an ambitious student. In 1939, Gurley graduated from high school as class valedictorian. She then worked at numerous clerical positions in Los Angeles, California, until 1948, when she was hired as a copywriter at Foote, Cone, and Belding, a large advertising agency. She quickly became proficient at writing advertising copy and won the Frances Homes Advertising Copywriters Award for three consecutive years, beginning in 1957.

In 1958, Gurley became an account executive at Kenyon & Eckhardt. On 25 September 1959, she married David Brown, a vice-president at Twentieth Century-Fox studios. Brown's book, *Sex and the Single Girl,* was published in 1962 and was an immediate best seller. She followed this success in 1964 with *Sex and the Office.* Brown also wrote a syndicated column, "Women Alone," which led her to write a third book, *Helen Gurley Brown's Outrageous Opinions,* published in 1966.

Brown had been doing various television and radio programs as well as lecturing, but found her métier in 1965 when the Hearst Corporation named her editor of *Cosmopolitan* magazine. Using the same clever, breezy style that had distinguished her books, Brown refocused the magazine and aimed it at a new audience—the working woman age eighteen to thirty-four. *Cosmopolitan* sales skyrocketed with Brown in charge. In 1965, circulation had hovered at about 800,000, but by 1969 newsstand sales (about 98 percent of total) hit 1,112,000.

Although Brown came under attack from feminists who decried what they saw as *Cosmopolitan*'s emphasis on frivolous matters, the straightforward, ambitious editor refused to admit offense. She also continued to publish the magazine in the format she had established. By 1985 it was flourishing, and Brown could point to a circulation of 2,987,970.

A tireless perfectionist, Brown has received many awards, including the Distinguished Achievement Award from the University of California School of Journalism (1971) and the Distinguished Achievement Award in Journalism from Stanford, which also made Brown an honorary alumna, in 1977. Brown did not abandon her own writing despite the demands of her career as an editor. In 1969, she published a cookbook; in 1970, she brought out *Sex and the New Single Girl,* a revised edition of her first best seller; and in 1982, she wrote *Having It All,* which is part autobiography and part self-help manual for working women of all ages.

---

2 February 1970
RELIGION. Sister Anita Caspary, president of the religious order Immaculate Heart of Mary, announces that nearly 315 of the order's 400 sisters have voted to renounce formal religious life and form a lay community.

23 February 1970
RELIGION. Two women from Iowa, Cornell Deeny and Mary Sandmann, are the first U.S. women permitted to distribute the Holy Eucharist at a Roman Catholic mass.

24 February 1970
HEALTH. At the Senate Subcommittee on Monopoly hearings, Dr. Elizabeth Connell, an associate professor of obstetrics and gynecology—and the first woman to testify—states that unfavorable publicity about birth control hearings is resulting in pregnancies in women concerned about using birth control pills.

14 March 1970
POLITICS. Democrat Bella Abzug, outspoken lawyer and peace activist, announces

her candidacy for the congressional seat from New York's 19th district.

18 March 1970
CIVIL RIGHTS.   A federal district court judge declares a Barnwell, South Carolina, plan for sex-segregated schools "racially motivated and unconstitutional."

19 April 1970
VIETNAM WAR.   Leaders of the Vietnam Moratorium Committee announce that the group is disbanding, partly due to lack of funding. However, leader Marge Sklencar says, "I don't think the antiwar movement is going to stop now."

2 May 1970
SPORTS.   Diane Crump is the first woman jockey in the Kentucky Derby at Churchill Downs.

5 May 1970
RELIGION.   Sister Nancy Ann Eagan, a nurse, becomes a second lieutenant in the Air Force Reserve and is assigned to the 932d Aeromedical Airlift Group, Scott Air Force Base, in Illinois. She is the first Roman Catholic nun to receive a military commission.

6 May 1970
WOMEN'S ISSUES.   Senator Birch Bayh (D-Indiana) opens congressional hearings on the Equal Rights Amendment to the U.S. Constitution.

15 May 1970
RELIGION.   The American Baptist Women express disappointment in the fact that, at its annual meeting, the American Baptist Convention bypassed the names of 10 qualified women when electing its president.

18 May 1970
JUDICIAL.   The U.S. Supreme Court refuses to upset a lower court ruling that Wheaton Glass Company in New Jersey must pay its male and female assembly-line workers equally.

4 June 1970
LABOR.   The Equal Employment Opportunity Commission announces that charges of sex and race discrimination have been filed against 4

companies and 15 labor unions in Houston, Texas.

9 June 1970
WOMEN'S ISSUES.   Elizabeth Duncan Koontz, Women's Bureau director, announces federal guidelines against sex discrimination applying to companies with government contracts of $50,000 or more, or companies with more than 50 employees.

11 June 1970
MILITARY.   U.S. Army Colonels Elizabeth P. Hoisington and Anna Mae Hays become the first women in military history to attain the rank of brigadier general.

1 July 1970
MEDICAL.   A New York City law permitting abortions during the first 24 weeks of pregnancy goes into effect.

2 July 1970
LABOR.   U.S. Labor Department figures show a decline in the jobless rate among women from 5.1 percent in May to 4.5 percent in June.

14 July 1970
HEALTH.   The Senate authorizes $991.25 million for a 5-year federal program to provide family planning services and population research. President Nixon's stated goal is to serve the 5 million U.S. women estimated to be in need of family planning services.

20 July 1970
JUDICIAL.   The Justice Department files suit charging job discrimination against women; Libbey-Owens-Ford Company is accused of hiring women at lower paying jobs than men and firing women first when layoffs occur.

10 August 1970
LEGISLATIVE.   In a vote of 350–15, the U.S. House of Representatives passes a proposed Equal Rights Amendment (ERA), the first time the House has voted on the ERA since it was introduced in 1923.

WOMEN'S ISSUES.   Betty Furness is named head of the New York State Consumer Protection Board.

13 August 1970
JUDICIAL. The American Civil Liberties Union represents a group of ABC-TV newswomen who charge that they have been discriminated against on the basis of gender.

15 August 1970
SPORTS. Patricia Palinkas of the Orlando Panthers is the first woman to play professional football in a game against the Bridgeport Jets.

23 August 1970
WOMEN'S ISSUES. A Susan B. Anthony stamp is issued by the U.S. Postal Service in honor of women and equality.

26 August 1970
WOMEN'S ISSUES. A 24-hour general strike is declared by many American women to honor the 50th anniversary of ratification of the Nineteenth Amendment. Feminists call for American women to unite "against the concrete conditions of their oppression."

1 September 1970
IDEAS/BELIEFS. Members of the Black Panthers, Women's, and Gay Liberation movements adjourn the first session of their "Revolutionary People's Constitutional Convention," in Philadelphia, Pennsylvania.

7 September 1970
SPORTS. After Orlando Panthers' female football player Pat Palinkas drops a pass, a male teammate, Wally Florence, states, "I'm out here trying to make a living and she's trying to make a folly of a man's game."

15 September 1970
WOMEN'S ISSUES. Phyllis F. Shantz is the first woman member of the Secret Service auxiliary formed to guard the president and his family in the Washington, D.C., area. She is the first of several women to join the Executive Protection Service.

17 September 1970
RELIGION. Seven hundred members of the Roman Catholic World Congress wind up a 5-day meeting, and some delegates call for backing a serious study of a female priesthood.

23 September 1970
SPORTS. The first Virginia Slims Tennis Tournament is held in Houston, Texas. This is the first time women professional tennis players have held a tournament separate from male players. Gladys Heldman, publisher of *World Tennis* magazine, is a primary organizer of the event.

24 September 1970
DEATHS. Edna Fischel Gellhorn, a founder of the League of Women Voters, dies in St. Louis, Missouri.

29 September 1970
POLITICS. Black lawyer Gwen Cherry is elected to the Florida House of Representatives. She is a member of the board of directors of the National Organization for Women.

4 October 1970
POPULAR CULTURE. Rhythm-and-blues and rock singer Janis Joplin dies in Los Angeles of acute heroin-morphine intoxication.

13 October 1970
CRIME. Black militant Angela Davis is arrested by the FBI following a 2-month hunt. She is sought in connection with the slaying of a California judge in August.

WOMEN'S ISSUES. Passage of the Equal Rights Amendment is jeopardized by addition of a rider to allow "nonpartisan prayer" in public schools.

14 October 1970
WOMEN'S ISSUES. A bomb explosion rips through Harvard University's Center for International Affairs in Cambridge, Massachusetts. Responsibility for the blast is claimed by the "Proud Eagle Tribe," a group of revolutionary women.

17 October 1970
RELIGION. Seven hundred deputies of the Protestant Episcopal Church narrowly defeat a motion to permit ordination of women to the priesthood. Those urging its passage note that 51 percent of church membership is female. Episcopal women attending the triennial convention in Houston, Texas, had voted 3 days earlier, 222–45 in favor of women's ordination.

22 October 1970
RELIGION. After actions pass that permit women to serve as deputies in the Protestant Episcopal Church House of Deputies, the group passes a bylaw permitting ordination of women deacons, the lowest rank in the Episcopal ministry.

24 October 1970
RELIGION. The American Lutheran Church votes 560–414 to approve the ordination of women.

29 October 1970
EDUCATION. A report issued by the Carnegie Commission on Higher Education calls for medical schools to provide more opportunities to women and minorities.

Leontyne Price, 1927–

Black soprano Leontyne Price was born Lary Violet Leontine in Laurel, Mississippi, on 10 February 1927. Her parents, James A. and Kate (Baker) Price, instilled a love of music in their daughter from an early age, and she sang at both school and church. Upon graduating from Oak Park High School in 1944, she entered Central State College in Wilberforce, Ohio. After earning a B.A. in June 1948, she traveled to New York City, where she studied at the Juilliard School of Music on a four-year scholarship.

It was at Juilliard that Price was noticed by Virgil Thompson, who had her sing the role of Saint Cecelia in his *Four Saints in Three Acts.* Following that, Price appeared as Bess in George Gershwin's *Porgy and Bess* both in the United States and on tour in Europe. During this time, Price married baritone William C. Warfield on 31 August 1952.

Price made her Town Hall recital in November 1954 and the following February was the first black opera star to appear on television in an NBC-TV production of *Tosca.* Numerous other debuts in a wide range of roles followed. She appeared in *Aïda* at the Vienna State Opera in 1958, and again in that role at La Scala in 1960. In January 1961, Price became the fifth black opera singer to perform in a major role at the Metropolitan Opera in New York City. Five years later, she performed at the opening of the new Metropolitan Opera House at New York's Lincoln Center for the Performing Arts in Barber's *Antony and Cleopatra.*

By 1970 Price had given 118 Metropolitan Opera performances and turned more and more frequently to recitals, appearing in many programs around the world. As late as February 1975, she sang the role of Manon Lescaut for the first time. In October 1977, she appeared at the San Francisco Opera in Strauss' *Ariadne auf Naxos;* her performance brought her wide critical acclaim.

For more than two decades, she has recorded many different types of music, from spirituals to popular songs to complete arias, all on the RCA label. She has won many Grammy Awards and is a member of the American Academy of Arts and Sciences. She has also received the Presidential Freedom Medal (1964), and was given the NAACP's coveted Spingarn Award in 1965.

After nearly twenty-five years of singing with the Metropolitan Opera, Price announced her retirement and made her final appearance at the Met in early 1985.

3 November 1970
POLITICS.   Gertrude W. Donahey is elected treasurer of the state of Ohio. It is the first time a woman has won state office in Ohio.

POLITICS.   Twelve women are elected to Congress, the largest number since 1960. Newly elected members are Bella Abzug (D-New York), Ella T. Grasso (D-Connecticut), and Louise Day Hicks (D-Massachusetts).

5 November 1970
MILITARY.   Navy Commander Robin L. Quigley is named to succeed Captain Rita Lenihan as the eighth head of the Women Appointed for Voluntary Emergency Service.

23 November 1970
LABOR.   The American Association of University Women reports that women do not have equal status with men in the academic world. The report indicates that women make up 22 percent of faculty in the nation's colleges and universities, but only 9 percent hold the rank of full professor.

29 November 1970
IDEAS/BELIEFS.   According to a Gallup poll, 40 percent of the nation's adults favor legalized abortions during the first 3 months of a pregnancy.

7 December 1970
JUDICIAL.   The Justice Department has successfully concluded a suit against Libbey-Owens-Ford Company, which was charged with sex discrimination. The government filed a consent decree, under which the company agrees to correct certain discriminatory employment practices.

10 December 1970
LABOR.   The Equal Employment Opportunity Commission recommends that American Telephone & Telegraph requests for a rate hike be denied because of the company's gross discrimination against women, blacks, and Hispanics.

27 December 1970
IDEAS/BELIEFS.   Susan LaMont, chair of the Young Socialist Alliance, opens the group's tenth annual convention. LaMont claims the organization has quadrupled in size since 1967, with nearly 5,000 members nationwide.

OTHER EVENTS OF 1970

SPORTS.   Shirley Fry Irvin is inducted into the National Lawn Tennis Hall of Fame.

POPULAR CULTURE.   Academy Awards for 1969 go to Maggie Smith, *The Prime of Miss Jean Brodie,* and Goldie Hawn, *Cactus Flower,* for Best Actress and Best Supporting Actress, respectively.

VIII

A Decade of Optimism and Growth
1971–1980

By far the most evident shifts in women's roles in America occurred during the 1970s as more women took a more active role in the political, economic, and cultural fabric of society. In the 1960s, women's increased participation in the work force and in politics provoked a snowball effect that manifested itself most fully in the following decade. By the mid-1970s there were many firsts for women in virtually every sphere—sports, science, medicine, religion, the military. The federal government responded to women's demands for equal treatment in a variety of ways, from eliminating gender discrimination in advertising and hiring for public jobs to legalizing abortion in the landmark Supreme Court decision *Roe* v. *Wade*. The latter brought American women a step closer to the total reproductive freedom for all women demanded by feminists.

The 1970s brought the first women FBI agents, Episcopal Church priests, Jewish rabbis, regularly scheduled commercial airline pilots, and state governors elected in their own right. Jeanne M. Holm became the first woman major general in the U.S. Army. And Roslyn Yalow won the prestigious Albert D. Lasker prize for her medical research. Another woman was literally in the news—Barbara Walters became the first female network news anchor, signing a $1-million-per-year contract.

Ms. magazine was launched in 1972, and the U.S. Government Printing Office accepted the title Ms. for use in federal publications. Another significant launching was of the STOP-ERA movement, a conservative response to the Equal Rights Amendment ratification drive that became a major force in the failure of the amendment to gain nationwide approval. Also, an avowed lesbian won election to public office in Massachusetts, a black woman was admitted to the Daughters of the American Revolution, and Sonia Johnson was excommunicated from the Mormon Church for her profoundly feminist views and her support of the Equal Rights Amendment.

In sports, Billie Jean King achieved prominence and led a successful campaign for establishment of a women's professional tennis circuit. She also delighted her fans in 1973 by defeating male tennis player Bobby Riggs in the much-publicized "Battle of the Sexes" tennis match. A different type of gender conflict ensued throughout the decade as female flight attendants at virtually all major airlines demanded legal redress for job discrimination. The flight attendants called for an end to differing standards of employment for women and men carrying out the same tasks. Military academies in all branches of the armed forces admitted women in 1976, and the first coed classes graduated four years later. In 1978, the National Aeronautics and Space Administration named six women astronauts for the Space Shuttle flights scheduled to begin in the early 1980s.

But there were still limitations to women's full and equal participation in American life. Despite a 10.6 percent increase in women in the labor force between 1950 and 1970, most Americans ended the decade as they began it, uncomfortable with the concept of working wives and mothers. And the U.S. Senate became an all-male body for a brief time beginning in 1972, when Senator Margaret Chase Smith of Maine lost her bid for reelection.

Probably the biggest disappointment to feminists during the 1970s was the failure to ratify the ERA. Congress granted an extension until June 1982, but ERA supporters worried that momentum built up during the decade would not sustain itself indefinitely. And poor women were often unable, even as late as 1980, to obtain adequate medical care, including abortions, despite apparent supports to the Medicaid program and to other federal health projects.

American women achieved a great deal during the 1970s, particularly in comparison to previous decades. But they looked ahead to the 1980s with realization of a greater need for adjustment in the legal, social, and economic structure of the nation. Whether women could effect the changes necessary through legislative and other acceptable means would require continued optimism, support, and involvement at levels from grass roots on up, by both men and women working together. The 1970s fostered growth and opportunity for reform and set the stage for continued progress during the next ten years. Women across the nation knew that they needed to put their hope into action in order to guarantee that the promise of the previous years would not be lost.

11 January 1971
EDUCATION. The College of the Holy Cross, a Roman Catholic institution in Worcester, Massachusetts, announces that it will admit women students beginning in 1972.

21 January 1971
POLITICS. Bella S. Abzug (D-New York) begins her first term in the U.S. House of Representatives.

25 January 1971
JUDICIAL. The U.S. Supreme Court rules that companies cannot deny employment to women with preschool children unless the same criteria apply to men.

21 February 1971
SPORTS. The $60,000 Sears Women's World Classic is won by golfer Ruth Jensen.

26 February 1971
RELIGION. The National Conference of Catholic Bishops endorses ordination of women deacons in the Roman Catholic Church.

8 March 1971
JUDICIAL. The Supreme Court rules that South Carolina does not discriminate against men by maintaining Winthrop College (all

female), since the state also supports all-male and coed schools.

11 March 1971

WOMEN'S ISSUES. President Nixon grants a 75-minute interview to 9 women news correspondents. Two dozen other women reporters excluded from the session stage a protest at the White House.

26 March 1971

LABOR. General Electric Company files suit for clarification of conflicts in federal and state employment laws regarding women.

27 March 1971

SPORTS. A New York State Education Department law goes into effect, permitting girls to compete as members of boys' teams in noncontact sports.

6 April 1971

POLITICS. Ilona Hancock, a San Francisco, California, homemaker, is elected to a seat on the city council.

8 April 1971

MILITARY. Second Lieutenant Susan M. Ocobock is the first woman military engineer in the U.S. Air Force.

WOMEN'S ISSUES. Four women are the first to graduate from the U.S. Treasury Department's Sky Marshall program.

24 April 1971

VIETNAM WAR. Women's liberation supporters join an antiwar protest of an estimated 500,000 people in Washington, D.C.

28 April 1971

WOMEN'S ISSUES. Seven members of the National Organization for Women call a news conference at which they denounce the Catholic Church as a "sexist institution."

12 May 1971

LABOR. The Civil Service Commission rules the sex specification of "men only" and "women only" in federal jobs must be eliminated.

14 May 1971

WOMEN'S ISSUES. Julie Price of Oklahoma, Paulette Desell of New York, and Ellen McConnell of Illinois are sworn in as the U.S. Senate's first female pages.

17 May 1971

LEGISLATIVE. Washington state enacts the first law in the nation to ban gender discrimination in employment. The law is effective 1 July.

27 May 1971

POLITICS. The Democratic National Committee reports that the percentage of women in policy-level federal jobs has increased by only 2 percent in the past 3 years.

1 June 1971

JUDICIAL. The 9th U.S. Circuit Court of Appeals rules that California laws permitting sex discrimination in employment violate the 1964 Civil Rights Act.

3 June 1971

CIVIL RIGHTS. Representative Shirley S. Chisholm (D-New York) states her knowledge of racial tension between Germans and U.S. black military personnel stationed in West Germany.

17 June 1971

MILITARY. Jeanne M. Holm is named to the rank of brigadier general in the U.S. Air Force. She is the first woman to reach this status in this branch of the armed forces.

10 July 1971

POLITICS. More than 200 women meet in the nation's capital to form the National Women's Political Caucus. Its goal is equal representation of men and women at all levels of the nation's political system.

12 July 1971

WOMEN'S ISSUES. Catherine M. Bedell is the first woman appointed chair of the U.S. Tariff Commission.

13 July 1971

RELIGION. The Lutheran Church–Missouri Synod votes to ask the church to reconsider its 1970 approval of ordination of women, declaring that "the word of God does not permit women to . . . exercise authority over men."

6 August 1971
WOMEN'S ISSUES. Senator Birch Bayh (D-Indiana) attempts to have the Equal Rights Amendment on the calendar for floor consideration, but his action is blocked by Senator Sam Ervin (D-North Carolina).

10 August 1971
WOMEN'S ISSUES. The Justice Department announces plans for a $500,000 model rehabilitation program for female inmates of federal, state, and city prisons.

21 August 1971
SPORTS. Sixteen-year-old Laura Baugh is the youngest winner of the U.S. Women's Amateur Golf tournament.

22 August 1971
SPORTS. Kerry Kleid is the first woman to be licensed as a professional motorcyclist.

24 August 1971
WOMEN'S ISSUES. Brereton Sturtevant is sworn in as the first woman examiner-in-chief of the U.S. Patent and Trademark Office.

26 August 1971
SUFFRAGE. Thousands of women march and rally nationwide in celebration of the 51st anniversary of woman suffrage.

6 September 1971
WOMEN'S ISSUES. More than 750 registered delegates and 200 observers attend the fifth national conference of the National Organization for Women in Los Angeles, California. NOW currently claims 15,000 members in 180 chapters throughout the country.

9 September 1971
LABOR. The Justice Department asks a federal court in East St. Louis, Illinois, to bring a suit of discrimination against the Obear-Nester Glass Company for job discrimination toward women and blacks.

Maggie Kuhn, 1905–

An ardent crusader for the rights of aged citizens, Maggie Kuhn was born in Buffalo, New York, on 3 August 1905. The daughter of Samuel F. and Minnie (Kooman) Kuhn, she lived with her family in Cleveland, Buffalo, and Memphis, but graduated from West High School in Cleveland, Ohio, in 1922. She attended Case Western Reserve University, graduating with a B.A. in English and sociology in 1926. Subsequently, Kuhn worked to improve conditions for women YWCA employees while working as a publications editor for the YWCA in New York City.

Her social conscience was well developed, even for that time period. She worked for the United Presbyterian Church: She wrote and edited *Social Progress,* a church journal. Kuhn admittedly made many attempts to challenge the existing church bureaucracy, and by 1970 she was urging the Presbyterian Church to mount an attack against *agism,* which she termed discrimination against an individual on the basis of age alone. Earlier, Kuhn had been active in the Vietnam-era protests. During this time she helped organize a group known as "Consultation of Older and Younger Adults for Social Change." Her concern was to find ways to bridge communications difficulties between age groups. In 1970, she faced mandatory retirement from the United Presbyterian Church.

In 1971, Kuhn was a speaker at the White House Conference on Aging, and

An ardent activist for the elderly, Maggie Kuhn, founder of the Gray Panthers, maintains an active schedule, operating from the organization's headquarters in Philadelphia. (Photo courtesy Gray Panthers)

Consultation for Social Change was dubbed the "Gray Panthers" by the news media, which saw parallels with the militant black-power group, the "Black Panthers." The Gray Panthers began lobbying for legislation to improve the nation's nursing homes, and in July 1973, Kuhn testified before a Senate Special Committee on Aging; she testified again in 1977 before the House Select Committee on Aging. Kuhn pointed out on these and many other occasions that America's elderly citizens represented the nation's greatest untapped resource.

In 1975, she received a service award from the American Speech and Hearing Association, in recognition of her lobbying for legislation to benefit those who wear hearing aids. Other awards she has received include the United Presbyterian Peace Fellowship Peaceseeker Award in 1977 and the Humanist of the Year Award from the American Humanist Association in 1978. Also in 1978, the Gray Panthers held its second biennial convention in Chevy Chase, Maryland. More than 350 delegates attended the convention, at which the Gray Panthers stated their opposition to customary mandatory retirement policies at most businesses and corporations across the nation.

Kuhn has been an advisor to the television series "Over Easy," which deals with issues related to age. And she appears regularly as a speaker at a wide variety of public and private functions. Kuhn maintains offices for the Gray Panthers in Philadelphia, Pennsylvania.

---

18 September 1971
POLITICS. The National Women's Political Caucus urges President Nixon to consider a woman appointee to the Supreme Court to fill a vacancy created by the retirement of Associate Justice Hugo Black.

26 September 1971
POLITICS. Representative Shirley S. Chisholm (D-New York) announces that she will enter the Democratic presidential primaries.

1 October 1971
WOMEN'S ISSUES. The 12 female members of Congress urge President Nixon to appoint one of "several highly qualified women" to the existing U.S. Supreme Court vacancy.

7 October 1971
POLITICS. Shirley Chisholm states that her decision to enter the presidential primaries is to guarantee that the Democratic nominee selection will not be a "white, male decision."

12 October 1971
LEGISLATIVE. By a 354–23 vote margin, the House approves and sends to the Senate an Equal Rights Amendment. The House rejects a proposal to include military draft exemptions for women in the proposed amendment.

29 October 1971
RELIGION. The bishops of the Protestant Episcopal Church end a 6-day session in Pennsylvania at which they discuss issues including that of the priesthood for women.

9 November 1971
JUDICIAL. The Supreme Court lets stand a U.S. circuit court decision ruling that company pension plans requiring women to retire earlier than their male counterparts were a violation of federal civil rights law. The Supreme Court ruling applies only in Indiana, Illinois, and Wisconsin, the jurisdictions of the 7th Circuit Court.

22 November 1971
JUDICIAL. The U.S. Supreme Court overturns legislation in *Reed* v. *Reed* that made a distinction based on sex in a case involving male estate executors.

1 December 1971
LABOR. In a 20,000-page report to the Federal Communications Commission, the Equal Employment Opportunity Commission charges that AT&T is guilty of job discrimination against women, blacks, and Hispanics. The

report terms AT&T, with nearly 1 million employees, "the largest oppressor of women workers in the United States."

3 December 1971
LABOR. The Equal Employment Opportunity Commission (EEOC) asks the Interstate Commerce Commission to ban hiring biases among 15,000 interstate trucking firms employing more than 1 million workers. The EEOC charges discrimination against women, blacks, and Hispanics.

4 December 1971
LABOR. The Department of Health, Education, and Welfare suspends federal contracts with Columbia University in New York City. These contracts, totaling $688,000, are suspended pending the outcome of charges that the university failed to submit an affirmative action plan to the federal government.

6 December 1971
WOMEN'S ISSUES. The Senate confirms Ramona Acosta Banuelos as treasurer of the United States.

OTHER EVENTS OF 1971

WOMEN'S ISSUES. President Nixon vetoes the proposed Child and Family Services Act, which would have provided federal support for child care programs.

SPORTS. Althea Gibson Darben, the first black woman tennis player to win the U.S. Open and Wimbledon championships in 1957 and 1958, and Elizabeth Moor are named to the National Lawn Tennis Hall of Fame.

POPULAR CULTURE. Oscars for 1970 go to Glenda Jackson, *Women in Love,* and Helen Hayes, *Airport,* for Best Actress and Best Supporting Actress, respectively.

13 January 1972
JUDICIAL. The New York State Court of Appeals finds that Bernice Gera, a professional baseball umpire, has the legal right to hold that position if she so chooses.

20 January 1972
WOMEN'S ISSUES. In his State-of-the-Union address, President Nixon vows to support

further equal opportunity for women in government and industry.

27 January 1972
DEATHS. Black gospel singer Mahalia Jackson dies in Evergreen Park, Illinois.

3 February 1972
LABOR. The Project on Corporate Responsibility announces expansion of its reform program. The project will target companies that allegedly practice job discrimination.

7 February 1972
POLITICS. Senator Margaret Chase Smith (R-Maine) announces her bid for election for a fifth term of office. She is currently the only woman in the U.S. Senate.

10 February 1972
WOMEN'S ISSUES. Outstanding Volunteer of 1971, Arnette Peters Giles, age 70, receives a $5,000 prize from President Nixon in ceremonies at Washington's Kennedy Center for the Performing Arts.

13 February 1972
POLITICS. In Nashville, Tennessee, nearly 400 women from 12 southern states meet at a conference called Women's Education for Delegate Selection. The group plans to work for changes in Democratic party delegate selection procedures.

28 February 1972
LEGISLATIVE. The U.S. Senate approves a 5-year education bill that will bar sex discrimination in all coed colleges and universities receiving federal funding.

29 February 1972
LABOR. The Department of Health, Education, and Welfare (HEW) accepts Columbia University's interim report on plans to comply with sexual and minority job rights requirements. HEW will now lift its freeze on federal contracts with the university.

20 March 1972
POPULAR CULTURE. A special issue of *Time* magazine is published entitled, "The American Woman."

22 March 1972
LEGISLATIVE. The U.S. Senate approves the Equal Rights Amendment by a vote of 84–8. It now goes to the states for a two-thirds majority ratification procedure.

27 March 1972
JUDICIAL. The trial of Angela Davis, a black militant accused of murder, kidnapping, and conspiracy, begins in San Jose, California.

28 March 1972
SPORTS. The New Jersey State Interscholastic Athletic Association approves a pilot program in which girls would be allowed to try out for varsity sports teams along with boys.

SCIENCE. Organizations representing 30,000 women scientists file a suit of sex discrimination against the National Institutes of Health (NIH). The plaintiffs charge that the percentage of women on all NIH advisory panels dropped from 5.4 percent in 1968 to 4.2 percent in 1971.

3 April 1972
JUDICIAL. The Supreme Court rules that unwed fathers as well as unwed mothers have the right to prove their fitness as parents before they can be denied custody of their children born out of wedlock.

8 April 1972
SPORTS. A group of 11 women parachutists perform a daring jump in which they form a star by all joining hands at 5,000 feet.

12 April 1972
SPORTS. Bernice Gera gets an umpire's contract with the association that governs minor league baseball. The contract goes to the National Association of Professional Baseball Leagues for approval. Gera had been denied a similar contract in 1969.

17 April 1972
SPORTS. Nina Kuscik is the first woman to run officially in the Boston Marathon. She finishes ahead of 800 male runners and 8 other women. Kathy Switzer had run unofficially in the 1968 Boston Marathon.

18 April 1972

LEGISLATIVE. A dozen women disrupt proceedings of the New York State Assembly, protesting the legalization of abortion in New York and demanding repeal of that state's abortion legislation.

22 April 1972

ARTS AND CULTURE. In Washington, D.C., more than 350 women wind up the first national conference for Women in the Visual Arts at the Corcoran Gallery.

27 April 1972

MILITARY. Alene B. Duerk, director of the Navy Nurse Corps, is named the first woman admiral in U.S. history.

11 May 1972

WOMEN'S ISSUES. The FBI announces that it will begin recruiting women for positions as special agents. The FBI names Barbara Lynn Herwig as special assistant in the Justice Department's Civil Division. She is the first woman to hold a major post in the FBI.

16 May 1972

LABOR. Fifty women editorial workers file a sex discrimination complaint against *Newsweek* magazine at the New York office of the Equal Employment Opportunity Commission.

31 May 1972

RELIGION. Union Theological Seminary's board of directors votes to require that one-half of its students, faculty, staff, and directors be women.

3 June 1972

RELIGION. Sally J. Priesand, the first woman rabbi in the United States and the second in the history of Judaism, is ordained in Cincinnati, Ohio.

7 June 1972

BUSINESS. Juanita Kreps is the first woman member of the New York Stock Exchange's board of directors.

Gloria Steinem, 1934–

Eloquent spokesperson and dedicated fighter for feminist goals in the United States, Gloria Steinem is descended from early twentieth-century suffrage leader Pauline Steinem. The daughter of Leo and Ruth (Nuneville) Steinem, she was born on 25 March 1934, in Toledo, Ohio, and she describes her childhood in bleak terms. Upon graduation from high school in 1952 she entered Smith College in Massachusetts. She received a B.A. degree, graduating magna cum laude in 1956. Steinem then studied in India for two years on a Chester Bowles fellowship. On her return to the United States, she worked as a researcher in Cambridge, Massachusetts, moving to New York City in 1960.

As a freelance writer in New York, Steinem was published in *Esquire* magazine. In 1963, she landed a one-month job as a Playboy Club bunny in order to write an exposé about the work as a hostess. Soon, her articles appeared in many different national magazines and she worked, in addition, as a scriptwriter at NBC-TV. Having majored in government at Smith College, Steinem was eager to write about U.S. politics. In 1968, she covered both the Democratic and the GOP presidential conventions, and came out in support of Robert Kennedy. She also became a contributing editor of *New York* magazine that year. By 1970 Steinem had aligned herself with the growing numbers of women who supported equal rights for both men and women.

Along with Betty Friedan, she helped organize the Women's Strike for Equality, held in August 1970. She was also a founder—along with Shirley Chisholm and Bella Abzug—of the National Women's Political Caucus. In 1971, Steinem became a founder and board member of the Women's Action Alliance.

Perhaps Steinem's most memorable, far-reaching, and lasting accomplishment was the launching, with Patricia Carbine, of *Ms.* magazine. Beginning publication in January 1972, *Ms.* magazine had by 1985 boosted its circulation to five hundred thousand a month, an overwhelming majority of which were paid subscriptions. Steinem continues to write extensively in many publications in addition to her responsibilities as editor of *Ms.* She is a sought-after speaker who appears on college campuses, before civic and political groups, and at other gatherings. She was named Woman of the Year by *McCall's* magazine in 1972 and has since appeared with regularity on lists of the most admired women in the nation. In 1984, she published *Outrageous Acts and Everyday Rebellions,* a collection of her essays and articles. Her biography of Marilyn Monroe was published in 1986.

Steinem has often been criticized as an enemy of traditional family values. She was a key supporter of the now-defunct Equal Rights Amendment and worked hard to promote reproductive freedom as a basic human right. A controlled, gracious, and meticulously well-prepared lecturer, Steinem often uses her dry wit to make a point and has disarmed many detractors with her sense of humor and gift for wry understatement. Of her long-term goals, Steinem was once quoted as hoping to be recalled as a fighter who "tried to humanize two caste systems that divide us most deeply—sex and race."

---

23 June 1972
POLITICS. After learning that the black caucus within the Democratic National Convention Rules Committee prefers a black for committee vice-chair, Representative Patsy Mink (Hawaii) withdraws her name from consideration. Mink is the first woman Japanese-American representative in U.S. history.

24 June 1972
SPORTS. Bernice Gera, the first woman umpire, resigns several hours after officiating at her first pro baseball game in Auburn, New York. Gera charges that "threats" she had encountered influenced her decision to resign.

25 June 1972
POLITICS. According to a *New York Times* tabulation, Representative Shirley S. Chisholm (D-New York) receives 28.65 percent of the votes for Democratic presidential nominee.

10 July 1972
JUDICIAL. A Chicago district court overturns a Board of Education ruling requiring pregnant teachers to take a 6-month unpaid leave after their fifth month of pregnancy.

14 July 1972
POLITICS. Frances Jean Miles Westwood of Utah becomes the first woman to chair the Democratic National Committee.

LABOR. Thirty-five newspapers in Connecticut seek a court order allowing them to continue classifying employment advertisements by gender.

17 July 1972
WOMEN'S ISSUES. Susan L. Roley and Joanne E. Pierce are sworn in as the first women FBI agents.

WOMEN'S ISSUES. Dixy Lee Ray is appointed to the Atomic Energy Commission; she is the first woman to be named to a full 5-year term. She is confirmed as a member on 2 August.

7 August 1972
MILITARY. The Women's Army Corps announces a decision to increase the 13,320 WAC force to 24,000 by June 1978.

8 August 1972
MILITARY. The U.S. Navy announces that women in the naval force will soon be named to general sea duty assignments.

11 August 1972
MILITARY. Colonel Norma E. Brown takes command of a mixed-gender unit of the U.S. Air Force at Fort Meade, Maryland.

Shirley Chisholm, 1924–

Former Congresswoman Shirley S. Chisholm, who ran for president of the United States on the Democratic ticket in the nation's primaries in 1972. Chisholm is currently on the faculty of Mount Holyoke College in Massachusetts. (Photo courtesy Shirley S. Chisholm)

An outspoken and energetic champion of minorities, the poor, and the undereducated, Shirley Chisholm was elected to the U.S. House of Representatives in 1968 from New York's twelfth district. In 1972, she became the first black woman to make a serious bid for the presidency of the United States, running as a Democrat in the nation's primaries. Born Shirley Anita St. Hill on 30 November 1924, in Brooklyn, New York, she was the daughter of Charles C. and Ruby (Seale) St. Hill. As a young child, she went to live with her maternal grandmother on Barbados. She was schooled with discipline, Christian virtue, and love, learning early to work hard and to take pride in her accomplishments. She learned to read at age three-and-a-half and to write at age four, which she credits to the Barbados school system.

After returning to the United States in late childhood, St. Hill graduated from high school and entered Brooklyn College. She earned a B.A. cum laude in sociology in 1945. Subsequently, she attended Columbia University while working as a child care aide, and earned an M.A. in education. On 8 October 1949, she married Conrad Q. Chisholm, a Jamaican. By 1953 Chisholm had been named director of a private day nursery in the Brownsville section of Brooklyn. The following year she moved to a directorship at Hamilton-Madison Child Care Center, an administrative post she held until 1959. This experience, as well as her efforts to become involved in local politics, helped her develop a reputation as a dedicated worker with high personal standards.

In 1964, Chisholm won a state assembly seat from Brooklyn; she was the first black woman to represent that district. She won again in 1965 and 1966, and was credited with supporting a series of education bills designed to benefit both the very young and the college-age student. Chisholm also took particular interest in the needs of domestic workers. In early 1968, Chisholm announced her intention to run for the U.S. House of Representatives from the twelfth district, which had been recently reapportioned and was now heavily Democrat, Puerto Rican, and black. She won by a margin of 2½:1, beating veteran U.S. Representative James Farmer.

Chisholm, a long-time foe of defense spending, worked hard to secure increased federal aid to state welfare departments, and she spoke out in favor of women in politics. In 1970, she published an autobiography, *Unbought and Unbossed*. The following year she was named to the House Education and Labor Committee, where she was able to draw on her years of professional experience.

In 1972, Chisholm announced her desire to win the Democratic presidential nomination. She campaigned long and hard, winning respect and recognition from virtually all quarters, although she had few illusions about her chances for victory. Chisholm proved, however, to women and to black Americans, the possibility of setting a goal and striving for it, no matter what the odds. In *The Good Fight* (1973), she details the experience of her campaign.

In 1976, Chisholm became the first woman and first black to serve on the House Rules Committee. Chisholm announced her retirement from public office in February 1982, and stated her desire to lecture, write, and teach. In the summer of that year, Mount Holyoke College in Massachusetts revealed that Chisholm had accepted its Purrington Professorship. She began her tenure at the school in February 1983. She maintained an active role in political campaigning, however, speaking out in favor of Jesse Jackson in the 1984 presidential race. Besides her two books, Chisholm has written numerous articles, and has received at least thirty honorary degrees.

---

23 August 1972
POLITICS. The Republican National Convention closes in Miami Beach, Florida. Of the 1,348 delegates, 29.8 percent were women.

25 August 1972
NATIONAL. George McGovern names 5 women as top campaign aides. They are Anne Martindell, Frances T. Farenthold, Anne Wexler, Bella Abzug, and Shirley MacLaine.

11 September 1972
WOMEN'S ISSUES. The first women graduates of the FBI police training school are Susan Roley and Joanne Pierce. They had been sworn into the FBI in July.

17 September 1972
RELIGION. In Northfield, Connecticut, Reverend Davida Crabtree is ordained in a ceremony at the United Church of Christ, in which all principals are women.

1 October 1972
SPORTS. Billie Jean King once again passes the $100,000 earnings mark by beating Margaret Court in the finals of the Virginia Slims

Tournament in Phoenix, Arizona. King was the first female tennis player to break $100,000 in 1971.

6 October 1972
MILITARY.   The Coast Guard announces it will accept women as officer candidates for the first time since World War II.

10 October 1972
JUDICIAL.   The U.S. Supreme Court announces that it will hear the case of Lieutenant Sharron A. Frontiero of the U.S. Air Force, who contends the constitutionality of military regulations denying male armed forces spouses the same benefits that wives of servicemen regularly receive.

15 October 1972
NATIONAL LABOR.   Census Bureau statistics indicate that in 1970, 39.6 percent of

all women over age 14 were in the labor force compared with 29 percent in 1950.

7 November 1972
POLITICS.   Barbara Jordan (D-Texas), Elizabeth Holtzmann (D-New York), Yvonne Braithwaite Burke (D-California), Pat Schroeder (D-Colorado), and Marjorie Holt (R-Maryland) are elected to the U.S. House, bringing the total of women there to 14.

POLITICS.   Republican Senator Margaret Chase Smith loses her bid for a fifth term as Senator from Maine, leaving the U.S. Senate with an all-male membership.

20 November 1972
DEATHS.   Hotel executive and entrepreneur Jennie Grossinger dies in New York.

Phyllis Schlafly, 1924–

Conservative opponent of the Equal Rights Amendment, Phyllis Schlafly, leader of the STOP-ERA movement. (Photo courtesy Phyllis Schlafly)

Of right-wing, ultraconservative individuals intent on blocking the goals of contemporary feminists, Phyllis Schlafly is perhaps the most outspoken and best known. Born Phyllis Stewart on 15 August 1924, in St. Louis, Missouri, she was the daughter of engineer John B. Stewart and his wife, Odile (Dodge) Stewart. She attended Roman Catholic schools and, after graduating first in her high school class of 1941, she entered Maryville College of the Sacred Heart. Transferring to Washington University, she was named to Phi Beta Kappa, received a bachelor's degree in 1944, and entered Radcliffe College in Cambridge, Massachusetts. She worked toward an M.A. in political science, which she received in 1945.

After graduation, she held a succession of jobs, including work as a campaign aide to Congressman Claude I. Bakewell (R-Missouri). On 20 October 1949, she married John F. Schlafly, Jr., a lawyer and political conservative from Illinois. Schlafly was active in the Republican party, and in 1952, she ran for U.S. Congress from Illinois' twenty-fourth district. Although defeated, she ran again (unsuccessfully) in 1960 after aligning herself closely with conservative, anticommunist groups, such as the Cardinal Mindszenty Foundation, which she helped organize in 1958. She also published a series of reading lists of conservative titles aimed at educating the public about the threat posed by communism.

Schlafly supported Senator Barry Goldwater's 1964 bid for the presidency, and that year wrote *A Choice Not an Echo,* a book about Goldwater. This volume sold more than 3 million copies. Schlafly continued to publish anti-Russian, pro-defense books throughout the 1960s, attacking liberals and blaming the Soviets for urban ghetto riots that plagued the United States in 1967.

Although she had been elected vice-president of the National Federation of Republican Women in 1964, her conservative stance led to her defeat for the presidency of that group in 1967. She then established the Eagle Trust Fund and started publishing the *Phyllis Schlafly Report*; both efforts were designed to build support for conservative political candidates nationwide. In 1970, Schlafly ran for the third time for Congress in Illinois, failing again.

In 1972, Schlafly turned her attention to the Equal Rights Amendment. Mounting a vociferous campaign, she fought ratification of the Constitutional amendment, setting up chapters of STOP-ERA—a conservative organization for men and women—throughout the country. In addition, she established the Eagle Forum, another group dedicated to defeating feminist goals. The Eagle Forum draws support from church groups, profamily and antichoice organizations, and some groups with reported connections to the right-wing John Birch Society. Schlafly also buttressed her considerably influential position as a conservative leader by earning a J.D. degree from Washington University Law School in 1978. In 1976, she had been granted an honorary Doctor of Laws degree from Niagara University.

Although the liberals of America have criticized Schlafly's seemingly outdated views on women, her organizations have been successful in drawing support from a wide variety of groups. By 1977 Schlafly was able to stage a large anti-ERA rally in Houston, Texas, that was timed to coincide with the National Women's Conference being held in that city. Beginning in 1978 she was named annually to a list of the twenty-five most influential women in the United States by World Almanac publications. Her STOP-ERA efforts were vindicated in 1982, when the ERA was still three states short of approval at the end of the extended period for ratification.

A staunch Republican and avid anti-communist, Schlafly has received many awards, including ten honor medals from the Freedoms Foundation at Valley Forge, Pennsylvania, the Woman of the Year designation from the Illinois Federation of Republican Women (1969), and the Brotherhood Award from the National Conference of Christians and Jews (1975). In 1980, Phyllis Schlafly was named by President Reagan as a member of his Defense Policy Advisory Group.

Schlafly has written many books, including *Kissinger on the Couch* (1975), a criticism of former Secretary of State Kissinger's pro-détente foreign policy, and *The Power of the Positive Woman* (1978), which was a Conservative Book Club selection. Her most recent book is *Child Abuse in the Classroom*. In addition to her writing and public appearances, Schlafly airs radio commentaries on 175 stations nationwide.

---

5 December 1972
BUSINESS. The Rand Corporation announces that 2 women have been named to its 21-member board of directors.

8 December 1972
WOMEN'S ISSUES. The Justice Department announces that Jewel Lafontant, a Chicago lawyer and member of the U.S. delegation to the United Nations, will join the department as a deputy solicitor general.

13 December 1972
AVIATION. Stewardesses for Women's Rights holds a news conference to protest "annoying and degrading" treatment by employers and passengers. The group claims 60 charter members among the nation's 48,000 flight attendants.

OTHER EVENTS OF 1972

Olympic Gold Medals

Micki King: Springboard diving
Sandra Neilson: Swimming—100-meter freestyle
K. Rothhammer: Swimming—800-meter freestyle
Cathy Carr: Swimming—100-meter breaststroke
Karen Moe: Swimming—200-meter butterfly
Melissa Belote: Swimming—100-meter backstroke
Melissa Belote: Swimming—200-meter backstroke
    Swimming—400-meter freestyle relay

women's team medal
    Swimming—400-meter medley relay women's team medal
Doreen Wilbur: Archery
Barbara Cochran: Alpine skiing—women's slalom
Anne Henning: Speed skating—500 meters
Dianne Holum: Speed skating—1,500 meters

Olympic Silver Medals

Shirley Babashoff: Swimming—100-meter freestyle
Shirley Babashoff: Swimming—200-meter freestyle
Dana Schoenfield: Swimming—200-meter breaststroke
Lynn Colella: Swimming—200-meter butterfly
Susie Atwood: Swimming—200-meter backstroke
Kathy Schmidt: Track and Field—javelin throw
    Track and Field—400-meter relay women's team medal

Olympic Bronze Medals

Keena Rothhammer: Swimming—800-meter freestyle
Ellie Daniel: Swimming—200-meter butterfly
Susie Atwood: Swimming—100-meter backstroke
Lynn Vidali: Swimming—200-meter individual medley
Kathy Hammond: Track and Field—400-meter run
Emma Gaptchenko: Archery

Dixy Lee Ray, 1914–

Former Atomic Energy Commission head and ex-governor of Washington state, Dixy Lee Ray has enjoyed an eventful career as a public servant. Born on 3 September 1914, in Tacoma, Washington, she was the daughter of Alvis M. and Frances (Adams) Ray. Her name was derived from a nickname, "The Little Dickens," and she had it legally changed to Dixy Lee when in her teens. A good student with a strong interest in nature, she enrolled in Mills College, majoring in zoology. She graduated with a B.A. in 1937, and in 1938 received an M.A. from Mills.

Ray taught science in California before deciding to pursue a Ph.D. at Stanford, which she earned in 1945. She then taught at the University of Washington and received a Guggenheim Fellowship for the years 1952 and 1953. Her interests and her research led to numerous papers, and by the early 1960s she was known as a supporter of careful, considerate treament of the environment. Between 1960 and 1962, Ray was a consultant to the National Science Foundation, and in 1963, she became assistant to the Foundation's director. In 1969, she was named by President Nixon to a Task Force on Oceanography.

Ray was head of the Pacific Science Center in Seattle, Washington, a position she had assumed in 1963, when President Nixon named her to the Atomic Energy Commission (AEC) in July 1972. She was the first woman to be designated to a full, five-year term of office. The only other woman member of the Commission, Mary I. Bunting, had filled a one-year vacancy between 1964 and 1965. Ray credited public support for the women's movement as the key to her appointment. In February 1973, she was named head of the AEC when James Schlesinger resigned to head the Central Intelligence Agency. She was in charge of a $3-billion agency and had direct responsibility for regulating privately owned nuclear power plants throughout the nation.

Ray, never known for extremely liberal views even when dealing with the environment, supported the need for expansion of nuclear power facilities, a position that brought her into conflict with many environmentalists. Consumer activist Ralph Nader dubbed Ray, "Ms. Plutonium," but she consistently defended her decisions as AEC head. Ray quit the post in 1975, and the following year mounted a successful campaign for governor of Washington state. After her election, she spent a stormy four-year term during which she seemed to anger and alienate most of her former supporters and to further enrage those who opposed her positions.

Ray lost a bid for reelection in 1980, subsequently leaving public life. In 1981, she began broadcasting over Seattle radio station KVI, speaking about environmental issues among other things. She also did private consulting work and announced that she would be working on a book about her term as governor.

Margaret Mead, 1901–1978

America's premier anthropologist and self-appointed overseer of human culture via her contributions to studies of human behavior and generational change, Margaret Mead was born on 16 December 1901, in Philadelphia, Pennsylvania. Her parents, Edward S. and Emily (Fogg) Mead, were dedicated academics—her father taught at the Wharton School and her mother was involved in many research projects. Mead's childhood was uneventful, and in 1919, she attended DePauw University, although she transferred to Barnard College in New York just a year later. At Barnard, Mead discovered her talent for leadership and innovation.

On 3 September 1923, she married Luther Cressman, a student who hoped to enter the ministry. In August 1925, Mead arrived with her husband, by now a sociologist, in Samoa—the first of Mead's many field trips. Her research there was recounted in her book, *Coming of Age in Samoa* (1928). In 1930, she published *Growing Up in New Guinea* and in 1935, she wrote *Sex and Temperament in Three Primitive Societies,* a book later translated into twelve languages.

Mead's work moved more smoothly than her personal life. In July 1928, she divorced Cressman and soon married fellow anthropologist Reo Fortune. The two did field work together but Mead was soon drawn elsewhere, and she divorced Fortune in 1935. Gregory Bateson and Margaret Mead were married on 13 March 1936. He was an avid researcher and the two began a study of Balinese culture. This formed the basis of several joint publications, including *Balinese Character: A Photographic Analysis.* In 1939, Mead's only child, Mary Catherine Bateson, was born.

Mead rapidly became recognized as a leader in her field and received many awards and honors. She was named to the faculty of Columbia University, and in February 1942 she was given a gold medal by the Society of Women Geographers. This award had been given to a woman only once before—to Amelia Earhart Putnam. In the 1940s, Mead published many books and articles, among them *And Keep Your Powder Dry* (1942) and *Male and Female* (1949).

Active in many causes and campaigns, Mead was particularly concerned with nutrition. She worked in various ways to end world hunger and was instrumental in establishing UNESCO. In October 1950, Mead and Bateson were divorced, although they maintained contact throughout the ensuing years. Mead published extensively during the 1950s: *Growth and Culture, The School in American Culture,* and *Soviet Attitudes Toward Authority* (all 1951), *Cultural Patterns and Technical Change* (1954), and *People and Places* (1959). In 1959, Mead also published *An Anthropologist at Work: Writings of Ruth Benedict.*

As time passed, Mead grew in prominence and authority. Consulted on major social issues by educators, government leaders, and religious leaders, she enjoyed her widespread recognition and the publicity it brought her. Some critics felt Mead's popularity was greater than her credentials, but despite these occasional differences of opinion, Mead was acknowledged to be at the pinnacle of her career. She was viewed as one of a handful of premier authorities in her field and was among the most accessible. Mead traveled extensively—to the South Seas, Europe, Asia, and across the United States, speaking, studying, and receiving accolades. She lectured frequently at Emory University, Fordham, Yale, New York University, the University of Cincinnati, and the Menniger Foundation. She published *Blackberry Winter,* an autobiography of her early years, in 1972.

In 1973, Mead was elected to the National Academy of Science, and she was named president of the American Association for the Advancement of Science in 1975. In 1976, she was honored by the establishment of the Margaret Mead Chair of Anthropology at the American Museum of Natural History, with which she had long been associated. In 1978, she wrote *Culture and Commitment: A Study of the Generation Gap.* It was based largely on her previous studies of intergenerational tensions and told how they related to contemporary issues. Increasingly active even as she aged,

Mead expected a great deal of herself and of others. But by the mid-1970s she was suffering from pancreatic cancer and was forced to slow her pace. She entered a New York hospital in October 1978 and died there on 15 November.

EDUCATION. Passage of Title IX of the Educational Amendments Act calls for equal educational opportunities for male and female students in programs receiving federal funds.

ARTS AND CULTURE. Judith Jamison is named to the board of directors of the National Endowment for the Arts.

POPULAR CULTURE. Gloria Steinem and Pat Carbine found *Ms.* magazine, which by 1973 will have a circulation of 350,000 and a readership of 1.4 million.

POPULAR CULTURE. Loretta Lynn gets the Entertainer of the Year Award from the Country Music Association.

POPULAR CULTURE Oscars for 1971 go to Jane Fonda, Best Actress, in *Klute,* and to Cloris Leachman, Best Supporting Actress, in *The Last Picture Show.*

3 January 1973
FINANCE. In a public report, the National Committee on Consumer Finance notes ''widespread instances'' of discrimination in granting consumer credit to women.

4 January 1973
LABOR. The National Labor Relations Board rules that separate local unions for men and women at the same plant do not violate federal law.

6 January 1973
POLITICS. The first electoral vote for a woman is cast for Theodora Nathan of Oregon, a vice-presidential candidate for the Libertarian party.

10 January 1973
MILITARY. The U.S. Navy announces that 8 women have been chosen for naval pilot training in Pensacola, Florida.

12 January 1973
AVIATION. Emily Howell is hired by Frontier Airlines. She is the first woman pilot to work for a scheduled U.S. carrier.

18 January 1973
LABOR. The Equal Employment Opportunity Commission and AT&T reach agreement on a plan for the company to pay $15 million to women and minority male employees as compensation for past discriminatory hiring and promotion practices. AT&T agrees also to develop programs toward a goal of 40 percent women at inside jobs and 19 percent at outside craft jobs.

22 January 1973
JUDICIAL. In a landmark decision, *Roe* v. *Wade,* the U.S. Supreme Court rules that the constitutional right to privacy ''is broad enough to encompass a woman's decision whether or not to terminate her pregnancy.''

MILITARY. Brigadier General Jeanne M. Holm of the U.S. Air Force is promoted to major general. She is now the highest-ranking woman in the U.S. armed services.

1 February 1973
WOMEN'S ISSUES. Joan Wyatt Stewart is named the first woman corrections officer at the Iowa State Penitentiary in Fort Madison, Iowa.

4 February 1973
IDEAS/BELIEFS. A Gallup poll shows that only 21 percent of women sampled feel that a family should have 4 or more children.

6 February 1973
WOMEN'S ISSUES. The Government Printing Office rules that the prefix ''Ms.'' is an acceptable optional identifying label in all government publications.

WOMEN'S ISSUES. After the resignation of James R. Schlesinger, Dixy Lee Ray is designated chair of the Atomic Energy Commission—the first woman in the 27-year history of the agency to assume this responsibility.

9 February 1973
POLITICS. The first convention of the National Women's Political Caucus meets in

Houston, Texas, with more than 1,200 women from 48 states attending. Frances T. Farenthold is voted chair of the caucus on 11 February.

LABOR. The Communications Workers of America petition in U.S. district court to be allowed to intervene against a consent decree under which AT&T agreed to a mass promotion and pay compensation program designed to improve conditions for female workers.

10 February 1973
MILITARY. The New Jersey Department of Defense announces that it will admit women into state national guard units.

16 February 1973
IDEAS/BELIEFS. The 70-man board of directors of the U.S. Jaycees votes to bar women from membership in the organization.

18 February 1973
WOMEN'S ISSUES. The National Organization for Women (NOW) holds its sixth annual convention in Washington, D.C. There are 2,200 delegates from 50 states attending. Wilma Scott Heide is reelected president of NOW.

21 February 1973
WOMEN'S ISSUES. Vermont becomes the 28th state to ratify the proposed Equal Rights Amendment. Approval by 10 more states is needed. The amendment has been ratified by Wyoming, South Dakota, Oregon, Minnesota, New Mexico, Alabama, California, Delaware, Hawaii, Idaho, Iowa, Kansas, Kentucky, Maryland, Mississippi, Massachusetts, Nebraska, New Hampshire, New Jersey, New York, Pennsylvania, Rhode Island, Tennessee, Texas, West Virginia, and Wisconsin.

22 February 1973
WOMEN'S ISSUES. President Nixon reaffirms his support of the proposed Equal Rights Amendment.

1 March 1973
SPORTS. Robyn Smith is the first woman jockey to win in a major stakes race at the Aqueduct Race Track in New York.

23 March 1973
POLITICS. The Democratic National Committee endorses 25 new members, including 8 women.

27 March 1973
EDUCATION. The Michigan Department of Education charges that social studies textbooks present women and Hispanics in an inadequate manner.

25 April 1973
ARTS AND CULTURE. Clare Boothe Luce's satire, *The Women,* opens in a Broadway revival at the 46th Street Theater in New York City.

30 April 1973
SPORTS. In a *Sports Illustrated* article, Westport, Connecticut, Little League chair Mrs. George McCarthy states, ''I wouldn't be against having a Little League for girls, but I think they should be segregated [from boys].''

5 May 1973
SPORTS. Rosemary Casals earns $30,000 by winning the NBC–Family Circle Cup Tennis Tournament in Hilton Head Island, South Carolina.

SPORTS. The University of Miami at Coral Gables, Florida, offers athletic scholarships to a woman, Terry Williams.

6 May 1973
SPORTS. Forty-five-year-old Althea Gibson, the first black to compete at Wimbledon, announces her intention to return to professional tennis.

14 May 1973
JUDICIAL. The U.S. Supreme Court rules 8–1 that female members of the armed services are entitled to the same dependency benefits for their husbands as servicemen are for dependent wives.

17 May 1973
MILITARY. Staff Sergeant Ruth Johnson, a french horn player, is the first woman to play in the U.S. Marine Corps band.

26 May 1973
SPORTS. Kathy Schmidt sets a record for women's javelin throwing—207 feet, 10 inches—in Modesto, California.

28 May 1973
SPORTS.   According to a report in *Sports Illustrated,* golfer Kathy Whitworth collected $65,063 in prize money during 1972 after playing in 29 tournaments. Top male golfer Jack Nicklaus won $320,542 for 19 tournaments during the same 12-month period.

4 June 1973
SPORTS.   In a series on women athletes, *Sports Illustrated* comments that there is the "insinuation that athletics will masculinize a woman's sexual behavior."

11 June 1973
SPORTS.   The Pennsylvania Supreme Court rules that women may be licensed to box or wrestle in that state.

21 June 1973
JUDICIAL.   The U.S. Supreme Court rules in favor of a Pittsburgh, Pennsylvania, ordinance that forbids listing help-wanted advertising by gender.

23 June 1973
RELIGION.   At its ninth biennial synod, the United Church of Christ elects Margaret Haywood as the first black woman to hold a top leadership position in a U.S. biracial denomination.

28 June 1973
SPORTS.   *Black Sports* magazine inducts 38 members into its Black Sports Hall of Fame, including Wilma Rudolph and Althea Gibson.

1 July 1973
SPORTS.   The California Interscholastic Federation rules that all high school sports teams must be coeducational.

2 July 1973
DEATHS.   Film star Betty Grable—the famous World War II pin-up girl—dies of lung cancer in Santa Monica, California.

7 July 1973
SPORTS.   The Kentucky Colonels of the American Basketball Association are headed by an all-woman board of directors chaired by Eleanor Brown.

19 July 1973
SPORTS.   The U.S. Open tennis championships will award equal prize money to men and women.

24 July 1973
SPORTS.   At the U.S./USSR track meet, Mary Decker, age 14, wins the 800-meter run with a time of 2:3:2, in Minsk, Russia.

25 July 1973
SPORTS.   The Pittsburgh, Pennsylvania, chapter of the National Organization for Women charges that Little League teams playing in city parks discriminate against girls, who are not allowed to play.

25 August 1973
SPORTS.   The Little League World Series in Williamsport, Pennsylvania, is picketed by members of the National Organization for Women.

26 August 1973
SPORTS.   Mary Boitano wins the 6.8-mile Dipsea Race in Marin County, California. This is the first time a female runner has won the race in its 68-year history.

5 September 1973
RELIGION.   Leadership among Conservative Jews votes 9–4 to allow women to be counted in the quorum of 10 or more adults required for communal worship.

11 September 1973
EDUCATION.   Hanna Holborn Gray is named the first woman provost of Yale University.

20 September 1973
SPORTS.   Billie Jean King meets Bobby Riggs in a $100,000 winner-take-all tennis match. King, age 29, bests Riggs—54 years old—in a series of wins, 6–4, 6–3, 6–3.

22 September 1973
EDUCATION.   Women in the University of California band march for the first time during the California–Illinois football game at Berkeley.

26 September 1973
MILITARY.   Captain Lorraine Potter, an American Baptist minister, is the first woman U.S. Air Force chaplain.

27 September 1973
SPORTS. In Houston, Texas, Rosemary Casals and Billie Jean King walk off the court at the Pacific Southwest Open tournament in protest of a lineman's call.

4 October 1973
DEATHS. Sculptor Anna Hyatt Huntington dies in Connecticut at age 97.

9 October 1973
RELIGION. At the Episcopal Church's 64th general convention, deputies defeat a vote permitting ordination of women.

13 October 1973
LABOR. A federal district court strikes down the Communications Workers of America's plan to block implementation of a $38-million employment settlement at AT&T.

26 October 1973
WOMEN'S ISSUES. Ruth Bates Harris is dismissed from her post as deputy assistant director for equal employment at the National Aeronautics and Space Administration after she relays complaints about discrimination in hiring practices at the federal agency.

7 November 1973
SPORTS. In Hoboken, New Jersey, the Civil Rights Division of the state supreme court rules that the Little League team must allow girls to join ball-playing ranks.

9 November 1973
SPORTS. Tennis pro Billie Jean King speaks before a Senate education subcommittee on discrimination in physical education in America's schools. She points out that girls' sports receive only 1 percent of the funding that boys' programs receive.

13 November 1973
JUDICIAL. A U.S. district court judge rules that Northwest Airlines is guilty of "willful violation of federal discrimination laws in favoring male pursers over women stewardesses in employment procedures."

19 November 1973
WOMEN'S ISSUES. Barbara Alice Ringer, former assistant register of copyrights, is named to the post of register in that federal agency.

30 November 1973
SPORTS. Kathy Whitworth is named Ladies' Professional Golf Association player-of-the-year for the seventh time in 8 years.

2 December 1973
EDUCATION. The Women's Equity Action League of San Francisco, California, demands that the Department of Health, Education, and Welfare monitor schools there to be sure that all sports facilities and coaching services are distributed equally between the sexes.

10 December 1973
MILITARY. Colonel Mary E. Bane of Normal, Illinois, is named commanding officer of the Headquarters and Service Command, Camp Pendleton, California, which has an enrollment of 2,150 men and women.

17 December 1973
FINANCE. The Federal Home Loan Bank Board issues a statement ordering an end to discrimination against women in granting mortgage loans.

27 December 1973
WOMEN'S ISSUES. The Census Bureau reports that of the 6.6 million female-headed households extant in 1972, 37 percent have incomes below $4,000.

OTHER EVENTS OF 1973

POPULAR CULTURE. Erma Bombeck wins the Mark Twain Award as top humorist in the United States.

POPULAR CULTURE. Oscars for 1972 go to Liza Minnelli, Best Actress, in *Cabaret,* and to Eileen Heckart, Best Supporting Actress, in *Butterflies Are Free.*

2 January 1974
JUDICIAL. In Atlanta, Georgia, a 3-judge federal panel voids as unconstitutional a portion of a state law prohibiting women from voting in the state if their husbands maintain legal residence elsewhere.

JUDICIAL. The U.S. Supreme Court rules 7–2 that public schools cannot force a pregnant teacher to take maternity leave until a few weeks prior to her expected delivery date.

7 January 1974
JUDICIAL. The Maryland State Police must hire more women and blacks, according to a Justice Department consent decree.

IDEAS/BELIEFS In Trenton, New Jersey, a woman sues State Farm Mutual Insurance Company for denying her auto insurance because she has been living with a man "without benefit of wedlock."

8 January 1974
LABOR. In El Paso, Texas, a natural gas company agrees on a program of increased job opportunities for women and minorities.

24 January 1974
WOMEN'S ISSUES. Shirley Plume of the Oglala Sioux tribe is named superintendant of Standing Rock, a Bureau of Indian Affairs agency in North Dakota.

30 January 1974
INTERNATIONAL. President Nixon issues a proclamation calling on Congress and all Americans to observe the United Nations International Women's Year for 1975.

4 February 1974
CRIME. Patricia Hearst, daughter of publishing magnate Randolph A. Hearst, is kidnapped from her Berkeley, California, apartment by a group calling itself the Symbionese Liberation Army.

12 February 1974
JUDICIAL. In the Washington, D.C., and Los Angeles, California, courts, judges rule that local and state prostitution laws discriminate against women by providing no punishment for the men involved in cases of soliciting.

18 February 1974
WOMEN'S ISSUES. Carla A. Hills, a Los Angeles, California, attorney, is nominated as assistant attorney general of the United States. She is the first woman of that rank in the Justice Department since the 1920s.

1 March 1974
POLITICS. The Democratic National Committee approves new rules for selection of delegates. This rule change will help promote full participation by women and minorities.

23 March 1974
LABOR. Union women numbering 3,200 meet in Chicago, Illinois, to establish the Coalition of Labor Union Women.

28 March 1974
DEATHS. Dorothy Fields, lyricist who wrote such hit songs as "I Can't Give You Anything but Love" and "On the Sunny Side of the Street," dies of a heart attack in New York City.

15 April 1974
LABOR. Nine major steel companies, the United Steelworkers, and the federal government sign agreements providing back pay and expanded job opportunities for women. According to the Justice Department, about 73 percent of the nation's raw steel is produced by these companies, which employ more than 10,000 women nationwide.

18 April 1974
EDUCATION. Dr. Virginia Trotter is appointed assistant education secretary at the Department of Health, Education, and Welfare.

Shirley Temple Black, 1929–

At the age of four, Shirley Temple stepped into the public view and has remained there, in various capacities, virtually ever since. Born Shirley Jane Temple on 23 April 1928, in Santa Monica, California, she was the daughter of George F. and Gertrude (Creiger) Temple. Enrolled in dance classes at three-and-a-half, she quickly

A top box-office draw as a child star in the 1930s, Shirley Temple Black was U.S. ambassador to Ghana in 1969, and later served as a member of the U.S. delegation to the United Nations' General Assembly. (Photo courtesy United Nations)

captured the attention of an agent working for Educational Pictures, Inc. By 1932 Temple was making short-subject comedy films. She was signed with Fox Film Corporation in 1934 after her hit song-and-dance number "Baby Take a Bow" in the movie *Stand Up and Cheer*. Her contract guaranteed Shirley $150 per week, but by mid-decade she was earning $10,000 per week. Her films included *Little Miss Marker*, *Bright Eyes, The Little Colonel, Heidi, Curly Top*, and *Rebecca of Sunnybrook Farm*.

By the 1940s, Temple was no longer the number-one draw at the box office, although she continued making movies until 1949. Among films featuring the adolescent Temple are *The Bachelor and the Bobby-Soxer* (1946) and *Fort Apache* (1948). In 1945, she graduated from the Westlake School for Girls in Los Angeles, California, and published her autobiography, *My Young Life*. She also married Sergeant John Agar, Jr. He was to appear in several movies with his wife, and the couple had a daughter, Linda born in 1947. By 1949 Temple had divorced Agar; she married San Francisco businessman Charles A. Black in 1950. During this marriage she had two more children.

During the Korean conflict Black lived with her family in Bethesda, Maryland, but later returned to California, where she once more became involved in show business. Between 1957 and 1959 she hosted an NBC-TV series, "Shirley Temple's Storybook," and in 1960 appeared in "The Shirley Temple Theatre" and "Shirley Temple Presents Young America." In 1967 Black received the Kiwanis International Award for her support of decency in motion pictures. She was also the sole woman candidate for a

Republican seat in the House of Representatives, from the eleventh district in California. Campaigning on a conservative platform that included a hawkish position toward the Vietnam War, she was defeated by Paul McCloskey although she received more votes than eight other contenders.

Black supported Richard Nixon's bid for the presidency in 1968, and in 1969, she was named as one of five delegates to the twenty-fourth session of the United Nations General Assembly. In 1968, Black was made a Dame in the Order of the Knights of Malta. In 1970, she was named a delegate to the United Nations Conference of Human Environment in Stockholm, Sweden. During that decade she was a member of several commissions on the environment and was named a member of the U.S. Commission for UNESCO in 1973.

Black was appointed U.S. ambassador to Ghana in 1974, a diplomatic post she held until 1976. She then became White House Chief of Protocol under President Gerald Ford. A founder of the International Federation of Multiple Sclerosis Societies, Black served on the board of the National Wildlife Federation, the National Multiple Sclerosis Society, and the American Academy of Diplomacy. She was awarded the Ceres medal by the Food and Agricultural Organization of the United Nations in Rome in 1975. In 1981, she became a member of the U.S. delegation on African Refugee Problems.

Currently living south of San Francisco, California, Black continues her work on behalf of various charitable and civic organizations, including the National Committee for U.S./China Relations.

---

22 April 1974
BUSINESS. Katherine Graham, publisher of the *Washington Post,* is named to the 18-member Associated Press board. She is the first woman to join that board of directors.

23 April 1974
WOMEN'S ISSUES. The Tennessee legislature attempts to rescind its prior ratification of the Equal Rights Amendment.

7 May 1974
POLITICS. The League of Women Voters votes to end its policy of banning men to full membership.

13 May 1974
EDUCATION. The Supreme Court refuses to disturb a lower court ruling allowing Eastern Kentucky University dormitory regulations that are more restrictive for women than for men.

20 May 1974
RELIGION. The Women's Lobby sues the U.S. Catholic Conference to force it to register with congress as a lobbying organization or to refrain from influencing legislation.

31 May 1974
DEATHS. Nutritionist and controversial yet popular food writer Adelle Davis dies of cancer at her home near Los Angeles, California.

3 June 1974
JUDICIAL. The U.S. Supreme Court rules 5–3 that an employer's retention of some traditional night shift differentials favoring male over female employees violates the Equal Pay Act.

12 June 1974
SPORTS. In Williamsport, Pennsylvania, a spokesperson for Little League Baseball, Inc., announces that the organization will now allow girls to play on previously all-boy teams.

RELIGION. The 12.3-million-member Southern Baptist Convention rejects a resolution to assure 10 percent black and ethnic representation and a 20-percent quota for women on church boards and commissions.

14 June 1974
LABOR. The National Labor Relations Board rules that having separate locals for men and

women in the same union at the same plant violates the National Labor Relations Act.

17 June 1974
JUDICIAL. The U.S. Supreme Court rules 6–3 that a California job disability insurance program does not discriminate against women by not including benefits for normal pregnancies.

19 June 1974
JUDICIAL. A U.S. District Court in Washington, D.C., rules that a "legitimate government interest" is served by refusing to admit women to the air force and naval academies.

25 June 1974
EDUCATION. Jill Ker Conway, an historian, is named the first woman president of all-female Smith College in Northampton, Massachusetts.

30 June 1974
DEATHS. Alberta Williams King, mother of slain civil rights leader Martin Luther King, Jr., is shot and killed by a black gunman at the Ebenezer Baptist Church in Atlanta, Georgia, where her husband is pastor.

1 July 1974
EDUCATION. The University of California at Los Angeles announces that all college athletics, including varsity football, are open to women.

3 July 1974
LABOR. The Census Bureau reports that the typical full-time year-round working woman earns $6,488. This is only 57 percent of what men earn: an average of $11,468.

10 July 1974
WOMEN'S ISSUES. A statue of Mary McLeod Bethune is dedicated in Lincoln Park in the nation's capital.

16 July 1974
MILITARY. Fifteen women are admitted to the U.S. Merchant Marine Academy; 5 of them are black.

29 July 1974
RELIGION. In North Philadelphia, Pennsylvania, 4 bishops ordain 11 women into the Episcopal Church priesthood. This ceremony

defies church law forbidding women to become priests. Two of the women are later suspended by their diocese bishops.

14 August 1974
RELIGION. The House of Bishops of the Protestant Episcopal Church rules that the ordination of 11 women priests is not valid. It urges also that the 1976 General Convention reconsider female ordination.

15 August 1974
WOMEN'S ISSUES. At its national convention in Honolulu, Hawaii, the American Bar Association votes to endorse the Equal Rights Amendment.

17 August 1974
JUDICIAL. The American Civil Liberties Union files suit in New York City to void Social Security regulations that discriminate against women.

18 August 1974
AVIATION. The National Aeronautics and Space Administration announces that it has rehired Ruth Bates Harris, a black woman dismissed in 1973. Harris had filed a complaint with the Civil Service Commission over her dismissal.

22 August 1974
HEALTH. The Food and Drug Administration recommends a continued ban on the intrauterine device known as the Dalkon Shield. There have been at least 11 deaths allegedly related to the use of the Dalkon Shield.

23 August 1974
WOMEN'S ISSUES. President Ford signs a proclamation that designates 26 August as "Women's Equality Day." He urges ratification of the Equal Rights Amendment.

3 September 1974
POLITICS. Republican Shirley Crumpler is the first woman ever nominated for governor of Nevada.

4 September 1974
POLITICS. Mary Louise Smith of Iowa is named chair of the GOP. She is the first woman to head the Republican party.

10 September 1974

POLITICS.   Mary Ann Krupsak, Democratic state senator from New York, wins the nomination for Lieutenant Governor with 42 percent of the vote. She defeats both Mario Cuomo and Antonio Olivieri.

16 September 1974

JUDICIAL.   A federal district court judge rules that Connecticut's state retirement system discriminates against men by allowing women to retire at 50 and requiring men to wait until age 55 to retire with the same pension benefits.

20 September 1974

WOMEN'S ISSUES.   Gail A. Cobb of Washington, D.C., is the first woman police officer to be slain in the line of duty.

29 September 1974

MEDICAL.   The National Cancer Institute finds that radical mastectomy is unnecessary in many cases of breast cancer. Currently, 95 percent of all women with breast cancer undergo this type of surgery to halt the spread of the disease.

3 October 1974

MEDICAL.   Betty Ford, wife of the president, enters Bethesda Naval Hospital for surgery to treat a recently discovered breast cancer.

17 October 1974

LABOR.   In Milwaukee, Wisconsin, a civil suit charges the police and fire departments with discrimination in hiring women and minorities. Of 2,200 police officers, only 58 are black and only 16 are women.

29 October 1974

FINANCE.   The Federal Deposit Insurance Corporation will be governed by a law, signed today by President Ford, that will prohibit credit discrimination on the basis of gender.

JUDICIAL.   The U.S. Supreme Court upholds the right of the U.S. Jaycees to continue to prohibit women from membership.

5 November 1974

POLITICS.   A record number of women are elected to public office nationwide. The House of Representatives now includes 18 women, an increase of 2.

POLITICS.   Elaine Noble (D-Massachusetts) is elected to the state legislature from the Sixth Suffolk District in Boston. She is the first avowed lesbian to achieve elected office.

POLITICS.   Millicent Fenwick (R-New Jersey) is the first grandmother to be elected to the U.S. Congress.

6 November 1974

RELIGION.   John Maury Allin, presiding bishop of the Protestant Episcopal Church, rejects a $672 contribution to a world hunger campaign. The money had been collected during a New York service at which 3 women priests had celebrated the eucharist.

8 November 1974

CRIME.   Singer and entertainer Connie Francis is raped and robbed in her Nassau, New York, hotel room.

10 November 1974

RELIGION.   In Washington, D.C., the Reverend Alison Cheek, an Episcopal priest, consecrates the eucharist at a service in St. Stephen and the Incarnation Church.

28 November 1974

WOMEN'S ISSUES.   The highest-ranking woman in President Ford's administration, Anne L. Armstrong, steps down as counselor to the president due to "pressing family responsibilities."

RELIGION.   Katherine Pappas, Lila Prounis, Zoe Cavalaris, Georgia Stathis, and Christine Peratis are named to the Greek Orthodox Archdiocesan Council of North and South America. They are the first women to serve in this capacity.

6 December 1974

RELIGION.   The Massachusetts Conference of the United Church of Christ (UCC) rules that it will accept women Episcopal priests as minister within UCC ranks.

10 December 1974

WOMEN'S ISSUES.   Representatives of 26 national organizations announce a campaign in 10 states to achieve ratification of the Equal Rights Amendment (ERA) in 1975. The ERA has been ratified by 33 of 38 states necessary, although Nebraska and Tennessee have voted to rescind ratification.

13 December 1974

POPULAR CULTURE. Fanne Fox, a stripper known as the ''blond bombshell,'' announces she is quitting the striptease business. She had been linked to an incident involving U.S. Representative Wilber Mills (D-Arkansas).

15 December 1974

FINANCE. The Federal Home Loan Bank Board announces regulations designed to prohibit sex discrimination in mortgage lending.

28 December 1974

DEATHS. Amy Vanderbilt, syndicated etiquette columnist, dies after a fall from a second-story New York City hotel window.

31 December 1974

RELIGION. The Reverend Betty Schiess is hired as a priest-associate at Grace Episcopal Church in Syracuse, New York.

OTHER EVENTS OF 1974

MILITARY. The Reverend Alice Henderson is the first black commissioned as a U.S. Army chaplain. She is the only woman chaplain in the army.

MILITARY. Jill Brown is the first black woman pilot in the armed forces and qualifies as a U.S. Navy pilot.

FINANCE. Passage of the Federal Equal Credit Opportunity Act makes it unlawful to deny credit on the basis of sex or marital status.

BUSINESS. Madeline H. McWhinney is the first president of the First Women's Bank, founded in New York City.

POPULAR CULTURE. At the Academy Award presentations, the Oscar for Best Actress of 1973 goes to Glenda Jackson in *A Touch of Class,* and the Best Supporting Actress Oscar goes to Tatum O'Neal in *Paper Moon.*

Women and Postsecondary Education

Postsecondary education of women was not common prior to the late nineteenth century. The first women's college in the United States that required a four-year course of study was Mary Sharpe College, founded in 1851 in Winchester, Tennessee. By the turn of the century, however, women could choose from diverse institutions, such as Elmira College (1855), Vassar (1865), Wellesley (1875), Smith (1875), Bryn Mawr (1880), Mills (1885), and Randolph-Macon (1891). Mount Holyoke College, founded in 1837 as a women's seminary, achieved college status a few years later. Also, many other institutions, among them Harvard, Stanford, and the University of Chicago, had become coeducational by 1900. At the University of Chicago, 24 percent of the students in 1893 were women. By 1902, the percentage of women at that school had increased to half of all students enrolled there.

But despite the proliferation of postsecondary institutions for women, in most cases they were designed to prepare women for the traditional roles of wife and mother. Careers, full-time permanent employment, and professions for women were not anticipated by the founders and trustees of the first women's colleges. Before postsecondary education offered women a wider range of opportunities, American women faced limited life choices. If they married, they might raise a family, but those who remained unmarried were usually dependent on parents or other relatives. By the early 1900s, this pattern was changing. Women college graduates were not marrying as soon as those without postsecondary educations—at that time one-quarter of college-educated women never married at all. By 1912, estimates indicated that 60 percent of women with college educations had obtained work, usually for a limited period of time. And although a growing number postponed marriage in favor of employment, there were virtually no middle-class women who could be classified as working wives. Once a woman married she left the work force for good, even if she had postsecondary training that qualified her for a professional position.

Concurrent with the growth of women's colleges and coeducational institutions was an upsurge in the number of women professionals. Their education prepared them for further study in law and medicine, for positions as librarians, teachers, social workers, engineers, and scientists. Across the nation settlement houses sprang up, many of which were affiliated with college and university social work programs. These settlements were real-life laboratories to which young women flocked. And in the course of their stay many became committed to the study of urban problems, immigrant culture, or labor organizing.

The number of college educated women in the United States enjoyed a steady increase from the beginning of the twentieth century, as indicated in the following chart. (All figures are rounded off to the nearest thousand.)

Year in which degrees conferred	B.A.	M.A.	Ph.D.
1895	4,400	200	30
1900	5,200	300	20
1910	8,400	600	40
1920	16,600	1,300	90
1930	49,000	6,000	400
1940	77,000	10,000	400
1950	103,000	17,000	600
1960	136,000	25,000	1,000
1970	343,000	83,000	4,000
1980	473,000	147,000	3,000

The chart figures indicate the continued interest in higher education by women early in the twentieth century. And by the 1960s, another change was occurring in women's education. Determining that the study of women was a valid and necessary discipline, many academic institutions established women's studies programs. The first such range of courses opened at San Diego State University in California in 1970, with five instructors and ten separate courses. There were approximately six hundred courses in women's history and related subjects offered at U.S. colleges by 1972. Ten years later, more than four hundred schools listed women's studies as a separate academic program and more than thirty thousand courses made up these programs.

5 January 1975
EDUCATION. Educational Testing Service releases a report based on a study of women Ph.D. recipients. The report states that male Ph.D.'s earn an average $18,700 5 to 6 years after receiving their degrees; women earn $16,400 under the same circumstances.

8 January 1975
LABOR. Betty S. Murphy is named chair of the National Labor Relations Board by President Ford. She is the first woman member of the board.

POLITICS. Ella Grasso is sworn in as the first woman state governor (Connecticut) not succeeding her husband into office. She was elected in November 1974.

9 January 1975
INTERNATIONAL. President Ford signs Executive Order #11832, creating the National Commission of the Observance of International Women's Year. He names Jill Ruckelshaus as chair of the commission and calls on the group to ''promote equality between men and women.'' The commission will prepare for a United Nations conference in Mexico City later this year.

RELIGION. One hundred fifty women ministers of the United Methodist Church call on their bishops to welcome the 11 women Episcopal priests into Methodism.

13 January 1975
CIVIL RIGHTS. The National Association for the Advancement of Colored People selects Margaret Bush Wilson as its chairperson.

15 January 1975
JUDICIAL. In two separate rulings, the U.S. Supreme Court determines that national political party rules concerning the seating of delegates prevails over conflicting state laws, and decides that the U.S. Navy's discharge policy favoring women over men is unconstitutional. Women had been permitted 13 years of commissioned service, but requirements stated that men were to be discharged after 9 years if they had been twice passed over for promotion.

19 January 1975
WOMEN'S ISSUES. In Wisconsin, the 9-member Menominee Reservation Committee is confronted with demands for a return to the older, patriarchal tribal system. Five of the committee members, including chair Ida Deer, are women.

21 January 1975
JUDICIAL. The Supreme Court declares that a Louisiana law excluding women from jury duty is unconstitutional.

SPORTS. Jackie Tonowanda is denied a boxing license by the New York State Athletic Commission.

22 January 1975
EDUCATION. The U.S. Commission on Civil Rights reports that the Department of Health, Education, and Welfare should monitor 25 percent of colleges receiving federal funds each year in order to check on opportunities offered women and minorities.

31 January 1975
RELIGION. Two women ordained as Episcopal priests are named to faculty positions at Episcopal Divinity School in Cambridge, Massachusetts.

4 February 1975
WOMEN'S ISSUES. The North Dakota legislature ratifies the Equal Rights Amendment.

8 February 1975
HEALTH. A jury in Wichita, Kansas, awards Connie L. Deemer $85,000 in damages after she charges that her use of the Dalkon Shield perforated her uterus.

17 February 1975
DEATHS. Ann L. Scott, a vice-president of the National Organization for Women, dies of cancer in New York City.

13 March 1975
CRIME. Patricia Hearst, missing since she was kidnapped in February 1974, is located at a Pennsylvania farmhouse hideout, according to FBI investigators.

19 March 1975
JUDICIAL. The U.S. Supreme Court votes unanimously to strike down a part of the Social Security law that provides survivors' benefits to widows and children but denies them to men who have lost their spouses.

SPORTS. Pennsylvania Supreme Court justices find that a ban on boy/girl competition in state-level athletics is unconstitutional.

24 March 1975
MILITARY. The U.S. Army reports that all women who join the army after 30 June will be required to become qualified with the M-16 rifle.

1 April 1975
RELIGION. William Creighton, Episcopal Bishop of Washington, announces that he will not ordain men to the priesthood if he cannot also ordain women.

2 April 1975
WOMEN'S ISSUES. Proponents of the Equal Rights Amendment (ERA) concede that North Carolina's refusal to ratify the amendment ends hopes that the ERA will become law by the end of 1975.

ARTS AND CULTURE. The Metropolitan Opera Company in New York City announces that Sarah Caldwell, founder of the Boston Opera Company, will be the first woman to conduct at the Met. Caldwell will lead 11 performances during the 1976 season.

10 April 1975
IDEAS/BELIEFS. Results of a Gallup poll indicate that 50 percent of Americans approve of the Equal Rights Amendment (ERA). Twenty-four percent oppose the amendment, and 18 percent have no opinion. Backing for the ERA is highest in the east and in the west.

14 April 1975
CRIME. Pretrial hearings begin for JoAnn Little, a black woman charged with slaying a white jailer. Little claims she killed Clarence Alligood in self-defense after he tried to rape her in her cell, where she awaited results of appeal on a breaking-and-entering conviction.

16 April 1975
WOMEN'S ISSUES. Margaret Mead receives the Woman of Conscience Award from the National Council of Women.

POLITICS. Lila Cockrell of San Antonio, Texas, becomes the first woman mayor in 1 of the nation's 10 largest cities.

17 April 1975
JUDICIAL. The Supreme Court rules that a Utah statute setting different majority ages for men and women is unconstitutional.

19 April 1975
WOMEN'S ISSUES. Joan Winn becomes the first black woman judge in Texas.

22 April 1975
LABOR. Mayor Richard P. Daly of Chicago, Illinois, announces that the city will hire 200 police officers, most of them women or minorities, in order to regain millions of dollars in federal revenue sharing.

FINANCE. The Federal Reserve approves antidiscriminatory banking rules that will give husbands and wives joint credit history and will not allow creditors to include sex or marital status in the "point system" used to determine credit worthiness.

25 April 1975
WOMEN'S ISSUES. Dr. Gloria E. A. Toote, the highest-ranking black woman in the Ford administration, resigns as assistant secretary for fair housing and equal opportunity in the Department of Housing and Urban Development.

6 May 1975
LABOR. The Civil Service Commission reports that certain federal agencies have been hiring and promoting employees without regard to guidelines designed to protect women and minorities from discrimination. Among agencies cited in the report were the Equal Employment Opportunity Commission, the National Science Foundation, the Small Business Administration, the Smithsonian Institute, the Social Security Administration, and the Atomic Energy Commission.

14 May 1975
LABOR. AT&T, the nation's largest employer, agrees to step-up its hiring and promotion of women.

19 May 1975
RELIGION. The United Presbyterian Church rules that seminarians seeking ordination must accept women as ministers. Currently, there are 189 women out of a total of 13,000 ministers in the Presbyterian Church.

21 May 1975
LEGISLATIVE. In Oregon, Governor Bob Straub signs a new rape law that prohibits

introduction of evidence about a rape victim's prior sexual relationship with persons other than the defendant.

27 May 1975
POLITICS. Democrat Thelma Stovall, Kentucky secretary of state, defeats 10 men to become the first woman nominated to run for lieutenant governor of Kentucky.

1 June 1975
EDUCATION. Sallie McFague Teselle of Nashville, Tennessee, is the first woman dean of the Divinity School at Vanderbilt University.

3 June 1975
EDUCATION. The Department of Health, Education, and Welfare issues antidiscrimination rules aimed at implementing Title IX of the 1972 Higher Education Act. Title IX requires schools to end discriminatory practices against women. This includes making funding available for equal sports opportunities for women athletes.

10 June 1975
WOMEN'S ISSUES. The Civil Rights Commission asks President Ford for an Executive Order declaring women a "socially and economically disadvantaged group eligible for special government aid in establishing businesses."

16 June 1975
POLITICS. A study released by the Capitol Hill chapter of the National Women's Political Caucus indicates that women congressional employees earn less than male employees. The median salary for women is $22,627; for men it is $28,091.

17 June 1975
WOMEN'S ISSUES. Helen Delich Bently resigns as Federal Maritime Commission chair. She had been under criticism for alleged partiality toward U.S. shippers.

29 June 1975
POLITICS. The National Women's Political Caucus ends a 4-day meeting in Boston with the election of Audrey Rowe Colom as the group's chair.

1 July 1975
POPULAR CULTURE. Personal advice columnist Ann Landers announces that she has filed for divorce after 36 years of marriage.

7 July 1975
MILITARY. The Pentagon announces that pregnant members of the military will have the choice of staying in the service, leaving it, or taking a "convalescent leave."

24 July 1975
RELIGION. Priests for Equality, a group of clerics in the Baltimore–Washington, D.C., area, calls for ordination of women to the Roman Catholic priesthood.

26 July 1975
IDEAS/BELIEFS. A recent Gallup poll indicates that 77 percent of the women asked said they were afraid to walk in their city neighborhoods at night.

27 July 1975
RELIGION. Six Episcopal women priests observe the anniversary of their ordination at St. Stephen and the Incarnation Church, in Washington, D.C. One, the Reverend Alison Cheek, had been invited to participate as a priest at St. Stephen's.

4 August 1975
LABOR. The New York State Division of Human Rights finds Stromberg Carlson Corporation guilty of denying pregnant women workers disability benefits.

7 September 1975
RELIGION. In defiance of Episcopal Church doctrine, 4 more women are ordained as priests, bringing the total number to 15.

14 September 1975
RELIGION. Canonization of Elizabeth Ann Seton takes place. Seton is the first American-born saint. She founded the first U.S. Order of Sisters of Charity of St. Vincent de Paul.

28 September 1975
MILITARY. Congress passes a bill that will allow women admittance to the nation's military academies beginning in 1976.

7 October 1975
RELIGION. Roman Catholic Archbishop
Joseph Bernardin of Cincinnati, Ohio, says that
although the church will suffer without women
in leading roles, "divine law" bars women from
the priesthood.

13 October 1975
POLITICS. A group of Democratic women
announces that they will seek to have a
"women's agenda" incorporated into their party
platform and that they will work for nomination
of a woman vice-president.

16 October 1975
FINANCE. The Federal Reserve Board issues
final regulations barring discrimination against
women in credit practices. The regulations,
which are effective on 28 October, include
banks, commercial institutions, finance
corporations, department stores, insurance
companies, and credit card companies.

20 October 1975
MEDICAL. A fetal test called amniocentesis,
a medical procedure for determining certain
defects in unborn babies, has been deemed safe
by the National Institute of Child Health and
Human Development.

21 October 1975
MILITARY. The U.S. Coast Guard Academy
is the first to admit women students.

26 October 1975
WOMEN'S ISSUES. Karen De Crow is
reelected to a second 1-year term of office as
president of the National Organization for
Women.

4 November 1975
POLITICS. Evelyn Gandy is elected the first
woman lieutenant governor of Mississippi.
Thelma Stovall is the first woman to win the
lieutenant governorship in Kentucky.

12 November 1975
WOMEN'S ISSUES. The Federal Manpower
Administration changes its names to the
Employment and Training Administration.

15 November 1975
WOMEN'S ISSUES. The National
Organization for Women (NOW) reports that a

group of present and former organization leaders
has formed a caucus, *Womensurge,* to combat
NOW's alleged movement "out of the
mainstream, into the revolution." The aim of
Womensurge is to "remobilize the membership
to concrete mainstream issues."

17 November 1975
JUDICIAL. The Supreme Court strikes down
a Utah law denying unemployment benefits to
women in their third trimester of pregnancy on
the grounds that they are automatically presumed
unable to work during this time.

26 November 1975
WOMEN'S ISSUES. President Ford
announces that a list of possible nominees for
Supreme Court Justice contains the names of
several women. Among them are Carla Hills,
Housing and Urban Development secretary, and
U.S. District Judge Cornelia G. Kennedy.

10 December 1975
LEGISLATIVE. Representative Bella Abzug
(D-New York) sees her bill, Public Law
94–167, passed by the House of
Representatives. This law will establish a
national women's conference in the United
States. It is passed by the Senate on 23
December, and President Ford signs it on 24
December.

26 December 1975
DEATHS. Sherry LaGace, a Kentucky strip-
miner, is the first woman miner to be killed on
the job. She dies when a scraper she is driving
overturns.

30 December 1975
WOMEN'S ISSUES. The city assembly of
Anchorage, Alaska, passes an ordinance barring
discrimination on the basis of sex or sexual
preference in employment, housing, public
accommodations, education, and finance.

OTHER EVENTS OF 1975

INTERNATIONAL. American delegates
attend the United Nations International Women's
Year Conference in Mexico City, Mexico. The
conference proclaims a United Nations Decade
for Women, 1975–1985.

POPULAR CULTURE. Academy Awards for
1974 go to Ellen Burstyn, Best Actress, in *Alice*

Doesn't Live Here Anymore, and Ingrid Bergman, Best Supporting Actress, in *Murder on the Orient Express.*

3 January 1976
DEATHS. Freida Kirchwey, editor and publisher of *The Nation* from 1937 to 1955, dies in St. Petersburg, Florida.

5 January 1976
LABOR. A federal district court judge in Chicago, Illinois, rules that the Chicago Police Department must establish hiring quotas that include 16 percent women officers.

9 January 1976
LABOR. The jobless rate for American women was 8 percent in December 1985, up from 7.8 percent in November.

12 Janaury 1976
HEALTH. According to a Department of Health, Education, and Welfare report, life expectancy among white women in the United States is 75.9 years; among nonwhite women, 72 years. For men, the expected average lifespan of whites is 67.4 years, and 62 years for nonwhites.

13 Janaury 1976
ARTS AND CULTURE. Sarah Caldwell is the first woman to conduct an opera at the Metropolitan Opera in New York City. She conducts *La Traviata.*

18 January 1976
DEATHS. Barbara Armstrong, said to have been the first woman law professor in the United States, at the University of California at Berkeley Law School, dies in Oakland, California, at age 85.

25 January 1976
POPULAR CULTURE Marabel Morgan's book, *The Total Woman,* is named to the *New York Times* best-seller list.

27 January 1976
BUSINESS. Libby Howie is named the first woman auctioneer in the 232-year history of Sotheby Parke Bernet, a New York art auction firm.

JUDICIAL. Jury selection begins in the bank robbery trial of Patricia Hearst, who was arrested on 18 September 1975, in San Francisco, California.

INTERNATIONAL. Marion Javits resigns a $67,500-per-year job as consultant to *Iran Air,* Iran's national airline, due to criticism of her position. Javits' husband, Senator Jacob Javits (R-New York), is a member of the Senate Foreign Relations Committee.

28 January 1976
INTERNATIONAL. President Ford announces that Anne Armstrong is to be U.S. ambassador to Great Britain. She is the first woman named to that post.

29 January 1976
EDUCATION. At Bennington College in Vermont, Gail Thain Parker, the nation's youngest woman college president, resigns from her post. She cites criticism and lack of trustee support as factors in her decision.

12 February 1976
BUSINESS. Roberta Kankus is named the first woman licensed operator of a commercial nuclear power plant.

13 February 1976
IDEAS/BELIEFS. Phyllis Schlafly, chair of the STOP-ERA group, states that the amendment threatens to turn all child care in the United States over to the federal government.

DEATHS. Metropolitan Opera singer Lily Pons dies at age 71 in Dallas, Texas.

18 February 1976
WOMEN'S ISSUES. The Kentucky House of Representatives votes 57–40 to rescind its 1972 approval of the Equal Rights Amendment.

25 February 1976
IDEAS/BELIEFS. A new group, ERAmerica, establishes its offices in Washington, D.C. The organization is headed by Liz Carpenter and Ellie Peterson.

1 March 1976
WOMEN'S ISSUES. The Arizona State Senate fails to approve the Equal Rights Amendment in a 15–15 vote.

4 March 1976
INTERNATIONAL. Jane Kennedy, an antiwar activist serving a 3-year prison term for destroying draft records, is nominated for the 1976 Nobel Peace Prize.

5 March 1976
WOMEN'S ISSUES. Frances Levine becomes the second journalist elected to membership in the Gridiron Club. She joins Helen Thomas, who was elected in February 1975.

7 April 1976
DEATHS. Mary Margaret McBride, radio talk-show host for more than 20 years, dies in West Shokun, New York, at age 76.

15 April 1976
FINANCE. The U.S. Justice Department files suit against 2 mortgage lenders for discrimination against women who have applied for loans.

22 April 1976
BUSINESS. Barbara Walters, co-host of NBC-TV's "Today" show, accepts an offer from ABC-TV to co-anchor the "Evening News" with Harry Reasoner. Walters will receive a 5-year, $1-million-per-year contract from ABC-TV.

30 April 1976
WOMEN'S ISSUES. The first bridge named for a woman, the Betsy Ross Bridge, is built across the Delaware River between Philadelphia, Pennsylvania, and Pennsauken, New Jersey.

8 May 1976
DEATHS. Marion B. Skaggs, 88 years old, founder of Safeway Store, Inc., the nation's largest supermarket chain, dies in Oakland, California.

12 May 1976
JUDICIAL. A U.S. district court judge rules that a Social Security law provision discriminates against men who were over age 62 by the end of 1974.

19 May 1976
ARTS AND CULTURE. Poet Gwendolyn Brooks is the first black woman inducted into the National Institute of Arts and Letters.

20 May 1976
INTERNATIONAL. Rosemary L. Ginn is confirmed as ambassador to Luxembourg, replacing Ruth Farkas, who announced her resignation on 14 May.

25 May 1976
POLITICS. The *Washington Post* reports that Representative Wayne Hays (D-Ohio) hired Elizabeth Ray for his staff in order to obtain sexual favors from her.

27 May 1976
WOMEN'S ISSUES. Charlotte Reid is named to the Federal Communications Commission.

POLITICS. Members of the National Women's Political Caucus charge that both major political parties fail to represent women and minorities in delegate selection for national conventions.

2 June 1976
CIVIL RIGHTS. The federal volunteer organization ACTION is charged with discrimination against women and blacks, especially against black women.

13 June 1976
POLITICS. Democratic presidential candidate Jimmy Carter issues a statement of support for the Equal Rights Amendment. He also announces establishment of a women's advisory committee to the Carter campaign staff.

29 June 1976
MILITARY. Warrant Officer Jennie A. Vallance, the first woman graduate of the U.S. Army Helicopter Flight School, resigns from the military due to alleged sex discrimination.

Barbara Walters, 1931–

A pioneering television newswoman, Barbara Walters is best-known for her many interviews of the world's most famous people. And for the fact that she became the highest-paid on-air reporter when she signed a $1-million contract with ABC-TV. Born on 25 September 1931, in Boston, Massachusetts, she was the daughter of nightclub owner Lou Walters and his wife, Dena (Selett) Walters. She attended both public and private schools and graduated with a B.A. from Sarah Lawrence College in 1954.

Walters worked at several jobs prior to landing a position on WRCA-TV in New York City, where she soon became a producer and writer. She then worked as a writer for the CBS-TV morning news program, a slot she left in favor of a public relations position. Hired in 1961 to write for the NBC "Today" show, Walters had no opportunities to do on-camera work until 1965, when she filled a temporary "Today" opening. Soon Walters had made a name for herself and became a regular on the show. She provided "Today" viewers with incisive, meticulously researched news stories and interviews with such notables as U.S. presidents and their wives and various film and stage stars.

On 8 December 1963, Walters married producer Lee Guber, and the couple adopted a daughter. The Gubers divorced in 1976. Walters' sense of professionalism and her warmth, coupled with a relentless ability to probe to the heart of a story, won her rave reviews from critics and co-workers alike. In 1970, she published *How to Talk with Practically Anybody About Practically Anything,* in which she revealed the stories behind many of her encounters with the rich and famous. Walters was made co-anchor of "Today" in 1974; she moved to ABC-TV in 1976 when that network's national evening news program expanded to a one-hour format. According to Walters, the greater opportunities presented by a sixty-minute show induced her to take the job. But a $1-million yearly contract was also an important factor in her decision.

With many television specials to her credit, she aired in-depth interviews with people such as Katharine Hepburn, Jihan Sadat, Jimmy Carter, Walter Cronkite, and Mamie Eisenhower. Walters has also contributed regularly to ABC-TV's weekly news program, "20/20." She has received numerous awards during her broadcasting career, including the Woman of the Year in Communications (1974), Broadcaster of the Year from the International Radio and Television Society (1975), and an Emmy award (1975). Walters continues to search out possible interview subjects, and has said repeatedly that she would like to do a television interview with Jacqueline Onassis, widow of President John F. Kennedy, and hopes also to be successful in persuading Greta Garbo, reclusive film star, to be interviewed. Barbara Walters is herself interviewed periodically, and many articles about her professional and private life appear in national magazines.

7 July 1976
EDUCATION. President Ford orders suspension of a Department of Health, Education, and Welfare ruling prohibiting father-son or mother-daughter events at public schools.

12 July 1976
POLITICS. Representative Barbara Jordan (D-Texas) opens the 1976 Democratic Convention. She is the first black and the first woman to be the party's keynoter.

POLITICS. Jimmy Carter meets in New York City with a women's caucus seeking commitment to women's fuller participation in future Democratic party activities.

7 August 1976
POLITICS. Women delegates to the 1976 GOP Convention number 31 percent. At the Democratic Convention, 33 percent of the delegates are women.

15 August 1976
POLITICS. Women journalists are permitted to cover a Sunday School class at Plains Baptist Church in Plains, Georgia. Democratic presidential candidate Jimmy Carter teaches the class.

27 August 1976
POLITICS. The American Independent Party platform calls for opposition to the Equal Rights Amendment. Former Georgia Governor Lester Maddox is the party's presidential nominee.

8 September 1976
WOMEN'S ISSUES. At the Federal Communications Commission, Margita E. White succeeds Glenn O. Robinson as commissioner.

15 September 1976
RELIGION. At its 65th triennial general convention, the Episcopal Church votes in favor of the ordination of women. More than 200 of the 912 delegates sign a declaration rejecting recognition of women priests.

23 September 1976
WOMEN'S ISSUES. Susan Gordon is named assistant secretary of the Department of Health, Education, and Welfare.

1 October 1976
LEGISLATION. Congress approves an unemployment bill that will bar the denial of jobless benefits merely on the basis of normal pregnancy.

4 October 1976
JUDICIAL. In *Stearns* v. *VFW*, the U.S. Supreme Court refuses to review lower court rulings denying a female World War II veteran membership in the all-male Veterans of Foreign Wars.

7 October 1976
POLITICS. In Los Angeles, California, Jimmy Carter meets with a women's rights group as part of his presidential campaigning.

18 October 1976
JUDICIAL. The Supreme Court agrees to review a sex-discrimination case involving a challenge to Philadelphia's system of sexually segregated high schools for the academically gifted.

21 October 1976
LABOR. Two coal mines in Kentucky agree to hire women as miners and to pay back wages of $29,000 to 2 women who had been denied employment. The Kentucky Commission on Human Rights orders the hirings.

RELIGION. In Detroit, Michigan, at the Assembly of American Roman Catholics, 1,340 delegates—of whom 520 are women—adopt resolutions supporting ordination of women and the marriage of priests.

22 October 1976
POLITICS. Vice-presidential candidate Walter Mondale accuses the Ford administration of neglecting millions of unemployed American women.

2 November 1976
POLITICS. As a result of national elections, there are now 18 women in the House of Representatives, down 1 from the last election.

POLITICS. Dixy Lee Ray, former head of the Atomic Energy Commission, is elected governor of Washington state.

9 November 1976
LABOR. New York's Department of Health, Education, and Welfare Office for Civil Rights charges that the New York City public schools discriminate against women and minorities.

16 November 1976
WOMEN'S ISSUES. Bernice Sandler is winner of a Rockefeller public service award. Sandler is project director of the Association of American Colleges project on Women in Work, and has campaigned for increased job opportunities for women.

17 November 1976
SCIENCE. Dr. Rosalyn S. Yalow is awarded the Albert Lasker prize for her work using radioimmunoassay. Yalow is the first woman ever to win this award.

28 November 1976
RELIGION. St. Mary's Episcopal Church in Denver, Colorado, votes to secede from the Episcopal Church over the recent church decision to ordain women priests.

29 November 1976
RELIGION. The Polish National Catholic Church announces a 30-year affiliation with the Episcopal Church over the latter's decision to ordain women.

7 December 1976
JUDICIAL. In a 6–3 decision, the U.S. Supreme Court rules that federal civil rights law does not require company disability plans to provide pregnancy or childbirth benefits. Women's rights advocates criticize this ruling.

13 December 1976
JUDICIAL. The U.S. Supreme Court unanimously votes to uphold a Social Security law that denies divorced mothers of dependent children certain payments made to married mothers whose husbands are eligible for Social Security.

19 December 1976
INTERNATIONAL. Women won 13 of the 32 Rhodes Scholarships awarded in 1976, the first time that the funding was made available to women. Winners receive 2 years' study at Oxford University in England and annual stipends of $5,400.

OTHER EVENTS OF 1976

Olympic Gold Medals

Jennifer Chandler: Springboard diving
Swimming—400-meter freestyle relay women's team medal
Luann Ryan: Archery
Mary Ann Tauskey: Equestrian team
Dorothy Hamill: Figure skating
Sheila Young: Speed skating—500 meters

Olympic Silver Medals

Sheila Young: Speed skating—1,500 meters

Olympic Bronze Medals

Sheila Young: Speed skating—1,000 meters

POPULAR CULTURE. Oscars for 1975 go to Louise Fletcher, Best Actress, in *One Flew Over the Cuckoo's Nest,* and to Lee Grant, Best Supporting Actress, in *Shampoo.*

3 January 1977
JUDICIAL. A federal appeals court in New Orleans rules that members of Congress are not constitutionally immune from charges of sex discrimination.

10 January 1977
LABOR. The Labor Department reaches agreement with Prudential Insurance Company: The firm will triple the number of women on its sales force by 1979.

Rosalyn S. Yalow, 1921–

Only the second woman ever to win the Nobel Prize in physiology or medicine (Gerty T. Cori was the first), physicist Rosalyn S. Yalow developed an important technique used to detect and diagnose a variety of medical conditions. The technique, known as radioimmunoassay, was described by Yalow, and her associate Dr. Solomon A. Berson, in 1959. Born on 19 July 1921, in the Bronx, New York, she was the daughter of Simon and Clara (Zipper) Sussman, both of whom encouraged her to study hard in school. During her high school years, she became interested in science, so much so that she went on to graduate from Hunter College in 1941 with a degree in physics and chemistry.

Dr. Rosalyn S. Yalow, winner of the
1977 Nobel Prize in physiology or medicine. Dr. Yalow is recognized as a pioneer in radioimmunoassay techniques.
(Photo courtesy Rosalyn S. Yalow)

After entering graduate school on an assistantship in physics at the University of
Illinois at Urbana—the only woman on the engineering faculty—she married fellow
student A. Aaron Yalow on 6 June 1943. After their Ph.D.'s were awarded in 1945,
the couple moved to New York City. In 1947, Dr. Yalow went to work at the Veterans
Administration hospital in the Bronx, where she currently holds the title of senior
medical investigator. She took part in a program involving the use of radioactive
materials in biomedical investigation and clinical medicine. She was joined by Dr.
Solomon A. Berson in 1950, and the pair worked together to develop their unique
method of radioimmunoassay (RIA). In 1959, RIA was successfully used to measure
insulin levels in humans. Yalow and Berson went on to use the RIA techniques in
studying other hormones in human circulation, and helped promote use of the procedure
in virtually all areas of medicine.

Yalow was named chief of the RIA Reference Laboratory at the Bronx Veterans
Administration Hospital in 1969, and by 1973 she was named director of the Solomon
A. Berson Research Lab (her colleague had died in 1972). In addition, she was on
the research faculty of the Mount Sinai School of Medicine, where she was named
Distinguished Service professor in 1974. She currently holds the title of Solomon A.
Berson Distinguished Professor-at-Large.

The Albert Lasker Prize for Basic Medical Research went to Yalow in 1976.
She was the first woman to receive this award. And in 1977, she received the coveted
Nobel Prize in Physiology or Medicine. At her acceptance of the award in Stockholm,
Sweden, Yalow spoke out on behalf of women's opportunities. "We still live in a

world in which a significant fraction of people, including women, believe that a woman belongs and wants to belong exclusively in the home; that a woman should not aspire to achieve more than her male counterparts and particularly not more than her husband.''

Yalow has received many awards in addition to the Nobel Prize. In 1978, she was given the Veterans Administration's Exceptional Service Award, which she had also received in 1975. She declined the *Ladies' Home Journal* Woman of the Year Award in 1979, however, saying that it was ''inconsistent and unwise to have awards restricted to women or to men in fields where excellence is not inherently sex-related.''

Yalow is a member of the National Academy of Sciences and of the American Academy of Arts and Sciences. She sits on the editorial boards of many professional journals. She has received thirty-nine honorary degrees, including those from Princeton, Columbia, Johns Hopkins, and from several foreign universities. She generally works up to seventy hours a week, and credits the publicity she received following the Nobel Prize with giving her more flexibility and greater opportunities for involvement in public affairs. Yalow is a staunch supporter of nuclear energy and hopes to play a continuing part in educating the public about the benefits of this power source.

---

14 January 1977
RELIGION. Dissident Episcopalians announce formation of a separate denomination opposed to women priests. The new U.S. Episcopal Church claims ordination of women is ''heresy.''

WOMEN'S ISSUES. President Carter names 2 women to top aide posts on his White House staff. They are Margaret Constanza, presidential assistant, and Martha H. Mitchell, special assistant for special projects. Mitchell is the only black among 11 aides named.

19 January 1977
WOMEN'S ISSUES. Indiana becomes the 35th state to ratify the Equal Rights Amendment with a state senate vote of 26–24. Ratification by 38 states by 22 March 1979 is required for the amendment to be added to the Constitution.

WOMEN'S ISSUES. The Department of Health, Education, and Welfare announces that Dr. Mary Berry is named assistant secretary for education, and Eileen Shanahan is named assistant secretary for public affairs.

20 January 1977
WOMEN'S ISSUES. The U.S. Senate confirms Patricia Roberts Harris as secretary of the Department of Housing and Urban Development and Juanita Kreps as secretary of commerce.

27 January 1977
WOMEN'S ISSUES. The Virginia State Senate votes on the Equal Rights Amendment but the measure receives only 20 votes, 1 short of the constitutional minority required for passage.

RELIGION. The ordination of women as Roman Catholic priests is definitely prohibited by the Vatican, causing American women and others supporting female ordination to denounce the policy.

8 February 1977
WOMEN'S ISSUES. The state of Idaho votes to rescind ratification of the Equal Rights Amendment, which was approved by the state in 1972. The legality of this and other state votes on rescission has not been tested in court. Nebraska and Tennessee have also voted to invalidate their earlier approval of the amendment.

9 February 1977
WOMEN'S ISSUES. The Senate Operations Committee reports that on many federal regulatory agencies, women and minorities are ''woefully under-represented'' among the commissioners.

11 February 1977
WOMEN'S ISSUES. The Nevada State Assembly defeats the Equal Rights Amendment by a vote of 24–15.

12 February 1977
WOMEN'S ISSUES. Rose Elizabeth Bird is named chief justice of the California Supreme Court. North Carolina's Susie Sharp is the only other woman currently holding such a judicial position.

13 February 1977
LABOR. NBC-TV agrees to a $2-million out-of-court settlement of a sex discrimination suit brought by women employees.

17 February 1977
EDUCATION. Joseph Califano, secretary of the Department of Health, Education, and Welfare, announces that he will order cut-offs of aid to public schools if districts are not in compliance with federal civil rights laws affecting women and minorities.

22 February 1977
BUSINESS. Former Department of Housing and Urban Development Secretary Carla A. Hills is elected to the board of directors of IBM.

26 February 1977
WOMEN'S ISSUES. In Montpelier, Vermont, more than 1,000 women attend the first International Women's Year state meeting to plan for the National Women's Conference in Houston, Texas.

1 March 1977
POPULAR CULTURE. The American Film Institute presents its Life Achievement Award to Bette Davis. She is the first woman recipient of this award.

2 March 1977
JUDICIAL. The U.S. Supreme Court rules that a provision of the Social Security law that gives automatic benefits to widows but not to widowers is unconstitutional.

3 March 1977
AVIATION. U.S. District Court Judge Robert Merhige, Jr., rules that Eastern Airlines' weight requirements for flight attendants be allowed to stand. Women flight attendants have challenged the requirement as discriminatory.

4 March 1977
WOMEN'S ISSUES. The U.S. Senate confirms several women to White House appointments: Barbara Babcock, assistant attorney general of the Civil Division of the Justice Department; Barbara Blum, deputy administrator of the Environmental Protection Agency; Mary King, deputy director of ACTION; Patricia Wald, assistant attorney general for legislative affairs.

MILITARY. Ensign Janna Lambine is the first woman airplane pilot in the U.S. Coast Guard.

5 March 1977
WOMEN'S ISSUES. President Carter, answering calls from a radio audience during a televised broadcast of statements to the nation, emphasizes that only if necessary for national security would be draft women into military service.

9 March 1977
WOMEN'S ISSUES. The Illinois House of Representatives votes 100–66 to retain requirement of a three-fifths vote for ratification of the Equal Rights Amendment.

DEATHS. Frances Payne Bolton, who served 14 consecutive terms in the Ohio House of Representatives from 1939 to 1968, dies in Lyndhurst, Ohio, at age 91.

14 March 1977
DEATHS. Fannie Lou Hamer, civil rights leader, dies of cancer in Mound Bayou, Mississippi.

WOMEN'S ISSUES. The Equal Rights Amendment (ERA) will not make it to the floor of the Senate for vote. The chief sponsor of the ERA moves to refer the amendment to committee due to apparent lack of sufficient votes for its approval.

15 March 1977
WOMEN'S ISSUES. Missouri's State Senate rejects the Equal Rights Amendment, 22–12.

EDUCATION. Nearly two-thirds of the nation's schools and colleges have not submitted statements of assurance that they are in compliance with a 1972 federal sex discrimination law.

AVIATION. Frontier Airlines, a Denver-based carrier, is sued by the Equal Employment Opportunity Commission for discriminatory practices, including the exclusion of men and married women from flight attendant jobs.

18 March 1977
WOMEN'S ISSUES. The Senate confirms Eula Bingham as assistant secretary of labor for the Occupational Health and Safety Administration.

23 March 1977
DEATHS. Anne W. Wheaton, the first woman to serve as associate press secretary to a president, appointed to this post by Dwight D. Eisenhower, dies in Dallas, Texas.

RELIGION. At least 200 delegates to the National Federation of Priests' Councils Convention in Louisville, Kentucky, vote to ask Pope Paul VI to reconsider his ban on women priests in the Roman Catholic Church.

24 March 1977
MILITARY. Twenty-two women Marine Corps officers begin combat training in Quantico, Virginia.

27 March 1977
SPORTS. Chris Evert wins her fourth Virginia Slims tennis title at New York City's Madison Square Garden.

28 March 1977
WOMEN'S ISSUES. President Carter issues an Executive Order that designates former U.S. Representative Bella Abzug (D-New York) as presiding officer of the National Commission on Women.

DEATHS. Elizabeth Ames, founder and director of Yaddo, a creative arts retreat, dies in Saratoga Springs, New York.

29 March 1977
HEALTH. A report issued by the Population Council indicates that the combined effects of cigarette smoking and birth control pills increase death rates among pregnant women over age 30.

31 March 1977
EDUCATION. Department of Health, Education, and Welfare Secretary Joseph

Califano states that he had mistakenly advocated quotas for school admissions and job-hiring as a way to rectify past or current discrimination against women.

4 April 1977
IDEAS/BELIEFS. A *Time* magazine poll indicates that 66 percent of those surveyed feel that President Carter is making a good start on women's appointments to government posts.

WOMEN'S ISSUES. President Carter appoints Esther Peterson to be special White House assistant for consumer affairs.

11 April 1977
EDUCATION. The U.S. Commissioner of Education states that his office intends to "enlarge the access to education of minorities and women and other historically bypassed groups."

23 April 1977
WOMEN'S ISSUES. Nan Waterman is named board chairperson of Common Cause.

24 April 1977
WOMEN'S ISSUES. Eleanor Smeal is elected to a 2½-year term as president of the National Organization for Women. She is the group's first salaried president and will earn $17,500 annually.

6 May 1977
RELIGION. A Gallup poll reports that 41 percent of those surveyed support the idea of Roman Catholic ordination of women priests.

9 May 1977
LABOR. A 1975 job-bias suit against Adolph Coors Company is dropped when the Colorado brewer agrees to hire more women and minorities.

10 May 1977
MEDICAL. The National Cancer Institute issues new guidelines on the use of X-ray in detecting breast cancer in women. The institute advises restricting mammograms for women under age 50 to those with a personal or close family history with the disease.

16 May 1977
JUDICIAL. The U.S. Supreme Court refuses to review a case concerning disclosure under the Freedom of Information Act. The case, *Prudential Insurance Co.* v. *NOW,* involves a suit to obtain affirmative action records.

17 May 1977
JUDICIAL. U.S. Supreme Court Chief Justice Warren Burger says that between 1969 and 1976 the Court has issued full opinions on 21 women's rights cases.

29 May 1977
SPORTS. Janet Guthrie, the only woman to qualify for the Indianapolis 500, is forced to drop out of the race after completing only 27 laps. Her car's fuel pump is discovered to be defective.

31 May 1977
JUDICIAL. The U.S. Supreme Court rules against the defendant in *United Airlines* v. *Evans.* The case concerns a flight attendant who left the airline to be married, was rehired in 1972, but lost her seniority. She had failed to file a complaint against her employer within 90 days of her initial retirement as required by law in such circumstances.

22 June 1977
MILITARY. Ensign Beverly Kelley and Third Class Petty Officer Debra Lee Wilson are the first women to serve on Coast Guard ships other than hospital ships.

6 July 1977
FINANCE. The U.S. Comptroller of the Currency grants national charters to 2 groups planning to open banks managed and directed chiefly by women. They are Women's Bank, N.A., in Denver, Colorado, and Women's National Bank in Washington, D.C. A number of state-chartered women's banks are already operating.

9 July 1977
DEATHS. Alice Paul, founder of the National Women's party, dies at age 92 in Moorestown, New Jersey.

18 July 1977
WOMEN'S ISSUES. The Justice Department announces plans to screen all federal laws, regulations, and policies for sex discrimination.

27 July 1977
JUDICIAL. The U.S. Supreme Court strikes down an Alabama law setting minimum height and weight standards for state corrections officers. The standards are found in violation of the 1964 Civil Rights Act since they disqualify 40 percent of Alabama's women, but only 1 percent of its men. The requirements set 5 feet 2 inches and 120 pounds as minimum statistics for applicants.

28 July 1977
AVIATION. Elizabeth E. Bailey is confirmed as the first woman member of the Civil Aeronautics Board.

4 August 1977
POLITICS. The latest Capitol Hill Women's Political Caucus survey shows that U.S. senators pay women 56 percent of the median wages paid to men.

6 August 1977
LABOR. Negotiations for AT&T and the American Federation of Labor and Congress of Industrial Organizations–Communications Workers of America reach contract agreement. Included is a provision that pregnancy will be treated as a disability.

15 August 1977
CIVIL RIGHTS. The U.S. Commission on Civil Rights charges that the television industry is guilty of job discrimination and of perpetuating racial and sexual stereotypes. ABC-TV and NBC-TV disagree with these allegations, but CBS-TV has no immediate comment.

26 August 1977
WOMEN'S ISSUES. In Washington, D.C., about 3,000 marchers supporting the Equal Rights Amendment launch the National Organization for Women nationwide effort to gain ratification of the amendment by March 1979, the current deadline.

7 September 1977
WOMEN'S ISSUES. Dr. Carolyn Robertson Payton is named the first woman to head the Peace Corps.

POLITICS. In Wisconsin's first judicial recall election, Dane County Judge Archie Simonson is defeated by Moira M. Krueger, Madison's first woman judge. During a rape trial over which he presided, Simonson had remarked that women's sexually provocative clothing had been the basis for rape as a "normal" response to that clothing.

9 September 1977
WOMEN'S ISSUES. The Republican leadership of the House of Representatives calls for changes in the Social Security system. Included would be a 25 percent increase in benefits to a working wife.

12 September 1977
WOMEN'S ISSUES. Azie Taylor Morton becomes the first black woman treasurer of the United States.

16 September 1977
LEGISLATIVE. The U.S. Senate, in a 75–11 vote, passes a bill requiring employers who offer medical benefits not to exclude pregnancy and childbirth from coverage under their plans. The bill also bars employers from forcing pregnant workers to quit their jobs.

23 September 1977
MILITARY. The U.S. Air Force announces that women will soon be assigned to launching crews of Titan 2 intercontinental ballistic missiles housed in underground silos.

25 September 1977
IDEAS/BELIEFS. Lillian Carter, the president's mother, becomes the first woman to win the Synagogue Council for American Peace Prize.

29 September 1977
WOMEN'S ISSUES. The Torch Relay of the National Women's Conference begins in New York City. Kathy Switzer is the first runner in the relay. The 51-day, 2,600-mile journey ends in Houston, Texas, on 18 November.

SPORTS. Eva Shain is the first woman to judge a heavyweight championship fight— between Muhammad Ali and Ernie Shavers.

30 September 1977
RELIGION. Episcopal Church head Bishop John Allin offers to resign due to his personal opposition to the ordination of women priests. The 125-member House of Bishops issues a vote of confidence for Allin on 3 October.

3 October 1977
JUDICIAL. The U.S. Supreme Court declines to review a lower court ruling stating that the Kiwanis International organization can withdraw the charter of any local branch for admitting women to membership.

RELIGION. The Episcopal House of Bishops, meeting at their annual General Convention, votes to table a resolution to rebuke Bishop John Moore of New York, who had ordained the Reverend Ellen Barrett, a lesbian, on 10 January.

HEALTH. After having been denied an abortion due to Medicaid funding restriction, Rosie Jimenez dies from complications following an illegally performed abortion.

9 October 1977
DEATHS. Ruth Elder, an aviator who was the first woman to attempt transatlantic flight, dies in San Francisco, California, at age 73.

29 October 1977
WOMEN'S ISSUES. A Joint House Resolution is introduced in Congress, specifying that the Equal Rights Amendment be given an extension of its ratification period for 7 years beyond the current 22 March 1979 deadline.

3 November 1977
CRIME. Francine Hughes, who allegedly had murdered her husband by pouring and igniting gasoline underneath his bed, is acquitted by reason of temporary insanity. Hughes is known to have been physically abused by her husband.

14 November 1977
WOMEN'S ISSUES. The National Organization for Women supports economic boycotts aimed at affecting convention cities in non-ERA states as a way to promote ratification of this amendment.

17 November 1977
WOMEN'S ISSUES. President Carter urges federal officials to seek "aggressively and creatively" to promote career opportunities for women in the Civil Service.

18 November 1977
WOMEN'S ISSUES. Registration begins for the National Women's Conference in Houston, Texas.

19 November 1977
WOMEN'S ISSUES. The National Women's
Conference officially opens in Houston, Texas.
There are 1,403 delegates and 370 delegates-at-
large; each state is represented. In addition,
there are 186 alternates and 20,000 more men,
women, and children present. Also in the city,
about 15,000 Equal Rights Amendment
opponents hold a "pro-family" rally at
Houston's Astrodome. This group is headed by
Phyllis Schlafly.

21 November 1977
WOMEN'S ISSUES. The National Women's
Conference holds its final session in Houston,
Texas.

22 November 1977
POLITICS. In Houston, Texas, Kathryn
Whitmire is elected city comptroller. She is the
first woman to hold city office there.

3 December 1977
IDEAS/BELIEFS. Karen Farmer is the first
black woman to become a member of the
Daughters of the American Revolution (DAR).

6 December 1977
JUDICIAL. In *Nashville Gas Co.* v. *Satty,*
the U.S. Supreme Court rules that an employee
who takes maternity leave cannot be deprived of
accumulated job seniority.

10 December 1977
EDUCATION. Hanna Holborn Gray, acting
president of Yale University, is named president
of the University of Chicago.

17 December 1977
WOMEN'S ISSUES. The 1977 edition of the
Labor Department's Dictionary of Occupational
Titles eliminates gender and age references in its
20,000 job classifications.

19 December 1977
DEATHS. Nellie Tayloe Ross, first woman
governor in U.S. history, dies in Washington,
D.C., at age 101.

21 December 1977
MILITARY. The U.S. Navy backs expanded
sea duty for women to alleviate a labor shortage
and to help end charges that the navy offers very
narrow opportunities for women's advancement.

OTHER EVENTS OF 1977

WOMEN'S ISSUES. The Department of
Commerce names Anne Wexler to chair the
newly formed Interagency Task Force of
Women Business Owners.

POPULAR CULTURE. Oscars for 1976 go
to Faye Dunaway, Best Actress, in *Network,*
and to Beatrice Straight, Best Supporting
Actress, in the same film.

1 January 1978
WOMEN'S ISSUES. Marie M. Lambert is
the first woman judge of the New York County
Surrogate Court.

4 January 1978
LABOR. Equal Employment Opportunity
Commission Chair Eleanor Holmes Norton
announces a campaign to root out "systematic
patterns and practices" of discrimination in big
business.

8 January 1978
DEATHS. Rose Halprin, leader in the Zionist
organization Hadassah, dies in New York City
at age 82.

9 January 1978
SPORTS. A federal judge in Kansas City,
Missouri, rejects a challenge by the National
Collegiate Athletic Association (NCAA) to Title
IX regulations of the 1974 Higher Education
Act. The judge rejects NCAA contentions that
providing equal funding for male and female
athletic programs would pose economic
hardships to schools.

12 January 1978
CIVIL RIGHTS. A coalition of women's and
minority groups asks the Federal
Communications Commission to reconsider its
approval of the sale of WJAL-TV in
Washington, D.C., due to the owner's
unwillingness to seek out minority purchasers
for the station.

16 January 1978
AVIATION. The National Aeronautics and
Space Administration names 35 people,
including 6 women, to take part as astronauts in
the Space Shuttle program. The women are
Anna L. Fisher of Rancho Palos Verdes,

California; Shannon W. Lucid of Oklahoma City, Oklahoma; Judith A. Resnik of Akron, Ohio; Sally K. Ride of Stanford, California; Margaret R. Seddon of Memphis, Tennessee; and Kathryn D. Sullivan of Paterson, New Jersey.

19 January 1978
WOMEN'S ISSUES. In his State-of-the-Union address, President Carter pledges to eliminate barriers that restrict the "opportunities available to women, blacks, Hispanics, and other minorities."

25 January 1978
POLITICS. Muriel Humphrey, widow of Senator Hubert H. Humphrey, is appointed to her late husband's Senate seat by Minnesota Governor Rudy Perpech. Humphrey declines to say whether she will run in a special November election concerning the remaining 4 years of the 6-year term of office.

26 January 1978
WOMEN'S ISSUES. Angela Davis, black activist and Communist party member, begins teaching a required course in feminism at San Francisco State University in California.

30 January 1978
POLITICS. *U.S. News & World Report* issues results of a study showing 25-year changes in Congressional membership. In 1953, 12 women served in the House of Representatives and 1 served in the Senate. In 1978, the House has 18 women members and the Senate has none until Muriel Humphrey's appointment to her late husband's seat.

1 February 1978
WOMEN'S ISSUES. The first postage stamp to honor a black woman, Harriet Tubman, is issued in Washington, D.C.

7 February 1978
ARTS AND CULTURE. The American Academy and Institute of Arts and Letters announces the election of sculptor Marisol and writer Joyce Carol Oates to membership. There are now 35 women members out of a total 250 in the institute, from which the academy's 50 members are chosen. The 2 groups merged in 1977.

13 February 1978
POPULAR CULTURE. Jacqueline Kennedy Onassis becomes an associate editor at Doubleday & Company, after leaving a similar position at Viking Press. Her departure from the latter company was due to a 1977 dispute over possible Viking Press publication of a book about her former brother-in-law, Edward M. Kennedy.

14 February 1978
MILITARY. The Defense Department intends to ask Congress to repeal legislation barring the use of female military personnel in combat.

16 February 1978
POPULAR CULTURE. At an auction, the belongings of actress Joan Crawford bring a total of $80,000 in bids.

17 February 1978
WOMEN'S ISSUES. At a town meeting in Bangor, Maine, President Carter says he will sign the ratified Equal Rights Amendment "with pleasure."

21 February 1978
JUDICIAL. The U.S. Supreme Court declines to review a lower court decision in *Northwest Airlines* v. *Laffey*. The suit alleges that stewardesses denied jobs as pursers should receive the same pay as pursers, who are male, since both stewardesses and pursers perform the same job tasks.

28 February 1978
LABOR. AT&T employs 385,000 women, more than any other U.S. company, according to a report issued by *Women's Studies Journal*.

20 March 1978
WOMEN'S ISSUES. Leaders of the Equal Rights Amendment movement request that Congress extend the 7-year ratification deadline of the amendment. The National Organization for Women predicts a loss of $200 million as a result of convention city boycotts in states that have not yet ratified.

JUDICIAL. The U.S. Supreme Court declines to review a decision upholding a United Airlines regulation requiring stewardesses to take unpaid maternity leave of at least 7 months.

22 March 1978
POLITICS. President Carter meets with a delegation from the National Women's Conference at which former Representative Bella Abzug (D-New York) presents the official report of the conference.

23 March 1978
RELIGION. The National Council of Churches reports that the total number of women Protestant ministers in the United States in 1977 was 10,470. Women are believed to make up between 20 and 50 percent of the enrollment at some major American divinity schools.

25 March 1978
SPORTS. The UCLA women's basketball team wins the national championship after beating Maryland, 90–74. The contest was held before more than 9,000 fans, the largest crowd ever to watch a women's championship game.

1 April 1978
RELIGION. Mormon Elder Neal A. Maxwell tells a church conference that a woman's primary role as mother is equal in importance to the roles assigned to men.

2 April 1978
RELIGION. Canon Mary Simpson of New York speaks at Westminster Abbey in London. She was the first American Episcopal nun to be ordained (December 1976).

6 April 1978
MILITARY. Marine Corps Brigadier General Margaret Ann Brewer is nominated by President Carter to be director of the Division of Information.

7 April 1978
RELIGION. Jessica Marks, a member of the Church of Scientology, claims that she was forcibly held by a deprogrammer for the "malicious purpose of interfering with religious belief."

10 April 1978
HEALTH. Betty Ford enters Long Beach Naval Hospital in California for treatment of an addiction to arthritis medication.

13 April 1978
POLITICS. The U.S. Census Bureau reports

that about 59 percent of all women voted in the 1976 presidential election.

19 April 1978
WOMEN'S ISSUES. President Carter announces that Anne Wexler, currently deputy undersecretary in the Commerce Department, will take over for public liaison work in the White House.

AVIATION. Jill E. Brown becomes the first black woman pilot for a major U.S. airline, Texas International Airlines, Inc.

25 April 1978
JUDICIAL. In *Los Angeles* v. *Manhart,* the U.S. Supreme Court rules 6–2 that an employer who charges women more than men to participate in a pension plan is guilty of discrimination under the Civil Rights Act of 1964.

3 May 1978
POLITICS. Consumer Action Now (CAN) organizes Sun Day, which leads to the formation of a solar energy lobby in Washington, D.C.

5 May 1978
HEALTH. Betty Ford leaves California's Long Beach Naval Hospital after treatment for drug and alcohol dependency.

RELIGION. Barbara B. Smith, president of the Relief Society of the Mormon Church, notes that the church favors "women's rights in principle. We just feel that the Equal Rights Amendment is not the way to achieve these things."

7 May 1978
LABOR. The Labor Department implements new affirmative action rules designed to promote women hirees at 3.1 percent of the construction industry's total employment levels. These regulations affect hard-hat positions in federal contracts totaling more than $10,000.

8 May 1978
LABOR. The Rand Corporation releases the results of a study revealing differences in earnings between white and black women. In 1947, black women's earnings were 33 percent of white women's. In 1975, black women earned 98.6 percent of white women's earnings.

15 May 1978
POPULAR CULTURE. Jordanian officials announce the upcoming marriage of King Hussein of Jordan to an American woman, Elizabeth (Lisa) Halaby.

24 May 1978
HEALTH. The Centers for Disease Control report that in 1976 there were 312 legal abortions for every 1,000 live births. Sixty-five percent of women obtaining abortions are under 25 years old, 75 percent are unmarried, and 67 percent are white.

26 May 1978
WOMEN'S ISSUES. Equal Rights Amendment supporters press Congress to rule out permission for states to rescind prior favorable votes on the amendment.

28 May 1978
SPORTS. Women on the Penn State women's lacrosse team beat the University of Maryland in a 9–3 game in the first championship tournament of the U.S. Women's Lacrosse Association.

29 May 1978
SPORTS. Janet Guthrie takes ninth place in her second Indianapolis 500 race. She averages a speed of 152.96 miles per hour.

31 May 1978
LEGAL. According to a *Wall Street Journal* report, women attorneys make up more than 9 percent of the legal profession. In 1970, fewer than 3 percent of practicing lawyers were women.

4 June 1978
LABOR. The National Commission of Working Women reports that 8 percent of all working women are employed in low-status jobs, and that two-thirds of adults living below the poverty level are women.

9 June 1978
RELIGION. Although the Mormon Church announces that black males can now be members of the Mormon priesthood, women are still excluded from the ranks of the ordained.

15 June 1978
WOMEN'S ISSUES. The White House reports that of 1,140 appointments made by

President Carter, 10 percent went to blacks, 4 percent to Hispanics, and 18 percent to women.

20 June 1978
HEALTH. A *New York Times* report shows that 17 states and Washington, D.C., continue to fund all, or nearly all, abortions for low-income women despite the loss of federal matching funds for abortions in these cases.

22 June 1978
EDUCATION. Karen Hansen is the first woman graduate of the Webb Institute of Naval Architecture.

29 June 1978
WOMEN'S ISSUES. Susan B. King is appointed chair of the Consumer Product Safety Commission.

1 July 1978
MILITARY. Brigadier General Mary Clarke becomes the first woman named by the U.S. Army to the 2-star rank of major general. She is commander of the army's military police school at Fort McClellan, Alabama.

3 July 1978
JUDICIAL. The U.S. Supreme Court declines to review a lower court decision upholding a compensation settlement between AT&T and 15,000 women and minority employees.

9 July 1978
WOMEN'S ISSUES. Nearly 100,000 marchers in Washington, D.C., support an extension of the ratification period for the pending Equal Rights Amendment. Three more states must ratify the amendment before the 22 March 1979 deadline.

12 July 1978
WOMEN'S ISSUES. President Carter writes to the House Judiciary Committee urging members to vote for an extension of the Equal Rights Amendment ratification deadline.

23 July 1978
HEALTH. A U.S. Public Health Department survey shows that women on a diet of only liquid protein run a 30-times greater risk of fatal heart attack than nondieters using this protein supplement.

24 July 1978
LABOR. The Labor Department reports that nearly 48 percent of all wives are employed or are looking for work outside the home. A record 30.4 million U.S. families now have at least 2 wage earners.

27 July 1978
JUDICIAL. U.S. District Court Judge John Sirica strikes down as unconstitutional a law barring U.S. Navy women from serving aboard other than transport or hospital vessels.

1 August 1978
WOMEN'S ISSUES. Margaret (Midge) Constanza announces her resignation as presidential assistant.

9 August 1978
HEALTH. The American Bar Association House of Delegates approves the use of Medicaid funding for indigent women seeking abortions.

15 August 1978
WOMEN'S ISSUES. The House of Representatives votes 223 to 189 to give states an additional 39 months to ratify the Equal Rights Amendment. This pushes the ratification deadline to 30 June 1982.

18 August 1978
AVIATION. Rosalynn Carter pilots the dirigible *America* while taking a flight over northern Virginia on her 51st birthday.

28 August 1978
WOMEN'S ISSUES. Nancy Hays Teeters is nominated to the Federal Reserve System Board of Governors. She is the first to be selected for this slot and is sworn in on 18 September.

SPORTS. Fifteen-year-old Tracy Caulkins sets 14 individual American swimming records and wins five gold medals at the World Swimming Championships.

30 August 1978
CRIME. Maria Elaine Pitchford is found not guilty by reason of insanity in a case charging her with criminally aborting her own fetus.

31 August 1978
WOMEN'S ISSUES. Sarah T. Weddington is named an assistant to President Carter. Weddington will specialize in women's issues. She earned recognition in 1973 as the lawyer who won the Supreme Court case *Roe* v. *Wade*.

12 September 1978
POLITICS. Connecticut Governor Ella T. Grasso wins renomination to a second term of office.

13 September 1978
BUSINESS. Jane Cahill Pfeiffer is named board chairperson of NBC-TV as well as a director of RCA Corporation, the NBC parent company. Pfeiffer will be the highest-ranking woman executive in the broadcast industry.

14 September 1978
POPULAR CULTURE. Betty Ford undergoes cosmetic surgery in Palm Springs, California. "I wanted a nice new face to go with my beautiful new life," says Ford.

25 September 1978
SPORTS. U.S. District Court Judge Constance Baker Motley rules that major league baseball and the New York Yankees management cannot legally bar a woman sportswriter from the locker room after a game. The suit was brought by *Sports Illustrated* reporter Melissa Ludtke.

6 October 1978
WOMEN'S ISSUES. The U.S. Senate votes 60–36 to extend the ratification deadline for the Equal Rights Amendment to 30 June 1982.

WOMEN'S ISSUES. Phyllis Schlafly announces that the Equal Rights Amendment deadline extension will be challenged in the courts.

7 October 1978
RELIGION. The Mormon Church announces that women will be allowed to offer certain prayers previously given only by male priests.

10 October 1978
WOMEN'S ISSUES. Congress authorizes minting of a Susan B. Anthony copper-nickel clad dollar. It is first issued in December at the Philadelphia, Pennsylvania, mint.

15 October 1978
SPORTS. Irene Miller of Palo Alto,

California, and Vera Komarkova of Boulder, Colorado, are the first Americans and the first women to conquer Annapurna One, a 26,545-foot mountain in Nepal. Two other women in the party die in a fall on 17 October attempting the final ascent.

17 October 1978
ARTS AND CULTURE. Marian Anderson receives a special gold medal authorized by Congress, which salutes Anderson's "unselfish devotion to the promotion of the arts."

26 October 1978
SPORTS. Beverly Johnson of Wyoming becomes the first woman to scale El Capitan, in Yosemite National Park.

31 October 1978
LABOR. President Carter signs a bill protecting women from occupation discrimination because of pregnancy. Employers are now required to provide pregnancy disability payment in their medical disability plans.

1 November 1978
MILITARY. Eight female ensigns are the first women (other than nurses) to be assigned to sea duty in the U.S. Navy.

SPORTS. Four former National Football League cheerleaders criticize the management of the Baltimore, New Orleans, San Diego, and Chicago teams for allegedly encouraging the cheerleaders to pose nude in *Playboy* magazine. Each woman was subsequently fired by the teams.

3 November 1978
LABOR. The National Labor Relations Board rules that a union has the right to an employer's job data broken down by race and gender.

7 November 1978
DEATHS. Janet Flanner, writer and *New Yorker* correspondent for almost 50 years, dies of a heart attack in New York City.

13 November 1978
JUDICIAL. The U.S. Supreme Court rules 5–4 that a lower court had erred in a job discrimination case, *Board of Trustees* v. *Sweeney*. The case concerned denial of

promotion for women instructors at Keene State College in New Hampshire.

17 November 1978
LABOR. The city of Chicago is ordered to pay nearly $3 million in damages to 225 women public works employees who charged the department with sex discrimination.

22 November 1978
WOMEN'S ISSUES. The National Advisory Committee for Women cancels a scheduled meeting with President Carter in protest of the 15-minute limited time-slot for the meeting.

24 November 1978
WOMEN'S ISSUES. Dr. Carolyn Payton, the first woman and the first black director of the Peace Corps, resigns.

29 November 1978
MILITARY. The U.S. Army announces that it has given its commanders the authority to get rid of soldiers, married or unmarried, if child care responsibilities interfere with their military duties. About 15,000 soldiers are "sole parents," and about 37,000 are married to other soldiers, often creating assignment conflicts with regard to child care.

9 December 1978
SPORTS. The Women's Professional Basketball League (WBL) opens with a game between the Milwaukee Does and the Chicago Hustle. Chicago wins, 92–87. Salaries in the WBL range from $5,000 to $15,000. The minimum National Basketball Association salary is more than $30,000.

11 December 1978
DEATHS. In Hawaii, Iolani Luahine, a dancer regarded as the last exponent of the sacred hula ceremony—and officially proclaimed a living treasure by the state of Hawaii—dies at age 63.

16 December 1978
DEATHS. Blanche Calloway Jones, the first woman to lead a major American dance band in the 1930s, dies in Washington, D.C., at age 76.

27 December 1978
JUDICIAL. A Marion County Oregon Circuit Court jury acquits a man of first-degree rape

charges brought by his wife. If convicted, he could have been sentenced to 20 years in prison.

OTHER EVENTS IN 1978

ARTS AND CULTURE. The Coalition of Women's Arts Organizations holds its first formal meeting. The coalition seeks greater recognition for women in the arts and equal opportunity for women in arts programs and institutions.

POPULAR CULTURE. Academy Awards for 1977 are presented to Diane Keaton, Best Actress in *Annie Hall,* and to Vanessa Redgrave, Best Supporting Actress in *Julia.*

2 January 1979
MILITARY. The Pentagon expects the number of women in the nation's military to double to 12 percent by 1984.

9 January 1979
JUDICIAL. The U.S. Supreme Court rules that a law excusing women from jury duty on the basis of sex is unconstitutional.

10 January 1979
SPORTS. The National Collegiate Athletic Association meets in San Francisco, California, to discuss ways to counter Title IX of the 1974 Higher Education Act. The Act bans sex discrimination in sports.

Billie Jean King, 1943–

In 1967, tennis star Billie Jean King made headlines when she captured the Wimbledon titles—singles, doubles, and mixed. In 1971, she won $100,000 in prize money, the first woman to receive this great a sum. In 1981, King made news again as she acknowledged having a brief affair with a former secretary and companion, Marilyn Barnett. Born in Long Beach, California, on 22 November 1943, she was the only daughter of Willard and Betty Moffitt. Extremely active as a child, she showed natural athletic ability as early as her sixth year. By age eleven, her parents had encouraged her to take tennis lessons. Soon, Moffitt was completely absorbed by the sport and expressed her goal of playing someday at Wimbledon.

In 1958, Moffitt won the Southern Championship and was coaching with former tennis great Alice Marble. In 1960, she ranked fourth in the nation, and the following year she and Karen Hantze won the women's doubles title at Wimbledon, the youngest pair ever to do so. Moffitt attended California State College at Los Angeles beginning in 1962, and although she tried for the women's singles championship at Wimbledon the next year, she was defeated by Margaret Smith. She traveled to Australia to coach with Mervyn Rose, and in December 1964 ranked second among U.S. women tennis players. Playing exceptionally well during 1965, she did not lose a single match to any American rival, although she was defeated that year by Maria Bueno at Wimbledon.

On 17 September 1965, she married Larry King, and throughout 1966 she effected a long string of tennis victories. She was by now ranked at the top of the ladder in women's tennis—sharing the number-one spot with Nancy Richey. In June 1966, King won her first women's singles title at Wimbledon. King had by now achieved a certain degree of notoriety for her outspoken, ambitious demeanor both on and off the court. Described by some as lively, she was also taken to task by critics for showing too much emotion during (and after) a game. But no one could rightfully deny King the credit she deserved. By the early 1970s she had become the greatest American woman tennis player ever. In 1971, she was the driving force behind the establishment of women's professional tennis; the first competition was the Virginia Slims Circuit.

By 1979 King had taken twenty Wimbledon titles, six of them in women's singles. She had also captured many world titles, including the U.S. Singles, the U.S. Indoor Championships, and the French Open. She had also won the U.S. Doubles title, first in 1964, with Karen Hantze Susman, and then in 1980, teamed with Martina Navratilova. One of King's most publicized matches was against Bobby Riggs in 1973, a game that was billed as the "Battle of the Sexes." King won this match.

By her own admission, at age thirty-seven in 1981 King was no longer the top U.S. woman tennis player. But she was still a star attraction on the court. She was also, with her husband, an indefatigable worker on behalf of women's tennis. Together they established *WomenSports* magazine and the Women's Sports Foundation. And when a favorable judgment was handed down in the Barnett case (Marilyn Barnett had sued unsuccessfully for lifetime support, charging that King had promised to provide for her financially), King put the incident behind her, wrote her autobiography *Billie Jean* (1982), and joined her sports-producer husband in pushing for establishment of World Team Tennis.

SPORTS. The Association for Intercollegiate Athletics for Women holds its annual convention in Los Angeles, California. At the meeting, Ann Meyers, UCLA basketball player, is honored as the Outstanding Women College Athlete of 1978.

12 January 1979
WOMEN'S ISSUES. President Carter dismisses Bella Abzug as co-chair and member of his National Advisory Committee on Women due to Abzug's critical statements about the president. The women's panel terms Carter's action "a terrible mistake," and co-chair Carmen Degado Votaw resigns in protest.

16 January 1979
WOMEN'S ISSUES. The Nevada Senate votes 14–3 to reject the proposed Equal Rights Amendment.

BUSINESS. A *Newsweek* magazine article reports that fewer and fewer male executives are willing to uproot their families in order to relocate or to obtain a job promotion.

January 1979
LABOR. A federal report states that AT&T is in "substantial compliance" of government orders to end job discrimination against women and minorities. Women managers at AT&T now represent 6.9 percent of all such positions compared to 2.1 percent in 1973.

WOMEN'S ISSUES. A Virginia State Senate committee fails to approve a vote on the proposed Equal Rights Amendment.

19 January 1979
MILITARY. A Defense Department recommendation advises that the armed forces remove sexist language from their command jargon.

20 January 1979
HEALTH. The Centers for Disease Control announce that a new antibiotic effective in the treatment of gonorrhea has been developed. About 100,000 women are rendered sterile each year by gonorrhea infections.

24 January 1979
BUSINESS. Sears Roebuck & Company files a class action suit against 10 federal agencies charging that Equal Employment Opportunity laws are so confusing that the company cannot comply with them.

30 January 1979
RELIGION. A special commission of the Conservative branch of Judaism recommends that qualified women be ordained as rabbis.

31 January 1979
HEALTH. The *New England Journal of Medicine* reports that women who take estrogen during and after menopause have a lower risk of uterine cancer if they stop taking the hormone.

2 February 1979
RELIGION. Sally J. Priesand, the first American woman rabbi, resigns as associate rabbi of a New York Reform synagogue.

15 February 1979
WOMEN'S ISSUES. A federal study panel suggests changes in the Social Security system to eliminate discrimination against women.

21 February 1979
WOMEN'S ISSUES. A Kansas City, Missouri, District Court upholds the right of the National Organization for Women to promote a convention boycott against states not having ratified the Equal Rights Amendment. Judge Elmo Hunter rules that this boycott is not a violation of antitrust laws.

27 February 1979
ARTS AND CULTURE. Historian Barbara Tuchman is the first woman to be elected president of the American Academy and Institute of Arts and Letters.

9 March 1979
FINANCE. The Department of Housing and Urban Development (HUD) opens a drive to prevent discrimination against women who seek mortgage loans. Secretary of HUD, Patricia Roberts Harris, states "too few women know their rights in the matter."

MILITARY. More than 1,000 women U.S. Air Force Service pilots who flew for the Army Air Corps between September 1942 and December 1944 are recognized as service veterans with full Veterans Administration benefits.

25 March 1979
SPORTS. Old Dominion beats Louisiana Tech, 75–65, for the women's national basketball championships.

27 March 1979
POPULAR CULTURE. Promoters of the Miss New York State contest agree to reimburse losing entrants who prove financial loss as a result of the contest's practices.

29 March 1979
SPORTS. Nancy Lieberman, Old Dominion's All-American Guard, receives the Wade trophy as college basketball's outstanding female player.

7 April 1979
POLITICS. Lila Cockrell is elected mayor of San Antonio, Texas—her third 2-year term.

9 April 1979
MILITARY. The U.S. Army lowers many standards for women volunteers to help thwart a downward trend in women's enlistment.

18 April 1979
POPULAR CULTURE. Michelle Triola loses her breach of contract "palimony" suit against actor Lee Marvin. But Marvin is ordered to pay $104,000 "for rehabilitative purposes."

23 April 1979
JUDICIAL. The U.S. Supreme Court refuses to review an appeals court decision denying $225,000 in back pay to 238 women factory workers in Kentucky since the group cannot prove individual damages.

24 April 1979
BUSINESS. Sears Roebuck & Company announces that it will no longer bid for or accept federal contracts. This action, spurred by recent problems with the Equal Employment Opportunity Commission, will cost Sears about one-tenth of 1 percent of its $18 billion sales volume in 1978.

3 May 1979
ARTS AND CULTURE. The National Gallery of Art in Washington, D.C., elects Ruth Carter Johnson as its first woman trustee.

9 May 1979
WOMEN'S ISSUES. Lynda Bird Johnson Robb is named to head President Carter's National Advisory Committee for Women panel. She replaces Bella Abzug.

12 May 1979
RELIGION. A leader of the Protestant Episcopal Church urges a gathering of 50 followers to remain in the church although they disagree with the ordination of women priests.

15 May 1979
JUDICIAL. A U.S. district court judge dismisses a suit brought by Sears Roebuck & Company challenging federal equal employment laws as contradictory. The judge states the alleged conflict is not "sufficiently concrete."

18 May 1979
JUDICIAL. A federal jury in Oklahoma City, Oklahoma, awards $10.5 million in damages to the estate of Karen Silkwood, a lab technician contaminated by radiation in 1974 while employed at the Kerr-McGee Corporation Cimarron plutonium plant. Silkwood was killed in an auto accident on 13 November 1974 en route to meet with a *New York Times* reporter concerning the radiation contamination.

Judy Chicago, 1939–

Perhaps most famous for her large-scale ceramic piece *The Dinner Party,* artist and feminist Judy Chicago has spent her career exploring ways in which to promote female imagery in art. Born Judy Cohen on 20 June 1939, in Chicago, Illinois, she was encouraged to draw by her parents, Arthur M. and May (Levenson) Cohen. By the time she graduated from high school in 1957 she had already spent a decade of Saturdays in classes at The Art Institute of Chicago. Cohen obtained a B.A. and an M.A. from UCLA in 1962 and 1964, respectively.

During her formal studies, Cohen found virtually no support for her highly individualized style of painting, which showed soft "biomorphic" images. She instead became adept at Plexiglas sculpture and in 1966 had a solo show in Los Angeles. She also exhibited that year in New York City at the Jewish Museum. At the Pasadena Museum of Art in 1969, another one-artist showing enabled Cohen to display her ever-more-intricate sculptures, although critics' reactions were mixed. In 1970, she had her name legally changed to Judy Chicago as a symbol of her break with male-oriented society.

After a minimally successful show at California State College in Fullerton, Chicago spent time helping to establish a women's art program at Fresno State College, also in California. She helped mount *"Womanhouse,"* a show in Los Angeles that was attended by ten thousand people during its month-long run in 1972. In the early 1970s, Chicago was increasingly inspired by women's imagery and her work reflects this. Many of her paintings and prints of the period focus on a feminist message that was only just beginning to be accepted by the larger art community.

At the California Institute of the Arts, she organized a nationwide Conference for Women Artists in 1972. A year later, she produced a large painting entitled *Let It All Hang Out,* which was aimed at women specifically and which was designed to address issues of female empowerment. Chicago set up the "Woman's Building" in Los Angeles in 1973, which drew five thousand people to its opening. The Woman's Building was a joint venture designed to provide performance space for feminist theater groups as well as studio space and exhibition areas for writers, painters, and other artists. In 1973, she was the recipient of *Mademoiselle* magazine's "Woman of the Year" award.

Chicago's work relies on form, color, and texture for its impact. And she has drawn heavily on the growth of women's consciousness for her subjects, reaching into women's history for themes as well as projecting ideals for the future. In 1975,

Chicago published her autobiography, *Through the Flower,* which was both hailed as an important study of the world of feminist art and criticized for its weak style.

On 16 March 1979, her first showing of *The Dinner Party* was unveiled at the San Francisco Museum of Modern Art. In this ceramic and textile piece, Chicago interpreted the lives of thirty-nine women from classical through modern times. The exhibit moved to Houston, Texas, after several other facilities had canceled their showing of the work. Critics termed Chicago's creation innovative and definitive, as well as saying it was trivial and degrading to the women whose lives it represented. In two books and a documentary film, Chicago gave full credit to the more than four hundred women who had helped produce *The Dinner Party.* And her success with this large-scale work encouraged her to attempt another, similar project involving a team of women artisans. She chose the subject of birth for her second multiartist piece. The tapestry series *The Birth Project* was completed and first exhibited in 1984. A book about *The Birth Project* was published in 1985.

---

5 June 1979
JUDICIAL. The U.S. Supreme Court rules 7–2 in favor of veterans receiving an advantage in public service employment without discrimination against women. Ellie Smeal, president of the National Organization for Women, terms the decision "devastating."

MEDICAL. A University of California at San Diego study reports that male doctors take medical complaints of men more seriously than the complaints of women.

6 June 1979
MEDICAL. A National Cancer Institute panel recommends that surgeons abandon radical mastectomy when treating cancer of the breast. Currently, this form of surgery is performed on about 25,000 women per year.

8 June 1979
MILITARY. U.S. Coast Guard Lieutenant Susan Ingalls Moritz assumes command of the USS *Cape Current.* Moritz is the first woman to command a ship on regular Coast Guard patrol.

11 June 1979
LABOR. According to a report made public by the Supreme Court, women are not hired in equal proportion to male Court employees. Currently, there are 27 male law clerks and only 5 females. All these employees are white.

19 June 1979
MEDICAL. A *New York Times* article reports that midwifery is increasing in the United States and that there are currently about 2,500 individuals certified by the American College of Nurse Midwives.

25 June 1979
JUDICIAL. The Supreme Court rules that a provision of the Social Security Act providing benefits to families with unemployed fathers is unconstitutional because it denies such benefits to families whose mothers are out of work.

27 June 1979
JUDICIAL. The Supreme Court rules 5–4 that denial of Social Security benefits to unwed mothers is not a violation of equal protection under the Fifth Amendment.

30 June 1979
SPORTS. Mary Decker is the first woman to run a mile in less than 4.5 minutes. She competes in the Brooks Meet of Champions in Philadelphia, Pennsylvania. Her time is 4:23:5.

1 July 1979
WOMEN'S ISSUES. Circulation of the Susan B. Anthony dollar begins.

15 July 1979
POLITICS. More than 1,000 women meet for the fourth biennial convention of the National Women's Political Caucus in Cincinnati, Ohio. Iris Mitgang, a California lawyer, is elected to a 2-year term as president.

6 August 1979
POPULAR CULTURE. In a *Newsweek* article, first lady Rosalynn Carter is termed a

"one-woman Kitchen Cabinet, Carter's most trusted senior hand."

7 August 1979
WOMEN'S ISSUES. Joyce Londor Alexander is sworn in as the first black woman U.S. magistrate, in Boston, Massachusetts.

10 August 1979
WOMEN'S ISSUES. Sarah T. Weddington, assistant to President Carter, is promoted to senior aide status.

20 August 1979
SPORTS. Long-distance swimmer Diana Nyad completes an 89-mile swim from the Bahamas to Florida in 27 hours, 38 minutes.

23 August 1979
JUDICIAL. Former Representative Otto Passman (D-Louisiana) settles a sex bias suit brought against him in 1974 by Shirley Davis, who claimed she had been fired because she was a woman.

3 September 1979
LABOR. More than 1,000 labor leaders gather for a White House picnic, which President Carter states especially honors women workers.

9 September 1979
INTERNATIONAL. Karen Stevenson becomes the first black woman to win a Rhodes Scholarship. She plans to study French and Russian literature at Oxford University in England.

SPORTS. The Indiana Pacers waive Ann Meyers at the close of preseason rookie basketball camp. This ends her hope of being the first woman National Basketball Association player.

10 September 1979
MILITARY. Twenty-five women of the 1980 graduating class at the U.S. Air Force Academy are scheduled to be the first women to enter pilot training.

11 September 1979
MILITARY. Female U.S. Navy personnel go overseas on a warship for the first time. The *Vulcan* carries a crew of 730, of which about 55 are women.

12 September 1979
LITERATURE. Author Judith Krantz receives the largest book advance payment ever recorded—$3 million.

2 October 1979
DEATHS. Marilyn J. McKusker is the first woman killed in a coal mine disaster. She dies in the Rushton Mining Company mine cave-in in Coalport, Pennsylvania.

4 October 1979
WOMEN'S ISSUES. Commerce Secretary Juanita M. Kreps resigns her cabinet post for personal reasons.

9 October 1979
MILITARY. More than 70 percent of female West Point cadets want to be both officers and wives, according to a study sponsored by the U.S. Military Academy.

30 October 1979
WOMEN'S ISSUES. President Carter names Shirley Hufstedler to the newly created cabinet post of education secretary.

4 November 1979
SPORTS. The U.S. wins its tenth Wightman Cup with a 7-game sweep over Great Britain in tennis matches in West Palm Beach, Florida.

9 November 1979
MILITARY. The U.S. Military Academy in West Point, New York, admits that hazing traditions had accelerated into malicious "sophomoric antics," which included forcing women cadets to kill chickens by biting them across the tendons of the neck.

13 November 1979
MILITARY. The Carter Administration urges Congress to remove its ban on women in combat. Air Force Major General Jeanne M. Holm (retired) says women can fight as well as men in nearly all combat except ground fighting, where women lack physical strength.

14 November 1979
SPORTS. Ann Meyers, recently dropped by the Indiana Pacers, signs a 3-year contract with the New Jersey Gems of the Women's Professional Basketball League.

24 November 1979
LABOR. The Commerce Department reports that female wage earners had a median income of $4,048 in 1978.

25 November 1979
CRIME. The American Civil Liberties Union reports that 556 people, including 6 women, await execution in penitentiaries across the nation.

29 November 1979
WOMEN'S ISSUES. Stopping at the University of Iowa on a campaign tour, Senator Edward M. Kennedy (D-Massachusetts) promises to push hard for equal rights for women. He terms the Carter administration "passive and insensitive" in this area.

POLITICS. Rosalynn Carter tours New Hampshire on behalf of her husband's campaign for reelection.

3 December 1979
MILITARY. The U.S. Army takes disciplinary action in 30 cases of sexual fraternization among women trainees and male drill instructors at Fort Dix, New Jersey.

4 December 1979
SPORTS. The Department of Health, Education, and Welfare issues final Title IX guidelines concerning expenditures of male and female athletic programs at colleges and universities receiving federal funding.

5 December 1979
RELIGION. Sonia Johnson of Sterling, Virginia, an outspoken leader of Mormons for ERA, is formally excommunicated by the Mormon Church. Johnson terms her trial a "witchhunt."

7 December 1979
ARTS AND CULTURE. Louise Nevelson, sculptor, is elected to the American Academy and Institute of Arts and Letters.

11 December 1979
POLITICS. Dianne Feinstein becomes the first woman elected mayor of San Francisco, California.

23 December 1979
DEATHS. Expatriate millionairess and art collector Peggy Guggenheim dies in Italy, leaving an estate worth more than $35 million.

OTHER EVENTS OF 1979

POPULAR CULTURE. Oscars for 1978 go to Jane Fonda, Best Actress, in *Coming Home,* and to Maggie Smith, Best Supporting Actress, in *California Suite.*

1 January 1980
BUSINESS. Sherry Lansing is named president of Twentieth Century–Fox Productions. She signs a 3-year contract for $300,000 per year, thus becoming the first woman to head a major motion picture studio.

4 January 1980
POPULAR CULTURE. Actress Butterfly McQueen sues Greyhound Bus Lines, Inc., for $300,000 after she had been falsely arrested in April 1979 by Greyhound Security guards. McQueen, best known for her role as Prissy in *Gone With the Wind,* had been charged with being a pickpocket.

8 January 1980
SPORTS. The National Collegiate Athletic Association adopts a proposal to sponsor championship tournaments for women in Divisions II and III in 5 sports: basketball, swimming, field hockey, volleyball, and tennis.

SPORTS. Nancy Lieberman is named outstanding female athlete of 1979 by the Association of Intercollegiate Athletics for Women. Lieberman was an all-American basketball player at Old Dominion University.

9 January 1980
POLITICS. Chicago Mayor Jane M. Byrne appoints her husband, Jan McMillan, to a dollar-a-year position as her press secretary.

EDUCATION. A San Jose State University professor is fired for allegations of sexual harassment of women. He had been accused by 5 women students of various sexual incidents since 1977. Another faculty member is also cited for similar incidents and suspended.

10 January 1980
SPORTS. At its annual convention, the Association for Intercollegiate Athletics for Women (AIAW) responds with outrage to recent

National Collegiate Athletic Association (NCAA) proposals that would support women's championship tournaments sponsored by the NCAA. AIAW delegates express fears of takeover by the NCAA and wish to keep women's events separate from those of men.

13 January 1980
WOMEN'S ISSUES. More than 6,000 women march in Richmond, Virginia, in support of the Equal Rights Amendment. President of the National Organization for Women Ellie Smeal states, "We here in Virginia are kicking off the 1980 ratification drive."

14 January 1980
HEALTH. The U.S. Surgeon General states that lung cancer among American women is rising in incidence and could, within 3 years, be the leading cancer killer of women.

15 January 1980
WOMEN'S ISSUES. The U.S. Civil Rights Commission reports that households headed by women are discriminated against by "disproportionately high costs for flawed, deteriorating, and overcrowded housing."

LABOR. Washington Governor Dixy Lee Ray calls for the state's Department of Personnel to pay attention to salary differences between women and men with similar jobs and responsibilities.

17 January 1980
WOMEN'S ISSUES. An anti-ERA demonstration at the Virginia state capitol in Richmond draws about 1,000 supporters. The Equal Rights Amendment needs ratification of three more states before the deadline of 30 June 1982.

21 January 1980
CRIME. The FBI reports that crimes of all kinds committed by women went up 6.2 percent between 1973 and 1978. The number of women involved in white-collar crimes rose at rates of 2–3 times faster than white-collar crime committed by men.

23 January 1980
WOMEN'S ISSUES. In his State-of-the-Union address, President Carter announces his strong support of equal rights for women.

25 January 1980
HEALTH. A University of California study indicates that daughters of women who took the drug diethylstilbestrol (DES) have an increased risk of miscarriage or premature birth.

26 January 1980
SPORTS. Runner Mary Decker breaks her own world record by completing the mile in 4:21:7 at Mount Smart Stadium in Auckland, New Zealand.

28 January 1980
CIVIL RIGHTS. Rosa Parks is awarded the Martin Luther King, Jr. Non-Violent Peace Prize in Atlanta, Georgia. Parks, who now lives in Detroit, Michigan, was the Alabama woman who refused to give up her bus seat to a white person in 1955, provoking the now-famous Montgomery, Alabama, bus boycott.

MILITARY. Senator Ted Stevens (D-Alaska) says that "we will support [draft] registration for women as well as men, but we have to take a hard look at conditions under which women should be drafted." Stevens' remark is directed at President Carter's desire to increase U.S. military strength, especially in the Middle East.

8 February 1980
MILITARY. President Carter issues a draft registration plan that would include women as well as men. Registration of women would require congressional authority.

11 February 1980
MILITARY. Army Major General Mary E. Clarke, commander of Fort McClellan, Alabama, reports that sexual harassment is a definite problem in her branch of the armed services.

15 February 1980
ARTS AND CULTURE. Writer Lillian Hellman files a $2.25 million defamation suit against novelist Mary McCarthy. While appearing on a television talk show, McCarthy had called Hellman a "dishonest writer."

16 February 1980
SPORTS. Mary Decker breaks the indoor mile world record and takes the world title, finishing the race in 4:17:55 at Houston's Astrodome Invitational.

19 February 1980
JUDICIAL. The U.S. Supreme Court votes 6–3 to lift a stay on a lower court order that would require the government to fund abortions under Medicaid. States were notified of the resumption of Medicaid financing for medically necessary abortions.

21 February 1980
LABOR. The American Federation of Labor and Congress of Industrial Organizations votes to reserve 2 seats on its 35-member executive council for a woman and a member of a minority group.

MILITARY. Marine Sergeant Bambi Lin Finney is honorably discharged after it is revealed that she posed for *Playboy* magazine.

26 February 1980
ARTS AND CULTURE. Marta Casals Istomin is named artistic director of the John F. Kennedy Center for the Performing Arts in Washington, D.C.

28 February 1980
WOMEN'S ISSUES. Mary Foley Bitterman receives Senate confirmation as the first female director of the radio station Voice of America.

6 March 1980
MILITARY. By a vote of 8–1, the House Armed Services Military Personnel Subcommittee rejects President Carter's proposal to register women for the military draft.

ARTS AND CULTURE. Marguerite Yourcenar, a novelist and naturalized American citizen, is the first woman to be elected to the French Academy.

11 March 1980
POPULAR CULTURE. Jean S. Harris, headmistress of the Madeira School in Virginia, is arrested and charged with the murder of Dr. Herman Tarnower, author of the best-selling book, *The Complete Scarsdale Medical Diet.*

2 April 1980
MILITARY. The Defense Department extends full military veteran status to women who served in the Women's Auxiliary Army Corps during World War II. This provides benefits to 16,000 women who joined the Army Corps beginning in 1942.

8 April 1980
WOMEN'S ISSUES. Florida Governor Robert Graham calls for passage of the Equal Rights Amendment.

11 April 1980
WOMEN'S ISSUES. Eleanor Holmes Norton, chair of the Equal Employment Opportunity Commission, issues regulations that prohibit sexual harassment of workers by supervisors in government and private industry.

15 April 1980
EDUCATION. According to an Education Commission of the States study, more girls of high school age are showing increased interest in mathematics.

21 April 1980
JUDICIAL. The Supreme Court hears arguments involving 3 Illinois cases that deal with federal aid for abortions for poor women.

23 April 1980
MILITARY. General Frederick Kroesen, commander of the U.S. 7th Army in Europe, orders a crackdown on sexual harassment, saying he wants women "to be proud and happy to serve in the army."

7 May 1980
EDUCATION. At a White House ceremony, former federal judge Shirley Hufstedler becomes the first U.S. secretary of education.

9 May 1980
CRIME. Patricia Hearst Shaw is taken off probation after serving 2 years of a 7-year sentence for bank robbery.

20 May 1980
JUDICIAL. A federal judge awards nearly $6 million in back pay and $10 million in increased future salaries to 324 women bindery workers at the U.S. Government Printing Office.

IDEAS/BELIEFS. A U.S. district court judge rules that the army cannot discharge Sergeant Miriam Ben-Shalom solely because she has admitted to being a lesbian.

21 May 1980
MILITARY. The first woman to graduate from the U.S. Coast Guard Academy, Jean Marie Butler of Hershey, Pennsylvania, is one of 14 women graduating in a class of 156.

28 May 1980
MILITARY. In 3 first-time events at major services academies, 60 women graduate from the U.S. Military Academy in West Point, New York; 55 women graduate from the U.S. Naval Academy in Annapolis, Maryland; and 97 women graduate from the U.S. Air Force Academy in Colorado Springs, Colorado.

5 June 1980
DEATHS. In Los Angeles, California, Special Agent Julie Cross is the first woman Secret Service agent killed on duty.

6 June 1980
HEALTH. A report by Dr. William Foege of the Centers for Disease Control details a recently discovered disease called Toxic-Shock Syndrome. The disease is thought to be connected with the use of tampons by women.

10 June 1980
MILITARY. The Senate rejects by a 51–40 vote an amendment by Senator Nancy Landon Kassebaum (R-Kansas) to include women in a Selective Service registration plan. The House rejected a similar plan by voice vote in April.

12 June 1980
BUSINESS. Judy Hendren Mello is elected president and chief executive officer of the First Women's National Bank in New York City, after the January resignation of Lynne D. Salvage.

15 June 1980
SPORTS. Madeline Manning wins her fifth national outdoor title in the championship games in Walnut, California. Manning comes in with a time of 1 minute, 58.75 seconds in the women's 800-yard run.

18 June 1980
WOMEN'S ISSUES. The Illinois House of Representatives defeats the ratification of the Equal Rights Amendment (ERA) with a vote of 102–71, 5 short of the majority needed (107) for ratification. Among the ERA's opponents is Phyllis Schlafly, national STOP-ERA founder.

28 June 1980
MILITARY. The U.S. Navy institutes proceedings against 6 women discharged for allegedly being lesbians. Earlier, investigations of lesbian activity on the USS *Norton Sound,* a missile test ship, were criticized by feminists.

MILITARY. Captain James Kelly of the U.S. Navy reports that the women-at-sea program begun in 1978 has been a mixed success. Approximately 600 women are currently serving on noncombat ships.

30 June 1980
JUDICIAL. The U.S. Supreme Court rules 5–4 that neither the federal government nor state governments are constitutionally required to fund abortions for poor women. The decision upholds the Hyde Amendment used to limit Medicaid abortions.

7 July 1980
WOMEN'S ISSUES. Pauline Frederick, NBC-TV correspondent to the United Nations from 1954 to 1974, is the first woman to receive the Paul White Award, the highest honor of the Radio-Television News Directors Association.

10 July 1980
BUSINESS. Jane Cahill Pfeiffer resigns as NBC-TV chair and board member of the RCA Corporation. She had joined NBC in 1978 and reportedly received a $500,000 settlement. According to insiders, Pfeiffer had been at odds with RCA Chair Edgar Griffiths.

11 July 1980
MILITARY. A U.S. Navy officer is court martialed for sexual harassment after being charged by 4 female sailors on the ship *Norton Sound.*

14 July 1980
WOMEN'S ISSUES. A pro-ERA demonstration of 3,000 people takes place in Detroit, Michigan, as the GOP Convention gets under way in that city.

15 July 1980
POLITICS. The Republican National Convention reports that its party platform is

committed to equal rights for women but not to the Equal Rights Amendment.

18 July 1980
JUDICIAL. A 3-judge panel in Philadelphia, Pennsylvania, rules that draft registration excluding women is unconstitutional.

8 August 1980
DEATHS. Jacqueline Cochran, pilot and director of the Women's Air Force Service Pilots during World War II, dies of a heart attack in California.

13 August 1980
POLITICS. The Democratic party platform, including support for women's draft registration, is formally adopted by the National Convention in New York City.

21 August 1980
MILITARY. The U.S. Navy drops charges against alleged lesbians assigned to the *Norton Sound*.

LABOR. The American Federation of Labor and Congress of Industrial Organizations elects Joyce Miller as the first woman member of its executive council. Miller was a vice-president of the Amalgamated Clothing and Textile Workers and president of the Coalition of Labor Union Women, a 12,000-member group.

30 August 1980
POLITICS. National Unity Party candidate John B. Anderson issues his party's platform, which pledges support for the Equal Rights Amendment.

4 September 1980
HEALTH. Pregnant women are urged by the Food and Drug Administration to stop or reduce consumption of caffeine-containing products because of alleged links to birth defects.

22 September 1980
HEALTH. A Procter & Gamble Company tampon, "Rely," is recalled from the market after federal studies link its use to toxic-shock syndrome.

6 October 1980
JUDICIAL. The U.S. Supreme Court lets stand a lower court ruling that an economic boycott by the National Organization for Women (NOW) against the state of Missouri does not violate the Sherman Anti-Trust Act. NOW urges organizations not to hold conventions in states where the Equal Rights Amendment has not been ratified.

9 October 1980
BUSINESS. Mary E. Cunningham, vice-president for strategic planning at Bendix Corporation, resigns after rumors that her rapid promotions were linked to a romantic attachment to her boss, Chief Executive Officer William Agee.

21 October 1980
WOMEN'S ISSUES. Barbara S. Thomas is sworn in as commissioner of the Securities and Exchange Commission. Thomas is the youngest and the second woman to be named to the post.

27 October 1980
ARTS AND CULTURE. Beverly Sills gives her final opera performance at New York City's Lincoln Center. She sings the role of Rosalinda in *Die Fledermaus*.

1 November 1980
SPORTS. Wightman Cup players retain the U.S. team championship for the 11th straight year. It is the 43d U.S. victory since the competition was begun in 1923.

4 November 1980
POLITICS. Women now hold 19 seats in the House of Representatives. Paula Hawkins (R-Florida) joins Nancy Landon Kassebaum (R-Kansas) in the U.S. Senate.

7 November 1980
WOMEN'S ISSUES. Wanda Brandstetter, a former volunteer for the National Organization for Women, is fined $500 for offering a $1,000 bribe to an Illinois lawmaker to vote for the proposed Equal Rights Amendment.

12 November 1980
SPORTS. The Women's Tennis Association announces it will drop plans to boycott the 1981 U.S. Open championships because the U.S. Tennis Association has agreed to increase purse money for the women's open.

22 November 1980
DEATHS.   Mae West, stage, film, and nightclub star and legendary sex queen, dies in Hollywood, California, at age 87.

25 November 1980
LABOR.   Ford Motor Company announces settlement of a job discrimination case involving women and minority employees. Ford will provide $23 million for developing special job training programs. Also, women are to be hired for 30 percent of openings for nonskilled workers.

26 November 1980
WOMEN'S ISSUES.   The co-chair of Ronald Reagan's presidential campaign denies that she will accept any post in the newly elected president's cabinet.

1 December 1980
WOMEN'S ISSUES.   Outgoing president of the National League of Cities, Jessie M. Rattley, of Newport News, Virginia, states that the ''era of the New Deal is coming to an end.''

JUDICIAL.   The Supreme Court agrees to decide the case of *Department of Education* v. *Seattle University* in which violation of Title IX of the Education Amendment of 1972 is charged. Title IX prohibits gender-based discrimination by educational institutions receiving federal funds.

JUDICIAL.   The Supreme Court agrees to review the case of *Rostker* v. *Goldberg.* The case deals with the constitutionality of the all-male military draft.

3 December 1980
CRIME.   Bernadine Dohrn, a former leader of the Weather Underground, surrenders to federal

authorities in Chicago, Illinois, after hiding out for 11 years.

4 December 1980
INTERNATIONAL.   The bodies of 4 Roman Catholic missionaries are found in an unmarked grave in El Salvador. The women, Maryknoll sisters Ita Ford and Maura Clark, Ursuline sister Dorothy Kazel, and lay missionary Jean Donovan, are believed to have been murdered by Salvadoran soldiers.

POLITICS.   Connecticut Governor Ella T. Grasso announces her resignation due to ill health. Her departure from office is effective 31 December. Grasso is the first woman governor to be elected without succeeding her husband.

14 December 1980
SPORTS.   Nancy Lopez wins the mixed teams golf championship with Curtis Strange in Largo, Florida.

20 December 1980
WOMEN'S ISSUES.   Attorney Elizabeth Hanford Dole is named by Ronald Reagan as presidential assistant for public liaison. She is a former Federal Trade Commission member.

OTHER EVENTS OF 1980

Olympic Silver Medals

Linda Fratianne: Figure skating
Leah Mueller: Speed skating—500 meters
Leah Mueller: Speed skating—1,000 meters

Olympic Bronze Medals

Beth Heiden: Speed skating—3,000 meters

POPULAR CULTURE.   Oscars for 1979 go to Sally Field, Best Actress in *Norma Rae,* and to Meryl Streep, Best Supporting Actress, in *Kramer vs. Kramer.*

IX

SUCCESS BUILDING ON SUCCESS
1981–1987

The 1980s opened with a move toward conservatism in the country that promised little real support for advancing women's rights. A Republican administration confident that it spoke for all women nevertheless implemented many policies that contradicted its expressed concern about women's issues. Still, women maintained a high level of visibility in many areas, and strong support continued for helping women achieve greater economic, political, and social powers.

In a reassuring move, President Reagan named a woman to fill a U.S. Supreme Court vacancy, and designated another as U.S. ambassador to the United Nations. Although neither woman satisfied completely the desires of liberal feminists, in a general way the very fact of a woman associate Supreme Court justice could be considered a victory for equal representation. Other firsts during the early 1980s included a black Miss America; a woman U.S. Navy commander at the Great Lakes Training Center, the navy's largest such facility; and a woman police chief in Portland, Oregon, a major U.S. city. A woman also designed the Vietnam War memorial in Washington, D.C., and as a commentary on the results of some women's liberation activities Betty Friedan published *The Second Stage*.

In sports, Tracy Caulkins became the top medalist in swimming, topping Johnny Weissmuller's record number of championship titles. A woman won Alaska's 1,827-kilometer Iditarod dogsled race for the first time, and Joan Benoit won the first Women's Olympic Marathon. Another Olympic star later became the first woman to join the Harlem Globetrotters basketball team.

After lengthy lawsuits, women flight attendants won retroactive awards and reinstated seniority from several major airlines guilty of sex discrimination. In another settlement, Dalkon Shield maker A. H. Robins Company, Inc., established a fund for women injured while using the birth control device. Doctors also identified a new medical phenomenon known as toxic-shock syndrome. Affecting tampon users, toxic-shock resulted in legislative measures requiring warning labels on certain tampon products.

Perhaps the most exciting issues of the early 1980s were the Equal Rights

Amendment (ERA), the first woman in space, and a woman vice-presidential running mate in the 1984 Democratic campaign. Although its supporters numbered in the hundreds of thousands, the ERA failed to gain sufficient votes for ratification by the June 1982 deadline. And attempts at its revival pointed out that the ERA was unable to regain the vitality it had enjoyed in the previous decade. Its failure was a bitter disappointment to feminists throughout the nation, but a cause for rejoicing among conservatives who had feared wholesale upheaval in women's lives as a result of the amendment. Symbolically, at least, things looked up for American women when Sally K. Ride became the first woman astronaut in space in 1983. Her successful shuttle flight was followed by those of several other women astronauts, and in mid-1985, a woman teacher, Christa McAuliffe, was chosen to be the first civilian in space.

The most dramatic event in U.S. politics during the early 1980s was the selection of Geraldine Ferraro as Walter Mondale's running mate in the 1984 Democratic presidential campaign. Sixty-four years after being granted the vote, American women could attempt to put one of their own in the number-two elected office in the nation. For many, it seemed the culmination of women's best efforts, and although the Mondale–Ferraro ticket did not win, it proved something. It showed that women could be competent, qualified, flawed, courageous, human, ambitious, fallible, and talented. And it also proved that the twentieth century might yet witness the fruition of women's quest for executive office, just as the preceding years had seen women learn to drive cars, fly planes, excel at sports, obtain voting rights, win election to office, scale mountains, swim the English Channel, win Nobel Prizes, be ordained Episcopal priests, head corporations, decide Supreme Court cases, and explore outer space.

2 January 1981
POLITICS. Eileen Anderson becomes the mayor of Honolulu, Hawaii. She is the city's first woman chief executive since 1893.

6 January 1981
IDEAS/BELIEFS. A study prepared for the President's Advisory Committee for Women indicates a positive shift in public acceptance of working women.

WOMEN'S ISSUES. President Reagan names Karna Small as a deputy press secretary.

8 January 1981
SPORTS. Julie Shea, a track star at North Carolina State University, is named top woman college athlete for 1980 by the Association of Intercollegiate Athletics for Women.

9 January 1981
SPORTS. The Association of Intercollegiate

Athletics for Women (AIAW) winds up a 4-day convention in Detroit, Michigan. The convention adopts a resolution to urge the National Collegiate Athletic Association to postpone plans for championship tournaments at small colleges. Donna Lopiano of the University of Texas is installed as AIAW president.

13 January 1981
HEALTH. Results of a 3-month study link the use of high-absorbency tampons to toxic-shock syndrome.

15 January 1981
INTERNATIONAL. Jeane J. Kirkpatrick tells the Senate Foreign Relations Committee that she will present the administration's policy at the United Nations without "bluster." Kirkpatrick is confirmed on 29 January as chief U.S. delegate to the United Nations.

16 January 1981
POPULAR CULTURE. The estate of Mae West, the actress who died in 1980, leaves an estimated $1 million, mostly to West's sister.

22 January 1981
EDUCATION. Ruth B. Love is named superintendent of schools of the Chicago Public School System, the nation's third largest. The black educator's salary of $120,000 makes her the highest-paid official in Illinois.

24 January 1981
SPORTS. Evelyn Ashford sets an American record for the indoor 60-yard dash at 6.65 seconds.

5 February 1981
DEATHS. Former Democratic Governor of Connecticut, Ella T. Grasso, dies of cancer in Hartford, Connecticut.

6 February 1981
WOMEN'S ISSUES. More than 3,000 women's rights advocates lobby Congress on Women's Rights Day.

18 February 1981
JUDICIAL. The Massachusetts Supreme Court rules that the state is required to pay for all medically necessary abortions for women on welfare, even if their lives are not in danger.

23 February 1981
SPORTS. A Detroit federal judge rules that educational institutions receiving federal funding do not have to provide equal athletic programs for men and women. The ruling is termed "disastrous" by those favoring equal funding for women's sports.

24 February 1981
JUDICIAL. A White Plains, New York, jury convicts Jean S. Harris of second-degree murder in the death of her lover, Dr. Herman Tarnower.

25 February 1981
WOMEN'S ISSUES. The Directors Guild of America files sex discrimination charges against 3 major television networks, 11 independent TV production companies, and 6 movie studios. According to the guild, only 1.3 percent of directors' jobs in the top 19 film and TV companies went to women during the past decade.

26 February 1981
WOMEN'S ISSUES. The Older Women's League is established in New York City to address needs of women aged 45 to 65.

2 March 1981
JUDICIAL. The U.S. Supreme Court refuses to review a decision that Eastern Airlines could require flight attendants to take maternity leave after the 13th week of pregnancy. It also refuses to interfere with a decision that the city of Chicago had discriminated against female employees. The decision in *Chicago* v. *National Organization for Women* included a judgment exceeding $3 million.

3 March 1981
LABOR. The Working Women's Association and the American Federation of Labor and Congress of Industrial Organizations Service Employees Union form a new District 925 to conduct a national organizing drive among office workers.

5 March 1981
SPORTS. Elaine Zayak, a 15-year-old student from New Jersey, wins the silver medal in the World Figure Skating Championships in Hartford, Connecticut.

6 March 1981
WOMEN'S ISSUES. At a news conference, the president states that a constitutional amendment prohibiting abortion is unnecessary if Congress can determine that the fetus is a human being.

18 March 1981
WOMEN'S ISSUES. Ford Foundation program officer Susan V. Berresford reports that the foundation is examining 300 U.S. and foreign aid projects with a "feminist lens."

23 March 1981
JUDICIAL. The Supreme Court rules 6–3 that the state may require a doctor to inform parents of a dependent teenage girl before performing an abortion.

31 March 1981
SPORTS. Lynette Woodard, a University of Kansas senior, receives the Margaret Wade Trophy from the Associated Press. Woodard is named the Outstanding Women's College Basketball player of the year.

1 April 1981
IDEAS/BELIEFS. In New York City, the National Organization for Women Legal Defense and Education Fund sponsors a National Convocation on New Leadership.

3 April 1981
HEALTH. The American Medical Association reports that the use of spermicides is linked to an increase in birth defects and spontaneous abortions.

20 April 1981
SPORTS. The Nebraska Wranglers win the Women's Basketball League title with a 99–90 victory over the Dallas Diamonds in Omaha, Nebraska.

SPORTS. Patti Catalano comes in second in the Boston Marathon, setting a new record for an American woman in a marathon with a time of 2:27:51.

23 April 1981
WOMEN'S ISSUES. Six women are arrested after they interrupt a Senate hearing on abortion with shouts of "Not the church, not the state, women must decide their fate."

25 April 1981
POPULAR CULTURE. Maureen Reagan, the president's oldest daughter, is married to Dennis Revell, in Beverly Hills, California.

27 April 1981
JUDICIAL. The U.S. Supreme Court lets stand an Indiana law that makes it a felony for second-trimester abortions to be performed anywhere but in a hospital.

1 May 1981
SPORTS. Billie Jean King holds a press conference and announces that she had a lesbian affair with her former secretary, Marilyn Barnett.

Sandra Day O'Connor, 1930–

In a break with tradition, Sandra Day O'Connor was named associate justice of the United States Supreme Court in July 1981. Historically, the nation's highest judicial body had been all-male, but O'Connor's unanimous Senate approval in September 1981 guaranteed that American women could feel truly represented in the federal justice system.

Born on 26 March 1930, in El Paso, Texas, she was the daughter of Harry A. and Ada (Wilkey) Day. The family ranch, on which she grew up, was in an isolated corner of Arizona, and she was sent at age five to live with her grandmother in El Paso. She attended a private girls' school, and later went to Austin High School. By 1950 she had graduated cum laude from Stanford University in California with a B.A. in economics and in 1952 was awarded an LL.B. At Stanford, Day met fellow law student John J. O'Connor III, and the two were married in June 1952.

Despite her sterling academic record, O'Connor recalled later that the social climate of the 1950s made it impossible for a woman lawyer to obtain a position in a private law firm. As an alternative she worked as a deputy attorney for San Mateo County in California. By 1959, however, she opened her own law practice in Maryvale, Arizona, and followed conventional dictates by also raising a family—the O'Connors have three sons. She worked in several appointed positions, including the Governor's Committee on Marriage and Family in 1965. O'Connor was named assistant attorney general of Arizona and served until 1969, when she was selected as a replacement for Senator Isabel A. Burgess, who had vacated her state senate seat to take an appointment in Washington, D.C. In 1970 and 1972, O'Connor mounted a successful campaign for

Associate Justice of the United States Supreme Court Sandra Day O'Connor, the first woman ever named to the high court bench. (Photo courtesy U.S. Supreme Court Public Information Office)

election to that senate seat, and in 1972, she was the first woman elected majority leader in any state senate. She served her constituents capably, and gained the respect of her colleagues, both male and female. O'Connor voted in a conservative manner, although she did work to revise Arizona laws that discriminated against women and also voted in favor of ratification of the Equal Rights Amendment.

O'Connor left the state senate in 1974 and won a seat on the Maricopa County Superior Court. Although she was involved in Republican politics, having served as an alternate to the 1972 GOP Convention, she was not anxious to enter the political arena again. In 1979, she was named to the Arizona Court of Appeals. When Ronald Reagan chose O'Connor as his first Supreme Court appointment in July 1981, she was not immediately endorsed by all women's groups. She was not considered conservative enough to please members of antiabortion and profamily groups, yet some feminists found her record decidedly less than liberal.

Nonetheless, when O'Connor was sworn in on 26 September 1981, she was seen as representative of a positive action taken on behalf of women. And although not an outspoken champion of women's rights, O'Connor's position on the U.S. Supreme Court has enabled her to provide a more balanced, less inherently sexist judicial voice for all Americans.

2 May 1981
SPORTS. Avon Products and Toyota Motor Works announce that they will not withdraw their sponsorship of women's professional tennis because of Billie Jean King's recent disclosures about her personal life.

5 May 1981
WOMEN'S ISSUES. Anne McGill Gorsuch is confirmed by the Senate as administrator of the Environmental Protection Agency.

6 May 1981
SPORTS. Martina Navratilova announces that she supports Billie Jean King's recent stance on making public the fact of her previous affair with a woman. "People always seem to just talk about the women . . . men seem exempt from this," said Navratilova.

8 May 1981
SPORTS. The Women's Tennis Association board of directors rejects Billie Jean King's offer to resign as the group's president.

14 May 1981
POPULAR CULTURE. Diana Ross announces that she has signed an exclusive contract with RCA after 20 years of recording exclusively with Detroit's Motown Records.

IDEAS/BELIEFS. Actress and model Brooke Shields is dropped as the centerpiece of a government antismoking campaign. The Department of Health and Human Services states that Shields' image is not sufficiently "family-oriented."

20 May 1981
HEALTH. Antiabortionist Dr. Mildred F. Jefferson testifies in front of Congress that life begins with the meeting of sperm and egg. The hearings on this subject relate to proposed antiabortion legislation that would overturn the 1973 *Roe* v. *Wade* Supreme Court decision that made abortion legal.

23 May 1981
WOMEN'S ISSUES. The U.S. Census Bureau reports that as of April 1980, there are 6 million more women in the United States than men. Women outnumbered men 3–2 in the over-65 age group.

31 May 1981
SPORTS. Pam Spencer sets an American women's high jump record by leaping 6 feet 5¼ inches.

6 June 1981
WOMEN'S ISSUES. Maya Yang Lin wins a national competition for design of a Vietnam War memorial to be located in the nation's capital. The 21-year-old Yale student receives a prize of $20,000.

8 June 1981
JUDICIAL. The Supreme Court rules 5–4 that women can sue their employers for wage discrimination even if their jobs are not identical to those of male employees. This decision, in *County of Washington* v. *Gunther,* increases the rights of women to sue over job bias.

12 June 1981
WOMEN'S ISSUES. Anne Gorsuch, newly appointed head of the Environmental Protection Agency, announces a reorganization of the agency.

14 June 1981
SPORTS. At Kings Island, Ohio, Donna Caponi wins the 27th Ladies Professional Golf Association championship.

17 June 1981
HISTORY. The fifth biennial Berkshire Conference on the History of Women opens at Vassar College. There are more than 1,500 participants.

18 June 1981
LEGISLATIVE. The Senate ends 8 days of hearings on a bill designed to ban abortions. No conclusive action is taken on the legislation.

25 June 1981
JUDICIAL. In *Rostker* v. *Goldberg,* the U.S. Supreme Court rules that the Constitution permits excluding women from draft registration and from the military draft itself. Eleanor Smeal, president of the National Organization for Women, states that this means "women can be discriminated against, that it upholds the myth of this country that all men are better than all women."

7 July 1981
JUDICIAL. President Reagan nominates Sandra Day O'Connor as the first woman Supreme Court justice.

8 July 1981
WOMEN'S ISSUES. Eleanor Smeal of the National Organization for Women praises Reagan's nomination of Sandra Day O'Connor as a "victory for women's rights."

14 July 1981
IDEAS/BELIEFS. Patti Davis, younger daughter of President Reagan, is the featured speaker at a Southern California Alliance for Survival rally in Los Angeles.

LABOR. In San Jose, California, a 9-day strike by municipal workers ends when the city agrees to bring women's pay up to the level of men's for comparable work. Mayor Janet Gray Hayes cites the agreement as "a giant step toward fairness."

17 July 1981
HEALTH. The Food and Drug Administration publishes a report recommending that pregnant women abstain from drinking alcohol.

18 July 1981
INTERNATIONAL. Linda Arrigo, of Los Angeles, California, is arrested in Taiwan for her actions in protest of the death of Chen Wen-Cheng, a U.S. professor visiting Taiwan.

19 July 1981
SPORTS. The U.S. Wightman Cup team beats Great Britain's team in the 53d Wightman Cup playoffs. It is the 44th American victory in this 2-nation match, established by Hazel Hotchkiss Wightman.

20 July 1981
HEALTH. A study published in the *New England Journal of Medicine* indicates that women using birth control pills have an increased risk of heart attack, even after they have stopped taking the oral contraceptives.

26 July 1981
SPORTS. Pat Bradley wins the U.S. Women's Open Golf Tournament by 1 stroke over Beth Daniel. Her score is a record 279 for the 72-hole event.

31 July 1981
WOMEN'S ISSUES. The House and Senate approve federal budget cuts affecting more than 200 domestic aid programs, including the Women, Infants, and Children supplemental nutrition program.

16 August 1981
SPORTS. Mary T. Meagher breaks 2 world records—for the 100-meter and the 200-meter butterfly event—at the U.S. Long-Course Championships. Tracy Caulkins wins 4 races to boost her overall career title to 35, the most ever held by a woman and only 1 less than the record number of titles by a male swimmer.

23 August 1981
WOMEN'S ISSUES. More than 6,000 supporters of the Equal Rights Amendment rally in Los Angeles, California, and in more than 100 other cities nationwide.

SPORTS. Beth Daniel takes the World Championship of Women's Golf title in Shaker Heights, Ohio. The prize money is $50,000—the richest purse in women's pro golf history.

27 August 1981
IDEAS/BELIEFS. In San Francisco, California, Mary Morgan is named by Governor Edmund G. Brown as that state's first acknowledged lesbian judge.

1 September 1981
LABOR. The Equal Employment Opportunity Commission reports that women's earnings lag 60 percent behind those of men. This number has remained relatively stable since the early 1960s, according to the study.

2 September 1981
JUDICIAL. If confirmed as a Supreme Court justice, Sandra Day O'Connor will be among the wealthiest of bench members. Her net assets are reportedly more than $1.1 million.

4 September 1981
LABOR. According to Labor Department statistics, the unemployment rate for adult women fell from 6.7 percent in July to 6.5 percent in August.

8 September 1981
JUDICIAL. The American Bar Association

endorses the nomination of Sandra Day O'Connor.

12 September 1981
SPORTS.   Tracy Austin wins the U.S. Open Singles Tennis Championship by defeating third-seeded Martina Navratilova.

17 September 1981
BUSINESS.   Paige Rense becomes editor-in-chief of *Geo* magazine. Rense is the person whose efforts have changed the look of both *Architectural Digest* and *Bon Appétit* magazines.

25 September 1981
JUDICIAL.   Sandra Day O'Connor takes the oath of office and becomes the first woman member of the U.S. Supreme Court. Associate Justice O'Connor is the first woman in the court's 191-year history.

7 October 1981
DEATHS.   Emma Bugbee, one of the first women reporters on the *New York Herald Tribune* staff in 1911 and a founder of the Newspaper Women's Club of New York, dies at age 93 in Warwick, Rhode Island.

POPULAR CULTURE.   The Wonder Woman Foundation is established by Warner Communications. It marks the 40th anniversary of the comic book heroine, and will give financial aid to women over age 40.

12 October 1981
WOMEN'S ISSUES.   Betty Friedan, author of *The Feminine Mystique,* publishes a new book on feminism entitled *The Second Stage.*

SPORTS.   The Women's Sports Foundation holds its second annual dinner in New York City. The event raises nearly $80,000 to help promote women in sports.

POPULAR CULTURE.   Barbara Mandrell wins the Country Music Association's Entertainer of the Year Award.

18 October 1981
POPULATION.   Census Bureau statistics indicate that the number of unmarried couples in the United States tripled between 1970 and 1980. The median age for men to marry is now set at 24.6 years; for women, the median marriage age is 22.1 years.

AVIATION.   Anne Morrow Lindbergh receives the Achievement Award from the National Aviation Club at a Washington, D.C., ceremony.

20 October 1981
CRIME.   Kathy Boudin, a radical activist and leader in the Weather Underground (a 1960s militant group), is arrested at a shoot-out in Nyack, New York.

22 October 1981
CRIME.   Recently arrested fugitive Kathy Boudin has reportedly been living in a New York apartment with a year-old baby. Boudin has allegedly been receiving $177.75 weekly in welfare benefits under a false name.

11 November 1981
POLITICS.   Maureen Reagan announces her intention of running in 1982 for the U.S. Senate seat currently held by S. I. Hayakawa (R-California).

16 November 1981
WOMEN'S ISSUES.   Mary Louise Smith is named vice-chair of the U.S. Civil Rights Commission. She is a former chair of the Republican National Committee, serving from 1974 to 1977.

HEALTH.   The Senate votes 68–24 to confirm Dr. C. Everett Koop as surgeon general of the United States. Koop is an outspoken antiabortionist.

17 November 1981
IDEAS/BELIEFS.   A World Almanac poll of news personalities finds that Billie Jean King and Katharine Graham are the most influential women in the United States.

POLITICS.   Democrat Kathryn J. Whitmire, city controller for 4 years in Houston, Texas, wins 62.5 percent of the vote and becomes mayor.

23 November 1981
POPULAR CULTURE.   A New York State Supreme Court judge rules that photographs of a nude Brooke Shields at age 10 are "not pornographic" and can be published by photographer Garry Gross.

Sonia Johnson, 1936–

When Sonia Harris was growing up in a devoutly Mormon family, she had no thoughts of becoming a public figure and a principal player in the fierce debate on women's role in society. She was born on 27 February 1936, in Malad, Idaho. Her parents were teachers, and the family was typically Mormon—patriarchal and all-controlling, with an emphasis on religious doctrine. In 1957, Harris received a B.A. from Utah State University and entered graduate school, where she met Rick Johnson, another graduate student. They were married on 21 August 1959. She worked as her husband completed graduate studies, taking classes as well. By 1965 she had two children and had completed a doctoral degree in English at Rutgers University in New Jersey, where the family now lived.

Soon, the couple was traveling throughout Southeast Asia, teaching and doing Mormon missionary work. They moved to Virginia in 1975, and by 1977 Johnson had discovered both the women's movement and what she felt was a major flaw in Mormonism—its condemnation of the Equal Rights Amendment (ERA). Johnson helped found Mormons for ERA, an activist group that joined a march in Washington, D.C., in July 1978. The one hundred thousand people who assembled wanted to extend ratification time for the ERA to 1982. Johnson was now in direct conflict with her church and found that Mormon leaders—an all-male group—saw her as undermining

Sonia Johnson, a Mormon feminist who was excommunicated from her church because of her outspoken support of equal rights for women. Johnson drew public attention during 1982 as she fasted with seven others in Springfield, Illinois, during a thirty-seven-day "Women's Fast for Justice." (Photo courtesy Sonia Johnson)

church authority. She was tried by church elders in December 1979 and excommunicated from the Mormon church. The charge was "Serious defection from the church and its doctrines." Until this point, her husband had stood beside her as she supported the ERA. But following the excommunication came his demand for a divorce.

After this point, Johnson became an even more vehement speaker on behalf of women's rights. She published *From Housewife to Heretic* in 1981 and worked tirelessly to promote the ERA before the extended deadline for ratification was reached. She and seven other women staged a thirty-seven-day "Women's Fast for Justice" in May 1982 at the state capital building in Springfield, Illinois. Johnson was hospitalized several times during this fast. In Washington, D.C., at the National Organization for Women (NOW) convention in October 1982, Johnson received 40 percent of the vote cast for NOW president, losing her bid for leadership of that organization to Judy Goldsmith.

In 1984, Johnson ran for U.S. President as the Citizens Party candidate, making clear her stand on justice and her opposition to "war, pollution, poverty, inequality, and powerlessness." Johnson raised more than $180,000 in private campaign contributions, becoming the first of any third-party candidate to qualify for federal matching funds. And although Johnson did not succeed at the polls in November 1984 (receiving less than 1 percent of the national vote), she was satisfied that her efforts helped in many ways to "change peoples' values . . . I would consider that winning."

---

23 November 1981
DEATHS. Actress Natalie Wood, 3-time Academy Award nominee, drowns after falling from a yacht in waters off Catalina Island, California.

29 November 1981
BUSINESS. Pam Johnson becomes the first black woman to head a general circulation daily newspaper—Gannett's *Ithaca*.

30 November 1981
SPORTS. In *O'Connor* v. *Board of Education,* the Supreme Court refuses to review a ruling in a case involving the right of a public school system to prevent girls from trying out for boys' athletic teams.

4 December 1981
LABOR. The Labor Department reports that unemployment for adult women went from 7 percent in October to 7.3 percent in November.

POPULAR CULTURE. In a book describing her abduction in 1974, Patricia Hearst Shaw tells of being kidnapped by the Symbionese Liberation Army in *Every Secret Thing.*

11 December 1981
SPORTS. Los Angeles Superior Court Judge Julius M. Title rules that Marilyn Barnett, the

former lover of Billie Jean King, is not entitled to King's Malibu, California, beach property. Barnett had brought suit against King in a "palimony" charge, demanding recompense for their one-time intimate relationship.

22 December 1981
WOMEN'S ISSUES. President Reagan creates a Federal Task Force on Legal Equality for Women. He names Carol E. Dinkus as chair of the task force.

23 December 1981
JUDICIAL. A federal judge in Idaho, Marion J. Callister, rules that Congress violated the Constitution by extending the Equal Rights Amendment ratification deadline. The National Organization for Women announces that it will appeal this district court decision directly to the Supreme Court of the United States.

3 January 1982
WOMEN'S ISSUES. The White House makes clear that the Reagan administration is opposed to "rigid" quotas for minorities and women in hiring and promotion.

5 January 1982
JUDICIAL. The Justice Department announces it will oppose efforts of the National

Organization for Women to seek an expedited ruling from the U.S. Supreme Court concerning possible extension of the Equal Rights Amendment ratification deadline.

6 January 1982
CRIME. Patricia Hearst Shaw drops a 7-year legal appeal to win a new trial in her 1976 conviction for bank robbery.

8 January 1982
LABOR. The Labor Department indicates that the unemployment rate for adult women had risen to 7.5 percent in December 1981.

10 January 1982
WOMEN'S ISSUES. In a letter signed by 90 U.S. Representatives, President Reagan is urged to seek expedited review of the recent Idaho court ruling concerning ratification deadline–extension for the Equal Rights Amendment.

12 January 1982
AVIATION. A federal district court judge orders United Airlines to rehire up to 1,800 female flight attendants who lost their jobs when they married during the 1960s.

14 January 1982
JUDICIAL. The Justice Department files a proposal urging the U.S. Supreme Court to nullify a lower court's ruling that would effectively prevent ratification of the Equal Rights Amendment.

19 January 1982
WOMEN'S ISSUES. The Oklahoma State Senate votes 27–21 to reject the Equal Rights Amendment and not reconsider its ratification.

20 January 1982
WOMEN'S ISSUES. The Georgia House of Representatives rejects the Equal Rights Amendment by a vote of 116–57 despite requests for its support from former presidents Carter and Ford.

26 January 1982
WOMEN'S ISSUES. In his State-of-the-Union message, President Reagan reaffirms

support for extension of the Voting Rights Act and says his administration's commitment to equal rights for women is "firm and unshakeable."

10 February 1982
JUDICIAL. Judge Betty Roberts becomes the first woman supreme court justice in Oregon.

11 February 1982
DEATHS. Former tap-dance star Eleanor Powell dies of cancer at age 69 in Beverly Hills, California.

13 February 1982
WOMEN'S ISSUES. In Missouri, a senate committee rejects the Equal Rights Amendment.

16 February 1982
WOMEN'S ISSUES. In Washington, D.C., 10 women demonstrators are arrested as they attempt to climb a White House fence. The women are trying to obtain support for passage of the Equal Rights Amendment.

17 February 1982
POLITICS. First Lady Nancy Reagan announces that she will no longer accept free designer-originals' clothing. Critics say that the Reagans should be taxed for the gifts of clothing valued in the thousands of dollars.

18 February 1982
CIVIL RIGHTS. Julia Wilder, age 69, receives a 5-year jail term for her role in a 13-day civil rights demonstration. Wilder, and another activist, Maggie Bozeman (who also receives a 5-year sentence) were helping elderly, illiterate blacks to fill out absentee voting ballots in Georgia.

22 February 1982
WOMEN'S ISSUES. At a luncheon at the Cosmos Club in Washington, D.C., Patricia Roberts Harris and Maria Wolfe, both members of Women's Economic Roundtable, note that the Cosmos Club continues to decline women's applications for membership.

24 February 1982
LABOR. The U.S. Supreme Court rules

unanimously that TransWorld Airlines' female flight attendants fired prior to 1971 because of pregnancy are entitled to back pay and retroactive seniority.

2 March 1982
POLITICS. Senator Bob Packwood (R-Oregon) expresses concern that "the Republican party has just about written off those women who work for wages." His statements draw criticism from Republican colleagues.

4 March 1982
WOMEN'S ISSUES. President Reagan establishes National Women's History Week.

Alice Walker, 1944–

Pulitzer Prize–winning writer Alice Malsenior Walker was born in Eatonton, Georgia, on 9 February 1944. Her father, Willie Lee Walker, earned $300 a year as a sharecropper, and her mother, Minnie (Grant) Walker, supplemented the family income by working as a domestic servant. Although her childhood was marked by poverty, Walker excelled in school. Due to an eye injury received when she was eight years old, Walker was left blind in one eye, but this potential handicap resulted in her attending Spelman College on a special scholarship. At Spelman she was drawn to radical politics and soon she transferred to Sarah Lawrence College, where her involvement in civil rights grew. She traveled to Africa in 1964; this journey resulted in her writing a series of poems later published in the volume, *Once*.

Walker's B.A. was awarded in 1965, and she then moved to Mississippi, where she continued civil rights work. She also wrote steadily, and married Melvyn R. Leventhal on 17 March 1967, in New York City. But in September of that year they moved again to Mississippi, where between 1968 and 1971 Walker was a writer-in-residence at several colleges.

In 1970, Walker's novel, *The Third Life of Granger Copeland*, was published, and it received mixed reviews. Walker lectured at several Massachusetts colleges in the early 1970s, and in 1973 published *In Love and Trouble: Stories of Black Women*. This collection of short stories won the Rosenthal Award from the American Institute of Arts and Letters. In 1974, Walker and her husband returned to New York City, where she joined the staff of *Ms.* magazine as contributing editor.

Although Alice Walker published a number of essays, poetry collections, and stories during the 1970s, her third novel, *The Color Purple*, published in 1982, brought her the widest acclaim, winning both the American Book Award and the Pulitzer Prize. A film version of *The Color Purple*, starring actress Whoopi Goldberg, was released in late 1985. In it, both the delicate and brutal qualities of a woman's life are explored, and an emphasis on women's reliance on, and love for, other women is detailed.

In 1983, Walker published a book of essays, *In Search of Our Mothers' Gardens*, and in 1984, her fourth poetry volume appeared—*Horses Make a Landscape More Beautiful*. Walker divorced her husband in 1976. She lives in San Francisco, California, with her daughter, Rebecca. She continues to write and remains active in social issues, notably the antinuclear movement.

6 March 1982
DEATHS. Author and philosopher Ayn Rand dies in New York City. Her books included *Atlas Shrugged* and *The Fountainhead*.

13 March 1982
SPORTS. Elaine Zayak wins the women's world figure skating championships.

17 March 1982
WOMEN'S ISSUES. As the Virginia legislature adjourns this session without action on the Equal Rights Amendment, women express hope that the amendment will pass in Florida and Illinois.

28 March 1982
SPORTS. Louisiana Tech and Rutgers University win the national women's basketball championships. Lady Techsters beat Cheyney State in the first National Collegiate Athletic Association Division I tournament. At the Association for Intercollegiate Athletics for Women championships, Rutgers defeats the University of Texas, 83–77.

9 April 1982
SPORTS. Swimmer Tracy Caulkins wins a record 37th national championship, making her the top titlist in history.

27 April 1982
SPORTS. Virginia Slims announces that it will return as a sponsor of women's professional tennis in 1983.

28 April 1982
BUSINESS. Christie Hefner is promoted to president of Playboy Enterprises, Inc.

29 April 1982
WOMEN'S ISSUES. Critics of President Reagan's Women's Educational Equity Act program charge that funding goes only to "radical feminists."

3 May 1982
WOMEN'S ISSUES. In a commencement address at Columbia College in South Carolina, Associate Supreme Court Justice Sandra Day O'Connor states that women can combine careers with a family, but they must work harder than men to achieve the same goals.

28 May 1982
WOMEN'S ISSUES. In Springfield, Illinois, 7 women are in the tenth day of a fast to bring attention to hoped-for passage of the Equal Rights Amendment. Among the hunger strikers is Sonia Johnson, former Mormons for ERA leader.

3 June 1982
WOMEN'S ISSUES. In Illinois, 7 women on a hunger strike are cited as a reason Senator Forest D. Etheredge may not vote in favor of the Equal Rights Amendment.

4 June 1982
WOMEN'S ISSUES. The Equal Rights Amendment (ERA) hunger-strikers chain themselves together at the Illinois Senate chamber to protest anti-ERA sentiments.

5 June 1982
WOMEN'S ISSUES. In North Carolina, the senate sets aside consideration of the Equal Rights Amendment. This is considered a death blow to hopes of state ratification by the June deadline.

7 June 1982
WOMEN'S ISSUES. In Illinois, thousands of marchers, including Betty Ford and Chicago Mayor Jane Byrne, push for ratification of the Equal Rights Amendment.

13 June 1982
IDEAS/BELIEFS. The National Organization of Italian-American Women meets to discuss ways of eliminating stereotyping on the basis of ethnicity. Dr. Aileen Riotto Sirey is president of the group.

16 June 1982
WOMEN'S ISSUES. In Illinois, supporters of the Equal Rights Amendment voice their fears of a lack of sufficient votes for ratification.

20 June 1982
WOMEN'S ISSUES. In Illinois, Equal Rights Amendment supporters ask for a change in the rules that would permit a ratification vote by simple majority rather than the three-fifths majority now required.

As the ratification deadline for the Equal Rights Amendment (ERA) drew to a close, thousands of women nationwide drew together in public support of the Constitutional change. The deadline passed in June 1982, without passage of the ERA, which fell just three votes short of the necessary two-thirds required for ratification. (Photo courtesy Dorothea Jacobson-Wenzel)

22 June 1982
WOMEN'S ISSUES. In Florida, the senate defeats ratification of the Equal Rights Amendment.

24 June 1982
BUSINESS. In New York City, women connected with the founding of *Ms.* magazine gather to celebrate the tenth anniversary of the publication.

26 June 1982
WOMEN'S ISSUES. In Illinois, the senate rejects passage of the Equal Rights Amendment. Angry demonstrators spray a red substance on the state capital building as an expression of their disappointment.

27 June 1982
WOMEN'S ISSUES. Eleanor Smeal warns Democratic party leaders that women's votes should not be taken for granted. The National Organization for Women (NOW) identifies 101 Democratic legislators who are termed "anti-ERA," and whose reelection NOW will oppose.

28 June 1982
POLITICS. The Democratic party leaders from New York state refuse to seat Bella Abzug at the Philadelphia, Pennsylvania, conference. She is denied her seat on the grounds that she is "disruptive."

30 June 1982
WOMEN'S ISSUES. The Equal Rights Amendment dies after failing to gain the necessary ratification of 3 final states.

SPORTS. The Association for Intercollegiate Athletics for Women discontinues operations.

2 July 1982
JUDICIAL. The U.S. Supreme Court upholds 9–0 a New York state law prohibiting the use of children in pornographic films.

4 July 1982
SPORTS. Martina Navratilova defeats Chris Evert Lloyd at Wimbledon for the women's championship.

5 July 1982
WOMEN'S ISSUES. President Reagan claims he appointed a record number of women and minorities to state posts while governor of California.

19 July 1982
WOMEN'S ISSUES. The Women's Rights National Historical Park opens in Seneca Falls, New York. The park specifically honors Elizabeth Cady Stanton.

2 August 1982
WOMEN'S ISSUES. The National Organization for Women and the National Women's Political Caucus suspend a boycott of political conventions in states where the Equal Rights Amendment went unratified.

IDEAS/BELIEFS. In Washington, D.C., the Family Forum, sponsored by the Free Congress Research and Education Foundation and the Moral Majority Foundation, debates ways to keep women from working outside the home.

11 August 1982
WOMEN'S ISSUES. The National Governor's Association promotes a new drive for ratification of the Equal Rights Amendment.

15 August 1982
WOMEN'S ISSUES. President Reagan designates 26 August as Women's Equality Day.

27 August 1982
POLITICS. The National Organization for Women announces a $3-million fund drive to finance political action on behalf of American women.

28 August 1982
POLITICS. In Skowhegan, Maine, papers and tapes of long-time Republican politician Margaret Chase Smith, are part of a library dedicated to the former state Senator and Representative.

1 September 1982
WOMEN'S ISSUES. Feminists voice concern over President Reagan's appointment of Dee Jepson as White House liaison on women's issues. At issue is her work on the proposed Family Protection Act.

3 September 1982
LABOR. The Labor Department reports that unemployment rates for adult women fell from 8.4 percent in July to 8.2 percent in August.

5 September 1982
POPULAR CULTURE. Actresses Mary Martin and Janet Gaynor (the first Best Actress Oscar winner) are seriously injured in a San Francisco, California, automobile accident.

7 September 1982
JUDICIAL. In Manhattan's South Court District, Prudence Beay Abram is sworn in as the first woman bankruptcy court judge in the district. She is 1 of 4 such women judges among 200 in the nation.

12 September 1982
SPORTS. Chris Evert Lloyd wins the U.S. Open women's championship by defeating Hana Mandlikova.

14 September 1982
POLITICS. President Reagan, meeting with religious editors, states that infants had been born after only 3 months of gestation and had grown up "normal." Reagan's remarks are made in connection with a discussion of the abortion issue, and are later termed "mistaken" by a White House spokesperson.

15 September 1982
LEGISLATIVE. The U.S. Senate votes to table the antiabortion amendment sponsored by Senator Jesse Helms (R-North Carolina).

LEGISLATIVE. The Senate votes to kill a proposal that would ban use of federal funds for abortion.

29 September 1982
JUDICIAL. Marie L. Garibaldi is named by New Jersey Governor Kean as a candidate for the state supreme court. She will be the first woman to hold that post. Her nomination is unanimously confirmed on 19 October.

5 October 1982
JUDICIAL. The U.S. Supreme Court declares moot a National Organization for Women lawsuit against Utah's Supreme Court decision on the Equal Rights Amendment ratification procedure.

8 October 1982
LABOR. Unemployment statistics indicate that there has been a rise of one-tenth of a percentage point in the rate of women's unemployment since 1 September.

10 October 1982
WOMEN'S ISSUES. Judy Goldsmith is elected president of the National Organization for Women at its 15th annual convention in Indianapolis, Indiana.

WOMEN'S ISSUES. The National Council for Research on Women is founded in New York City.

17 October 1982
HEALTH. The American Cancer Society reports that all women, even those free of identified risk factors, should be considered likely candidates for breast cancer.

18 October 1982
DEATHS. Bess Truman, widow of President Harry S Truman, dies at age 97 in Kansas City, Missouri.

31 October 1982
WOMEN'S ISSUES. The Women's Rights Information Center opens in Englewood, New Jersey.

18 November 1982
JUDICIAL. Marie L. Garibaldi is sworn in as the first woman on the New Jersey Supreme Court.

20 November 1982
DEATHS. Catherine Mackin, the first woman to cover a national political convention for a television network in 1972, dies of cancer in Towson, Maryland.

22 November 1982
LABOR. In Los Angeles, California, waterfront employees and the International Longshoreman's and Warehouseman's Union agree to hire women at rates that will make them 20 percent of the job force there by 1997.

WOMEN'S ISSUES. The Older Women's League holds its first convention in Louisville, Kentucky.

23 November 1982
WOMEN'S ISSUES. Eighteen women are chosen as recipients of the first Wonder Woman Foundation Awards.

28 November 1982
JUDICIAL. Connecticut State Supreme Court Justice Ellen A. Peters wins the first Ella Grasso Distinguished Service medal.

30 November 1982
WOMEN'S ISSUES. Eleanor Smeal steps down as president of the National Organization for Women; Judy Goldsmith is formally inducted as the organization's president.

LABOR. In the District of Columbia, a federal district court judge rules that Northwest Airlines must pay $52.5 million in back pay to stewardesses for settlement of job discrimination charges.

6 December 1982
SPORTS. The Athletics Congress names Olympia, Washington, as the site of the 1984 U.S. Olympic marathon trials for women. This will be the first time this event has been included as part of the Olympic Games.

20 December 1982
BUSINESS. Sherry Lansing resigns as head of Twentieth Century–Fox Film Studios. Lansing had been the only woman named to head a major motion picture studio.

OTHER EVENTS OF 1982

POPULAR CULTURE. At the Academy Awards, Oscars for Best Actress and Best Supporting Actress of 1981 go to Katharine Hepburn and Maureen Stapleton for their roles in *On Golden Pond* and *Reds*, respectively.

Jeane J. Kirkpatrick, 1926–

Her proven scholarship, political activism, and commitment to a conservative, yet aggressive foreign policy made Jeane J. Kirkpatrick President Reagan's choice for permanent representative to the United Nations. He announced her appointment on 22 December 1980, and her unanimous Senate confirmation followed in January 1981. This distinguished Kirkpatrick as the first Democrat to achieve a cabinet-level position in the Reagan administration.

Born on 19 November 1926, in Duncan, Oklahoma, Jeane Jordan received an A.A. from Stephens College in 1946 and a B.A. from Barnard in 1948. Following her graduation from Columbia University (where she received an M.A. in political science) in 1950, Jordan became an analyst for the State Department. Subsequently, she obtained a fellowship to study at the Institut de Science Politique in Paris, France, between 1952 and 1953, and then worked for both the Economic Cooperative Administration at the Governmental Affairs Institute and the Human Resources Research Office at George Washington University.

She married Dr. Evron M. Kirkpatrick in February 1955 and spent time raising three sons while she was a research associate for the Fund for the Republic from 1956 to 1962. Her work at the Fund was with the Communism in Government project.

Jeane J. Kirkpatrick, U.S. ambassador to the United Nations from 1983 to 1985. She resigned due to increasing disagreements with the Reagan administration, particularly over U.S. military support to El Salvador. (Photo courtesy United Nations)

At this time, she also consulted with the departments of State, Defense, and Health, Education, and Welfare. In 1962, Kirkpatrick assumed a position as assistant professor of political science at Trinity College in Washington, D.C., and in 1967 became associate professor at Georgetown University's political science department. Awarded a Ph.D. from Columbia in 1968, Kirkpatrick became Leary Professor in the Foundation of American Freedom at Georgetown in 1978.

Kirkpatrick quickly became well known for her strong anticommunist position, partly due to her contributions to publications such as the *New Republic* and the *APS Review*. In 1974, she wrote *Political Women,* an investigation of characteristics of fifty women state legislators elected in 1972. A staunch supporter of strong political parties, she also published *Dismantling the Parties* in 1978. This book detailed her concern over the fracture of the U.S. political system through single-issue organizations. In 1972, Kirkpatrick ran unsuccessfully for the House of Representatives in Maryland in the hopes of stemming what she saw as a rising tide of counterculture opinion. That year, she also helped establish the Coalition for a Democratic Majority—a group of neoconservatives committed to reclaim the Democratic party from what they termed the antiwar/antibusiness faction.

Throughout the mid-to-late 1970s, Kirkpatrick supported first Senator Henry Jackson and then Jimmy Carter. Ultimately she became disillusioned with the Carter administration's position on foreign policy and published her criticisms in the November 1979 issue of *Commentary* in an article, "Dictatorships and Double-Standards." After backing Ronald Reagan's candidacy for president in the 1980 election, she was named to the permanent United Nations position. She consistently defended U.S. support of El Salvador's military junta and condemned proposed economic sanctions against South Africa's apartheid government.

By 1983 she was continually at odds with many of President Reagan's advisors with whom her views clashed. In June 1985, she resigned from her assignment at the United Nations to return to a faculty position at Georgetown University. Her objective became "to speak out clearly on behalf of shared foreign policy objectives." In November 1985, President Reagan named Kirkpatrick to a fourteen-member intelligence panel headed by former U.S. Ambassador to Great Britain Anne Armstrong.

---

12 January 1983
WOMEN'S ISSUES. Margaret M. Heckler is named secretary of the Department of Health and Human Services by President Reagan.

30 January 1983
SPORTS. Fourteen-year-old Melissa Brown of Scarsdale, New York, is named the best tennis player in her age group by the U.S. Tennis Association.

7 February 1983
WOMEN'S ISSUES. Rita Lavelle of the Environmental Protection Agency is dismissed from her post as head of the toxic waste program.

WOMEN'S ISSUES. At a special conference for middle-aged women in New York City, Betty Furness speaks on issues dealing with mid-life concerns.

3 March 1983
IDEAS/BELIEFS. League of Women Voters lobbyist Sally Laird states that Congress is shifting its attitude on issues and legislation involving women.

11 March 1983
POLITICS. National Federation of Republican Women leaders ask President Reagan's administration to help solve the economic problems facing women.

13 March 1983
JUDICIAL. In Connecticut, a Superior Court judge rules that National Organization for Women members' rights to free speech are protected by the state constitution.

28 March 1983
SPORTS. Martina Navratilova defeats Chris Evert Lloyd in the Virginia Slims New York tennis tournament. On 15 August, Navratilova defeats Lloyd again at the Virginia Slims Los Angeles tournament.

4 April 1983
LABOR. District 65 of the United Auto Workers pushes for union organization of the Legal Defense and Education Fund of.the National Organization for Women. Executive Director Stephanie J. Clohesy states that the fund is not engaged in an antiunion campaign.

11 April 1983
SPORTS. Martina Navratilova defeats Tracy Austin at the Family Circle Magazine Cup tennis tournament in Hilton Head Island, South Carolina.

14 April 1983
JUDICIAL. In Connecticut, a judge finds retailers at Westfarms Mall in Hartford in contempt of court for preventing National Organization for Women (NOW) members from petitioning shoppers there. NOW had been seeking support of the Equal Rights Amendment during early 1982.

16 April 1982
WOMEN'S ISSUES. The Maine State Senate votes 22–0 to send the proposed Equal Rights Amendment to the state constitution to voters.

25 April 1983
IDEAS/BELIEFS. Writer Betty Friedan speaks at Cambridge University in England where she notes the benefits to men that have resulted from the women's movement.

2 May 1983
WOMEN'S ISSUES. The American Civil Liberties Union issues a revision of its handbook on women's rights.

11 May 1983
WOMEN'S ISSUES. The National Organization for Women (NOW) ends a 6-year boycott of Florida's convention facilities. NOW plans to hold its 1984 convention in Miami as a gesture of thanks to the city for supporting the Equal Rights Amendment.

9 June 1983
LABOR. District 65 of the United Auto Workers wins the right to represent staff at the Legal Defense and Education Fund of the National Organization for Women.

18 June 1983
AVIATION. Astronaut Sally K. Ride is the first woman to fly into outer space. She is one of the crew on the space shuttle *Challenger* and will spend 6 days in space.

30 June 1983
IDEAS/BELIEFS. National Organization for Women leaders announce they have formed a "Women's Truth Squad on Reagan," aimed at revealing the "devastating" impact of the president's programs on American women's lives.

SPORTS. Andrea Jaeger defeats Billie Jean King at the women's semifinals at Wimbledon.

3 July 1983
SPORTS. Martina Navratilova defeats Andrea Jaeger to win the women's tennis title at Wimbledon.

9 July 1983
POLITICS. In San Antonio, Texas, the National Women's Political Caucus holds a convention where 2,000 women gather. The theme of the meeting is how women can gain political advantage through the use of the ballot in 1984.

Sally K. Ride, 1951–

About the time that the National Aeronautics and Space Administration (NASA) had succeeded in putting the first American in space, a young girl named Sally K. Ride was enjoying a carefree, athletic childhood in Encino, California. Born on 26 May 1951, Ride proved early that she had determination and strength. At age ten she began tennis lessons and within a few years excelled at that sport, ranking eighteenth in the nation's junior tennis circuit.

She entered Westlake School for Girls, a college preparatory school in Los Angeles, on a partial tennis scholarship and while there studied science under Dr. Elizabeth Mommaerts. During her high school years Ride's interest in science blossomed, and in 1968 she enrolled in Swarthmore College as a physics major. After several months, she left college to work more intensively on her tennis game, but gradually decided against professional tennis. She enrolled at Stanford University in 1970. Graduating in 1973 with a double major—a B.A. in English literature and a B.S. in physics—Ride continued her academic studies with graduate work in astrophysics at Stanford.

For the first time since the 1960s, NASA was accepting new applicants for its astronaut program. Because women were now being considered and Ride believed

Sally K. Ride, the first American woman astronaut. Ride was part of the NASA team that investigated the causes of the space shuttle *Challenger* disaster. (Photo courtesy National Aeronautics and Space Administration)

she had the qualifications NASA wanted, she filled out an application in 1977. One of 8,000 applicants of whom 1,000 were women, Ride was, by October 1977, one of 208 finalists for the NASA program. Ride was chosen in January 1978 as one of six women among thirty-five total new recruits for astronaut training. In 1980, two more women were added, bringing the numbers to eight women and seventy-eight men.

At the Johnson Space Center, Ride began mission training that included water survival, radio communications, navigation, and extensive work on the flight simulator, a facsimile space craft. During this time she learned to fly a jet and also obtained her pilot's license. Ride was capsule commander for the second and third space shuttle missions in November 1981 and March 1982. Part of her work was relaying information to the shuttle crew from the flight director.

During the spring of 1982, Captain Robert Crippen selected Ride to be a mission specialist on the seventh flight of the space shuttle *Challenger*. Her job would be to help test a remote robot arm developed for use in space retrievals. In addition, Ride would act as flight engineer. Prior to the flight, she and the rest of the crew logged weeks of training time, sometimes more than fifty hours at a stretch, designed to acquaint them with and prepare them for any emergency while in space.

On 18 June 1983, the shuttle *Challenger* left Cape Canaveral, Florida, at 7:33 A.M. (EST) for a six-day flight. *Challenger* carried a crew of five, including Dr. Sally K. Ride, the first American woman astronaut in space. During the flight Ride repaired equipment, conducted experiments, and worked with the robot arm to test retrieval, repair, and return to orbit of existing satellites. After *Challenger* landed at Edwards Air Force Base on 24 June, Ride repeatedly emphasized her role as a team member rather than as the first American woman in space. She refused to capitalize on the novelty of her position and turned down requests to license her name and image to sell products.

Ride has remarked in interviews, "I'm just another astronaut." She was assigned, after her shuttle flight, as a liaison officer between NASA and private groups wanting to purchase shuttle space. In response to questions about her desire to fly in space again, Ride said, "I'd like to do it as many times as NASA will let me."

In July 1982, Ride married fellow astronaut Steven Hawley, and the couple share a home in Clear Lake City, Texas. In 1986, following the *Challenger* space shuttle disaster, Ride participated as a member of a NASA investigatory team. In her spare time, Ride flies a Grumman Tiger, works out at the Johnson Space Center gym, and usually runs several miles a day.

---

10 July 1983

WOMEN'S ISSUES. Outside the White House in Washington, D.C., the National Organization for Women sponsors a rally to illustrate the impact of Reagan's policies. About 300 people join the demonstration.

POLITICS. National Women's Political Caucus chair Kathy Wilson asks President Reagan not to run for reelection. Wilson states that she is voicing the sentiments of most other Republican women in the 73,000-member organization.

11 July 1983

POLITICS. In San Antonio, Texas, Kathy Wilson is reelected president of the National Women's Political Caucus at its annual convention. Four presidential hopefuls address the gathering and express their desire to see ratification of the now-defunct Equal Rights Amendment.

20 July 1983

BUSINESS. Angela Buchanan is named chair of President Reagan's new advisory committee on women's business ownership.

2 August 1983
WOMEN'S ISSUES. President Reagan addresses the American Bar Association and states that his administration has achieved an "unparalleled record" on women's rights. Critics term his speech simplistic and misleading.

14 August 1983
WOMEN'S ISSUES. Some observers note that a growing interest on Capitol Hill in the Equal Rights Amendment could mean new efforts to pass the amendment.

23 August 1983
WOMEN'S ISSUES. Barbara Honegger, special assistant to the Justice Department, resigns from her assigned project on eliminating sex discrimination in federal and state laws. Honegger terms the project "a sham."

24 August 1983
POLITICS. Maureen Reagan, the president's daughter, becomes a consultant to the Republican National Committee.

25 August 1983
IDEAS/BELIEFS. A White House spokesperson comments unfavorably on the recent behavior of Barbara Honegger, who resigned after criticizing Reagan's record on women's rights.

WOMEN'S ISSUES. Transportation Secretary Elizabeth H. Dole announces that 26 August is Women's Equality Day at the Department of Transportation.

26 August 1983
IDEAS/BELIEFS. Speaking at a news conference, Barbara Honegger further criticizes President Reagan for his role in diminishing the power of American women.

WOMEN'S ISSUES. President Reagan gives a speech on Women's Equality Day in which he pledges to reduce inflation and improve the economy.

27 August 1983
POLITICS. At a meeting of the Republican Women's Leadership Forum in San Diego, California, President Reagan defends his

programs and policies on women. Two hundred demonstrators protest the president's appearance.

30 August 1983
SPORTS. Martina Navratilova faces a $2-million damage suit brought against her by a photographer. He charges that Navratilova took his camera at the U.S. Open tennis tournament in 1982.

1 September 1983
WOMEN'S ISSUES. Reports indicate that Dee Jepson is planning to leave her $52,000-a-year job at the White House Office of Public Liaison. Some speculate that her departure results from women's groups' criticism of President Reagan's policies.

9 September 1983
FINANCE. Barbara Davis Blum is elected president and chief executive officer of the Women's National Bank in Washington, D.C.

WOMEN'S ISSUES. Assistant Attorney General of the United States William Reynolds notes that the present administration's planned changes in sexist language in federal laws are cosmetic. Reynolds defends the Reagan administration's enforcement of existing laws on behalf of women as an "impressive record."

11 September 1983
SPORTS. Chris Evert Lloyd is defeated by Martina Navratilova at the U.S. Open tennis tournament. Navratilova's total career winnings now stand at $6,089,756—the most any tennis player has ever received.

25 September 1983
WOMEN'S ISSUES. In Connecticut, the Permanent Commission on the Status of Women celebrates its tenth anniversary.

4 October 1983
EDUCATION. At the University of Oregon, the Center for Study of Women in Society receives a $3.5-million grant in memory of feminist writer Jane Grant.

24 October 1983
DEATHS. Jessica Savitch, newswoman for NBC-TV, drowns after her car plunges into the Delaware Canal outside a restaurant parking lot.

Barbara McClintock, 1902–

Winner of the 1983 Nobel Prize for physiology or medicine, Barbara McClintock received wide recognition for her genetic research. But for years prior to the award McClintock had worked alone, in relative obscurity, with little encouragement from colleagues. Born on 16 June 1902, in Hartford, Connecticut, she was one of four children of Thomas and Sara (Handy) McClintock. Her father was a physician, her mother a conventional homemaker absorbed by caring for her family. As a child, McClintock spent a great deal of time living with relatives in Massachusetts, and when she entered school found her interests rested more in sports than in academics. By adolescence she had become an avid scholar and recalls that she "loved to know things. I loved information."

She received a B.A. in 1923 from Cornell University and entered the graduate program. Majoring in cytology, with minors in genetics and zoology, she was awarded an M.A. in 1925 and a Ph.D. in 1927. During these years she studied the morphology of maize chromosomes, subsequently publishing nine scholarly papers on her research between 1929 and 1931. McClintock and her colleague Harriet Creighton were urged by geneticist Thomas Hunt Morgan to present the results of their work together in the *Proceedings of the National Academy of Sciences.*

In 1931, McClintock received a fellowship from the National Research Council, and in 1933, she was awarded a Guggenheim Fellowship. She traveled to Germany to study but was repelled by Nazism. She returned home to Cornell but was denied a faculty appointment because she was a woman. McClintock was given a short-term research position at Cornell, funded by the Rockefeller Foundation, and in 1936 left for an assistant professorship at the University of Missouri. In 1939, she was elected vice-president of the Genetics Society of America.

Facing entrenched prejudice against women academics, McClintock left the University of Missouri in 1941 and went to work for geneticist Milislav Demerec, director of the Carnegie Institute of Washington at Cold Spring Harbor Laboratory on Long Island. In 1944, she became president of the Genetics Society of America, and was the third woman in history elected to the National Academy of Science.

McClintock's genetic research and the dismissal of her results continued, however. When she announced her discovery of movable genetic elements in 1951, she was termed "crazy" by her colleagues. But the advent of molecular biology helped vindicate her findings, proving that her theory of "jumping genes" was, in fact, viable. McClintock was finally to reap the recognition and praise that she had long been denied.

In 1967, she won the Kimber Genetics Award; she received the National Medal of Science in 1970. The Albert Lasker Award and Israel's Wolf Foundation Prize were awarded her in 1981. She also received a MacArthur Foundation grant in 1981, which provided her a lifetime annual sum of $60,000. McClintock continues to work long hours in the field and in the laboratory, but enjoys the outdoors, often taking walks during which she identifies wildlife. She shuns publicity, reads extensively, and lives, very simply, alone in Cold Spring Harbor.

31 October 1983
WOMEN'S ISSUES. Radcliffe College holds a ceremony honoring 9 outstanding achievers among American women. They are Dr. Mary S. Calderone, Barbara Tuchman, Georgia O'Keeffe, Esther Peterson, Jean E. Fairfax, Lucy Somerville Howorth, Dr. Helen B. Taussig, Professor Chien-Shuing Wu, and Eudora Welty.

2 November 1983
JUDICIAL. The U.S. Justice Department sues to obtain medical records of "Baby Jane Doe." The infant has been born with severe birth defects and the court has been asked to require surgery that the baby's parents have decided against.

8 November 1983
POLITICS. Democrat Martha Layne Collins is elected the first woman governor of Kentucky. Kathy Whitmire and Diane Feinstein are elected mayors of Houston, Texas, and San Francisco, California, respectively.

15 November 1983
WOMEN'S ISSUES. Representative Thomas P. O'Neill (D-Massachusetts) attempts to revive the Equal Rights Amendment but receives a vote of 278–147, 6 votes short of the number needed to send the amendment to the states for ratification once again.

WOMEN'S ISSUES. The Wonder Woman Foundation presents awards to 17 women for outstanding contributions to American society. Each woman receives $7,500.

16 November 1983
JUDICIAL. Federal Judge Leonard Wexler denies court requests for medical intervention on behalf of "Baby Jane Doe." The severely handicapped infant born on 11 October has become the focus of right-to-life efforts designed to force parents and doctors to provide surgery that would most likely be of little use in helping the child.

30 November 1983
FINANCE. The Women's Bank of Richmond, Virginia, announces its planned takeover by First Virginia Banks, Inc.

1 December 1983
CRIME. Rita Lavelle, former head of the Environmental Protection Agency's toxic-waste program, is convicted of perjury and obstruction of congressional investigation in hazardous waste clean-up.

4 December 1983
IDEAS/BELIEFS. In a *New York Times* survey, 26 percent of women surveyed state that motherhood is the "best part" of being a woman. In 1970, 53 percent of women questioned answered that motherhood was best.

WOMEN'S ISSUES. In San Diego, California, Republican women gathering at a bipartisan meeting demand that President Reagan extend his support to the Equal Rights Amendment.

Women and the Olympic Games

Although we now expect women's participation in the Olympic Games, in 1892, when the modern Games were established, women did not compete. In 1900, Margaret Abbot of the Chicago Golf Club won a gold medal—the first ever awarded to a woman. In 1904, an archery competition for women was included, although only on an unofficial basis. Archery was not included in the Games again until 1972.

By 1920 U.S. women competed in swimming and diving, as well as in figure skating events. And despite the conservatism of Olympic founder Baron Pierre de Coubertin, who vehemently opposed women's participation in Olympic events, women were fully involved by 1928. They competed in track and field, tennis, and fencing.

In early decades the presence of women was viewed by some Olympic organizers as adding an excessive number of athletes, but this was clearly an attempt to keep women out of competition. In 1939, the International Olympic Committee ruled against including women's gymnastics in the 1940 Games; field hockey was ruled out for 1946. In 1949, Avery Brundage favored elimination of five major women's categories from the Olympic Games—including track and field and gymnastics—at the 1952 Helsinki competition.

In spite of the considerable lack of support for women athletes, they made a good showing in most Olympic Games. When American women joined the track and field competition in 1928, it was widely felt that women lacked the physical and emotional stamina to compete safely. For the most part, women athletes disagreed. In the October 1928 issue of *The Sportswoman,* one writer said, "Even the stupidest mortal must by this time realize that a few women are capable of developing into such experts . . . that to watch them is a great pleasure." Although it is only fair to note that the Women's Division of the National Amateur Athletic Federation made a concerted effort during the 1920s and 1930s to ban women athletes from the Olympic Games, this objection stemmed largely from philosophical conflicts over both the nature of amateur sports and the varying standards of femininity at the time.

Swimming, diving, and track and field are the three areas in which American women have traditionally made the best showing at the Olympic Games. For the winter Games, alpine skiing, speed skating, and figure skating, in that order, have proved the best areas for American female athletes. The talent of American women in the Olympic competitions blossomed fully in the years following World War II. There had been few really outstanding women competing before then—with the exception perhaps of Babe Didrikson in 1932. But by 1960 women athletes such as Wilma Rudolph, Tenley Albright, Patricia McCormick, and Andrea Lawrence were well known.

The television broadcast of selected women's Olympic events garnered even more public support and enthusiasm for women athletes. When Peggy Fleming won a gold medal at the 1968 winter Olympics, thousands watched and applauded at home. By the time Joan Benoit won the first-ever Olympic Marathon for women in 1984, the view of female athletes as anachronisms had been discarded.

---

10 December 1983
SPORTS. Martina Navratilova wins the Australian Open women's tennis championship.

19 December 1983
IDEAS/BELIEFS. Two-thirds of women surveyed by the *New York Times* state that the feminist movement has done nothing to improve their lives.

29 December 1983
POLITICS. Presidential candidate Sonia Johnson comments on her aim of furthering the impact of feminism by running for executive office. Johnson is the founder of Mormons for ERA and was excommunicated by the Mormon Church for her radical views.

OTHER EVENTS OF 1983

POPULAR CULTURE. Oscars for 1982 go to Meryl Streep, Best Actress, in *Sophie's Choice,* and to Jessica Lange, Best Supporting Actress, in *Tootsie.*

5 January 1984
CIVIL RIGHTS. Linda Chavez is named the new staff director of the U.S. Commission on Civil Rights. Chavez urges a study on the "radical" principle that men and women should receive equal pay for equal work.

6 January 1984
LABOR. The Labor Department reports that the jobless rate for adult females dropped in

December 1983 to 7.1 percent from a rate of 7.2 percent the previous month.

9 January 1984
JUDICIAL. The U.S. Supreme Court agrees to rule on the case *Gomez* v. *U.S. Jaycees.* The suit deals with charges of gender discrimination against women. They are denied full membership in the civic group, which currently has 300,000 members.

CRIME. Rita Lavelle, former Environmental Protection Agency official, is sentenced to 6 months in prison.

13 January 1984
JUDICIAL. Christine Craft, a television newswoman, is awarded $325,000 in damages after a retrial of her sex discrimination and fraud case against Kansas City, Missouri, station KMBC-TV.

WOMEN'S ISSUES. New York Governor Mario Cuomo pledges his support of a state constitutional amendment that will guarantee equal rights for women.

20 January 1984
POLITICS. While campaigning in Iowa, Democratic presidential-hopeful Walter Mondale speaks out against Ronald Reagan and calls the chief executive a foe of women's rights.

23 January 1984
IDEAS/BELIEFS. Thousands of people gather in the nation's capital for a "March for Life" antiabortion demonstration.

15 February 1984
DEATHS. Ethel Merman, musical comedy star, dies in New York at age 76.

16 February 1984
WOMEN'S ISSUES. On the 165th anniversary of Susan B. Anthony's birth, President Reagan defends his administration's efforts on behalf of women.

17 February 1984
IDEAS/BELIEFS. At a feminist rally in Claremont, New Hampshire, the most popular button sold carries the slogan, "If we can send a man to the moon, why not send them all there?"

WOMEN'S ISSUES. The National Organization for Women gives out the first Elizabeth Cady Stanton Awards for role models to Mary Johnson Lowe, Joyce D. Miller, and Kay Wight. Fifth Annual Awards for grass-roots activists, the Susan B. Anthony Awards, go to Luz Allende, Carol Burt-Beck, Chris Almvig, Dr. Alexandra Symonds, and Brenda Berkman.

28 February 1984
JUDICIAL. The U.S. Supreme Court rules 6–3 that Title IX of the 1972 Education Amendments Act is enforceable only upon programs specifically receiving federal funds. The National Organization for Women calls the decision a "terrible setback."

29 February 1984
JUDICIAL. Chief U.S. District Court Judge Miles W. Lord approves a $4.6-million lawsuit involving the Dalkon Shield. A. H. Robins Co., Inc., maker of the intrauterine device, is accused of causing "catastrophic" harm to thousands of women.

4 March 1984
SPORTS. Martina Navratilova beats Chris Evert Lloyd in the finals of the Virginia Slims Tennis Championships in New York City. The crowd of 15,309 is the largest ever to turn out for a women's tournament.

5 April 1984
RELIGION. The 230,000-member Reorganized Church of Jesus Christ of Latter-Day Saints votes to authorize ordination of women priests.

6 April 1984
BUSINESS. Speaking at a conference sponsored by the Women Business Owners of New York, President Reagan admits that he is perceived as not concerned enough about women's issues.

14 April 1984
POLITICS. In Los Angeles, California, Walter F. Mondale campaigns for the presidency and calls Ronald Reagan's views on women's issues "abominable."

20 April 1984
LEGISLATIVE. The U.S. Senate passes a bill designed to rid federal laws of nearly 100 instances of gender bias.

24 April 1984
SPORTS. Seventeen women finalists are tapped for the U.S. Olympic basketball team. The roster will be cut to 12 by mid-July.

25 April 1984
SPORTS. Joan Benoit, U.S. Olympic women's marathon hopeful, announces that she will undergo arthroscopic knee surgery. Some question Benoit's ability to run in the August Olympics.

CRIME. In Los Angeles, California, police report that some women posing as prostitutes are luring guests to hotel rooms, where they then drug their victims and rob them.

6 May 1984
WOMEN'S ISSUES. Transportation Secretary Elizabeth H. Dole urges Republicans in Delaware to "turn up the volume" on President Reagan's record on women.

8 May 1984
DEATHS. Lila Acheson Wallace, co-founder of *Reader's Digest*, dies at age 94 in Mount Kisco, New York.

10 May 1984
SPORTS. Recovered from her arthroscopic surgery, Joan Benoit reports that she will compete in the U.S. Olympic Marathon trials in Olympia, Washington.

12 May 1984
LEGISLATIVE. U.S. Representatives Patricia Schroeder (D-Colorado) and Olympia Snowe (R-Maine) call for congressional action on legislation that will help working and divorced mothers.

13 May 1984
SPORTS. Joan Benoit wins the U.S. Olympic Marathon trials in Olympia, Washington. Julie Brown and Julie Isphording also place.

16 May 1984
RELIGION. At its annual convention, the Rabbinical Assembly of Conservative Judaism rejects the second membership application of Beverly Magidson, a woman rabbi. The vote is 230–99, which is 22 votes less than the 75 percent majority required. Action on another woman rabbi's application is tabled until the 1985 convention.

17 May 1984
POLITICS. Representative Geraldine A. Ferraro (D-New York), chair of the Democratic Platform Committee, states that guaranteed rights for women should be mentioned in the platform, but specific reference to the Equal Rights Amendment should be avoided.

23 May 1984
WOMEN'S ISSUES. The U.S. Senate confirms the nomination of Aulana Peters as a member of the Securities and Exchange Commission (SEC). Peters will be the first black ever to serve on the SEC.

24 May 1984
WOMEN'S ISSUES. In Albuquerque, New Mexico, presidential candidate Senator Gary Hart (D-Colorado) promises to make the Equal Rights Amendment part of the U.S. Constitution by 1988.

12 June 1984
JUDICIAL. The Supreme Court rules 6–3 that valid seniority systems cannot be altered to protect minority workers hired under affirmative action.

WOMEN'S ISSUES. In New York, Republicans block action on a proposed Equal Rights Amendment to the state constitution.

13 June 1984
IDEAS/BELIEFS. Peace activists and feminist leaders race from the Capitol to the White House. They are led by Representative Pat Schroeder (D-Colorado), who calls for President Reagan's defeat in November.

17 June 1984
WOMEN'S ISSUES. In New York, women's rights groups campaigning in support of a state Equal Rights Amendment charge that Governor Mario Cuomo is not giving the amendment enough support to ensure its passage.

18 June 1984
SPORTS. Two women, Valerie Zimring and Michele Berube, are named to the U.S. Olympic rhythmic gymnastics team.

22 June 1984
JUDICIAL. A federal appeals court announces that it will not order Olympic officials to permit women in the 5,000- and 1,000-meter races at the 1984 Games. Women from 27 countries, including the United States, contend that their rights are being violated by Olympic policy, which doesn't permit them 2 distance races but does provide such races for men.

24 June 1984
SPORTS. At the Olympic track and field trials, Mary Decker qualifies for the U.S. Olympic team by winning the 3,000-meter run.

30 June 1984
DEATHS. Lillian Hellman dies at her home in Martha's Vineyard, Massachusetts.

SPORTS. Tracy Caulkins beats Nancy Hogshead in the 200-meter individual medley at the U.S. Olympic swimming trials.

1 July 1984
POLITICS. The National Organization for Women passes a resolution that calls for nomination of a woman vice-president of the United States in the 1984 elections.

EDUCATION. At Douglass College in New Brunswick, New Jersey, about 5,000 women meet for 5 days at the sixth annual conference of the National Women's Studies Association.

3 July 1984
JUDICIAL. The U.S. Supreme Court rules 7–0 that the U.S. Jaycees cannot exclude women from full membership.

12 July 1984
POLITICS. Representative Geraldine A. Ferraro (D-New York) is chosen by Walter F. Mondale (D-Minnesota) as his vice-presidential running mate.

16 July 1984
POLITICS. Kentucky Governor Martha Layne Collins becomes the permanent chair of the Democratic Convention in San Francisco, California.

LEGISLATIVE. President Reagan signs a bill that obligates states to legislate on behalf of court-ordered child support. States must pass laws requiring employers to withhold wages from parents falling one month behind in making these payments.

19 July 1984
POLITICS. Geraldine A. Ferraro is nominated by acclamation as the vice-presidential candidate at the Democratic convention.

Joan Benoit, 1957–

Joan Benoit set an American record for women's marathon running in 1979, when she won the Boston Marathon with a time of 2:35:15. A senior at Bowdoin College in her native Maine, Benoit shunned the resulting publicity and continued to train. She won again in Boston in 1983, setting a world's record with her time—2:22:42. The daughter of André and Nancy Benoit of Cape Elizabeth, Maine, she became most prominent in 1984, when she won a gold medal in the first Olympic Games marathon event for women on 5 August. She ran the third-fastest time ever for a woman, 2:24:52, and her victory was shared by the 77,000 people crowded into the Los Angeles Memorial Coliseum. Early in the race, Benoit set her pace and by the time she hit the three-mile mark had left the pack behind and was running alone, finishing 430 meters ahead of world champion Grete Waitz of Norway.

Inclusion of a women's marathon for the first time in modern Olympic history made Benoit's success even more notable. And her awareness of her victory's symbolic importance was clear as she prepared to enter the Coliseum through a tunnel leading in from the street. "When you come out from underneath the tunnel, you're going to be a different person. Do you want to come out of the tunnel?" Benoit recalled asking herself.

At one point Benoit's participation in the 1984 Olympic Games was uncertain, however. She had arthroscopic surgery to remove an inflamed plica from her right knee just seventeen days before the Olympic trials. Her coach, Bob Sevene, agreed then that Joan was in less than optimum shape for the 26-mile, 385-yard race. But she easily won the trials and made history in Los Angeles by winning a gold medal. In September 1984, Benoit was honored by the Women's Sports Foundation and received the Amateur Sportswoman of the Year Award, along with Olympic gold-medal gymnast Mary Lou Retton. A runner of exceptional stamina, Benoit has said, "I don't know where my competitiveness comes from."

She continues to train and compete, despite the Olympic highpoint, which would perhaps have caused some athletes to retire from amateur sports. On 16 September 1984, Benoit won the Philadelphia Distance Run (a 13.1-mile half-marathon) with a time of 1:08:34, her personal best for a marathon. Benoit is working toward her goal of breaking 2:20 in a marathon, and observers expect to see her compete in the first 10,000-meter women's Olympic event in Seoul, South Korea, in 1988.

Until her marriage to Scott Samuelson on 29 September 1984, Benoit lived in Cape Elizabeth. She and her husband make their home in a renovated 1850s farmhouse in Freeport, where she can be seen running ninety miles a week, picking berries, and enjoying the peace and solitude of her native surroundings. In 1985, Benoit won the women's division of the America's Marathon in Chicago, with a time only slightly over one minute more than 2:20—a goal Benoit hopes to reach.

---

23 July 1984
POPULAR CULTURE. The first black Miss America, Vanessa Williams, gives up her title after it is revealed that she had previously posed for nude photographs.

26 July 1984
POLITICS. Third-party presidential-hopeful and former Mormon feminist leader Sonia Johnson qualifies for federal matching campaign funds.

30 July 1984
SPORTS. Tracy Caulkins sets an American record for the 400-meter individual medley at the 1984 Olympic Games. Her time is 4:39:24.

1 August 1984
INTERNATIONAL. In Jerusalem, Betty Friedan takes part in opening a conference promoting dialogue between American and Israeli women.

9 August 1984
CIVIL RIGHTS. Speaking before the American Bar Association convention in Chicago, Illinois, Deputy Attorney General Carol E. Dinkus defends President Reagan's "colorblind" policy on civil rights, which rejects racial and gender quotas.

14 August 1984
POPULAR CULTURE. Patti Davis, daughter of President Reagan, is married to Paul Grilley, a yoga instructor, in Los Angeles, California.

17 August 1984
POLITICS. In Seattle, Washington, Geraldine Ferraro greets 10,000 supporters as she campaigns for vice-president.

POLITICS. At the GOP Convention, the party platform committee blocks attempts to include endorsement of the Equal Rights Amendment in the party statement.

23 August 1984
WOMEN'S ISSUES.   The president signs the Retirement Equity Act, which will make it easier for women to earn retirement benefits under private pension plans.

26 August 1984
IDEAS/BELIEFS.   The National Organization for Women holds an outdoor celebration in Washington, D.C., to observe the anniversary of woman suffrage and the birthday of Representative Geraldine A. Ferraro.

30 August 1984
AVIATION.   Judith A. Resnick is one of 6 astronauts to take the space shuttle *Discovery* on its maiden flight. Resnick is the second U.S. woman in space.

13 September 1984
JUDICIAL.   A federal judge rules that a policy of Burning Tree Club in Rockville, Maryland, will cost the club $186,000 per year in tax exemptions. The exclusive club bars women as members, guests, and even kitchen workers. Judge Irma S. Raker declines to rule on the legality of Burning Tree's gender-restrictive membership.

28 September 1984
WOMEN'S ISSUES.   Transportation Secretary Elizabeth H. Dole reports that she has suspended her fight for passage of the Equal Rights Amendment due to President Reagan's strong feelings against the amendment.

8 October 1984
WOMEN'S ISSUES.   Columbia Law School Library announces that former Secretary of State

Cyrus R. Vance has donated to its collection the first English-language book on women's marital and property rights. The book was printed in 1632.

13 October 1984
IDEAS/BELIEFS.   The American Association of University Women and 59 other national women's organizations hold a New York City conference on the International Women's Decade and Beyond.

15 October 1984
WOMEN'S ISSUES.   Nancy Clark Reynolds, the U.S. Representative to the United Nations Commission on the Status of Women, speaks to the American Association of University Women–sponsored conference in New York City. Reynolds notes that the United States will emphasize development at the Nairobi, Kenya, World Conference next year.

17 October 1984
DEATHS.   Black jazz singer and songwriter Alberta Hunter dies in New York City. She is 89.

18 October 1984
LABOR.   William Nikasen of the President's Council of Economic Advisors denounces the concept of comparable worth. He speaks at a meeting of the Women in Government group.

21 October 1984
POPULAR CULTURE.   Diane Sawyer debuts as the first woman correspondent on the CBS-TV show "60 Minutes."

Geraldine Ferraro, 1935–

Geraldine Ferraro, the New York congresswoman, who was the first woman ever to be nominated for vice-president by a major political party, was born in Newburgh, New York, on 26 August 1935. The bright, determined daughter of Dominick and Antonetta (Corrieri) Ferraro, she was educated at the Marymount School and later graduated from Marymount College in 1956 with a B.A. in English. Ferraro taught school in Queens, New York, but soon tested her ambition and considerable intellect by attending Fordham University Law School in the evenings. She received her J.D. in 1960, and married John Zaccaro on 16 July of that year.

While raising three children, Ferraro also practiced civil law and was active in the local Democratic party. In 1974, she became assistant district attorney in the Investigations Bureau of Queens, and the following year she worked for the Special Victims Bureau. These career appointments helped her develop further a liberal consciousness, since many of her clients were poor and disadvantaged. In 1978, Ferraro quit the D.A.'s office and ran for a seat in the House of Representatives from the ninth district. She won then, and was also victorious in her bids for reelection in 1980 and 1982.

After gaining a reputation for hard work and skilled speaking, she was instrumental, as chair of the Platform Committee, in constructing the Democratic campaign platform at the July 1984 Democratic National Convention. She was also singled out as one of the most appropriate running mates for Walter Mondale, despite the fact that no woman had ever before been selected for this slot. Her confirmation was one of the more dramatic early moments in a relatively quiet election campaign. Ferraro acquitted herself well in campaign efforts. She debated Republican Vice-President George Bush on national television, parrying neatly and effectively the verbal attacks on her inexperience on foreign policy issues.

Ferraro has always emphasized her indebtedness to her family. To her mother, Antonetta, who supported her children after the early death of her husband, Ferraro acknowledges much of her own drive and sense of self-worth. In addition, she has made clear that although she has chosen a career in the public eye, her private life with her husband and three children is also important. When John Zaccaro was investigated for fiscal irregularities in his real estate business, Ferraro firmly accepted the resulting adverse publicity as her due. She proved during long months in the limelight that she was both strong-willed and intelligent, and a canny politician.

After the Mondale–Ferraro defeat to Reagan–Bush in 1984, Ferraro carried out her remaining public duties with cheer and enthusiasm. It was only late in 1985 that she finally announced her decision not to run for the New York Democratic Senate seat, though few supporters doubted her ability to wage a strong campaign. Also in late 1985, she published her autobiography, *Ferraro: My Story,* with Linda Bird Francke, in which she discussed the challenges inherent in being a woman in high-level politics.

---

28 October 1984
INTERNATIONAL. Commenting on her recent experiences at a conference on Israeli-American women, author Betty Friedan notes that the choice of Geraldine Ferraro as Democratic vice-presidential candidate indicates a struggle for human freedom similar to that occurring in Israel and Egypt.

WOMEN'S ISSUES. In Westchester County, New York, the League of Women Voters decides to hold evening meetings to accommodate the needs of working mothers.

29 October 1984
POLITICS. Elizabeth L. Chittick, president of the National Women's party, resigns from the

Republican Business Women of New York. Chittick is angered by the group's use of the initials "ERA" to promote the slogan, "Elect Reagan Again."

2 November 1984
DEATHS. Margie Velma Barfield is the first woman executed in North Carolina since 1944. No women have been executed in the United States in 22 years.

5 November 1984
IDEAS/BELIEFS. An article in the *New York Times* debates the question of Eleanor Roosevelt's commitment to feminism. Most

women's rights leaders agree that she embodied the spirit of women's rights while not speaking out strongly on specifics, or disagreeing with certain key issues.

6 November 1984
POLITICS. Madeline M. Kunin is elected governor of Vermont. She defeats Attorney General John Easton in a close vote of 116,245 to 112,505.

POLITICS. Arlene Violet, a former Roman Catholic Sister of Mercy, becomes the first woman attorney general in Rhode Island. She is also the only woman state attorney general in the nation.

8 November 1984
LEGISLATIVE. President Reagan signs a bill allowing former spouses of federal employees to collect survivor benefits.

WOMEN'S ISSUES. In Maine, voters reject a proposed state Equal Rights Amendment.

9 November 1984
AVIATION. Dr. Anna L. Fisher, a physician, is the first American mother (and the third woman) to fly into space on the shuttle *Discovery.*

14 November 1984
JUDICIAL. A $38-million settlement is announced in the suit against Dalkon Shield maker A. H. Robins Company. The firm has recently begun a recall of the intrauterine device and offers to pay costs for having it removed.

15 November 1984
WOMEN'S ISSUES. Rosa L. Parks receives 1 of 14 awards from the Wonder Woman Foundation. The annual awards for women over age 40 recognize public service achievement.

16 November 1984
LABOR. U.S. Civil Rights Commission member Clarence Pendleton states that the concept of comparable worth is "the looniest idea since Looney Tunes came on the screen."

20 December 1984
WOMEN'S ISSUES. In speaking to the Woman's Forum in New York City, U.S. Ambassador to the United Nations Jeane J. Kirkpatrick observes that "sexism is alive" at the United Nations and in U.S. government.

28 December 1984
JUDICIAL. The Justice Department files suit against the Las Vegas, Nevada, Police Department for failing to "hire, assign, transfer, and promote" females and minorities on the same basis as "whites, Anglos, and males."

31 December 1984
ARTS AND CULTURE. Soprano Leontyne Price is reported to be planning her final Metropolitan Opera performance for January 1985 prior to her retirement. Price has been with the Metropolitan Opera for nearly 25 years.

OTHER EVENTS OF 1984

POPULAR CULTURE. At the Academy Awards, Oscars for 1983 go to Shirley MacLaine, Best Actress, in *Terms of Endearment,* and to Linda Hunt, Best Supporting Actress, in *The Year of Living Dangerously.*

Olympic Gold Medals
Mary T. Meagher: Swimming—200-meter butterfly
Mary T. Meagher: Swimming—100-meter butterfly
Tiffany Cohen: Swimming—400-meter freestyle
Tiffany Cohen: Swimming—800-meter freestyle
Tracy Caulkins: Swimming—400-meter individual medley
Carrie Steinseifer and Nancy Hogshead: Swimming—tie for 100-meter freestyle
Theresa Andrews: Swimming—100-meter backstroke
Mary Mayte: Swimming—200-meter freestyle
    Swimming—400-meter medley relay women's team medal
Evelyn Ashford: Track and Field—100-meter dash
Benita Brown-Fitzgerald: Track and Field—100-meter hurdles
Valerie Briscoe-Hooks: Track and Field—200-meter dash

Joan Benoit: Track and Field—Marathon
   Track and Field—400-meter relay women's
   team medal
   Track and Field—1,000-meter relay women's
   team medal
Connie Carpenter: Cycling—individual road race
Mary Lou Retton: Gymnastics—all-around best
Pat Spurgin: Shooting—air rifle
   Equestrian—3-day event women's team medal
   Equestrian—team jumping women's team
   medal
   Basketball—women's team medal
   Rowing—eight oars women's team medal
Debbie Armstrong: Alpine skiing—giant slalom

Olympic Silver Medals

Amy White: Swimming—200-meter backstroke
Betsy Mitchell: Swimming—100-meter
backstroke
Jenna Johnson: Swimming—100-meter butterfly
Cynthia Woodhead: Swimming—200-meter
freestyle
Alice Brown: Track and Field—100-meter dash
Florence Griffith: Track and Field—200-meter
dash
Kim Gallagher: Track and Field—800-meter run
Jackie Joyner: Heptathlon
Julie McNamara: Gymnastics—floor exercises
Mary Lou Retton: Gymnastics—vault
   Gymnastics—women's team medal
Rebecca Twigg: Cycling—individual road race
Leslie Deniz: Discus
Ruby Fox: Shooting—pistol
Karen Stives: Equestrian—3-day individual
event
   Volleyball—women's team medal
Charlotte Geer: Rowing—single sculls
   Rowing—quadruple sculls with coxswain
   women's team medal
Rosalynn Sumners: Figure skating
Kitty Carruthers: Figure skating—pairs with
Peter Carruthers
Christin Cooper: Alpine skiing—giant slalom

Olympic Bronze Medals

Kim Turner: Track and Field—100-meter
hurdles
Mary Lou Retton: Gymnastics—floor exercises
Kathy Johnson: Gymnastics—balance beam
Mary Lou Retton: Gymnastics—uneven parallels
Joni Huntly: Track and Field—long jump
Wanda Jewell: Shooting—small-bore, 3
positions
   Field Hockey—women's team medal

9 January 1985
LABOR. The Labor Department reports that
unemployment rates for adult women fell in
December 1984 to 6.4 percent from 6.5 percent
in the previous month.

10 January 1985
POLITICS. Madeline M. Kunin is sworn in
as governor of Vermont.

12 January 1985
MILITARY. Commodore Roberta Hazard is
named the first woman commander of the U.S.
Naval Training Center in Great Lakes, Illinois.
It is the country's largest naval training facility.

14 January 1985
JUDICIAL. The U.S. Supreme Court lets
stand a ruling setting payment of $60 million in
back wages to Northwest Airlines' female flight
attendants. The women had brought a sex
discrimination suit against the airline.

17 January 1985
EDUCATION. Smith College announces that
Mary Maples Dunn, dean of Bryn Mawr
College, will replace outgoing college president
Jill Ker Conway on 1 July.

19 January 1985
SPORTS. Runner Mary Decker sets a world
indoor record of 5:34:52 for the 2,000-meter run
in Los Angeles, California.

20 January 1985
WOMEN'S ISSUES. Geri B. Larson is the
first woman forest supervisor in the U.S. Forest
Service. She is in charge of the Tahoe National
Forest in Nevada City, California.

21 January 1985
LABOR. At Yale University in New Haven,
Connecticut, a 10-week strike by clerical and
technical workers ends with approval of a 3-year
contract, increasing salaries by an average of 35
percent. More than 80 percent of the striking
workers are women.

22 January 1985
IDEAS/BELIEFS. President Reagan speaks at
an antiabortion rally in Washington, D.C. Up to
71,500 people gather for a "March for Life."

23 January 1985
IDEAS/BELIEFS. Betty Ford, Rosalynn Carter, and Dr. Jeane J. Kirkpatrick will be among the speakers at a symposium on Women in a Changing World, sponsored by American University. Jihan el-Sadat, widow of former Egyptian president Anwar Sadat, will chair the gathering.

24 January 1985
WOMEN'S ISSUES. Penny Harrington is sworn in as chief of police in Portland, Oregon. She is the first woman to head a major city's police department and has been with the force since 1964.

29 January 1985
CIVIL RIGHTS. Chair of the U.S. Civil Rights Commission Clarence Pendleton reports that "quotas are a dead issue."

30 January 1985
INTERNATIONAL. U.S. Ambassador to the United Nations Jeane J. Kirkpatrick announces that she is resigning her diplomatic post.

BUSINESS. Anne Sutherland Fuchs is named publisher of *Woman's Day* magazine.

31 January 1985
POLITICS. Republican Muriel Siebert, first woman member of the New York Stock Exchange, invites leaders of New York women's groups to her home. Siebert hopes to form a coalition of women to lobby for more women in public office and to support day care, among other issues.

HISTORY. In Chicago, Illinois, it is announced that the Lexington Hotel will become a museum honoring women. The building's renovation is slated for completion by 1992, the year the World's Fair will be held in Chicago.

4 February 1985
WOMEN'S ISSUES. Jennifer Hirshberg is named White House press secretary to Nancy Reagan. Hirshberg is currently director of the Federal Trade Commission Office of Public Affairs.

10 February 1985
SPORTS. Patty Sheehan wins the Ladies Professional Golf Association's Sarasota,

Florida, Classic with a 10-under-par score of 278 for 72 holes.

14 February 1985
RELIGION. The U.S. Rabbinical Assembly of Conservative Judaism announces that it will accept women as rabbis in its organization. The vote is 636–267, exceeding the two-thirds majority required after an amendment to the assembly's constitution. Previously, women have been denied admission to the assembly.

19 February 1985
DEATHS. Carol Sutton, who became the first woman to head the news staff of a major daily paper, the Louisville *Courier-Journal,* dies at age 51 of cancer.

25 February 1985
POPULAR CULTURE. A 2-hour movie, *A Bunny's Tale,* airs on ABC-TV. The film is based on Gloria Steinem's work as a reporter posing as a cocktail waitress at a New York City Playboy Club.

26 February 1985
WOMEN'S ISSUES. Marjory E. Mecklenburg, head of the Health and Human Services Family Life program, resigns amid accusations of having used public funds for private travel.

1 March 1985
WOMEN'S ISSUES. The Vermont House of Representatives approves an equal rights amendment to the state constitution.

3 March 1985
DEATHS. Sarah Blanding Gibson, first female president of Vassar College, dies at age 86 in Newtown, Pennsylvania.

5 March 1985
WOMEN'S ISSUES. The U.S. Postal Service issues a commemorative stamp honoring Mary McLeod Bethune.

8 March 1985
INTERNATIONAL. The State Department announces that Maureen Reagan, the president's daughter, will head the U.S. delegation to the

United Nations Women's Conference in Nairobi, Kenya, in the summer.

18 March 1985
ARTS AND CULTURE.   Sculptor Louise Nevelson announces that she will donate 25 of her works to 11 different institutions. The collages and sculptures are valued at more than $5 million.

20 March 1985
SPORTS.   In Alaska, Libby Riddles becomes the first woman to win the 1,827-kilometer Anchorage-to-Nome Iditarod Trail International Race. The dogsled event is the world's longest and richest. Riddles receives $50,000 after nearly 18 days of racing.

23 March 1985
POPULAR CULTURE.   Fashion model Christie Brinkley and singer-songwriter Billy Joel are married in New York City.

DEATHS.   Patricia Roberts Harris, the first black woman cabinet member, dies of cancer at age 60.

24 March 1985
SPORTS.   Jan Stephenson wins the Ladies Professional Golf Association tournament in Glendale, California. She is the ninth woman on the tour to reach career earnings of $1 million.

SPORTS.   Martina Navratilova wins the New York Virginia Slims Championship by beating Czech Helena Sukova.

26 March 1985
JUDICIAL.   The U.S. Supreme Court upholds a lower court ruling that an Oklahoma law permitting a teacher's dismissal for speaking out on gay rights is unconstitutional.

27 March 1985
POLITICS.   A Rutgers University study finds that women account for 14.7 percent of the nation's state legislators. In 1975, the figure was about 8 percent. New Hampshire has 33 percent women lawmakers, and Mississippi has only 2.3 percent. Black women legislators make up 6.7 percent of the total number; Hispanic women, 1.2 percent.

2 April 1985
HEALTH.   The A. H. Robins Company establishes a multimillion-dollar fund for women who were injured while using the Dalkon Shield.

9 April 1985
WOMEN'S ISSUES.   Cibella R. Borges is ordered reinstated as a New York Police Department (NYPD) officer after having been dismissed in 1983 for posing nude for magazine photos. Borges had been a civilian employee of the NYPD at the time the pictures were taken.

10 April 1985
WOMEN'S ISSUES.   *USA Today* heads the list of 11 newspapers carrying signed articles by women writers. Altogether, 23.7 percent of all front-page pieces in the newspapers surveyed were written by women. *USA Today* had 45.1 percent of the total women's pieces. The *New York Times* had only 10 percent of its front-page stories by-lined by women.

11 April 1985
LABOR.   The U.S. Civil Rights Commission rejects, on a 5–2 vote, the concept of comparable worth pay. Two commission members, Mary Frances Berry and Blandina Cardenas Ramirez, cast votes against the policy.

14 April 1985
LABOR.   The Justice Department announces it is stepping up its campaign against the use of numerical goals and quotas by public employers. This decision follows in the wake of the current presidential administration's lack of support for hiring quotas relative to women and minorities.

15 April 1985
BUSINESS.   Dawn Steel is named president of production for Paramount Pictures Corporation in Hollywood, California.

23 April 1985
DEATHS.   Texas Federal District Judge Sarah T. Hughes dies in Dallas. Hughes was the only woman judge to swear in a president of the United States at the time of Lyndon Johnson's assumption of power after John F. Kennedy's death.

28 April 1985
SPORTS.   For the first time, two women, Kathy Whitworth and Mickey Wright, compete in the Liberty Mutual Legends of Golf tournament held in Austin, Texas.

29 April 1985
LABOR. At a meeting of the New York State Chapter of the National Organization for Women (NOW), Brooklyn District Attorney Elizabeth Holtzman points out certain progress she has made concerning hiring of women. Judy Goldsmith, NOW president, notes the importance of comparable worth and pay equity policies.

1 May 1985
SPORTS. According to *Runner's World* magazine, Joan Benoit is the highest-paid woman track athlete. She reportedly earned $402,000 during 1984.

WOMEN'S ISSUES. *Essence* magazine celebrates its 15th anniversary. The publication promotes the interests of black women.

5 May 1985
WOMEN'S ISSUES. Eleanor Smeal states that she is anticipating running against current president of the National Organization for Women, Judy Goldsmith, at the convention to be held in the summer.

7 May 1985
WOMEN'S ISSUES. The Older Women's League lobbies in Congress against funding cuts in programs for older women.

12 May 1985
IDEAS/BELIEFS. Results of a Gallup poll indicate that 72 percent of American women find the role of wife and mother is ideal. And 38 percent of women surveyed state they would also like a full-time job outside the home.

15 May 1985
LEGISLATIVE. A bipartisan group of lawmakers introduces the Economic Equity Act into Congress. This proposed bill deals with enhancing economic status of women and changing discriminatory laws regarding child care, credit, and health insurance.

16 May 1985
DEATHS. Actress Margaret Hamilton, best-known for her role as the Wicked Witch of the West in the 1939 film *The Wizard of Oz,* dies in Salisbury, Connecticut.

18 May 1985
IDEAS/BELIEFS. The Girls Clubs of America celebrate their 40th anniversary. There are about 200,000 girls enrolled in club programs.

19 May 1985
WOMEN'S ISSUES. A National Network of Women's Funds is established in New York City to promote fund-raising for women's groups.

26 May 1985
WOMEN'S ISSUES. Betty Friedan criticizes Eleanor Smeal for her bid to replace Judy Goldsmith as the president of the National Organization for Women in the upcoming elections.

27 May 1985
LEGISLATIVE. The Congressional Caucus for Women's Issues announces its plans to campaign for passage of the Economic Equity Act of 1985, which contains 22 pieces of legislation designed to help women achieve economic parity.

13 June 1985
LABOR. The Labor Department reports that 53 percent of all married women are in the labor force compared to less than 17 percent in 1940.

17 June 1985
LABOR. The Equal Employment Opportunity Commission rejects any cases of job discrimination based on comparable worth. The commission states that unequal pay for similar jobs is not sex discrimination.

18 June 1985
WOMEN'S ISSUES. Four women receive MacArthur Foundation Grants. They are Joan Abrahamson, Marian Wright Edelman, Jane Richardson, and Ellen Stewart.

28 June 1985
JUDICIAL. A federal appeals court overturns a lower court award of $325,000 to former TV anchorwoman Christine Craft. She had brought suit against a Kansas City, Missouri, television station after she was demoted in 1981 due to her appearance.

30 June 1985
POLITICS. The National Women's Political Caucus elects Irene Natividad as its chairperson.

RELIGION.   Reverend Maria-Alma Copeland is ordained in St. Paul, Minnesota. She is the first black woman pastor of the American Lutheran Church and serves at the Fellowship Lutheran Church in Jacksonville, Florida.

1 July 1985
JUDICIAL.   Due to a 1984 U.S. Supreme Court decision obligating the Jaycees to admit women to membership, the *Jaycee Women* disbands.

DEATHS.   The first black woman Episcopalian priest, Pauli Murray, dies at age 74. Murray had also served as deputy attorney general of California and was a civil rights activist. She was a founder of the National Organization for Women.

15 July 1985
INTERNATIONAL.   In Nairobi, Kenya, 13,500 women from more than 100 countries gather for the United Nations Conference on the Status of Women. The 10-day event signals the end of the United Nations Decade for Women.

19 July 1985
CRIME.   In New York, Sydney Biddle Barrows pleads guilty to fourth-degree promotion of prostitution. The so-called "Mayflower Madam" had been arrested after it was learned that she ran a high-class prostitution ring. Several of her ancestors came to this country on the Mayflower.

20 July 1985
AVIATION.   Sharon Christa McAuliffe, a high school teacher from Concord, New Hampshire, is chosen as the National Aeronautics and Space Administration's first civilian to fly on a space shuttle flight. McAuliffe dies on 28 January 1986 when the *Challenger* explodes minutes after takeoff.

21 July 1985
WOMEN'S ISSUES.   Eleanor Smeal is reelected as president of the National Organization for Women. She had served as the organization's head from 1977 to 1982, and had been replaced by outgoing president Judy Goldsmith. Smeal defeats the incumbent on a vote of 839–703. Eleven votes were cast for Sonia Johnson, a former Mormon active in feminist causes, especially the antipornography campaign.

28 July 1985
SPORTS.   Julie Janke wins the logrolling contest at the Lumberjack World Championships in Hayward, Wisconsin.

30 July 1985
DEATHS.   Julie Robinson, the first woman mathematician to be elected to the National Academy of Arts and Sciences, dies at age 65.

8 August 1985
DEATHS.   Actress Louise Brooks dies in Rochester, New York.

10 August 1985
POLITICS.   In Charlestown, West Virginia, Marie Prezioso is elected the first woman president of the Young Democrats of America.

13 August 1985
LABOR.   In Philadelphia, Pennsylvania, women guards will be allowed to work in men's prisons. The city also pays women guards back wages of $950,000 denied them when they could not work in all-male penal institutions.

14 August 1985
LABOR.   An Executive Order drawn up for President Reagan's signature would, if enacted, free federal contractors from all numerical quotas in hiring women and minorities. The White House states the order is in "early stages of discussion."

16 August 1985
WOMEN'S ISSUES.   Jennifer Hirshberg resigns as secretary to First Lady Nancy Reagan. She has been involved in a misunderstanding over press reports concerning the president's health, and will be replaced by Elaine Crispen in early September.

25 August 1985
DEATHS.   Thirteen-year-old Samantha Smith of Auburn, Maine, dies in a plane crash. She is famous for her letter writing to Soviet leader Yuri Andropov and her concern for world peace. Smith had traveled to the Soviet Union as Andropov's guest, and was later chosen for a television series, "Lime Street."

26 August 1985
SPORTS.   Elizabeth Balsley becomes a member of the North Hunterdon, New Jersey,

high school football team. This move is made possible by the New Jersey Commissioner of Education's decision to allow girls' participation in contact sports.

28 August 1985
DEATHS.   Stage and screen actress Ruth Gordon dies in Edgartown, Massachusetts. She received an Oscar for Best Supporting Actress in *Rosemary's Baby*.

30 August 1985
POPULAR CULTURE.   Phyllis George, co-anchor of the "CBS Morning News," announces her resignation. She had been named to the post in January. Maria Shriver, niece of former President John F. Kennedy, will replace George in the co-anchor spot.

5 September 1985
SPORTS.   The Women's International Professional Tennis Council gives final approval to guidelines governing tournament participation by girls under age 14.

6 September 1985
JUDICIAL.   The National Organization for Women's Legal Defense and Education Fund files a complaint with the Federal Communications Commission against ABC-TV and CBS-TV due to the networks' refusal to run public service announcements offering birth control information. The networks later agree to run revised versions of the spots that have been produced by the American College of Gynecologists and Obstetricians.

12 September 1985
RELIGION.   At its biennial general convention, the Episcopal Church House of Bishops states that it overwhelmingly supports election of a female bishop by any church diocese.

15 September 1985
RELIGION.   At the National Conference of Catholic Bishops, Bishop James W. Malone calls for enhancement of women's roles in the Roman Catholic Church.

19 September 1985
POLITICS.   The Republican party establishes an Alliance for Opportunity to aid women in

overcoming issues that could block personal and career success.

23 September 1985
SPORTS.   The Women's Sports Foundation holds its annual Hall of Fame banquet in New York City. Honored as outstanding sports figures of the year are Libby Riddles, first woman to win the Iditarod Trail Sled Race; Michelle Mitchell, Amateur Sportswoman of the Year; Dawn Fraser, swimmer; and Ann Meyers, the only woman to sign a contract with a National Basketball Association team, the Indiana Pacers.

1 October 1985
LEGISLATIVE.   Montana is the first state to have passed legislation, effective today, that prohibits different insurance rates for men and women. The so-called unisex insurance rates mean that women in Montana will no longer be charged the higher rates for health and other insurance that they have paid up until now.

WOMEN'S ISSUES.   The White House announces that Health and Human Services (HHS) Secretary Margaret M. Heckler will resign her cabinet post. She will become U.S. ambassador to Ireland. Heckler has been HHS secretary since January 1983 and has been considered by some to be inadequately supportive of some Reagan administration policies.

2 October 1985
DEATHS.   Alberta E. Crowe, a founder of the Women's International Bowling Congress and its president between 1960 and 1981, dies of cancer in Syracuse, New York.

5 October 1985
DEATHS.   Special Agent Robin L. Ahrens is the first woman FBI agent to be killed in the line of duty. She is shot while making an arrest in Phoenix, Arizona.

6 October 1985
POLITICS.   Gerald R. Gereau joins the National Women's party. He is the first man to do so in the party's 72-year history.

7 October 1985
SPORTS.   Former University of Kansas basketball star Lynette Woodard is signed as the first woman player on the Harlem Globetrotters.

Woodard was also on the U.S. Olympic basketball team in 1984.

8 October 1985
POLITICS. Geraldine A. Ferraro's book, *Ferraro: My Story,* is published.

16 October 1985
INTERNATIONAL. Betty F. Bumpers, president of Peace Links, welcomes a delegation of 15 Soviet women on a 2-week visit to the United States. Their trip is part of the group's peace program.

18 October 1985
DEATHS. Tish Sommers, co-founder of the Older Women's League, dies of cancer in Oakland, California.

20 October 1985
SPORTS. Joan Benoit wins the women's race at the America's Marathon in Chicago, Illinois. Her time, 2:21:21, is her fastest ever for a marathon event.

24 October 1985
RELIGION. The Women's Ordination Conference in St. Louis, Missouri, holds a convocation for those women who want to become Roman Catholic priests.

30 October 1985
LABOR. At its 16th convention, held in Anaheim, California, the American Federation of Labor and Congress of Industrial Organizations fails to elect any new female members to the 35-member executive council. Women make up 30 percent of union membership but only 6 percent of the council.

5 November 1985
POLITICS. In Virginia, Mary Sue Terry is the first woman elected to state office as state attorney general. In Houston, Texas, Kathy Whitmire is elected to a third term as mayor.

POPULAR CULTURE. Patty Duke Astin is elected president of the Screen Actors Guild, receiving 56 percent of the vote. She replaces outgoing president Ed Asner.

19 November 1985
POLITICS. Representative Patricia Schroeder (D-Colorado) berates Donald T. Regan for his remark that arms control and other summit talk issues are too complicated for women to understand. Schroeder says, ''women deserve an apology.''

20 November 1985
POPULAR CULTURE. Effie Lederer—better known as Ann Landers—receives the coveted Albert Lasker Award for her efforts on behalf of cancer research and other medical work.

14 December 1985
WOMEN'S ISSUES. In Tahlequah, Oklahoma, Wilma Mankiller is sworn in as principal chief of the Cherokee Nation of Oklahoma. She is the first woman in history to head a major Native American tribe.

19 December 1985
JUDICIAL. A federal jury rules that singer Dolly Parton did not copy the words of her hit tune, ''Nine to Five,'' from a song claimed to have been written by a husband-and-wife songwriting team.

22 December 1985
SPORTS. Runner Mary Decker Slaney is named the Associated Press Sportswoman of the Year.

OTHER EVENTS OF 1985

POPULAR CULTURE. The Academy Awards for Best Actress and Best Supporting Actress of 1984 go to Sally Field in *Places in the Heart,* and Dame Peggy Ashcroft in *A Passage to India,* respectively.

Georgia O'Keeffe, 1887–1986

Considered the preeminent American woman artist, Georgia O'Keeffe was born on 15 November 1887, in Sun Prairie, Wisconsin, one of seven children of Francis and Ida (Totto) O'Keeffe. Attending Madison High School for one year, she graduated from Chatham Episcopal Institute in Virginia in 1904, and then studied at The Art Institute of Chicago. Ill with typhoid, O'Keeffe left the Institute in 1905 and only recovered sufficiently to resume her studies in 1907, when she attended the Art Students' League in New York City until 1908.

O'Keeffe studied at Teacher's College, Columbia University, and at the University of Virginia. In 1916 she went to Amarillo, Texas, where she was a public school supervisor. But she left teaching that year after her work was exhibited—without her consent—by Alfred Stieglitz at his Fifth Avenue gallery in New York City. On 29 January 1923, O'Keeffe mounted her first big New York exhibit at Anderson galleries. On 11 December 1924, she married Alfred Stieglitz for whom she subsequently posed in thousands of photographs.

Predominated by bold flower forms and organic movement, her work was embraced by a public willing to pay high prices for the young artist's unique paintings. She exhibited yearly at Stieglitz's gallery in New York City from 1923 until 1946. In 1929, O'Keeffe traveled to Taos, New Mexico, where she was instantly drawn to the stark, harsh, yet seductive landscape. Her paintings reflected these qualities, and during the 1930s, much of her work was dominated by animal skulls and bones, and reflections of the hard-edged desert landscape. In 1938, O'Keeffe received an honorary doctorate from the College of William and Mary.

In 1946, O'Keeffe had a major retrospective showing of her work at The Museum of Modern Art in New York City. Also, her husband died that year. Thereafter, she moved permanently to New Mexico. She made her home in Abiquiu, near Santa Fe. During the 1950s, O'Keeffe gave four one-woman shows and was featured again at The Museum of Modern Art in 1958 in a show entitled, "Fourteen American Masters."

The artist continued painting and exhibiting at museums and galleries throughout the 1960s, and received many awards. In 1963, Brandeis University gave her the Creative Arts Award. In 1970, she received the Gold Medal for painting from the National Institute of Arts and Letters. She mounted a major retrospective at the Whitney Museum of American Art in New York City in 1970, which showed 121 of her works spanning fifty-five years. In 1971, she displayed similar exhibits at The Art Institute of Chicago and at the San Francisco Museum of Art in California.

In 1973, O'Keeffe received the McDowell Medal from the famous artist colony in New Hampshire, and in 1977, she was awarded the Medal of Freedom by President Carter. O'Keeffe had arranged for the National Park Service to assume responsibility of her home and studio after her death, but by 1983 she had canceled this takeover. She continued to live in New Mexico up until the time of her death on 6 March 1986. She was ninety-eight years old, and was called a "national treasure" and the "most important woman artist in America" when she died.

---

2 January 1986

HEALTH. Mary Lund, the first woman to receive an artificial heart, emerges from a coma. Doctors say she has at least a 50 percent chance of survival.

EDUCATION. Columbia University Law School appoints Barbara Aronstein Black as its dean. She is the first woman to head an Ivy League law school, and will assume her duties on 4 February.

DEATHS. Silent screen star Una Merkel dies at age 82.

3 January 1986

HEALTH. Searle & Company announces the end of domestic sales of two intrauterine devices

(IUDs), virtually ending the marketing of IUDs in the United States. "Unwarranted product litigation" was stated to be a major cause for the removal.

5 January 1986
BUSINESS. Vernett Bludson-Francis is named Minority Advocate of the Year by the United States Commerce Department Minority Business Development Agency. Bludson-Francis is director of Citicorp's Minority Vendor Program.

7 January 1986
WOMEN'S ISSUES. The League of Women Voters names its first male executive director. The 66-year-old organization has nearly 5,000 male members on its 120,000-total membership rolls.

POLITICS. Representative Barbara Mikulski (D-Maryland) is reported to lead in the polls over her rivals in the race for a U.S. Senate seat being vacated by Charles Mathias.

8 January 1986
EDUCATION. The University Cottage Club at Princeton votes to consider women for membership. The move is taken after a lawsuit was filed by Princeton alumna Sally Frank, who charged discrimination.

9 January 1986
MEDICAL. According to a Harvard University study, women who exercise regularly significantly lower their risk of developing breast and reproductive cancer.

14 January 1986
DEATHS. Screen and television actress Donna Reed dies of pancreatic cancer. Reed won an Oscar in 1953 for Best Supporting Actress for her role in *From Here to Eternity*.

17 January 1986
WOMEN'S ISSUES. At the 48th annual PEN Congress held in New York City, author Grace Paley reads a joint statement of protest against the low number of women panelists at the gathering. According to 1 count, only 16 out of 117 speakers at the week-long conference are women.

20 January 1986
CIVIL RIGHTS. Coretta Scott King leads a march through Atlanta, Georgia, to commemorate her slain husband's birthday, which is celebrated for the first time this year as a national holiday.

22 January 1986
WOMEN'S ISSUES. President Reagan addresses a group of 36,000 antiabortion demonstrators at the White House.

24 January 1986
DEATHS. Flo Hyman, age 31, a championship volleyball player, suffers a heart attack and dies in Japan during a volleyball match. Hyman led the U.S. Olympic team to a second-place victory in the 1984 Olympics.

26 January 1986
MILITARY. According to a California news report, U.S. Air Force women were part of flight crews that airlifted supplies and troops to Grenada in 1983. Air Force officials deny that this was a violation of prohibitions against using women in combat.

28 January 1986
DEATHS. Astronaut Judith A. Resnick and teacher Christa McAuliffe perish as the space shuttle *Challenger* explodes shortly after takeoff. McAuliffe, of Concord, New Hampshire, was to be the first civilian in space. Resnick would have been the second U.S. woman astronaut to travel in space.

30 January 1986
JUDICIAL. The U.S. Justice Department reports that it will not proceed in further investigations of Representative Geraldine Ferraro's finances, nor bring charges against her.

3 February 1986
JUDICIAL. A Chicago federal court judge dismisses a sexual bias suit against Sears, Roebuck & Company. The suit had been brought by the Equal Employment Opportunity Commission in the late 1970s, and charged that women enjoyed fewer hirings and promotions than their male counterparts.

6 February 1986
JUDICIAL. New Jersey Judge H. Lee Sarokin rules that Kiwanis International cannot revoke

the Ridgewood, New Jersey, chapter's charter simply because the club admitted a woman to membership. Kiwanis International, which refuses to recognize Julie Fletcher as a Kiwanis member, will appeal the ruling.

8 February 1986
SPORTS. Debi Thomas is the first black woman to win the Senior Singles U.S. Figure Skating Championship. Caryn Kadavy places second, and Tiffany Chin third.

9 February 1986
WOMEN'S ISSUES. The House Select Committee on Children, Youth, and Families issues a report focusing on teen pregnancy. The report notes that there will be 1 million teen pregnancies annually. More than one-half of the 500,000 births would be to unmarried mothers. Twenty-six states surveyed in the study noted that services and funding for pregnant teenagers and mothers are inadequate.

10 February 1986
EDUCATION. Frances Daly Ferguson is named the ninth president of Vassar College in New York.

12 February 1986
JUDICIAL. Jan Kemp, a former University of Georgia instructor, is awarded more than $2.5 million in a lawsuit after she was dismissed from her duties. She was dismissed after she had criticized the university for allowing athletes with failing grades to stay in school in order to play football.

13 February 1986
AVIATION. The National Aeronautics and Space Administration announces that Barbara Morgan, the backup teacher-in-space candidate, would be offered a chance to fly on the next space shuttle that takes a civilian on board.

POPULAR CULTURE. Evelyn Marie Adams wins nearly $1.5 million in her second New Jersey State lottery win. She is the first person to twice win the million-dollar prize. Her first winnings were in October 1985, when she claimed $3.9 million.

14 February 1986
SPORTS. Jackie Joyner wins the long jump event at the 79th Annual Millrose Games with a distance of 21 feet 11½ inches.

17 February 1986
POLITICS. Senator Paula Hawkins (R-Florida) emerges from a 10-day hospitalization to dispel rumors that poor health will force her to avoid reelection.

CRIME. A New York state woman dies after taking a cyanide-laced Tylenol capsule. Since 1982, Dian Elsvoth is the seventh person to die after taking over-the-counter drugs that had been tampered with.

24 February 1986
JUDICIAL. The U.S. Supreme Court strikes down an Indianapolis, Indiana, antipornography law.

SPORTS. Joan Benoit Samuelson is the 7th woman to win the Sullivan Award, presented annually by the American Athletic Union.

28 February 1986
DEATHS. Author Laura Hobson, who wrote the best seller *Gentlemen Prefer Blondes,* dies in New York City of cancer.

1 March 1986
DEATHS. Katherine A. Towle, first woman dean of students at the University of California at Berkeley, dies of a heart attack. Towle had also been the first director of the Women's Marine Corps between 1948 and 1953.

SPORTS. Diane Dixon earns the highest number of points among women in the Mobil Grand Prix tour. Her specialty is the 440-yard run.

3 March 1986
JUDICIAL. The U.S. Supreme Court refuses to hear television anchor Christine Craft's suit in a bid for reinstatement of a $325,000 damage award. Craft had brought the suit against a Kansas City, Missouri, station, charging discrimination and fraud.

8 March 1986
SPORTS. Martina Navratilova wins the U.S. Women's Indoor Tennis Championship.

Nationally known figures in the quest for women's equality, Gloria Steinem (*third from left*); Bella Abzug (*third from right*); Eleanor Smeal (*far right*). The three were joined by thousands of others at a "March for Women's Lives" in the nation's capital in March 1986. (Photo courtesy Dorothea Jacobsen-Wenzel)

9 March 1986
WOMEN'S ISSUES. Pro-choice demonstrators rally in Washington, D.C., at a march sponsored by the National Organization for Women which draws between 85,000 and 125,000 people. The "March for Women's Lives" is deemed proof that there is renewed activism by women, for women.

13 March 1986
EDUCATION. Brown University accuses the press of sensationalizing stories that several women students at the Rhode Island institution were involved in a prostitution ring.

SPORTS. Susan Butcher is the second woman to win the 1,827-kilometer Iditarod dogsled race in Nome, Alaska. She makes a record time run of 11 days, 15 hours, 6 minutes.

21 March 1986
SPORTS. Debi Thomas becomes the first black woman to win the women's World Figure

Skating Championship. Tiffany Chin comes in third.

23 March 1986
SPORTS. Lynn Jennings takes second place in the women's World Cross Country Championships in Colombier, Switzerland. Jennings comes in behind South Africa's Zola Budd.

26 March 1986
POLITICS. According to a newspaper survey, Nancy Hoch (R) and Helen Boosalis (D) are leading contenders in the race to succeed outgoing Nebraska Governor Bob Kerrey.

30 March 1986
SPORTS. The Lady Longhorns of the University of Texas win the National Collegiate Athletic Association's women's basketball championship by beating the USC Women of Troy, 97–81. Texas freshman Clarissa Davis is named the game's most valuable player.

1 April 1986
POPULAR CULTURE.   Trina Robbins, an artist from San Francisco, California, becomes the first woman to draw Wonder Woman comic books.

6 April 1986
DEATHS.   Sculptor Dorothea Greenbaum dies at age 92 in Princeton, New Jersey.

10 April 1986
IDEAS/BELIEFS.   IBM Corporation drops charges of trespassing against Amy Carter, daughter of former President Jimmy Carter. She and 13 others had been arrested at a Providence, Rhode Island, antiapartheid sit-in.

17 April 1986
POLITICS.   Maxine Waters of the Democratic National Committee joins 2 other prominent Democrats and the Reverend Jesse Jackson in forming the National Rainbow Coalition. Its purpose is to provide a liberal, progressive voice within the Democratic party.

LITERATURE.   Elizabeth Frank receives the Pulitzer Prize for biography for her book, *Louise Bogan: A Portrait.*

20 April 1986
RELIGION.   Atheist Madalyn Murray O'Hair announces her retirement as president of the American Atheist Center.

22 April 1986
JUDICIAL.   Jan Kemp, the University of Georgia instructor who blew the whistle on unfair grading practices, has her initial court award of $2.5 million reduced to $680,000. A federal judge determines that Kemp's actions had affected contract negotiations at the university.

24 April 1986
DEATHS.   Wallis Warfield Simpson, the Duchess of Windsor, dies in Paris, France, at the age of 89.

26 April 1986
POPULAR CULTURE.   Maria Shriver, daughter of Eunice Kennedy and Sargent Shriver, marries Austrian-born actor and strong-man, Arnold Schwarzenegger.

30 April 1986
JUDICIAL.   The U.S. Supreme Court dismisses *Diamond* v. *Charles,* a case that sought to defend an Illinois law restricting abortion.

1 May 1986
JUDICIAL.   Pamela Golden, former weathercaster at a Duluth, Minnesota, television station, sues her former employer for $8 million, charging discrimination and sexual harassment.

SPORTS.   Ann Bancroft is among 6 people who are the first explorers since Admiral Robert Peary to reach the North Pole assisted by only dogsled.

6 May 1986
POPULAR CULTURE.   Joan Rivers announces that she will host a 1-hour nighttime entertainment show on the Fox Broadcasting Company's network beginning in the fall. Rivers, long-time permanent guest of Johnny Carson's "Tonight Show" is the first woman to attempt competing with Carson's show.

7 May 1986
BUSINESS.   Transportation Secretary Elizabeth Hanford Dole is named a director of Conrail, replacing Daniel Burke.

20 May 1986
DEATHS.   Dr. Helen Brooke Taussig dies at age 87. Dr. Taussig was the pioneer pediatric cardiologist who developed an operation that saved lives of children born with a certain heart defect. She was injured in a West Chester, Pennsylvania, car accident and dies as a result of those injuries.

21 May 1986
ARTS AND CULTURE.   Lynne Cheney is named chair of the National Endowment for the Humanities. She was senior editor at *Washington* magazine.

23 May 1986
POPULAR CULTURE.   Actress Tatum O'Neal and tennis star John McEnroe announce the birth of their son, Kevin John McEnroe.

24 May 1986
SPORTS. The first "Women on Wings" air show is held at Dulles International Airport in Washington, D.C. The show is organized by Nanci Callahan.

1 June 1986
SPORTS. Golfer Pat Bradley is the first player to win all 4 major women's golf tournaments as she wins the Ladies Professional Golf Association Championship in King's Island, Ohio.

2 June 1986
POLITICS. Penny Harrington, chief of police in Portland, Oregon, announces her resignation. She notes that her decision was influenced by the results of a city commissioners' report criticizing her abilities. Harrington, named to the post in January 1985, was the first woman to hold this position in a major U.S. city.

6 June 1986
LITERATURE. Poet Adrienne Rich is awarded the first annual Ruth Lilly Poetry Prize. The award of $25,000 is the nation's largest offered to poets.

9 June 1986
WOMEN'S ISSUES. The National Organization for Women seeks an injunction against antiabortion activists at a federal district court in Delaware.

11 June 1986
JUDICIAL. The U.S. Supreme Court strikes down a Pennsylvania law that was considered unconstitutional restraint against abortion. The 5–4 ruling reaffirms the 1973 *Roe* v. *Wade* decision.

13 June 1986
WOMEN'S ISSUES. The National Organization for Women (NOW) opens its 19th annual convention in Denver, Colorado. President Eleanor Smeal delivers the keynote address and criticizes claims that NOW has neglected issues of child care, pregnancy benefits, and other factors that make up the reality of working women's lives.

17 June 1986
WOMEN'S ISSUES. White House Chief of Staff Donald Regan is criticized for remarking

that sanctions against South Africa would be asking women of America to "give up their jewelry."

DEATHS. Kate Smith, the singer who made "God Bless America" famous, dies at age 79 in Raleigh, North Carolina.

19 June 1986
JUDICIAL. The U.S. Supreme Court rules that sexual harassment of an employee violates federal law. The ruling, *Meritor Savings Bank* v. *Vinson,* deals with Mechelle Vinson's case against a supervisor at the bank. She claims that she was dismissed from her position after refusing the supervisor's sexual advances. This ruling paves the way for a new trial.

30 June 1986
POPULAR CULTURE. The last three Playboy Clubs owned by Playboy Enterprises, Inc., close. The organization, owned by Hugh Hefner, cites changing moral standards as a reason for the failing revenues that prompted the closings. More than 25,000 women had been employed as Playboy Club bunnies. There are still several franchised clubs operating in the Midwest and in Japan.

1 July 1986
MEDICAL. Feminists and others criticize an American Psychiatric Association decision to add Premenstrual Syndrome (PMS) to its official diagnostic manual. The term PMS was added only to an appendix after pressure prompted a compromise action.

DEATHS. The first woman bishop of the United Methodist Church, Reverend Marjorie S. Matthews, dies of cancer at her home in Grand Rapids, Michigan.

5 July 1986
SPORTS. Martina Navratilova wins the Wimbledon Tennis Singles title for the fifth straight year. It is her seventh Wimbledon victory overall.

9 July 1986
IDEAS/BELIEFS. The U.S. Attorney General's Commission on Pornography releases a 1,960-page report stating that pornography leads to sexual violence and aggressive behavior toward women. Critics of the report call the findings "bizarre." The National Organization

for Women expresses concern that action against pornography might be used by the nation's "religious right" to spread hatred of America's gay and lesbian population.

19 July 1986
POPULAR CULTURE. Caroline Bouvier Kennedy, daughter of President John F. Kennedy, marries Edward Schlossberg in a ceremony in Cape Cod, Massachusetts.

3 August 1986
SPORTS. Jackie Joyner sets a new world record in the women's heptathlon by achieving 7,161 points at the 10-day U.S. Olympic Festival held in Houston, Texas.

5 August 1986
POLITICS. Lieutenant Governor Harriett Woods (D) of Missouri wins 75 percent of the votes cast in a primary election for senator. Woods' candidacy is important to the future of a Democratic-controlled Senate in 1988 and to the position of women in government.

14 August 1986
MILITARY. Rear Admiral Grace Murray Hopper retires from active duty in the U.S. Navy. Hopper, an expert on computer language and an author of COBOL, is 79, and was the oldest officer still on active duty at the time of her retirement.

CRIME. A 13-year-old student, California's Deanna Young, turns her parents in to law enforcement officers for possessing a trash bag of pills, marijuana, and cocaine. Officials noted that the girl had tried unsuccessfully to persuade her parents to stop their involvement with drugs and that her action was a last resort.

16 August 1986
AVIATION. The National Aeronautics and Space Administration (NASA) announces that Sally K. Ride, the first U.S. woman astronaut in space, has been named special assistant to the administrator of NASA. Ride was a member of the Presidential commission to investigate the space shuttle *Challenger* explosion.

RELIGION. The triennial convention of Lutheran Church Women has requested its leaders to name more Lutheran churches after women of the early church. The group notes that the Roman Catholic Church, generally less progressive in areas concerning women, often names its churches after female saints.

17 August 1986
SPORTS. The U.S. women's basketball team beats the Soviet Union's team, 108–88, to win the world championship. Cheryl Miller scores 24 points.

22 August 1986
IDEAS/BELIEFS. Janice Hart, conservative Democratic candidate for secretary of state in Illinois, is fined $500 on disorderly conduct charges. The fine results from a 1985 incident in which Hart presented a Roman Catholic bishop with a piece of raw liver. Hart suggested that the liver symbolized blood shed due to the bishop's support of the International Monetary Fund.

31 August 1986
DEATHS. Children's author Elizabeth Coatsworth dies at her home in Nobleboro, Maine. Coatsworth won the prestigious Newbery Medal in 1931 for her book, *The Cat Who Went to Heaven.*

6 September 1986
RELIGION. The Roman Catholic Archbishop of Miami, Florida, Edward A. McCarthy, issues a pastoral letter offering absolution to women who have had abortions. The offer extends also to those who have assisted in performing abortions.

POPULAR CULTURE. Barbra Streisand performs in public for the first time in 6 years at a Democratic political benefit held at her Malibu, California, estate.

8 September 1986
CRIME. Deanna Young, the teenager who reported her parents to law officers on drug-use charges, is allowed by an Orange County California Juvenile Court judge to return to her home. Officials express confidence that the teen's relationship with her parents will remain a positive one despite the incident.

10 September 1986
POLITICS. Elections across the nation result in many women winning area primaries. Among them is Kathleen Kennedy Townsend (D-Maryland), who wins the race for a

congressional seat. Bella S. Abzug wins a narrow victory in the House Democratic primary in Westchester County, New York. Abzug is a 3-term former congresswoman from Manhattan and a leader in feminist causes. Altogether, 7 women are now in the race for U.S. Senate, 61 for the House of Representatives. In various states there are 9 women running for governor, 15 for lieutenant governor, and 2 for attorney general. In Maryland, Barbara Mikulski (D) and Linda Chavez (R) vie for the Senate seat. This is only the second time in U.S. history that 2 women have challenged each other for national office. The first occasion was when Margaret Chase Smith (R) defeated Lucia Cormier (D) for the Senate seat from Maine.

11 September 1986
WOMEN'S ISSUES. In Hackensack, New Jersey, Mary Beth Whitehead, a surrogate mother, loses her suit to keep custody of a child born to her in March. Whitehead had been artificially inseminated with sperm from a man whose wife was unable to conceive. Whitehead had contracted to bear the child for $10,000, but changed her mind after the baby's birth. Whitehead's lawyer will appeal the court ruling.

13 September 1986
POPULAR CULTURE. Kellye Cash, Miss Tennessee, grand-niece of country-western singer Johnny Cash, is crowned Miss America in Atlantic City, New Jersey.

14 September 1986
WOMEN'S ISSUES. First Lady Nancy Reagan joins her husband on nationwide television and radio in an appeal against drug abuse.

22 September 1986
POPULAR CULTURE. A first printing of the unauthorized biography about Frank Sinatra— *His Way*—written by Kitty Kelly, reaches U.S. bookstores.

MEDICAL. Dr. Rita Levi-Montalcini, of Rome's Institute of Cell Biology, is 1 of 2 researchers to receive the 1986 Lasker Basic Medical Research Award. Levi-Montalcini holds dual citizenship in the United States and Italy.

24 September 1986
INTERNATIONAL. Journalist Claire Sterling is acquitted of charges of aiding and abetting an official who had provided Sterling with documents later connected with the 1981 assassination attempt on Pope John Paul II.

29 September 1986
SPORTS. Mary Lou Retton, gold medal gymnast at the 1984 Olympic Games, announces her retirement from competition. Retton is pursuing an education at the University of Texas.

10 October 1986
DEATHS. Wilma Porter Soss, founder of the Federation of Women Shareholders in American Business, dies of a heart attack at age 86 in New York City.

13 October 1986
MEDICAL. Dr. Rita Levi-Montalcini is 1 of 2 researchers to be awarded the Nobel Prize for physiology or medicine. Levi-Montalcini shares this honor with her partner, Dr. Stanley Cohen.

15 October 1986
SPORTS. Martina Navratilova wins the 1,000th match of her tennis career during the Filderstadt (West Germany) Grand Prix tournament. Chris Evert Lloyd is the only other woman to win this number of pro tennis matches.

EDUCATION. Bequests made by the late heiress Liliore Green Rains of Beverly Hills, California, total $240 million and are to be divided among 6 separate educational institutions. Several of the recipient colleges and universities state that they had no connection with Rains but are grateful for her generosity.

21 October 1986
WOMEN'S ISSUES. Penny Harrington, former police chief of Portland, Oregon, is approved for a claim of stress-related disability in a 6–3 vote taken by the city's Police Disability and Retirement Board.

28 October 1986
POPULAR CULTURE. Marie Osmond, pop singer, marries for the second time at a Mormon Temple in West Jordan, Utah.

30 October 1986
SPORTS. The United States women's team takes the title in the Wightman Cup tennis competition after Bonnie Gadusek and Kathy Rinaldi win the doubles match. This is the eighth straight year that the United States has won the Wightman Cup and is the nation's 48th win overall in 58 years of Wightman Cup tournaments.

3 November 1986
JUDICIAL. In a 5–3 decision, the U.S. Supreme Court rules that Arizona cannot deny state funding to a private family planning group that provides abortions and abortion counseling. The case, *Babbitt* v. *Planned Parenthood,* was not voted on by Associate Justice Sandra Day O'Connor, a former judge and legislator from Arizona.

3 November 1986
SPORTS. High school girls' basketball player Christy Lee of Max Meadows, Virginia, breaks the national career record of 675 assists. The previous record of 670 was held by Tami Fick of California.

17 November 1986
POPULAR CULTURE. A spokesperson says that actress Gilda Radner is expected to recover completely following surgery for ovarian cancer.

19 November 1986
ARTS AND CULTURE. Tina Howe's play, *Coastal Disturbances,* opens at New York City's Second Stage Theater.

24 November 1986
IDEAS/BELIEFS. Amy Carter, daughter of former president Jimmy Carter, is arrested for being disorderly during an anti-CIA protest at the University of Massachusetts at Amherst.

17 December 1986
WOMEN'S ISSUES. In testimony before the House Judiciary Civil and Constitutional Rights Subcommittee, numerous women say that they were given pro-life lectures after seeking abortions at various clinics across the nation. Some of the clinics have been charged with fraud.

19 December 1986
CRIME. Judy A. Johnson, a mother who had

made charges in the alleged California child molestation case involving the Virginia McMartin Preschool, is found dead at her home in Manhattan Beach, California. Her own mental stability had been in question. The case against the preschool had involved more than a year of investigation and had required testimony from more than a dozen children who had attended the school.

23 December 1986
JUDICIAL. Convicted murderer Jean Harris, former headmistress of the exclusive Madeira School is denied clemency, although she has served 6 years of a life sentence for murdering Dr. Herman Tarnower. Harris's lawyer had unsuccessfully asked that New York Governor Mario Cuomo release Harris on the grounds that she has an excellent prison record and requires cardiac surgery.

27 December 1986
WOMEN'S ISSUES. *Time* magazine names President Corazon Aquino of the Philippines 1986 Woman of the Year.

OTHER EVENTS OF 1986

POPULAR CULTURE. Geraldine Page is awarded an Oscar as Best Actress of 1985 in *The Trip to Bountiful.* Anjelica Huston is named Best Supporting Actress, for *Prizzi's Honor.*

4 January 1987
DEATHS. Lauretta Bender, the psychiatrist who in 1923 developed the Bender Gestalt Visual Motor Test, dies in Annapolis, Maryland.

5 January 1987
POLITICS. The *New York Times* reports that when the 100th Congress convenes tomorrow, the Senate will be all white and will have only 2 female members. The House is 95 percent male and 92 percent white.

POPULAR CULTURE. Victoria Principal, star of television's popular series "Dallas" files a $3 million lawsuit against Joan Rivers. Principal charges that the talk-show host caused "humiliation and anguish" by making Principal's unlisted telephone number public during a talk show.

13 January 1987
JUDICIAL. The U.S. Supreme Court upholds a California law requiring employers to grant women disability leave for pregnancy and childbirth. The court determines that this law furthers women's equality in the workplace. Employers may also grant similar benefits to male workers wishing to participate in the birth and care of their infant. California is 1 of 10 states to provide these, or similar, benefits for workers.

14 January 1987
POPULAR CULTURE. Actress Elizabeth Taylor announces that she will participate in a $10 million advertising campaign to promote her new perfume, "Elizabeth Taylor's Passion." This is the first time that the veteran actress has agreed to commercial licensing of her name.

16 January 1987
SPORTS. Martina Navratilova is named Associated Press Female Athlete of the Year of 1986. Golfer Pat Bradley was second in the balloting, followed by Jackie Joyner, the track star. Navratilova's official earnings in 1986 were $1,905,841.

18 January 1987
POPULAR CULTURE. Maria Serrao is the first wheelchair-bound woman to compete in a beauty contest that leads to the title of Miss U.S.A. A model and actress, Serrao entered the Miss Solano pageant in California, although she lost to 18-year-old Terri Zorn.

MEDICAL. Dixie Schock of Gillette, Wyoming is the first woman to bear quadruplets as a result of in-vitro fertilization techniques.

20 January 1987
JUDICIAL. Betty Grissom, widow of U.S. astronaut Virgil "Gus" Grissom, urges families of those killed in the 1986 space shuttle *Challenger* explosion to file lawsuits against NASA. Grissom is critical of NASA's response to *Challenger* families' needs. She won $350,000 as a result of her lawsuit against the makers of the *Apollo* spacecraft in which her husband died in 1967.

21 January 1987
JUDICIAL. The U.S. Supreme Court rules unanimously that a state retains the right to deny unemployment benefits in cases where women leave work because of pregnancy. With this ruling, the court finds that the state of Missouri did not violate the terms of the 1976 Federal Unemployment Tax Act. The 1976 legislation stipulates that pregnancy is not to be treated differently than other disabilities. In Missouri, unemployment benefits are only payable to workers who quit their jobs because of work-related issues.

AVIATION. At Edwards Air Force Base in California, Lois McCallin flies an experimental plane, the 92-pound *Eagle*. She travels 10 miles in 37 minutes, 38 seconds. The *Eagle* is powered by pedaling. McCallin sets a duration record for women and also sets the first closed-course record for women.

22 January 1987
IDEAS/BELIEFS. Amy Carter appears in Hampshire District Court in Northampton, Massachusetts, where a trial date of 6 April 1987 is set in connection with Carter's arrest in November 1986. Carter was protesting CIA-recruitment at the University of Massachusetts in Amherst.

23 January 1987
POLITICS. Maureen Reagan, daughter of President Ronald Reagan, becomes co-chairperson of the Republican National Committee.

26 January 1987
POPULAR CULTURE. Vocalist Whitney Houston wins 5 American Music awards at the 14th annual presentation ceremony in Los Angeles, California. Houston had been nominated for 7 awards.

4 February 1987
SPORTS. The first National Women in Sports Day is celebrated in Washington, D.C. It was created by a joint congressional resolution in 1986. According to Representative Olympia Snowe (R-Maine), an original sponsor of the resolution, National Women in Sports Day attempts to fight gender discrimination in sports. At today's ceremonies, Martina Navratilova receives the first Flo Hyman Memorial Award. Hyman, who was captain of the 1984 U.S. Olympic Volleyball Team, died suddenly in 1986.

7 February 1987
SPORTS. Jill Trenary of Minnetonka, Minnesota, wins the U.S. ladies' figure-skating championship in Tacoma, Washington. She displaces current champ Debi Thomas, who comes in second. Caryn Kadavy places third.

8 February 1987
SPORTS. Golfer Nancy Lopez wins the Sarasota Classic and nears qualification for induction into the Ladies Professional Golf Association Hall of Fame. Lopez will meet the 10-year LPGA membership requirement in July of this year, and will then be eligible for entry into the Hall. She will be the 11th player to qualify, and the first since JoAnne Carner was inducted in 1982.

9 February 1987
POPULAR CULTURE. Talk-show host Oprah Winfrey takes her television production to Forsyth County, Georgia, where picketers protest Winfrey's broadcast. The picketers are angry that the show, which focuses today on alleged racism in all-white Forsyth County, did not include any blacks, with the exception of Winfrey.

13 February 1987
RELIGION. The first Roman Catholic chapter of the nationwide Episcopal Church laywomen's order, Daughters of the King, is established at Holy Family Catholic Church in Ashland, Kentucky. Thirteen women are installed as members there.

17 February 1987
POPULAR CULTURE. Michelle Royer, Miss Texas, wins the Miss USA pageant. She will compete in the 1987 Miss Universe pageant.

23 February 1987
SPORTS. Jackie Joyner is named the top amateur athlete of the year by the American Athletic Union. She is the eighth woman to receive the prestigious Sullivan Award and the 34th track-and-field star to be given this honor. Joan Benoit, 1986 winner of the Sullivan Award, presents Joyner with a trophy at ceremonies in Indianapolis, Indiana.

26 February 1987
EDUCATION. Nineteenth-century educator Mary Lyon, who founded Mount Holyoke

College in 1833, is recognized on a 2-cent stamp issued today by the U.S. Postal Service.

3 March 1987
POLITICS. In Tampa, Florida, Sandy Freedman is elected the city's first woman mayor. She receives 66 percent of the vote, claiming 177 of Tampa's 178 precincts. Freedman, a 12-year veteran of the City Council, stepped into the mayoral seat after Bob Martinez resigned in order to promote his gubernatorial campaign. Freedman says she has a mandate to address issues of concern to the city's black population.

4 March 1987
CRIME. In a Washington, D.C., federal district court, Anne Henderson Pollard, wife of convicted spy Jonathan Pollard, receives a 5-year prison sentence. She is convicted for her role in espionage activities involving the Israeli government and U.S. intelligence sources.

4 March 1987
POPULAR CULTURE. According to a report released by Metropolitan Life Insurance Company, American girls who are now 7 years old have 4 times as great a chance, statistically, to reach the age of 100 as American boys of the same age.

5 March 1987
POPULAR CULTURE. According to reports from both *Playboy* and *Penthouse* magazines, Fawn Hall, former secretary of Lt. Col. Oliver North, has been offered substantial sums to pose for photographs. Hall, who gained notoriety during the Iran-Contra scandal, has reportedly declined the offers.

7 March 1987
SPORTS. In Alaska, Susan Butcher, winner of the 1986 Anchorage-to-Nome Iditarod dogsled race, drew the first slot in the lineup for the 1987 race. Butcher, only the second woman to win the traditionally males-only race, came in second in 1984. Last year, she took more than 17 hours off the course record, crossing the finish line after 11 days and 15 hours. In 1985, Libby Riddles was the first woman to win the race. Riddles's position in this year's lineup of 63 racers is number 12. Butcher wins the 1987 race.

8 March 1987

WOMEN'S ISSUES. International Women's Day, which has been celebrated since 1911 as a way of recognizing and promoting women's causes, prompts marches, parties, rallies, and speakers' programs across the United States and throughout the world. Speaking in observance of International Women's Day, Pope John Paul II notes that the Roman Catholic Church aims at recognizing "social and civil rights in the light of the dignity and identity of each woman."

SPORTS. Lillie Leatherwood-King wins a silver medal for her second-place standing in the 400-meter run at the First World Indoor Championships in Indianapolis, Indiana. This makes her the only American woman to garner an award in this year's track competition.

12 March 1987

POPULAR CULTURE. Across the nation, Girl Scouts celebrate the 75th anniversary of Girl Scouting. Members of this organization, founded by Juliette Gordon Low, meet in special ceremonies at 4:00 P.M. in each of the nation's time zones.

ARTS AND CULTURE. An exhibition of photographs of black women of the 1950s and 1960s opens at Coppin State College in Baltimore, Maryland. The photographs, by Judith Sedwick, feature women such as Rosa Parks, civil rights activist, and Lucy Miller Mitchell, a black educator.

SPORTS. Bonnie Blair wins the 500-meter speed-skating World Cup title in Inzell, West Germany. Her time in this final race of the season is 39.85 seconds.

14 March 1987

POLITICS. In San Francisco, California, the first Eleanor Roosevelt International Caucus of Women Political Leaders convenes for a weekend meeting. More than 60 women leaders of nearly 4-dozen nations are represented at the caucus, which is chaired by Geraldine A. Ferraro, the 1984 Democratic vice-presidential candidate. The meeting is sponsored by the National Democratic Institute for International Affairs, an arm of the Democratic party.

SPORTS. Debi Thomas, who won last year's women's world figure-skating championship, comes in second in the 1987 competition at Cincinnati, Ohio. Thomas, who was the first black to win a world singles title, is a full-time student in pre-med at Stanford University.

15 March 1987

BUSINESS. A *New York Times* article includes statistics predicting that by 1990, 43 percent of all new business ventures will be headed by women. Last year, according to the article, women represented only 28 percent of the total new business starts in the United States.

INDEX

INDEX